ACKNOWLEDGEMENTS

Thanks to helpful friends at Mirvish Productions — John Karastamatis, Chris Dorscht, Jennifer Jenkins, J. Randy Alldread, Catherine Chang, Francis Sookradge and Dwight Griffin; to Hank Kates, Paul Elliott and Russ Lazar, who remembered the old days; to Ron Jacobson, gentlemanly manager of the Royal Alexandra Theatre; to Lee Dickson, who spent many hours in the public library; to Lee Ramsay, who keeps and cares for that library's splendid theatre collection; to St. Andrew's Presbyterian Church, the Salvation corner of the crossroads; to Eleanor Johnston and David Mirvish Books; to the editors and photo archivists of the *Toronto Star*, the *Globe and Mail* and the *Hamilton Spectator*; to the archivists of the City of Toronto and the Province of Ontario; to my daughter, Abigail, who walked the dog so I wouldn't have to; to my wife, Lida, and son, Michael, who talked me into doing this even though I didn't think there was enough time; to Ernie Schwarz and Brian Sewell, who first hired me to work for something called Alexandra Productions; and to Cawthra Mulock, Lol Solman, William Breen, Ernie Rawley and Ed, Anne and David Mirvish who gave us the Royal Alexandra Theatre and worked so hard to make sure it would live for a hundred years, and more.

The

ROYAL ALEXANDRA
THEATRE

A Celebration of 100 Years

ROBERT BROCKHOUSE

with a Photo Essay by Edward Burtynsky

McArthur & Company
TORONTO

This edition published in Canada in 2007 by
McArthur & Company
322 King St. West, Suite 402
Toronto, ON
M5V 1J2
www.mcarthur-co.com

Library and Archives Canada Cataloguing in Publication

Brockhouse, Robert   The Royal Alexandra Theatre : a celebration of
100 years / Robert Brockhouse.

Includes index. ISBN 978-1-55278-648-2

1. Royal Alexandra Theatre (Toronto, Ont.)--History. I. Title.
PN2306.T62R69 2007   792.09713'541   C2007-906532-5

Cover and text design by Tania Craan
Printed in Canada by Friesens

The publisher would like to acknowledge the financial support of
the Government of Canada through the Book Publishing Industry
Development Program (BPIDP) and the Canada Council for our publishing
activities. The publisher further wishes to acknowledge the financial
support of the Ontario Arts Council for our publishing program.

10 9 8 7 6 5 4 3 2 1

TABLE OF CONTENTS

INTRODUCTION

" Keep this for our sweet friendship sake."

IT'S NOT THAT OURS is the oldest theatre around. There are many North American houses older — the famous Walnut Street Theatre in Philadelphia, for example, was already 98 years old when the Royal Alexandra first opened — but what's different about this house is that it was designed and built as a legitimate theatre and, for a hundred years, has been just that and nothing else. There are few other theatres on this continent that have not, at some time, suffered the indignity of conversion to cinemas, concert halls, variety stages, community centres, garages, restaurants, roller rinks, offices, warehouses or retail shops. The Royal Alexandra has certainly been used to show motion pictures and stage concerts and lectures — at one time, when St. Andrew's Presbyterian, down the street, was closed for renovations, the theatre was used every Sunday as a church — but these conversions were just for a day or two; for one hundred years, the business of this theatre has always been theatre, legitimate theatre, and nothing else, never missing a single season of live plays and musicals; in that, the Royal Alexandra is one of a kind.

This is its story.

1

PROLOGUE

To BEGIN, the name of this theatre is the Royal Alexandra. It is
not, as many seem to think, the Royal Alexander. Nor is it, as
many others insist, the Royal Alexandria.

It is not named for a Macedonian emperor, or for an Egyptian
city. It is named for a Danish-born woman: Alexandra Carolina
Marie Charlotte Louise Julia, who lived from 1844 to 1925 and was
also known, at various stages of her life, as Her Serene Highness
Princess Alexandra of Schleswig-Holstein-Sonderburg-Glücksburg,
Her Royal Highness Princess Alexandra of Denmark, Her Royal
Highness The Princess of Wales and, during that brief less-than-
a-decade we call the Edwardian Age, as Her Majesty The Queen.
She was the wife of King Edward VII, mother of King George V,
grandmother of both Edward VIII and George VI and great-
grandmother of the present Queen. She was also, incidentally,
the sister of Maria Feodorovna, Empress of Russia, and dear
aunt to both the Kaiser Wilhelm II and the unfortunate Czar
Nicholas II.

Another misconception: those who do know that this is the
Royal Alexandra Theatre often mistakenly assume that it was so
named in honour of Queen Alexandra; in fact, it is the other way
around; the Queen honoured the theatre in allowing it to use
her name.

For the past 50 years or so, Torontonians have avoided the
name problem by calling this theatre "the Royal Alex" or even
just "the Alex," but that easy, colloquial familiarity would have
shocked their Edwardian ancestors; the theatre bore the name
of the Queen and one did not refer to the Queen — even at a dis-
tance — by a nickname. It's true that, in her lifetime, she was

often called "Alix" – and her husband, the King, was affectionately known as "Bertie" – but that was only within the Royal Family circle. For common folk to call the theatre named for her "The Alex" would have constituted *lèse majesté*, a social offence just marginally more acceptable than blasphemy.

Alexandra Carolina Marie Charlotte Louise Julia was born on December 1, 1844, in a grand house known as the Yellow Palace, at 18 Amaliegade, in Copenhagen. Her father was the Crown Prince Christian, later to become King Christian IX of Denmark.

In 1861, Albert Edward, Prince of Wales, turned 21 and his mother, Queen Victoria – concerned by his already widespread dark reputation as a drinker, roisterer, gambler, theatregoer and womanizer – decided he should settle down and marry, and the sooner the better. She chose the Princess Alexandra from a prepared list of acceptable possibilities; not her first choice, it's said, but one that would do.

Albert Edward was then an officer of the Grenadier Guards; Victoria had him sent off to Speyer, in Germany, to observe military manoeuvres. There, he attended a party given his sister, Victoria Adelaide Mary Louise (who had just married the Crown Prince of Prussia) and there met, by chance, as arranged, the 17-year old Alexandra. Whether or not it was love at first sight – whether or not they even liked one another – no one knows, but the Queen had decided they would marry, Prince Christian had agreed and that's all there was to say.

Alexandra arrived in Britain, for the first time, on March 7, 1863. As she stepped from the ship, she was greeted by Alfred Lord Tennyson, Poet Laureate of England, who read, through his bushy, white whiskers, to a musical accompaniment provided by Sir Arthur Sullivan, these words of greeting:

> *Sea-kings' daughter from over the sea, Alexandra!*
> *Saxon and Norman and Dane are we,*
> *But all of us Danes in our welcome of thee, Alexandra!*
> *Welcome her, thunders of fort and of fleet!*
> *Welcome her, thundering cheer of the street!*

Welcome her, all things youthful and sweet,
Scatter the blossom under her feet!
Break, happy land, into earlier flowers!
Make music, O bird, in the new-budded bowers!
Blazon your mottos of blessing and prayer!
Welcome her, welcome her, all that is ours!
Warble, O bugle, and trumpet, blare!
Flags, flutter out upon turrets and towers!
Flames, on the windy headland flare!
Utter your jubilee, steeple and spire!
Clash, ye bells, in the merry March air!
Flash, ye cities, in rivers of fire!
Rush to the roof, sudden rocket, and higher
Melt into stars for the land's desire!
Roll and rejoice, jubilant voice,
Roll as a ground-swell dash'd on the strand,
Roar as the sea when he welcomes the land,
And welcome her, welcome the land's desire,
The sea-kings' daughter as happy as fair,
Blissful bride of a blissful heir,
Bride of the heir of the kings of the sea—
O joy to the people and joy to the throne,
Come to us, love us, and make us your own:
For Saxon or Dane or Norman we,
Teuton or Celt, or whatever we be,
We are each all Dane in our welcome of thee, Alexandra!

Alexandra Carolina Marie Charlotte Louise Julia, Queen of England in the Edwardian Age and namesake of the Royal Alexandra Theatre.

Albert Edward and Alexandra married at St. George's Chapel, Windsor, three days later.

For the next 47 years, they lived, by all accounts, a relatively calm and contented married life. Alexandra appears to have been a kind, good-humoured, patient and forgiving wife. She endured, quietly accepted and even laughed at her husband's wandering ways, showing neither distress nor disapproval at the steady parade of royal mistresses — the actresses Lillie Langtry and Sarah Bernhardt, the exotic dancer known as "La Belle

Otero," the high-born Countess of Warwick, the wealthy socialite Agnes Keyser and the charming and beautiful American heiress Jennie Jerome, wife of Lord Randolph Churchill (and mother to Sir Winston Churchill) – even maintaining friendships with some. During the King's final days, in 1910, Alexandra sat at his bedside with her husband's last "official" mistress, Alice Keppel, seated discreetly behind her, there at her invitation. (Alice Keppel, by the way, had at that time a 10-year-old daughter, Sonia, whom many believed to have been the King's child. Sonia's granddaughter is Camilla Parker-Bowles, wife of the present Prince of Wales, but that's not really part of this story.)

The British public, while not necessarily clashing bells, warbling bugles and uttering jubilees, took well to Alexandra. She was a popular Princess of Wales and a warmly regarded Queen, seen as kind, gentle and giving, with a genuine concern for the poor and sick – evidenced by the free hospitals built under her patronage, the Royal Alexandra Hospitals, still in operation today in England, Scotland, Canada and Australia. March 7, the anniversary of her arrival in England, is still celebrated in Britain as Alexandra Rose Day – an event she initiated in 1912 – a benefit raising funds for London charities through the sale of artificial roses, made by the disabled. Traditionally, for the past 95 years, the first rose of Alexandra Rose Day is purchased by, and pinned to the lapel of, the Prime Minister.

Queen Alexandra died on November 20, 1925. On stage at the Royal Alexandra Theatre that night was the Rudolf Friml, Otto Harbach and Oscar Hammerstein II operetta *Rose-Marie*, with Virginia Johnson (as the beautiful Rose-Marie La Flamme), Paul Donah (as her love, "Wild Jim" Kenyon, falsely accused of the murder of Black Eagle, the villainous Métis), Walter Lawrence (as honest Sgt. Malone of the Mounties) and Houston Richards (as Jim's pal, Hard-Boiled Herman). *Rose-Marie* ran to sold-out houses, the biggest hit of the season.

SETTING THE SCENE

In 1905, when this story properly begins, the population of Toronto was roughly 300,000 — making it the second largest city in Canada, behind Montreal, at just under 400,000. These 300,000 people enjoyed regular evening and matinee performances at five large theatres, two of them of the category "first-class legitimate," which was really quite remarkable for a city of that size — Detroit and Buffalo, the two nearest cities of comparable population, for example, each had only one first-class legitimate theatre. But before we proceed any further, we should define just what was meant in 1905 by "first-class," "legitimate," "theatre" and even "large."

By "theatre," an urbane person of those times meant a structure specifically designed and built to house and display theatrical performances. Almost any building might be used, from time to time, temporarily, as a theatre. Toronto's Massey Hall, for example, had staged theatrical productions, as had the St. Lawrence Hall, but the former was built as a concert venue and the latter for public meetings and lectures; neither was intended as a permanent, full-time theatre, nor had either been built with the peculiar needs of theatre performance in mind, and those distinctions were already very important ones in 1905.

The Grand Opera House,
at 11 Adelaide St. West, had
been Toronto's leading legitimate
theatre until 1905, when it sank
to second-class status. Both the
Grand and the Majestic were
owned by Ambrose J. Small.

Photo courtesy of the Archives of Ontario.

By "theatrical performance," that same sophisticated city-dweller would have understood us to mean an entertainment in which living human actors (though they might have been supplemented from time to time, as they often were in the first years of the Royal Alexandra, by performing dogs, ponies, sheep, goats, camels or even yaks) stood upon a stage, in front of a comfortably seated audience, and acted out a story.

The acting out of a story could be accomplished by spoken words, or by song, or by dance, or by mime, or by any combination of any or all. The term "legitimate theatre" – or "legit," for short - referred to a performance wholly by the spoken word, a hold-over from the theatre licensing laws of 17th-century England. Performances involving song and dance were not considered "legit," but would fall into the categories "opera" (if they were wholly sung) or "operetta" (if they involved both talking and singing), or "ballet" (if they were wholly danced). What we

call "musicals" were then just beginning to be thought of as falling into a new category, all their own.

Of course, there were other forms still considered "theatrical performances" and worthy of being housed in buildings called theatres even though they did not always involve actors acting out stories: vaudeville and burlesque. We'll come back to those later.

So, there were five large theatres in Toronto in 1905 – the Grand Opera House, the Princess, the Majestic, Shea's and the Star – and by "large" we mean that each seated 1,500 or more people.

The one most remembered in the history books is the Grand Opera House – which, despite its name, was a legitimate theatre, a theatre of the spoken word, and not an opera house.

The Grand stood at 11 Adelaide St. West, on the south side of the street, just west of the Yonge St. corner. It was owned and

The Princess Theatre on a snowy morning in 1912. They're lining up down the block, past St. Andrew's and around the Simcoe St. corner, to see the famous William Farnum – soon to become one of Hollywood's first cowboy stars – in the American Civil War melodrama *The Littlest Rebel*.

Photo from the collection of the Royal Alexandra Theatre.

run by the eccentric Ambrose J. Small, who would vanish without a trace (but, some said, with a suitcase full of money) in 1919,
sparking an epic, but fruitless, police search that at one point
drew an offer of assistance from *Sherlock Holmes* author Arthur
Conan Doyle.

The Grand seated 2,100 and had been Toronto's undisputed
number one playhouse from 1880 until a fire destroyed the old
Academy of Music on King St. West and that concert hall was
rebuilt and re-opened (in 1895) as the Princess, an 1,800-seat legitimate theatre. With a larger stage than the Grand – and with
electric lighting (the first in any public building in Toronto) to
the Grand's gas – the Princess quickly took over as the city's
leading theatre and, by 1905, the Grand had declined to second-
class status.

The Princess sat on the south side of King St. West, halfway
between Simcoe and York streets (there was no University Ave.
then). In 1905, it was jointly owned, ostensibly, by Mr. F.C.
Whitney, of Detroit, and Mr. Oliver Barton Sheppard, of
Toronto. Sheppard had for many years been manager of the
Grand Opera House and had given Ambrose Small his first job
there, as an usher, sometime in the late 1870s (but there was no
bond for old-times' sake to soften their rivalry, for Sheppard had
also fired Small sometime in the 1880s – and the first thing Small
did after buying the Grand in 1903 was fire Sheppard).

The third great legitimate theatre of 1905 was the Majestic, at
27 Adelaide St. West, just a few doors west of the Grand Opera
House (and also owned by Ambrose Small). The Majestic was
Toronto's newest playhouse, built in 1903 and seating 2,200, but its
stage was too small for it to compete with the Grand and the
Princess for major shows. Instead, it functioned – as its builders
intended – as a "ten, 'twent, 'thirt" melodrama house. What this
meant was that ticket prices were 30 cents for the good seats, 20
cents for the middling seats and 10 cents for the poor seats and
that the bill-of-fare offered was melodrama, the 1905 equivalent of
modern daytime television – indeed, it was "daytime" even then;

the Majestic had daily matinees catering to almost exclusively female audiences. Melodrama was still considered legitimate theatre, but only barely so. The Majestic hadn't long to live in 1905; it would soon be converted to motion pictures and re named "the Regent."

Around the corner from the Grand and the Majestic, at 91 Yonge St., stood the 1,600-seat Shea's — the first of three Shea's theatres to operate in Toronto: Shea's Yonge St. opened in 1899; Shea's Victoria (at Adelaide East and Victoria streets) opened in 1910; and the gigantic Shea's Hippodrome (on Bay at Queen, right across the street from the old city hall), with 2,600 seats, calling itself "the largest theatre in the British Empire," opened in 1914.

The Shea's houses were part of a 23-theatre empire founded and run by the brothers Michael and Jeremiah Shea. Buffalo, New York, claims the Sheas as prominent native sons — Buffalo was their home base and there is still a Shea's Theater in business there — but the two actually came from St. Catharine's, Ontario, and Jerry, who managed the three theatres here, lived most of his adult life in Toronto.

A 1907 picture postcard view from Bay St., looking east down Adelaide, toward Yonge. The great arch centre-right is the Majestic Theatre. The tallest building on the street, just to the left of the Majestic, Is the Grand Opera House.

The Shea's theatres were vaudeville houses and not considered legitimate theatres. Vaudeville was variety entertainment – comedians, singers, dancers, acrobats, jugglers, magicians and dog and pony shows. It was lower-class entertainment, even lower on the social scale than melodrama (but everyone went).

Even further down the social scale was burlesque. If vaudeville was lower-class, burlesque was downright vulgar. Burlesque in those days, however, was not yet just strip-tease and girlie shows. It was essentially a theatre of comedy, but "low" comedy – slapstick, pie-in-the-face comedy performed by men in absurdly baggy pants and false whiskers, often mildly risqué, sometimes parodying popular fads and trends or satirizing current events and newsworthy personalities, with the stage decorated by pretty girls in costumes as skimpy as the law allowed (which was not all that skimpy in 1905).

Toronto's palace of burlesque then was the 1,600-seat Star – later known as the Empire – at 23 Temperance St.

These five were not the only theatres in Toronto in 1905. There were many smaller, more modest houses scattered about – one perhaps worth mentioning was the brand-new Theatorium, with 150 seats (if you can call wooden planks nailed between chairs "seats"), Toronto's first movie theatre – but the big five were the "real" theatres. Collectively, they gave Toronto the full range of what professional theatre had to offer. These were the competition when construction began on the Royal Alexandra.

3

ENTER THE PLAYERS

GIVEN THE RELATIVELY SMALL SIZE OF TORONTO IN 1905, and given the relative abundance of its theatres, why would anyone spend the huge sums of money necessary to build another one?

The answer to that question, unfortunately, died with the man who did it, Cawthra Mulock, in the great influenza pandemic of 1918, but there have been many guesses.

It has been suggested that Mulock's motive in building the Royal Alexandra Theatre was nothing but aristocratic conceit. He was a very wealthy, important and socially prominent young man and, the story goes, he had been miffed one night when turned away from the box office of the Princess Theatre — refusing to believe that the sign reading "sold out" applied to him — and had decided to build a theatre of his own so that he might never suffer such impertinence again.

Another suggestion — preferred by the Mulock family — is that he was moved by selfless patriotism and civic pride (and Mulock would himself speak of his desire to perform "a public and cultural service" to his city). He was well-travelled and knew that Toronto was regarded — by those who had even heard of it — as a provincial backwater. Even across the rest of Canada, the nickname "Hogtown" was still in common use — unfairly; the city

13

had banned pigs from its streets more than 70 years before. A great theatre, he reasoned, would help give Toronto the recognition it deserved as a centre of urbanity, taste and refinement.

It's entirely possible, of course, that Cawthra Mulock might have simply thought a new theatre a good investment. Theatre was a big business at the turn of the twentieth century and there was then no reason to think it would not continue to be so forever. And while Toronto might then have been small by the standards of New York or Boston or Chicago, it was growing, and growing quickly. There were many opportunities for the quick and daring.

As a well-travelled man, Mulock also knew that Toronto's best theatres fell well below the standards expected in London and New York. Our theatres belonged to the last century and were becoming not just worn and tattered, but obsolete, incapable of meeting the technical requirements of the big, new stage extravaganzas coming from Broadway. A large, modern, state-of-the-art theatre would capture business that might otherwise pass Toronto by entirely.

For whatever reason or reasons, one day in 1905 Cawthra Mulock decided to build a theatre.

Mulock was born in Toronto in 1882, the son of the Hon. Sir William Mulock, of Newmarket, then Member for North York in Ottawa, later to become — among other things - Postmaster General for Canada, Minister of Labour under Sir Wilfrid Laurier, Rector of the University of Toronto and Chief Justice of the Supreme Court of Ontario. His mother was Sarah Cawthra Crowther, through whom he became an heir to the considerable fortune of William Cawthra – "the Astor of Canada" – son of the prominent Loyalist settler Joseph Cawthra, who once owned much of what is now the City of Mississauga and who was reputed to have been the wealthiest man in Ontario. Cawthra Mulock was a graduate of the exclusive Upper Canada College and had attended — for one year — the University of Toronto, leaving to go into business as a stockbroker, his future already well assured.

In 1903, at the age of 21, Mulock had been the centre of much public tittle-tattle when he married the 19-year-old Adèle Baldwin Falconbridge, daughter of Sir William Glenholme Falconbridge, Chief Justice of the Court of King's Bench. Adèle was Roman Catholic and Cawthra, Anglican. The Catholic Archbishop of Toronto, Dennis O'Connor, who opposed such "mixed marriages," refused to allow them to marry in a Catholic church, much to the dismay of the Falconbridge family. Cawthra's father, Sir William, had enlisted the help of his influential friends Prime Minister Laurier and His Excellency Donato Sbarretti y Tazza, the Apostolic Delegate, to pressure O'Connor into backing down. It didn't work, but the attempt made for delicious gossip.

In 1905, the handsome 23-year old Cawthra was known to the press as "the boy millionaire." He was (or was soon to become) president of the National Iron Works, the Guardian Trust Co. and the Canada Bread Co.; the youngest member of the Toronto Stock Exchange; a director of the Confederation Life Association, the Imperial Bank of Canada and the National Trust Company; a member of the boards of Toronto General Hospital and the Toronto Guild of Civic Art; a director of the National Horse Show Association, owner of much of the "worthless" swampland shore of Ashbridge's Bay; and the world was his oyster.

At that time, he and Adèle were living, temporarily – they would move in 1907 to a much grander house at Jarvis and Isabella – in the beautiful Greek Revival mansion Cawthra House, built by his Uncle William, at the corner of King and Bay streets, only a block away from the Grand Opera House and a block and a half from the Princess Theatre. People with nothing more productive to do on a summer's evening used to wander by Cawthra House at dusk to watch the butler change the knobs on the big front door; the daytime doorknobs were made of gold – solid gold, it was rumoured – and the butler would unscrew them and replace them with brass ones as evening fell.

In August 1907, just before he opened the doors of the Royal

Cawthra Mulock, Toronto's "boy millionaire," in 1906.
Collection of Mike Filey.

Cawthra House in 1914. No Cawthras or Mulocks were still living there when this photo was taken. They had sold the house to Molson's Bank and, presumably, taken the doorknobs with them.

Photo courtesy of the *Toronto Star*

Alexandra Theatre, Mulock's name and face dominated the pages of Toronto's newspapers — not as builder of the city's newest and best theatre, but as owner of the yacht *Adele*, the city's hope in the annual, three-day Canada Cup Race on Lake Ontario. Unfortunately, the *Adele* lost — by a nose — to Rochester, New York's *Seneca*.

No one today knows why Mulock, with all the money at his disposal, sought partners for his theatre project. Perhaps the reason was that he didn't yet actually have the money at his disposal; his inheritance from the Cawthra estate was paid out in installments, over the course of several years. As it was, however, his idea of building a theatre found immediate, enthusiastic backing and support from two older and well-established friends of his own social circle.

The first was Robert Alexander Smith, a former president of the Toronto Stock Exchange and a senior partner in the influential brokerage (and railway, steamship, coal, iron and real estate) firm of Osler and Hammond (the Osler of which was Sir Edmund Osler, a boyhood friend and neighbour of Cawthra's father, Sir William Mulock, in the small town of Bond Head, Ontario). Smith was a self-made man, pulling himself up by his own boot-straps in the kind of success story people loved to tell in that Gilded Age. Born poor in Scotland, little education, a

Robert Alexander Smith, stockbroker and partner in the ferry business. He was a self-made man in the best Horatio Alger tradition who would add his financial and moral support to Cawthra Mulock's theatre project.

teen-aged immigrant, working as a labourer, studying hard by night, becoming a railway company clerk, saving and investing – and now a very wealthy man whom, his friends said, could have been even wealthier were it not for his exceptional public philanthropy and private generosity.

The second was Stephen Haas, the French-born (Alsace-Lorraine) head of George Hees and Son, Ltd. (manufacturers of awnings, draperies and upholsteries), vice president of the Union Bank, director of the Royal Bank and the Canadian General Electric Co. and Commodore of the Royal Canadian Yacht Club – making him the man in charge of the Canada Cup Race in which Cawthra Mulock's *Adele* ran and lost.

Both Robert Smith and Stephen Haas promised to invest in the theatre project and their weighty support helped dispel any notion that might have run through the city that the whole thing was nothing but the hare-brained scheme of an immature young man with more money than sense.

Haas, Smith and Mulock then approached a possible fourth partner, a man not of their class and circle of friends, but one of extensive theatre-building and operating experience, Ambrose Joseph "Amby" Small, a one-time theatre usher who had risen by dint of hard work, keen intelligence — and the fortuitous marriage to the daughter of a wealthy brewery owner — to become

Stephen Haas, Commodore of the Royal Canadian Yacht Club, banker and manufacturer of draperies, the latter two both good businesses for someone interested in theatre. He would be the third partner in the Alexandra Co.

Photo courtesy of the Archives of the City of Toronto.

Lawrence "Lol" Solman, restaurant manager, hotelier, amusement park developer, ferry boat operator and baseball fan. He would become the first manager of the Royal Alexandra.

owner of the Grand Opera houses of Toronto and London, Ontario, and head of a cross-Canada empire of 34 theatres.

Small – perhaps already too busy with his existing theatres; perhaps just not interested in seeing yet another legitimate theatre built in Toronto – declined participation. It's said, however, that it was he who suggested an alternate – although the suggestion may also have come from Robert Alexander Smith's partner, H.C. Hammond, who knew the man well – Lawrence "Lol" Solman. It was an odd choice; Lol Solman had no experience in theatre and little money to contribute. It's possible that it was all a mistake; Lol had a younger brother – "Sol" – who then managed the Majestic Theatre. Could the partners have misunderstood Ambrose Small, confused Lol and Sol and gone to see the wrong Solman?

Lol Solman was even farther outside Cawthra Mulock's social circle than was Ambrose Small. He was 20 years older than Mulock and had been born poor – in a small house at 146 John St. – and Jewish. His father, Samuel Solman, was one of the first Jews to settle in Toronto and a founding member of the city's first synagogue – the first in Canada west of Montreal, in fact – a tiny congregation that met in a second-floor rented room over Coombe's Drugstore, at Yonge and Richmond (but which eventually grew to become Holy Blossom Temple).

There had been no Upper Canada College for Solman; he was educated in Toronto's public schools and had attended the old Mechanics' Institute, a trade school for working-class boys at Church and Adelaide. On leaving school, he worked as an errand boy for a hardware store in the village of Yorkville, just north of the Toronto city limits, before being apprenticed to a baker.

Not much enjoying working at an oven, he moved to Detroit in the early 1880s and found work as a clerk in a mail-order business, where he did very well, rising over the next ten years to own his own small company in that trade.

Around 1893, Solman returned to Toronto, for reasons unknown, and took a job managing the restaurant at the Hanlan's Point Hotel, on the Toronto Island, where he met, fell in love with and married Emily Hanlan Durnan, widowed

J.W. Gorman's famous diving horse — an example of what in theatre is called a one-trick pony — performs beside the Hanlan's Point roller coaster in the summer of 1907.

Photo courtesy of the Archives of the City of Toronto.

younger sister of the hotel's owner, the famous sculler (and Toronto city alderman) Ned Hanlan.

The Toronto Island (it wouldn't add an "s" and become "the Islands" until Hurricane Hazel split it apart in 1954) was then a popular summer resort and the Hanlan's Point Hotel its best place to stay. Solman talked his somewhat reluctant brother-in-law into greatly expanding his resort business, building an amusement park — complete with roller coaster, Ferris wheel and sideshow arcade, starring the famous J.W. Gorman's Diving Horse — and sports stadium (which would become home to the Maple Leafs, Toronto's first professional baseball team, owned and managed by Lol Solman).

Financing for this venture was to have come from the stockbroker H.C. Hammond, Grand Opera House owner Amby Small — whose original idea the whole thing might have been — and the Hanlan family. When Small backed out at the last minute, Solman went to break the bad news to Hammond; without Small, the project was dead; he and the Hanlans could not afford to make up Small's share. Hammond, however, must have had a lot of faith in Lol Solman; he agreed to cover the shortfall himself, on the condition that Solman would take complete charge of the construction and agree to manage the park and stadium when they opened.

As work on the amusement park got underway, Solman and Ned Hanlan formed a separate partnership with H.C. Hammond and Robert Alexander Smith. Ned owned a ferry boat – Hanlan's Ferry Service – while Smith and Hammond owned controlling interest in another. They pooled their properties to form the Toronto Ferry Company; if you wanted to go to a ball game or ride the roller coaster or see the diving horse at "Canada's Coney Island," the only way there was by the Solman/Hammond/Smith ferries *Blue Bell* and *Trillium*. The ferry service would make Solman rich.

In later years, Lol Solman and his brother, Sol, would build two more sports complexes in Toronto – the Mutual Street Arena and the 20,000-seat Maple Leaf Stadium, at Bathurst and the Lakeshore – and an even bigger and grander amusement park at Sunnyside, but that's getting ahead of the story. In 1905, he was not yet counted among Toronto's wealthy – he and Emily still lived in the modest John St. house in which he had been born – but he was well on his way to becoming the city's amusements king and that may have given him all the credentials Mulock, Smith and Haas thought he would need to run a theatre. Solman himself demurred when he first heard the plans; he pointed out that he knew nothing at all about the theatre business, but Mulock is said to have answered that he regarded Solman as being "smart enough to learn it."

So, the four men – Cawthra Mulock, Stephen Haas, Robert A. Smith and Lol Solman - signed the papers to form a syndicate, the Alexandra Company. As the name would indicate, they already knew – before an architect had yet made a sketch, before they even knew where it would be built – what their theatre would be called. Mulock had already used his extraordinary social and family network – including, remember, Prime Minister Laurier himself – to obtain a Royal Patent from King Edward VII, giving him the right to carve the Queen's name into the stone face of the building, to display the Royal coat-of-arms on the house curtain and over the lobby doors and to call his theatre "Royal" – the only legally royal theatre on the continent.

THE FOUR 'NATIONS

CAWTHRA MULOCK AND THE ALEXANDRA COMPANY did not search long for a site on which to build their theatre. A perfect spot had already been on the market for quite some time. It was at King and Simcoe streets, only a block west of the Princess Theatre, three blocks from the Grand Opera House and the Majestic, right around the corner from Lol Solman's John St. house, a five-minute stroll from the golden doorknob of Mulock's own front door. Best of all, in an increasingly congested downtown Toronto, it was an empty lot, with no existing structure to tear down and no pre-existing foundations to dig up; there had never been anything there but grass.

The property in question belonged to Mulock's old *alma mater*, Upper Canada College, the exclusive, private school for the sons of Ontario's upper class. From the time of the school's founding in 1829 until 1891, when it moved to a new campus just past the edge of town, at Avenue Road and St. Clair, its athletic field had fronted along King St. West. The land that interested Mulock and his associates was a small piece — a lot 99 feet 11 1/2 inches wide by 185 feet 6 inches deep — that had been carved from that field.

In those days, one could stand at the corner of King and Simcoe and enjoy a splendid view all the way down to the lake.

The only structures that might partially obstruct that view to the south were the old Provincial Parliament Buildings along Front St. – Queen's Park was not quite finished then – and Government House, the official residence of Sir William Mortimer Clark, Lieutenant-Governor of Ontario, which sat in lonely splendour at the corner of a square block of parklike lawns, from King St. south to Wellington and from Simcoe St. west to John – the whole of the area now filled by Roy Thomson and Metro Halls.

On the southeast corner of King and Simcoe, right across the street from Government House, stood the only structure that still survives today, one of Toronto's oldest (1876) and most beautiful churches, a "Norman Scottish" building in sandstone – with the granite pillars framing its doors imported from Scotland – St. Andrew's Presbyterian.

There was only one eyesore, one blemish, one blight to challenge the gentility of the intersection. On the northeast corner,

Legislation. A stereopticon
slide view of Government House,
official residence of the Lieutenant-
Governor of Ontario, which once
stood on the site now occupied
by Roy Thomson Hall.
Photo courtesy of the Archives of Ontario.

Salvation. The only neighbourhood
landmark already there before the
building of the Royal Alexandra,
and still there, St. Andrew's
Presbyterian Church.
Photo courtesy of the Archives of Ontario.

Damnation. Doyle's Tavern was the "Damnation" corner of King and Simcoe. The posters on the side of the building date the photo for us; *The Blindness of Virtue*, a drama by Cosmo Hamilton, played the Royal Alexandra from September 8 to 13, 1913. The show starred the young (then only 21) British actor Leo G. Carroll, who would go on to a career in motion pictures and television.

Photo by F. Baird, the Archives of Ontario.

directly across the street from the doors of St. Andrew's, stood a shabby, two-storey wooden building known to its disreputable clientele as "Doyle's," a low tavern patronized by rowdy and depraved actors, artistes, stagehands and hangers-on from the theatres up the street (and by the equally debauched reporters from the new Toronto Daily Star building at 20 King St. West).

For these four buildings – the church, Government House, the school and the tavern – Torontonians had long ago nick-named the intersection of King and Simcoe "The Four 'Nations: Salvation, Legislation, Education and Damnation."

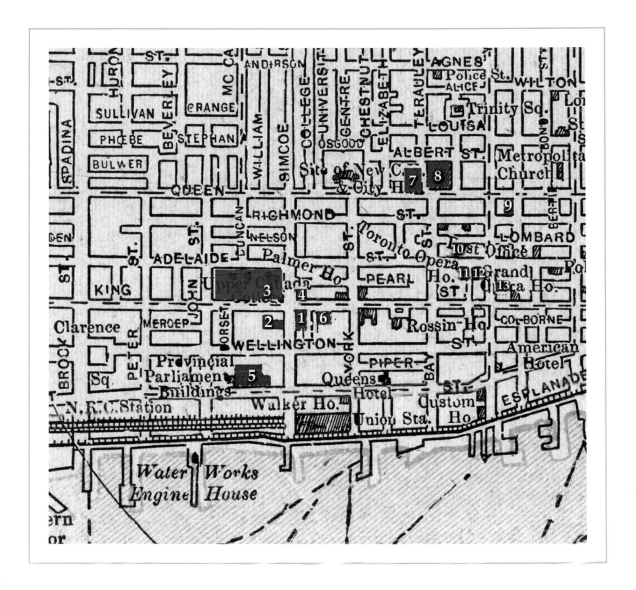

1) "Salvation": St. Andrew's Presbyterian Church, on the southeast corner of King and Simcoe.

2) "Legislation": Government House, official residence of the Lieutenant-Governor.

3) "Education": The campus of Upper Canada College, building site of the Royal Alexandra Theatre.

4) "Damnation": Doyle's Tavern.

5) The Ontario Provincial Parliament buildings.

6) The Princess Theatre.

7) Future site of Shea's Hippodrome, the biggest theatre in the British Empire.

8) Old City Hall — in 1905, "New" City Hall.

9) Site of Shea's Victoria, which would be replaced by the Hippodrome.

10) The Star Theatre, on Temperance St.

11) The Grand Opera House.

12) The Majestic Theatre.

13) The original site of Shea's Theatre, destroyed by fire in 1905.

THE BUILDER

In 1905, after buying his piece of land in the Four 'Nations, Cawthra Mulock took the train to New York to find a theatre architect. His first choice was the firm Carrère and Hastings, then one of the leading North American practitioners of Beaux-Arts — or "French Renaissance" — design, an elaborate mixture of Greek, Imperial Roman and Italian Renaissance architectural styles taught at the École des Beaux Arts, in Paris, that had been born in the grandiose plans of Napoleon III to remake all Paris as a glittering imperial capital — and that dominated as the preferred look for grand, public buildings in North America from about 1880 through 1920. Beaux-Arts design exuded wealth, elegance, taste, sophistication, solidity and permanence.

Carrère and Hastings had become famous for its designs for Chicago's "White City" for the World Columbian Exposition of 1893, as the builder of the landmark New York Public Library (1897) and as chief architects of the Pan American Exposition of 1901. The firm had also, at that point, one New York theatre to its credit, Abbey's Theatre (later the Knickerbocker), built in 1893.

Carrère and Hastings accepted the commission and handed full charge of the project over to one of the firm's brightest young associates, a Canadian architect named John MacIntosh

Lyle. Lyle, as it happens, had been planning — with the firm's support — to leave and open his own office in Toronto. The Royal Alexandra Theatre commission came along at exactly the right time; he would move to Toronto and set up his own independent business, but work on the theatre with the help, advice and resources of Carrère and Hastings at his disposal, whenever — if ever — needed.

The arrangement suited Cawthra Mulock well; having a Canadian chief architect was good public relations, but he would have, at the same time, both the cachet of the Carrère and Hastings name and the safety of the Carrère and Hastings back-up.

Mulock gave Lyle a preliminary budget of $350,000 and a simple set of instructions. Just what he said is disputed; it is variously reported as having been "Build me the finest theatre on the continent," or "Build me the most beautiful theatre on the continent," or "Build me the most modern theatre in the world." Whatever the exact words may have been, they implicitly negated the budget.

John MacIntosh Lyle was Northern Irish-born, from Connor, in County Antrim, just north of Belfast. His father, the Rev. Dr. Samuel Lyle, was a Presbyterian minister who moved his family to Canada in 1878 — when John was six — to take over the pulpit of the Central Presbyterian Church in Hamilton, Ontario, and to be among the founders of the Hamilton Public Library and the Hamilton School of Art.

John Lyle showed early artistic talent and his parents enrolled him in that same Hamilton School of Art, where he developed an interest in architecture. When he was 19, he won a scholarship for a year's study at Yale University and, the next year — 1892 — sailed to France to study at the fountainhead of the Beaux-Arts movement, the great École des Beaux-Arts itself.

Following his graduation, Lyle worked for the Parisian Beaux-Arts firm Blondel and Frémiet for a year before sailing back to North America to take a job with the New York architectural partnership of Howard & Cauldwell. A year later, he

John M. Lyle, architect of the
Royal Alexandra, in a picture taken
around the time of the opening of
Toronto's Union Station, in 1927.

became an associate with Carrère and Hastings and, himself, a
member of the prestigious Society of Beaux-arts Architects.
With an impressive education and 12 years of practical experience
with three first-class firms, Lyle was no novice. He had never,
however, built a theatre.

In those days, though, there were few North American
architects of anything like Lyle's background and experience
who *had* ever built a theatre. Theatre-building did not rank high
in the ambitions of architects of the Beaux-Arts school. Their
preferences went to monumental public buildings of serious
import and noble purpose – banks, museums, libraries, city halls
and railway stations (and Lyle would later crown his career with
one of the grandest of North America's Beaux-Arts railway stations, Toronto's Union Station). Theatres did not qualify; they

were mere playhouses, places of amusement, and beneath the dignity of real architects. In 1898, the British theatre architect Edwin Sachs had complained that most theatre design was "governed in its requirements by investors" who demanded of architects only "the qualification of being able to provide for a maximum audience at a minimum outlay." Beyond that, the bulk of the architect's job could be turned over to much less-expensive journeyman carpenters and such unimportant frills as acoustics, sightlines and fire safety, ignored.

Theatres at the turn of the 20th century were often built on the cheap and not intended to last for long. In 1908 — too late for Cawthra Mulock (who would end up spending more than $750,000 on the Royal Alexandra) to benefit from the advice — the Boston architect Clarence Blackall calculated that the average lifespan of a new theatre was only 12 years. He cautioned all would-be builders to never, under any circumstances, spend more than $600,000 (including the cost of the land) on a theatre if they entertained any hope of actually making their money back.

That Cawthra Mulock and John Lyle took a different attitude was due in large part to something that happened in Chicago on the afternoon of Dec. 30, 1903, during a matinee performance of the spectacular Christmas pantomime *Mr. Bluebeard, Jr.*, just as the second act began.

6

HOW NOT TO
BUILD A THEATRE

THE SINGLE MOST IMPORTANT FACTOR in driving down the average lifespan of theatres to Clarence Blackall's calculated 12 years was their unfortunate tendency to catch fire and burn down. That they burned down was very often the result of the fact that their builders had built cheaply and not employed qualified architects. That they caught fire in the first place was just the nature of the theatrical beast.

In the 17th century, theatres were lit by candles. In the 18th century, candles gave way to oil lamps. In the 19th century, oil lamps were replaced by gas lights. All used open flames, hung in the midst of cloth draperies, hempen ropes and wood-framed canvas scenery painted with oil-based — and flammable — paints.

Around 1850, there had been a revolution in theatre lighting with the invention of the limelight — also sometimes called the "calcium lamp" — which gave a light almost as bright as day, without benefit of electricity. The way it worked was this: a piece of calcium carbonate — a small chunk of ordinary limestone rock would do — was heated to incandescence in the very hot flame produced by a mixture of compressed hydrogen and oxygen gases. The result was a brilliant, white light that could be focused with lenses into a narrow spot or spread out to wash an entire stage. The limelight could also be coloured by placing pieces of dyed cloth over the lens. It was wonderful, but it generated a lot of heat and had to be constantly monitored; improperly tended limelights were known to explode.

And so, not surprisingly, theatres caught fire with great regularity. In Toronto, the Royal Lyceum – our first professional legitimate theatre – burned down in 1873, to be replaced by the Grand Opera House; the Grand itself burned down (to be rebuilt) in 1879; the Grand's neighbour, the Majestic Theatre, had been built on the lot once occupied by the old Toronto Opera House, which burned down in 1903; the Princess Theatre burned down and was rebuilt in 1895, and would burn and be rebuilt again in 1915; Shea's, the vaudeville house on Yonge St., burned in 1897 and did it again in 1905 (interestingly, the man who sounded the fire alarm in 1905 was Lol Solman's brother, Sol, who saw the smoke and flames from the window of *his* theatre, the Majestic). The all-time champion firetrap was probably New York's elegant Bowery Theatre, which burned down five times over the course of 17 years, always rebuilt until its owners finally gave up after the fire of 1929, sold the newly vacant lot and abandoned show business for good.

Theatre fires might have become a joke had they not often killed people, and killed them in appalling numbers. The worst fire of 19th century North America was that of New York's Conway Theatre, in 1876, in which three hundred people died; but the Conway fire seemed almost insignificant when compared with Europe's worst. In 1881, a fire in Vienna's Ringtheater may have killed as many as nine hundred – the box office records were destroyed and the victims so thoroughly incinerated it was not possible to count them.

In totalitarian Austria, the Ringtheater disaster led to a number of fire safety innovations being forced upon theatres: steel framing, reinforced concrete walls and floors, sprinkler systems and woven asbestos fire curtains (to seal off the stage, where most fires started, preventing flame and smoke from entering the auditorium).

In democratic, laissez-faire, capitalist North America, however, these new ideas were slow to catch on. They were expensive. They were complicated. They required hiring and paying architects and engineers. They took building costs too high for the owners to recoup within the 12-year life-span (before the place burned down anyway).

Fortunately for the Royal Alexandra Theatre-to-be, Cawthra Mulock did not think this way. If he had once so thought, what

A newspaper photographer just happened to be on hand right outside the Iroquois on the afternoon of December 30. The lucky people who made it out the fire escape doors are a panic-stricken blur on the sidewalk.

Eddie Foy, in his costume for
Mr. Bluebeard, Jr., was the hero
of the Iroquois fire of 1903.

happened at the Iroquois Theater in Chicago helped convince him – and hundreds of other North American theatre owners – otherwise.

The Iroquois was a brand-new theatre – opened only a month before the disastrous afternoon of December 30, 1903 – and had been widely advertised as (and believed by its patrons to be) "fire-proof." The theatre sat sixteen hundred, but there may have been as many as nineteen hundred in the house – mostly mothers and children – for a special holiday matinee of the pantomime extravaganza *Mr. Bluebeard, Jr.*, starring the great comedian Eddie Foy and featuring a live, performing elephant and a pony ballet.

Act II began with a song and dance number – "In the Pale Moonlight" – for which the scene appeared illuminated by a full moon hanging above the stage. The moon effect was created by a dimmed-down limelight hung behind a gauze scrim and must have been lovely to behold, until the lamp exploded.

The exploding limelight set fire to the scrim and the scrim set fire to the scenery flats and masking draperies hanging in the flies. The performers, with bits and pieces of burning cloth and wood raining down on them, ran for the big double doors – the loading doors – at the rear of the theatre. Eddie Foy, alone, remained on stage in a heroic – but vain – attempt to prevent panic, joking, making light of the situation and urging the audience to remain calm and move in an orderly fashion toward the fire exits.

A stagehand pulled the emergency lever to bring down the asbestos fire curtain, but the curtain jammed and stopped 20 feet above the stage – perhaps because the fleeing cast and crew had opened the loading doors and the wind created as the fire sucked in air caused the too-flimsy fire curtain to balloon out of its channels; perhaps because those channels were made of wood and were, themselves, on fire.

And then, the flames reached the tanks of compressed oxygen and hydrogen that fed the limelights and they exploded, sending a ball of fire rolling under the open asbestos curtain and into the house.

FIRE, PANIC AND DEATH IN CITY OF CHICAGO

Nearly Half an Audience Numbering Thirteen Hundred Souls Swept Into Eternity Yesterday Afternoon

THIRTEEN hundred happy and contented people attended a performance in the Iroquois Theater in Chicago yesterday afternoon. A fire started on the stage, an explosion resulted and a dread panic followed. This morning at 4 o'clock 623 bodies were recovered from the building, showing that nearly half the audience had perished. Chicago mourns today at the direful calamity and New Year will be a doleful day in thousands of homes in the great city.

Special to The Journal]

CHICAGO, Dec. 30. — One of the most terrible fires of the twentieth century occurred in the Iroquois Theater in this city today. Five hundred and sixty men, women and helpless little children were crushed, trampled and burned to death as a result of the awful and indescribable holocaust.

Tortured and incinerated, suffocated by smoke and gases and crushed while frantically attempting to escape impending doom is the manner in which over half a thousand frenzied human creatures met their awful end.

Hundreds of others are now lying between life and death, with limbs broken and bodies, features and form burned, at their homes and at hospitals, while every undertaking establishment in this big city is filled with bodies, many of which will never be identified.

The fire started at 2 o'clock this afternoon during the performance of "Mr. Bluebeard." Thousands of persons, out with their children, to attend the holiday matinees, were present.

It started either from a broken electric wire or the explosion of a calcium light. It spread with incredible rapidity through the inflamable scenery. In the excitement the doors of the theater were opened. This caused a draught which resulted in the huge asbestos curtain bulging out in such a manner that the employes could not lower it. With the draught adding fury to the flames they spread to the gas tanks, which exploded with tremendous force, sending a sheet of flame out over the crazed and panic-stricken audience.

Scores were killed in their seats by the escaping gas, but this only added more terror to those left alive and they used every effort of a desperate dying person to reach the doors and freedom.

Practically all those in the lower floor escaped, but in the balcony and gallery, where the flames were sent by the explosion, hundreds died. Men became lunatics at the fear of death, and trampled helpless women and children under their feet.

Near the entrance the crowd became jammed, and it was here that scores of bodies of people killed in the crush piled up. Clothes were literally torn from the bodies of the dead, and in many cases the faces were trampled into an unrecognizable mass.

One man's entire body from the waist up was gone, having been literally ground up by the feet of the panic-stricken people.

There were little children almost torn to pieces and beautiful women crushed beyond all recognition.

The dead were carried out and piled in rows on the sidewalk, to be carried off later to nearby stores and restaurants.

Police returns received from Chicago at 4 o'clock this (Thursday) morning give the number of bodies recovered thus far as six hundred and twenty-three.

There were thirteen hundred people in the theater when the fire broke out. The theater itself is fire proof and is practically unburned.

It was the blast of fire caused by the explosion of gas on the stage that cremated the helpless victims.

Nearly all the actors and employes back of the scenes and on the stage escaped.

Death of a Pioneer

Hampton Ede, an old and highly respected resident of Sierra Valley, died at Walla Walla, Washington, early yesterday morning.

Mr. Ede left Reno a short time ago to visit his daughter in the north. He was taken suddenly ill and died shortly afterwards.

The deceased was born at Brighton, Sussex county, England, January 5, 1826. He sailed for America in 1842 and settled in Wisconsin. In 1853 he crossed the plains and returned, but made two more trips to the coast, in 1859 and in 1864.

He leaves a daughter, Mrs. Dan McCloud, of Walla Walla, and a son, George Ede, of Loyalton. He is survived by a brother, Stephen Ede, of this city.

Nevada Club Party

The Leap Year party given at the Nevada Club last evening by Mrs. John Sunderland Jr. and Miss Maude Patterson was one of the most enjoyable events of the season. It was truly a Leap Year function and the men folk were at a disadvantage. They could not stroll across the floor without an escort.

The older members played cards on the first floor, while dancing was enjoyed by a younger generation in the story above. At the midnight hour refreshments were served and the guests departed.

WAR CLOUDS GATHER

Russia and Japan on the Eve of a Great Conflict

Special to The Journal]

LONDON, Dec. 30.—It was admitted today in official circles that the only hope of averting war between Japan and Russia lay in a concession by Russia. The French foreign minister is bringing all the possible pressure to bear in St. Petersburg and still hopes to be successful in bringing about a reconciliation. Such a settlement is not probable. Japan is determined to hasten matters, but Russia is not to be hurried. The January 10th reply is likely to be delivered.

Fearless Officer

Constable Gus Schlumpf, Truckee's fearless officer, visited Reno friends for a few hours last night. Mr. Schlumpf has done much to repress the lawless floating element in Truckee. It is due to his efforts that the town was saved from destruction by fire a few weeks ago. While making his rounds he discovered a series of fires that had been started by firebugs. Truckee is to be congratulated on having such an efficient officer.

A newspaper report on the Iroquois Theatre fire of 1903.

From the collection of Ed Mirvish.

the newspaper is unknown.

The worst was over within eight minutes. Miraculously, although the elephant and the dancing ponies died, Eddie Foy and all but one of the cast and crew – a tightrope walker caught in flies – survived. On the other side of the footlights, however, the policemen assigned to the sad recovery counted 623 dead. The Iroquois would hold the record for the worst single-building fire toll in North American history for the next 98 years.

The Iroquois Theater was owned and built by a New York-based organization called the Theatrical Syndicate, and that group would have a large part to play in the story of the Royal Alexandra. It had a twin theatre, of sorts, for the Syndicate, not wanting to spend any more than necessary on architects, copied its plans from those of the Opéra Comique, in Paris. The Opéra Comique also burned down.

7

HOW JOHN M. LYLE DID IT BETTER

THE BONES OF THE THEATRE

The Iroquois disaster might never have happened had the theatre's builders read and heeded one book, *Modern Opera Houses and Theatres* by Edwin O. Sachs.

Sachs was a British architect and engineer with a keen interest in theatres — everything to do with theatres, from their grand designs to the nuts and bolts of stage machinery, set construction and even scenery painting. Sachs had actually worked in theatres, as a stagehand, and there was little about them he did not know — and nothing about them on which he did not have a strong opinion. His book, published in 1898, studied, reviewed, analyzed and compared 55 European theatres built between 1875 and 1897 and included their plans, sections and elevations. It also included chapters on standard measurements, interior details, seating arrangement and configuration, stage construction, stage machinery, fly systems, lighting, hydraulics, electrification, acoustics and fire safety; in the latter were detailed analyses of 346 recent theatre fires with full instructions on how they could have been prevented.

Sachs' book was not popular with his fellow theatre architects, for his critical analyses of the work of his contemporaries

He built it better. Architect John M. Lyle's self-portrait, as "John M. T-Square."

often employed undiplomatic – even derisive – language. John M. Lyle, however, did read it and heed it. He would build the Royal Alexandra to meet, and even exceed, all of Sachs' fire-proofing standards.

To begin, the Royal Alexandra was built on a steel frame. It's been suggested that this method of construction – not yet common then – might have been the self-promoting idea of Cawthra Mulock, whose family and Alexandra Company partners had iron and steel interests. No Canadian company, however, was then equipped to produce the superior grade of steel specified by Lyle's structural engineer, William Fry Scott. Lyle had to have his framing supplied by a mill in Chicago that made channel steel for bridge builders.

The exterior walls and interior floors of the theatre were built of reinforced concrete. The steel and concrete walls of the auditorium and stage house were faced with yellow brick and the administration building – the part of the structure fronting on King St. – with sandstone. The concrete of the walls is two feet, five inches thick; that of the floors, two feet thick.

The entire building was wired for electricity. There would be no gas lighting and no limelights. For followspots - the spotlights moved by an operator to follow a performer on the stage – Lyle installed carbon-arc lamps. Although frightening and danger-ous-looking in operation – they produce light by means of a high-voltage spark jumping between two carbon-rod electrodes – carbon-arcs are far less likely to start a fire than limelights. Nevertheless, Lyle put the followspots in a separate, fire-proofed room of their own, at the rear of the upper balcony, so situated that audience members would not have to pass near them – would move away from them – to get to the fire-escape doors.

The fire code mandated two fire-escape doors – one on each side – on every level of the theatre. Lyle put four extra-wide doors on each level of the auditorium. It was theoretically possi-ble, absent panic, to empty a full house through the emergency exits within two and a half minutes.

Those emergency exits also opened outward and opened

easily, with push bars, to steel fire escapes. This might seem the obvious way to build an exit door today, but it was not so then; many of the bodies at the Iroquois were found piled up around inward opening exit doors that opened – if they had opened – into interior stairwells.

The fire curtain was specially manufactured to Lyle's exacting specifications: woven asbestos and steel wire, double-faced and heavily framed with iron. It could be operated electrically or manually – with levers on the stage, in the flies and at the stage door – or automatically, with a fuse designed to release if the temperature got too high. The asbestos curtain slid down inside steel channels – the "smoke pockets" – that overlapped its edges by six inches and would prevent smoke passing around them.

Backing up the fire curtain was a "water curtain," an automatic sprinkler system – fed by a 15,500-gallon cistern on the roof – designed to instantly soak everything in the fly tower, drench

The stage in 1907, with the fire curtain down. It was the custom to let the audience see the fire curtain as it entered the auditorium (it would then be raised to reveal the house curtain behind it) as the big letters spelling ASBESTOS reassured everyone. Today, they would be more likely to alarm the audience. Modern fire curtains are made of fibreglass, not asbestos.
Photo courtesy of the Toronto Public Library, Theatre Collection.

the draperies and flood the stage with water. For good measure, sprinkler heads were also discreetly hidden over the auditorium, in the ornate plasterwork of the ceilings.

The Royal Alexandra was the first — and, for a few years after its construction, the only — North American theatre that could with clear conscience call itself "fireproof." And it was only the second such in the entire English-speaking world — the first having been the Royal Opera House, Covent Garden, retrofitted and partially rebuilt (after a fire) in 1902 by Edwin O. Sachs.

PUTTING THE PARTS TOGETHER

It was Sachs who had once complained that the sole mandate given most theatre architects was to cram in as many ticket-buying patrons as physically possible, but building a truly first-class theatre — as John Lyle had been commissioned to do — was a bit more complicated.

If you stand outside the Royal Alexandra Theatre today, you might notice that there are three distinct parts to the building. In the rear is the stage house — the section containing the stage and the flies, the working part of the building. The stage house is a rectangular prism, wider than it is deep and taller than it is wide — like a shoebox stood on one end. In the centre is the auditorium — the seating area. This structure is a cube — equal in width, depth and height — or pretty close to it. The third part is the administration building — the part fronting on the street and containing the box office, lobbies, lounges and washrooms. It is also, roughly, a cube (but narrower than the auditorium).

THE STAGE HOUSE

The dimensions of the stage house were dictated by two factors beyond Lyle's control, the width of the lot and the theatrical set standards prevailing when the theatre was built. The latter were dictated by the Theatrical Syndicate (of which we hear more later), one of the more positive things the Syndicate did. Touring companies travelled with their own sets and scenery and it was crucial that these fit with the least necessary alter-

In the loft, at the top of the fly tower. If the scene reminds you of the deck of a sailing ship, you're right. The rigging and knots and the wooden belaying pins on which the lines are tied off are all based on the rigging of an 18th-century sailing ship.

Photo courtesy of the Toronto Public Library, Theatre Collection.

ation into every theatre; the Syndicate set standard dimensions to stage width and depth, the amount of wing space on each side of the stage, proscenium width and height and fly tower height and capacity.

Lyle's lot, remember, was about 100 feet wide. He chose to make his stage house 80 feet wide, leaving ample fire-escape room on either side, and a little extra space for a stage entrance on the east side. In this space, he met and surpassed the Syndicate's highest recommended standards by building a stage 42 feet wide and 35 feet deep — more than big enough for the most elaborate productions — with about 17 feet of wing space, with ramps and loading doors, on each side. Behind the stage, the stage house extended back another 22 feet to accommodate dressing rooms and washrooms of uncommonly generous and comfortable dimensions. Above the stage, the fly tower rose up 86 feet, high enough to handle any sets and scenery ever devised.

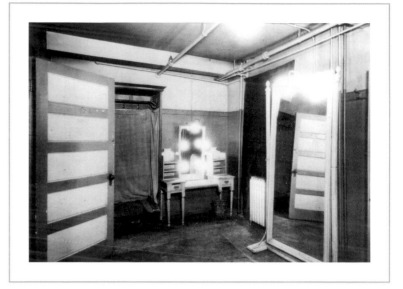

A backstage dressing room. Not particularly attractive, perhaps, but unusually spacious, warm, well equipped and lit by the standards of the time.

Photo courtesy of the Toronto Public Library, Theatre Collection.

While the 17 feet of wing space on either side of the stage was not much by the standards of the big New York and London theatres, Lyle reasoned that the Royal Alexandra would be a "road house," taking in touring shows arriving with their sets and scenery ready-made, ready to set up on the stage or hang in the flies; there would be no need for workshops and storage areas. It was far more important to give as much room as possible to the stage, and that's what he did.

THE AUDITORIUM

The second distinct part of the theatre is the auditorium, the centre section, where the audience sits. The dimensions of the auditorium were set for Lyle by two factors: the width of the stage – or, more properly, the width of the proscenium arch, the "picture-frame" of the stage – and the laws of acoustics.

The width of the arch determined the sightlines – and, thus, the maximum width – of the auditorium. Lyle calculated this to be 75 feet. Although he could have built his auditorium to the full width of the stage house and still left room on the sides for external fire-escape stairs, it would have put those theatregoers at the ends of the seating rows at too great an angle to the stage; the arch would obstruct their views. While most builders might have considered this an unfortunate necessity in the drive to maximize seating, Lyle – mindful of his mandate – did not. Not only did he stay within his calculated 75 feet, he did not even use all the room that gave him for seating; he cut out 86 potential seats that width would have allowed him in order to widen the side aisles, allowing easier access to the fire escapes.

The width of the auditorium determined the room's depth. Many years before Lyle set to work, theatre architects had discovered that the shape of an auditorium had an impact on its acoustic properties. The best shape for a legitimate theatre auditorium – for the acoustics of the human voice, speaking – was a cube. The closer the architect could come to a perfect square floor plan, the better the sound in the room. So, Lyle built the auditorium to be 75 feet wide by 72 feet deep by 65 feet high.

In that auditorium cube, he planned for three levels of seating, with a first – or "front" – balcony 23 feet above the orchestra and an upper balcony 21 feet above that. The steel framing of the building allowed Lyle a daring innovation in balcony construction. The balconies – also built of reinforced concrete on steel frames – were securely bolted to the side walls and, in a borrowing from bridge construction, cantilevered to the rear wall. This meant that full weight of the balconies could be borne by the steel frame of the building, with no visible supports. The Royal Alexandra would be the first theatre in North America to be built with no internal pillars and, thus, no obstructed-view seats.

A drawback to the cantilever principle – from the owner's point of view – was that it limited the depth of the balconies and, consequently, the number of balcony seats. Other theatres extended their pillar-supported balconies much farther over the orchestra, adding five or six more rows, but this had a negative impact on acoustics as well as sightlines. Lyle – with Mulock's approval – felt the improvements to the quality of the auditorium justified the reduction in potential revenue.

Another architect might also have found a way to squeeze three balconies – and an extra three hundred seats – into the space into which Lyle put two. This could have been accomplished by raising the ceiling and reducing the headroom between the levels. The latter, however, would also impact sightlines and acoustics; people in the back rows of the balconies

— and in the back rows of the orchestra level — would have been unable to see or hear clearly. Setting the balconies higher than normal allowed Lyle to actually improve the acoustics of the back rows, shaping the high ceilings under the balcony over-hangs to create a megaphone effect.

The shallow balconies, however, also meant that Lyle would have to build the uppermost level — the "gallery" or "the gods" — at a dizzyingly steep rake. In 1907, however, this was not a worry; the upper gallery was traditionally the student seating area — the lowest-priced and least comfortable, meant for the young, rowdy and adventurous, its steep seating adding to the fun, excitement and glamour of going to the theatre — and seen by many owners as more a public service than a revenue centre.

In the early days of the theatre, it became a tradition for uni-versity students to celebrate an annual Varsity Night at the Royal Alexandra, just before the spring exams, and pack the gallery. On one such night in 1911 — as the British actor Edward Terry attempted a performance of Pinero's *The Magistrate* — students in the gallery dumped bags of flour down onto the balcony and orchestra patrons below. The audience below that night includ-ed the Lieutenant-Governor, Sir John Gibson, the mayor, G.R. Geary, and Robert Falconer, president of the university. Falconer took to the stage to appeal for order, but both Gibson and Geary stood to cheer the students on. Manager Solman called the police, but ejecting the revelers from the steep gallery proved a very difficult task. In later years, as Ontario relaxed its blue laws and began allowing theatres to sell alcoholic beverages — absolutely forbidden in 1907 — the Royal Alexandra's gallery would remain dry; in the opinion of the Liquor Licensing Board, its stairs were too steep to be safely negotiated by the tipsy.

That steep rake had a great benefit; it gave every seat in the gallery an exceptionally good view of the full stage — a better view, in fact, than that enjoyed by the VIP patrons sitting in the stage-side boxes below. Box seats were then fading out of fashion and many new North American theatres of the early 20th centu-ry eliminated them altogether. The problem with boxes was that the drive to maximize seating left them, practically, useless; if the builder wished to extend the rows of orchestra seating as widely as possible – right up to the theoretical limits of sightlines – box seats would block the view from the orchestra sides. The only solution was to push the boxes back, away from the proscenium, and so angle them that those sitting in them would be facing the house, and not the stage. No one would want to sit in them if he could not see the show.

The function of box seating was social. These were the seats of the aristocracy – or, if a theatre owner were lucky enough, of royalty – the seats reserved for those who would not come to the theatre at all if they had to sit among the common people. While it was unlikely that King Edward and Queen Alexandra would ever show up for a play in Toronto (although they certainly did attend the theatre in London – and sit in a box), it was reasonable to expect the at least occasional attendance of such people as Sir William Mortimer Clark, the Lieutenant-Governor (who did, after all, live right across the street), or the prime minister, Sir Wilfrid Laurier (who was, after all, a close family friend of the Mulocks), or even His Excellency the Earl Grey, the Governor General (who, as it turned out, would come often in his capacity as patron of the Dominion Drama and Music Festival). It would be unthinkable to build a first-class theatre in Canada without box seats, but John Lyle's decisions not to maximize seating – to make the side aisles wider than normal and keep the orchestra rows well within the full limit of sightlines – solved the major problem in box placement. Not having to worry about hindering the views from side seats that did not exist, he could angle his boxes to face the stage and project them far enough out from the proscenium to allow those sitting in them a relatively decent view of the stage – not as good, perhaps, as that enjoyed by those sitting nearer the centre or up in the balconies, but actually better than what rival theatres could offer those viewers sitting in expensive seats on the sides of their orchestras.

Lyle's finished plan gave the Royal Alexandra a total of 1,525 seats – 300 fewer than the Princess, 600 fewer than the Grand

The house-left boxes, with their vice-regal draperies in place. Box seating was a social necessity in theatres of the British Empire in Edwardian times.

Photo courtesy of the Toronto Public Library. Theatre Collection.

ROYAL ALEXANDRA THEATRE, TORONTO, CANADA.

The brand-new Royal Alexandra Theatre. The show title displayed on the boards dates the photo for us: Clyde Fitch's drama *The Cowboy and the Lady* ran from October 21 to 26, 1907, a production of the Royal Alexandra Players starring Grace Mae Lamkin as Jessica Weston — the Lady — and Robert Conness as Teddy North, the dude cowboy with whom she finds happiness.

Opera House, almost 700 fewer than the Majestic — but he could boast that among those 1,525 there wasn't a bad seat in the house.

THE ADMINISTRATION BUILDING

After the shoebox of the stage house and the cube of the auditorium, John Lyle still had about 50 feet of building space left to take him to the King St. sidewalk. This he devoted to the third structure, the administration building — with a Beaux-Arts stone façade, slate-tiled mansard roof and copper trims that would have looked at home on the streets of Second Empire Paris — housing the theatre's lobbies, washrooms, lounges and offices.

The prevailing wisdom of theatre-building then was that any space given to lobbies and lounges was space wasted, unless it could be leased to rent-paying tenants. Most North American theatres either had no front-of-house space at all — the street doors opening directly into the auditorium — or had as "crush space" mere walkways between rows of shops. Lyle went against the current to build lobbies — and more — on all three levels.

On the orchestra level, the street doors opened into a large entrance way containing the box office wickets. The doors from this "ticket vestibule" opened into a lobby – the "foyer" – adjoining which were a gentlemen's smoking room, a gentlemen's washroom, a ladies' "retiring room," a sitting room, gentlemen's and ladies' coat-check rooms, a manager's office and the "owner's room" (which doubled as a private VIP lounge and party room).

The stairs on either side of the first-floor lobby led into a second-floor lobby, adjoining which was the "French Lounge," a spacious tearoom with huge windows and French balconies overlooking King St., with a beautiful view south to the lake. Up short flights of steps on either side of this lobby were two more washrooms. Two other sets of stairs would take a patron up to the gallery, at the top of the building, with a lobby and washrooms and a tiny apartment for the theatre janitor.

The newspapers of the day all commented on the unprecedented and luxurious size of the Royal Alexandra lobbies and lounges. In later years, they would not seem so big and might often feel crowded, but in 1907 they were enormous; after all, in the custom of that time, it was only gentlemen patrons who visited the lobbies at intermissions; ladies were expected to remain always in their seats and the retiring rooms were little used – and ladies, then as now, often made up the majority of the audience. Lyle's overkill in lobby and washroom space might have been evidence of clairvoyance, for those Edwardian rules of ladylike behaviour were going to change radically after the First World War, and his theatre would be ready for that change.

Within a year of the theatre's opening, John Lyle had to find space in his administration building for one more novel amenity. In those days, everyone wore a hat. Gentlemen were expected to remove their hats on entering and Lyle equipped the underside of each seat with a wire hat-rack, just the right size for a man's winter homburg or summer skimmer; ladies, however, kept their hats on. This did not present a problem – women's hats, while sometimes exuberant, were still relatively compact – until 1907, when an Austrian operetta called *The Merry Widow* premiered

The ladies' retiring room, the place to go to powder one's nose in 1907. The wall coverings — no colour photography yet then — were of green silk.

Photo courtesy of the Toronto Public Library, Theatre Collection.

The gentlemen's smoking room, with its masculine, brown leather furniture, was off-limits to ladies. This room is now the manager's office of the theatre, right behind the box office.

Photo courtesy of the Toronto Public Library, Theatre Collection.

The owner's room, a private reception room for VIP guests of the theatre. The room and its elegant fireplace are still there, just off the main lobby.

Photo courtesy of the Toronto Public Library, Theatre Collection.

in London. The show starred a very popular actress named Lily Elsie, whose costumes were designed by one of Britain's leading offstage fashion designers, "Madame Lucile," Lady Duff-Gordon (who grew up, by the way, in Guelph, Ontario). For Miss Elsie, Lady Duff-Gordon created a series of wide-brimmed, outrageously theatrical hats. When Lily Elsie wore them on stage she sparked the first great, worldwide fashion fad of the 20th century. While *The Merry Widow* would not be seen at the Royal Alexandra until 1910 (with Mabel Wilber wearing the hats), photos of Lily Elsie filled newspapers and magazines all over North America in 1907, and every woman of fashion *had* to have one of those *Merry Widow* hats. Suddenly faced with audiences filled with women in hats so wide that no one could sit beside them — much less see over them — John Lyle added a ladies' hat-check room to the first-floor lobby.

THE ICING ON THE CAKE

It's likely that John Lyle had already more than used up that preliminary $350,000 budget before he even began thinking about the theatre's façade and interiors. If that bothered him – or the Alexandra Company – it's not apparent. He handed the plans to John McEwan, his contractor, with the instruction "All of the materials necessary to carry out the work herein described are to be the best of their several kinds."

In those days, "the best" meant imported. In his later years, John Lyle would become a champion of a new, Canadian architectural style and of native materials, but then, he was still firmly of the French Beaux-Arts school. For the interior walls of the foyer he specified a dark green marble – *verde assoluto* – which McEwan had to order from Italy. The foyer floor was to be of mosaic tile, which McEwan had made in Venice. The walls and staircases of the main floor and first balcony lobbies were to be panelled in walnut, with hand-carved walnut trims, but not ordinary Canadian black walnut; for these, "the best" was Circassian walnut, imported from Turkey. The grand staircases leading up from the main lobby – banisters, balustrades and newel posts – were hand-carved of the best cherrywood, and the best cherry came from Central Europe.

Inside the auditorium, the wainscoting and doorways *were* of Canadian wood: oak. But Lyle specified that the oak be quarter-sawn, the most expensive grade. Above the wainscoting, the walls were "papered" in cream and gold silk and the boxes hung with red silk draperies, the fabrics imported from France. The seat coverings matched the colours of the walls, with a striped cream and gold wool and silk gabardine, specially woven for Lyle and McEwan by Burberry's, in England.

Not only were the materials largely imported, so were the artisans who shaped them. The team responsible for the decorative carvings in the main lobby came from Germany; the tile floor was the work of mosaicists from Italy; the elegant façade of the administration building, of stonemasons and stone-carvers from Britain; the ornate plasterwork of the ceilings, the proscenium

Mabel Wilber, wearing her *Merry Widow* hat at the Royal Alexandra, in November 1910.

Photo from the collection of the Royal Alexandra Theatre.

arch and the box and balcony fronts, of French craftsmen. Some of these people who came to Canada for this one job would stay; 80 years after the theatre opened, David and Ed Mirvish would add a new lounge and washroom area in the basement. Among the plasterers they found to duplicate the look of the auditorium above was one whose grandfather had come to Toronto from Paris in 1906 to work for John Lyle and John McEwan.

Speaking of the basement, it was there that Lyle put a heating plant of unique design that would make easier the difficult task of regulating winter temperatures in the huge, open auditorium above. It was an early version of a forced-air system. Two coal-fired boilers, which could be operated separately or together, generated the heat that was pushed by fans through brass-grilled vents in the auditorium floor, each vent capable of being opened, damped down or closed by the person sitting nearest it.

This heating system doubled in the hot Toronto summers as a cooling system. Lyle borrowed the basic idea — but greatly improved upon it — from Richard D'Oyly Carte's Royal English

Opera House, opened in London in 1891. In front of the boilers, he built a concrete pit. In the summer, workmen kept the pit filled with ice. The floor fans pushed cool air from the ice pit into the auditorium. Hidden away from sight, up in the ceiling, above the crystal chandelier, a huge, silent fan pulled the cooled air up and kept it circulating through the house. It was the first "air-conditioning" system to be seen in any theatre on this continent. As primitive an idea as it might seem today, Lyle's fans and ice pit could keep the temperature of the auditorium at about 20

The *Globe* comments on the theatre, August 22, 1907.

degrees C, even on an August afternoon, and that was a true marvel in 1907.

There was a possibly unexpected plus benefit in the heating/cooling system. Lyle may have planned it, but it may also have just been a happy accident. The gently moving column of air generated by the floor and ceiling fans actually improved the already exceptional acoustic properties of the room.

The final bill for the project came to $750,000 — more than twice the original, preliminary budget and 25 percent more than what Clarence Blackall would calculate, in 1908, to be the maximum any builder should dare spend. It was a huge sum, five times what had been spent 10 years before on Massey Hall. It's difficult to say precisely what its equivalent would be in today's money, but if one looks at average wages and the relative costs of food and housing, then and now, it would work out to be something between 50 and 60 million dollars — far more than the Alexandra Company could hope to recoup from ticket sales within that 12-year window. It looked as though Cawthra Mulock had been telling the truth when he described his theatre as "a public and cultural service" for Toronto.

But, before we begin selling tickets, there's one other aspect to the theatre's interior décor that deserves a chapter of its own.

THE MURAL

EVERY THEATRE AS OLD as or older than the Royal Alexandra has a proscenium, the decorative arch – the "picture frame" – around the stage. Actually, it's not just decoration. It defines the stage area; it hides all the machinery, wires, ropes, cables, props, costume racks, lights, sets and scenery and whatnot above the stage or in the wings; and, often, it's shaped like the bell of a horn and acts as a sound projector. In later years, many architects, mistakenly viewing the proscenium as mere decoration and seeking a stripped-down, sleek and "modern" look, would eliminate the old-fashioned arch and build arena or thrust stages, placing the audience around the stage rather than before it. This turned out to be a mistake, severely limiting what could be done in their theatres; but, those new-fangled notions had not yet come along in John Lyle's day, and he built a proscenium.

Up at the top of the proscenium, right in the centre, knowledgeable architects put a large, smooth, carefully angled and curved plaster surface called a "sounding board." As the arch is a sound projector, the sounding board is a sound reflector, designed to bounce the voices of actors on the stage into the balconies – especially, the gallery, "the gods."

As a reflector, the sounding board had to have a smooth surface – no plaster rosettes, vine leaves or pagan gods. But, rather than leave their sounding boards blank and empty and annoyingly distractive, theatre owners who could afford to do so hired artists to paint decorative murals on them. The richer the theatre owner, the more famous the artist. As cost was no problem for John Lyle, he had the Royal Alexandra's sounding board painted by a very famous artist – considered one of Canada's finest muralists and painters of allegorical and historical scenes – named Frederick Sproston Challener.

Challener was born in 1869, in Whetstone, England. His parents brought him with them to Toronto in 1870, but sent him back to Britain for his grammar school education, leaving him in a lonely boarding school until he was 14, then bringing him back to Canada and sending him off to work. He spent his teenage years working as a clerk in a brokerage house until he found a way to take advantage of a natural talent with pen, pencil and paintbrush, working at colouring and retouching photos for the famous studios of William Notman and John A. Fraser, while taking classes at the Ontario School of Art.

In 1889, Challener left Notman and Fraser to study with the well-known painter (and muralist) George A. Reid and work, part-time, as newspaper artist and as a draughtsman. In 1898, he left Canada again to make a grand tour of Europe and the Middle East, where he studied mural painting, coming home at the end of that year to open a mural studio of his own in a rented barn near Leamington, Ontario, and to begin work on his first commissions: the ceiling panels for McConkey's Restaurant, in Toronto; the proscenium mural for the Russell Opera House, in Ottawa; the proscenium mural for Ambrose Small's Grand Theatre, in London, Ontario; and *The French at Fort Rouillé*, a mural for the lobby of Toronto's new King Edward Hotel. In 1901, he won the Bronze Medal for painting at the Pan-American Exposition (where the chief architects had been John Lyle's firm, Carrère and Hastings). By 1903, he found himself doing well enough to leave the Leamington barn, build himself a house and studio at 87 Garden Ave., in Toronto, and get married.

The bride was a beautiful young woman named Ethel White, whom Challener had met in 1901, on a visit to Chicago. It is Ethel's face you see in the Royal Alexandra's proscenium mural; she served as basic body-model for all the female figures in the painting, but the woman at the right — with the dark hair and orange gown — is Ethel herself, her portrait.

Her portrait, but an allegorical one. The scene depicted is from Roman mythology, via the poet Ovid — *Venus and Attendants Discover the Sleeping Adonis*. In the myth, Venus, goddess of love and beauty, went out walking one day in the company of some nymphs and her son, Cupid. Cupid stumbled and accidentally shot his mother with one of his magic arrows. The arrow-wound caused Venus to fall in love with the first man she saw, who happened to be a handsome mortal named Adonis who was taking a nap in the grass. What the relevance of this scene is to a theatre is anyone's guess, but that wasn't considered important in 1906; a proscenium mural was meant to be beautiful, not meaningful.

Ethel was painted as Venus, but there is another person from Challener's life in the group. Cupid, on the far right, is a portrait (with some added, adult muscle) of "Hughie" Allward, the

Frederick S. Challener at work in 1917 on his mural *Orpheus Charming the Nymphs* for the proscenium arch of the Princess Theatre in Montreal.

seven-year-old son of one of Challener's closest friends from his art student days, the sculptor Walter Allward. Walter would later become internationally famous as the sculptor/architect of the Canadian war memorial at Vimy Ridge. Hughie would grow up to become an architect himself – dropping the "ie" to become Hugh – build Toronto's Sunnybrook Hospital and take charge of the 1963 renovations of the Royal Alexandra.

Although Ethel may have looked the part of the goddess of love, she acted the role of something else. By all accounts, she made poor Challener's life a misery. While it's certainly possible that their marital problems were all Challener's fault, contemporary accounts by his friends tell of a very pleasant and likeable fellow chained to a harpy. One of those friends – his old teacher, George Reid – wrote privately of his fear that Ethel was actually insane.

The Challeners separated in 1915 and Ethel moved back to Chicago (taking their five children with her), but they never divorced. Challener continued to support her until his death in 1959 – for the next 44 years – and, although his mural work should have made him rich, Ethel lived extravagantly and paying her bills kept him in near penury. To make ends meet, he took a day-job as a teacher at Central Technical School and, later, at the Ontario College of Art, where he remained until 1952.

When Frederick Challener died, at the age of 90, Ethel – still Mrs. Challener – came back to Toronto to claim the keys to the Garden Ave. house. Philip Clark, the executor of the estate, wrote that the vindictive widow went into the house and destroyed every painting, every drawing, every sketch she could find, almost wiping out 70 years of the artist's work.

Fortunately, there were enough paintings already hanging on other walls or stretched over theatre proscenia, beyond Ethel's reach, to save something of Frederick Sproston Challener's memory: the sounding-board mural of the Royal Alexandra; the earlier, larger mural at the Grand Theatre; the murals at Old City Hall; the painting *Canada's Grand Armada* at the War Museum, in

Ottawa; the famous, history textbook, paintings *The Fathers Of Confederation* and *Étienne Brûlé at the Mouth of the Humber* now hanging in Queen's Park; 14 painted wall panels at Parkwood, the museum/former home of Col. Robert McLaughlin in Oshawa; individual paintings at the National Gallery of Canada and the Art Gallery of Ontario; and, perhaps – just perhaps – the *Fort Rouillé* mural that once filled the lobby of the King Edward Hotel. No one knows what ever happened to the *Fort Rouillé* mural. There is no record of its ever having been taken down and the possibility remains that it's still there, hidden under more than one hundred years of wallpaper and paint.

9

THE ROAD

Around the time Edith Challener put on the orange gown to pose as Venus and little Hughie Allward stripped to his skivvies and shouldered Cupid's quiver and bow, Lol Solman took the train to New York City to start talking to actors, managers and booking agents about putting the Royal Alexandra on the first-class legitimate touring circuit.

New York, the biggest city on the continent, was then — even more so than it is today — the centre, the point of origin, of almost all professional theatre production in North America. It was not yet, however, the goal or endpoint of theatre performance; it was, rather, the hub from which theatre companies moved out onto the road. The day had not yet come — although it soon would — when shows would "try out" on the road with a hope of going to Broadway; many shows tried out in New York with the hope of then going on the road (even if the New York run was unsuccessful, they could still advertise themselves in Detroit or Chicago, Toronto or Montreal, as "direct from Broadway"). It was on the road, not on Broadway, that the real money was to be made.

"The road" meant the railroad. By the 1890s, the railroad went almost everywhere worth going to and any town with a

Canadian performers who went south to find stage work and stardom: Gladys Smith (also known as Mary Pickford), of Toronto; Donald Brian (above picture), of St. John's; and Ottawa-born Margaret Anglin.

railroad siding to park along, a theatre (or adequate approximation of a theatre) to play in and a hotel or boarding house to spend the night in had become a potential market for a touring troupe of actors – as long as the hotel would take them in; many would not, presuming all "play actors" to be drunkards and fornicators whose presence would drive away respectable guests.

At any given moment in the years between 1890 and 1914 – the "golden age" of touring theatre in North America – there might have been three hundred or more professional companies somewhere on the road; and we are talking only about "legitimate" theatre companies, not counting the hundreds more vaudeville, burlesque and minstrel show troupes or individual variety acts. The majority of these companies called New York home (or, at least, did their business out of New York). Although there might often be one or two British companies out there as well, they were few and far between; transatlantic travel costs were too high. As for Canadian companies, in most years then you could count them on one finger; while amateur theatre thrived across Canada, professional theatre was almost non-existent. Canadians who wanted to work on the stage – including such major stars of the day as Mary Pickford, Marie Dressler, Matheson Lang, Margaret Anglin and Donald Brian (whom the *New York Times*, in 1908, would crown "the king of Broadway") – went to New York or London.

The legitimate touring companies fell into one of three categories: multiple-show repertory companies, multiple-show stock companies and companies assembled for and travelling with a single show.

The latter category featured, generally, the biggest, most expensive, most lavish productions – large-scale musicals, revues, operettas and extravaganzas – with famous stars, big casts, eye-popping sets and costumes and elaborate special effects. These were the kind of shows that a theatre owner today might hope to settle into his house for a long run – several months, or even a year or two – but there was no such thing as a long-running, sit-down production in the road houses of the early 20th century. Shows went on the road with a prearranged schedule and even the biggest could seldom stop in any one theatre for more than a week. The preferred run was five days: open on Monday, close on Friday, travel on Saturday, set up in the next city on Sunday, open on Monday. A really popular show, however, might run for years on the road, returning again and again to all the cities on its circuit for yet another few days.

Thus, the Sigmund Romberg/Dorothy Donnelly "Viennese" operetta *Blossom Time* – based on the familiar music of Franz Schubert and said to be the only musical to see audiences whistling the show tunes *before* they entered the theatre – would reappear at the Royal Alexandra 21 times over a stretch of 27 years (with five of those stops billed as "the farewell engagement"). Its cast changed a little each time as exhausted performers dropped out, got too old for their parts, retired or died. The spectacular drama *The Bird of Paradise* – telling the story of the forbidden, miscegenational love of an American sailor and a Polynesian girl, and featuring a volcanic eruption and a raging typhoon, live, on stage (not to mention the all-native-Hawaiian orchestra that sparked a 20-year-long fad for ukeleles) came back to Toronto 11 sold-out times between 1913 and 1922, never playing more than five days. And the biggest of them all – the biggest show ever to play the Royal Alexandra – the stupendous 1919 musical *Chu Chin Chow*, a retelling of the story of Ali Baba and the 40 Thieves, with a cast of three hundred human actors and a performing menagerie of camels, donkeys and yaks – would return four times, with the same stars, in the course of a single three-year tour, with its longest Toronto run being only one week.

As desirable as these crowd-pleasing spectacles might have been for their effect on a theatre's bottom line, the touring companies most coveted by serious-minded owners and managers – such as Cawthra Mulock and Lol Solman – who had ambitions to see their houses regarded as high-class, cultural institutions, were the repertory – or "rep" – companies. These were the aristocrats of the road, troupes that travelled with a well-rehearsed group of plays (and scenery and costumes for

Laurette Taylor starred as Luana, the South Sea island maiden, in the perennial tour of the spectacular *The Bird of Paradise*.

The dashing James K. Hackett
as the heroic Rudolf Rassendyll
in the popular adventure
The Prisoner of Zenda.

all) that they would perform, one after the other, on successive evenings and afternoons.

The best rep companies emphasized acting – tour de force performance – over spectacle and literary quality over novelty. They were built around a famous actor, or group of famous actors – often a famous acting/managing couple, such as the husband-and-wife teams of E.H. Sothern and Julia Marlowe, or Johnston Forbes-Robertson and Gertrude Elliott, or Katharine Cornell and her director husband Guthrie McClintic, or Sir John Martin-Harvey and Nina de Silva.

Many specialized in certain plays or types of plays. Sothern and Marlowe, for example, were Shakespeareans, at their best with the comedies; Robert Bruce Mantell was a thundering tragedian, famed for his *King Lear*, his *Macbeth*, his wicked *Richard III* and, most of all, his evil *Richelieu*; the Marie Tempest Company brought new plays, sophisticated contemporary comedies; Minnie Maddern Fiske specialized in modern European drama (with emphasis on the controversial works of Ibsen); John Martin-Harvey was a swashbuckler, touring with such classic adventures as Sabatini's *Scaramouche*, the cavalier and roundhead drama *The Breed of the Treshams* and his dramatization of Dickens' *Tale of Two Cities*, *The Only Way*; the Maurice Colbourne and Barry Jones Company was famous for the comedies of Shaw; Johnston Forbes-Robertson was counted by many as the greatest *Hamlet* of all times; and the Canadian-born matinee idol James K. Hackett, who looked wonderful in tight military uniforms, was an unforgettable *Prisoner of Zenda*. A company such as Forbes-Robertson's might play for five nights, presenting four different plays (two classics and two modern works) and, on the fifth night, an evening of highlights – single acts – from all four, to a full house every time (with many in the audience coming every night).

Like rep companies, stock companies were usually built around one or two well-known actors and presented a variety of different plays over a short period of time. The principal difference was how short that time was. Stock companies would move into a theatre for an extended period – a month or two – and run each of the plays in their repertoires for several days, or even a week or two. Some might stay in one theatre for two months and then move to another; some did not tour at all, but would remain in a single theatre for a summer season and then disband, sometimes to regroup for another engagement, sometimes to disappear altogether; others would become resident companies, staying in a single theatre for years, yielding the stage to touring productions, but filling the gaps in between.

Originally, back in the good old days of the 19th century, stock companies were almost all resident companies and did not tour at all. Almost every city that had a theatre had a resident stock company – Toronto's Grand Opera House was built specifically for a stock company led by Charlotte Morrison, daughter of the American actor John Nickinson, who brought his company to Toronto for a two-week engagement in 1852 and stayed, setting up permanently at the Royal Lyceum (which burned down in 1874 to be replaced by the Royal Opera House, which burned down in 1883). But this was in the days before rep companies and big touring productions became commonplace; the basic job of a stock company was to provide a ready-made ensemble with which individual travelling "star" actors could play. A single famous actor – Sarah Bernhardt, for example – or famous acting family – such as John Drew, his sister Georgina and Georgina's husband, Maurice Barrymore – might come to Toronto to work for a few days with Mrs. Morrison's stock players before moving on to Buffalo or Cleveland or Detroit to play with a stock company there. The railroad changed all that, making it possible for the famous actors to form travelling companies of their own. As the touring circuits grew, and theatre owners realized they no longer had to keep actors on a regular payroll, most of the old stock players, to survive, went on the road themselves.

Stock productions tended to be lighter fare than rep – popular comedies and old favourite dramas and melodramas, usually the tried and true – and theatre managers regarded stock as a good, safe fallback that could always be relied upon to keep the lights

Margaret Anglin

Mary Pickford

on, especially in the slower summer seasons (hence "summer stock") when there were often fewer shows and rep companies on the road.

Some of the more successful stock companies – such as that led by Percy Haswell, whose photo you'll see on page one in this book – would actually take a theatre over for a summer, leasing it, paying all the bills and sending the regular management on holiday. Miss Haswell leased the Royal Alexandra for six summers in a row, from 1910 to 1915, mounting 66 family-friendly productions (she promised Toronto nothing but clean entertainment "free of the Ibsen taint") and enjoyed a lucrative side business selling autographed photos and her own brand of cosmetics in the lobby; she would empty cups-full of her Percy Haswell Perfumes into the basement ice pit, allowing her largely female audiences to sample her scents as they laughed to Ernest Denny's *All-of-a-Sudden Peggy* or wept to Frances Hodgson Burnett's *The Dawn of a Tomorrow*.

Stock – and stock players like Percy Haswell – would prove of immense value to Lol Solman after that first trip to New York, when he would be forced to turn the as-yet-unlaunched Royal Alexandra into the Canadian battleship in a North American theatre war.

THE SYNDICATE

IN THE LATE 19TH CENTURY, as the road became a bigger and bigger business, theatre managers competed for the attention of the brightest stars and the best shows. At the same time, the stars, the shows and the touring companies competed for bookings in the best theatres in the best towns (and bookings in enough of those theatres in enough of those towns to make a tour profitable). A new middleman business grew up in New York, "booking agents" who represented and negotiated with all involved – theatres, producers, acting company managers and even railroad lines – handling the complexities of organizing and scheduling; and the booking agents competed with one another. In spending so lavishly to build "the finest theatre on the continent," it's likely that Cawthra Mulock and his Alexandra Company partners believed that they could trump the competition of Toronto's lesser theatres and be in a position to pick and choose among the offers of competing booking agents. All they needed to do was let everyone know that the Royal Alexandra was open. Lol Solman took the train to New York for just that purpose, but found that times had changed; things were not as he imagined them to be.

Abraham Lincoln Erlanger.
In 1907, he was "the Napoleon of theatre" as head of the Theatrical Syndicate, the organization that controlled all legitimate theatre bookings all over North America.

Photo courtesy of the New York Public Library, Billy Rose Theater Collection.

In 1896, a group of theatre owners met over lunch at the Holland House, in New York, and formed a syndicate – the Theatrical Syndicate, also known as "the Theatres Trust" – for the purpose, they said, of rectifying problems in the touring theatre business that had been brought on by too much competition. The most important members of this group were Charles S. Frohman, a prolific producer and director who also owned a number of theatres in the American midwest and west; Abraham Erlanger and Marcus Klaw, who owned a chain of theatres in the American south; Samuel Nixon and Fred Zimmerman, who owned several theatres in the eastern United States; and Al Hayman, who owned theatres in New York and California. The way things were then organized – or disorganized – they felt to be "economically unsound" and hurting everyone in the business. Competition among theatre owners sometimes left them at the mercy of rapacious booking agents and often led to two or more first-class attractions running simultaneously in cities that could support only one at a time, resulting in "immense losses" for both theatres and players; too many independent booking agents led to dishonest theatre owners playing them off against one another, driving down the profits of the travelling companies and limiting their ability to book complete seasons; highly desirable star actors and star attractions could hold both owners and agents to ransom, threatening to switch to other agencies or tour circuits. In short, overcompetition had led to a situation in which contracts had become meaningless and were honoured only until a competitor offered a better deal. The grand idea of the men who met for lunch at the Holland House was to end wasteful competition by bringing all theatres into one cooperative organization, rationalizing and centralizing all tour bookings through one office and standardizing (and enforcing) all contracts. This, they argued, would benefit all.

All together, the Syndicate partners of 1896 controlled 37 theatres, but the numbers were less important than the locations. Touring companies moved step by step across the continent, trying to always end one engagement within a day or two's travel of the next; long delays between stops cost money and no company manager in his right mind would book a tour that took his players from, say, Montreal to Chicago without intermediate stops in Toronto and Detroit. The placement of those 37 theatres meant that no company could hope to make a profitable tour of the United States without playing at least a few Syndicate houses. No Syndicate house would accept a booking that had not been made through the Syndicate's central office, and this drove most of the independent booking agencies right out of the legitimate theatre business. As the independent bookers disappeared, more

Charles S. Frohman, one of Erlanger's partners and the leading theatre producer of his day.

Photo courtesy of the New York Public Library, Billy Rose Theater Collection.

Marcus Klaw, a lawyer by trade, was Abe Erlanger's business partner and third member of the Syndicate's ruling triumvirate.

theatre owners found themselves forced to sign Syndicate contracts; and, as the money started rolling in, the Syndicate partners bought or built more theatres. By 1905, when construction began on the Royal Alexandra, the Syndicate numbered five hundred theatres and had almost complete control of the legitimate touring business of North America.

In Toronto, in its drive to end wasteful competition, the Syndicate decreed that first-class productions would play only the Princess Theatre. The older Grand Opera House, which had been first-class, was assigned the role of second-class house and the new Majestic, that of third-class, or melodrama house. The three theatres would no longer compete, but would complement one another, to the advantage of all. These decisions were a bitter disappointment to Ambrose Small, who owned the latter two theatres. His status was diminished; the first-class honours went to the Princess's Oliver Barton Sheppard, whom he had once gleefully fired; but he had no choice except to acquiesce if he wanted to stay in business at all. What Small probably did not know — few did at this time — was that it was the Syndicate, not O.B. Sheppard, that actually owned the Princess Theatre. This, then, was the situation when Lol Solman went to New York to book shows for the Royal Alexandra.

Abe Erlanger, the man who ran the Syndicate's booking office — and who then liked to call himself "the Napoleon of theatre" — was quite happy to meet Solman. He knew all about the Royal Alexandra and was keenly interested in adding it to the Syndicate's family — not, however, as a legitimate theatre. He had no interest in seeing another legitimate house in Toronto, competing in that limited market with his own Princess Theatre. He had other plans.

Having conquered the legit world, Erlanger and his partners had ambitions to do the same with the world of vaudeville — the variety stage of singers, tap and soft-shoe dancers, jugglers, magicians, ventriloquists, comedians, acrobats, dog-and pony acts, minstrel shows and hypnotists. Toronto's first-class vaudeville house was Shea's, owned by the Shea brothers but controlled by vaudeville's own near-monopoly booking agency, the very Syndicate-like "KAO" (the Keith-Albee-Orpheum Organization — the Albee of which was Edward Albee, grandfather of the playwright). Erlanger and Marcus Klaw had put together a new first-class vaudeville booking agency of their own — Klaw and Erlanger's Advanced Vaudeville — with the aim of challenging, overthrowing and supplanting KAO. They were looking for theatres and thought the Royal Alexandra just the ticket. They would use it to drive the Sheas out of the Toronto market. When Lol Solman came to see him, Erlanger had already mapped out two full seasons of Advanced Vaudeville for the Royal Alexandra.

Had Erlanger presented his proposals to Solman in the latter's role as an amusement park owner, the man who had brought J.W. Gorman's Diving Horse to Hanlan's Point, he might have received an enthusiastic response. As representative of the Alexandra Company, which had just spent a fortune building the finest theatre on the continent, however, Solman took a different attitude. If the Royal Alexandra were to become a vaudeville house, half the money spent would have been wasted; vaudeville theatres did not need wide, deep stages or 86-foot-tall fly towers. Even more important than the money were the issues of status, class and prestige. Cawthra Mulock and his partners had built the Royal Alexandra as a centre for dramatic art. They would not surrender its elegant stage to slapstick buffoonery and performing collies. Solman politely declined Erlanger's offer and reminded him that there were still a few independents in legit theatre with whom he could talk – people like the Shubert brothers, who were beginning to produce their own shows for their own small chain of theatres. Erlanger's smile turned to a sneer. He put his feet on his desk, puffed on his cigar and told Solman to go right ahead; he could talk to anyone he wanted to; he was free to do as he pleased; the Syndicate, however, would consider itself free to do as it pleased with the Royal Alexandra. What the Napoleon of theatre had immediately in mind was bankrupting the Alexandra Co., buying their theatre on the cheap and turning it into a stable for the carriage horses of the upper-class patrons of the Princess, just up the street.

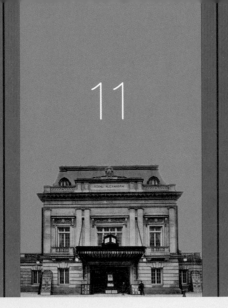

THE REBEL ALLIANCE

It was said of the many partners of the Theatrical Syndicate that there were two without whom the organization could not exist: Abe Erlanger and Charles S. Frohman. Erlanger was the businessman and deal-maker, the master organizer who maintained order throughout the complex empire. Frohman was the creative director, a producer and director of unerring judgement and boundless energy who kept the vast circuit of member theatres supplied with money-making product. The two had little in common, beyond their partnership, but they worked well together — Frohman as the Syndicate's velvet glove and Erlanger, its iron fist.

Charles Frohman, before the beginnings of the Syndicate, was already one of the best-known and most highly respected people in both North American and British theatre. A warm, good-humoured, likeable and somewhat shy man, he counted a startling number of the leading actors, directors, playwrights and composers of the Edwardian era among his close, personal friends; and as a producer, he seemed to have the Midas touch. Frohman's name at the top of the list of partners gave the Syndicate an air of legitimacy, quality and integrity — or, at least, the benefit of the doubt — and, alone, was sufficient to bring

Sarah Bernhardt

Maurice Barrymore

dozens of theatre's brightest stars into its fold. Those, however, who did not respond to Mr. Frohman's charm were dealt with by Mr. Erlanger.

It could be very unpleasant to be dealt with by Mr. Erlanger. Among the first to publicly question the goodwill and honest "for the benefit of all" intentions of the Syndicate were the playwright and publisher Harrison Grey Fiske and his wife, the prominent actress Minnie Maddern Fiske. Mr. Fiske published a theatrical trade newspaper, *The New York Dramatic Mirror* – the *Variety* of its day – and used its pages to criticize the Syndicate as a money-driven, would-be monopoly (and to publish alarmingly personal attacks on Mr. Erlanger and his partners). Erlanger responded by not only banning *The Dramatic Mirror* from all Syndicate theatres, but also threatening any actor seen reading the paper – anywhere – with instant dismissal. Mrs. Fiske was at that time starring in a play in a Syndicate-controlled theatre; she came to work and found the doors locked, her contract abruptly cancelled.

As Syndicate power grew, even daring to question its decisions could bring a harsh reprisal. The eminent actor James O'Neill (father of playwright Eugene O'Neill) was blacklisted, denied any work at all, as were the director and playwright David Belasco, the actor Maurice Barrymore (whose last speech on a stage ended – in a complete mental breakdown – with, "Down with the Trust! Death to the Syndicate! Charles Frohman is doomed!") and the Canadian-born actress Margaret Anglin (despite her star status and the fact that she had been a friend and protégé of Frohman's). Even the worldwide popularity and fame of "The Divine" Sarah Bernhardt was no armour against the wrath of Abe Erlanger. In 1905, she announced her intention of touring North America. Erlanger drew up a schedule, but Bernhardt rejected it; there was nothing objectionable about it, she explained, but she had always organized her own tours and would prefer to continue doing so; Erlanger responded by barring her from all Syndicate theatres. Bernhardt made the tour, but with theatres shut to her, performed in a hired circus tent. In one case, however, Mr. Erlanger's iron fist came down with unnecessary force on some people he really ought to have been nicer to.

Lee, Sam and Jacob J. Shubert were the sons of Polish immigrants who settled in Syracuse, New York, where the teenaged Sam got into show business, hired by the director David Belasco – ever after his friend, mentor and role model – to fill a small part in a play. Sam progressed from actor to theatre program boy, to box office clerk, to treasurer of the Wieting, Syracuse's best theatre and, along the way, got his brothers jobs in Syracuse theatres as well.

By 1900, the three Shuberts managed five theatres in upstate New York – owning outright the Baker, in Rochester, and the Grand Opera House, in Syracuse – and were good clients of the Theatrical Syndicate. They, however, had independent ambitions; they wanted to produce their own shows and mount their own tours. For that, they needed their own theatre circuit, operating outside Syndicate control. They borrowed money and bought the Herald Square, the Casino and the Princess, in New York City; the Hyperion in New Haven; the Dearborn in Chicago; and the Colonial in Boston. The Syndicate saw the Shuberts as impertinent upstarts and decided to make an example of them, as a warning to others. No Syndicate shows were allowed to play the Shubert houses; no Shubert-produced shows were allowed to play any Syndicate theatres. The Shuberts responded by opening their doors to actors, directors and producers – including the Fiskes, Margaret Anglin and David Belasco – whom the Syndicate had also barred. It was the Shuberts who rented the tent for Sarah Bernhardt, simultaneously thumbing their noses at Abe Erlanger and building their own legend as champions of art, free enterprise and free expression.

Shubert ambitions appeared to come to a sudden and tragic end in May, 1905. On his way home from Pittsburgh, Sam Shubert was horribly burned in a railroad accident; a few days later, on May 12, he died of his injuries. His grieving brothers, Lee and Jacob, lost the heart to continue the struggle. They went to see Erlanger and offered to sell him all their theatrical interests.

Jacob J. and Lee Shubert, of Syracuse. They had decided to get out of the theatre business, until Abe Erlanger behaved rudely to them.

Photo courtesy of the Shubert Archives.

David Belasco

Negotiations were almost complete when the three came to a sticking point; Sam had made a number of contracts that his brothers insisted the Syndicate, as new owner of the Shubert theatres, honour. In particular was an agreement with Sam's close friend, David Belasco. Erlanger refused. Belasco was a bitter enemy and he would have no dealings with him. He saw no reason, he said, why he should be obliged to honour a third-party contract "made by a dead man."

Thus did the great Theatre War begin. The gratuitous insult to their brother's memory enraged the Shuberts. They left the table. Negotiations were over. They would not sell. They would rally the remaining independent theatre owners and blacklisted actors, directors and producers together under their flag in a rebel alliance. They vowed to fight the Syndicate and bring it down. And thus it was that when Lol Solman found the Syndicate's doors closed, the Shubert doors were wide open.

Indeed, the Shuberts offered what they called an "open door" policy; any theatre in their alliance could play whatever it wished – it would not be restricted to Shubert-produced shows; and any theatre, inside or outside the alliance, could book Shubert shows. They promised Lol Solman that if he would turn his theatre's bookings over to them, they would guarantee the Royal Alexandra from 25 to 40 weeks of first-class legitimate attractions per year, both their own shows and those of other independent managers and producers. No one could ask for more, and Solman signed the contract.

Meanwhile, in Toronto, up King St. at the Princess Theatre, manager O.B. Sheppard closed down operations as the Syndicate poured in money to widen and deepen the stage, raise the roof, extend the fly tower, revamp the lighting and renovate the auditorium. He girded for battle.

12

THE OPENING
A Rocky Start

The Royal Alexandra Theatre opened to the public on Monday, August 26, 1907, with an extravagant world premiere, a new musical produced in the style of an English pantomime by Lee and Jacob Shubert — Mark Swan and James O'Dea's (book and lyrics) and Manuel Klein and Anne Caldwell's (music) *Top O' Th' World*.

August 26 was the day before the opening of the Canadian National Exhibition, the event that marked the end of the summer and the date by which everyone was expected to be home from holidays. The opening of the Ex was the traditional beginning of the Toronto theatre season, with managers hoping to take advantage of the thousands of visitors crowding the city. Cawthra Mulock and Lol Solman, in choosing the day before, had hoped not only to avoid competition with any Ex events, but that their opening night audience might include the Earl Grey, the Governor General, and Prime Minister Laurier, both of whom were to be in town for the first day of the fair. In this, they were disappointed. Laurier telegraphed his regrets that same afternoon and business held the Earl Grey in Ottawa until the next day. As it was, however, Solman opened the doors that evening to the delight of the cream of Toronto

King Street and Royal Alexandra Theatre, Toronto, Canada

A 1907 picture postcard view along tree-lined King St. West, with the brand-new Royal Alexandra Theatre one of the only buildings on the block.

society — including Lieutenant-Governor Sir William Mortimer Clark, Justices Mulock and Falconbridge and the four founders, sitting in what would for many years to come be their family boxes.

As for the play, Mulock may have been a little disappointed; *Top O' Th' World* was less a work of the high-class theatre art he desired for the Royal Alexandra than a commercial blockbuster bomb devised by the Shuberts to stun and awe their Syndicate rival at the Princess Theatre. Four boxcars full of spectacular scenery and a fifth full of gorgeous costumes were parked on the rail siding along Front St. Their contents — including a giant globe inside a spiral ramp (by which the characters in the tale made an ascent by airship to the North Pole) — were trundled by horsecart up Simcoe St. and through the intersection of the Four 'Nations to Pearl St. and the theatre's loading doors. There were 63 actors in the cast — and that was just for the first week. Twelve more joined in the second week — as well as a troupe of performing collies (a little vaudeville-like, but perhaps acceptable in the context of a legitimate show).

Syndicate theatres had had a recent hit in New York and on the road with a spectacular musical adaptation of *The Wizard of*

Oz. The Shuberts commissioned Mark Swan and James O'Dea (who had been *The Wizard*'s lyricist) to out-do that show with something similar, but with more extravagant sets, costumes and special effects. *Top O' Th' World* had a plot uncannily like that of the earlier show: a young girl travels magically to a distant land of fantasy (in this case, the North Pole), where she overcomes an evil witch-queen with the aid of a friendly bear, a man made of candy and a Jack-in-the-box. The star of *Top O' Th' World* was a young actress named Anna Laughlin who, not coincidentally, had come to fame in the role of Dorothy in *The Wizard of Oz.*

Top O' Th' World, however, had its intended effect. It packed the Royal Alexandra, leaving the Princess – then playing a middling comedy – half empty, and everyone in Toronto who might not yet have heard the news knew that there was now a splendid new theatre in town.

The Syndicate countered by rushing the Princess a new fairy-tale-pantomime-musical costume, scenery and special effects extravaganza of its own, the hastily assembled *The Land of Nod* – so hastily assembled that the songs of the first and second acts were written by two different composers, so dissimilar in their

MUSIC AND THE DRAMA.

The opening of the Royal Alexandra Theatre last night was an event of sufficient importance and interest to attract a fashionable audience that exhausted the seating capacity. The house looked very handsome when seen under the full illumination of the electric lights, from the onyx walled entrance hall to the auditorium, in which the tasteful harmony of the color scheme showed to great advantage. The management in selecting a musical extravaganza for the opening acted no doubt wisely, as this is a popular form of entertainment with the large numbers of visitors who come to Toronto during the Exhibition weeks. The audience, however, last night was essentially a city gathering, and the extravaganza does not secure an enthusiastically favorable verdict from a Toronto audience. It must be said in favor of "The Top o' th' World," which was the piece presented last night, that it was nevertheless received with convincing marks of favor, quite a number of the songs and dances, and much of the broad comedy business being greeted with demonstrative applause. There is no coherent plot or design in the piece, but it introduces a number of characters who act and speak in a manner suggestive of a fairy tale made grotesque by whimsical perversion. The play is handsomely staged, and there is a large number of principals, chorus singers and dancers in the company. The successes of the evening were made by Anna Laughlin, an attractive little soubrette, with a voice of juvenile charm; Kathleen Clifford, another light-

voiced soprano; Blanche Wayne, a soprano with more substance to her voice, and John D. Gilbert, the principal comedian, who had the feminine role of Aurora Borealis. Mr. Gilbert kept the audience well amused by his suggestive style of broad comedy and by his ludicrous poses and gestures. His business might, however, be shortened to some extent, as the first act is extremely long. The music, which is by Manuel Klein and Anna Caldwell, is obviously tuneful, and therefore such as is appropriate to an extravaganza. Much of the performance will be enjoyed by juveniles, as there are introduced Kris Kringle, the toymaker, got up much in the state of Father Christmas; the friendly bear, taken by Arthur Hill; Jack-in-the-box, the wonderful toy; Jack Frost, king of the north wind, who causes people to shiver, and Anna Laughlin, herself dressed up as an Eskimo belle. The orchestra numbers twenty-five, a more generous combination than is usually offered with light entertainments. "Top o' th' World" is billed for two weeks, and may be expected to draw crowded houses. Veteran theatre-goers present last night were congratulating themselves that Toronto has now a new first-class theatre, and one, moreover, thoroughly up-to-date.

—•—

The management of the Princess had the gratification of seeing a crowded house last night when the theatre was reopened for the season with the comedy, new to Toronto, "Before and After." The plot of what is really a succession of laughter-creating incidents is hinged on the practical test of a humor-producing mixture of drugs by one medical man on a fellow-practitioner of the severe type, who is a nerve specialist. The result is that the specialist, called to attend a charming French lady, while still under the in-

A *Globe* review.

Anna Laughlin, in her full rabbit-skin costume as Kokomo, daughter of Kankakee, the Eskimo, in *Top O' Th' World*, the first show to play the Royal Alexandra. It must have been excruciating to wear under the lights.

Photo from the collection of the Royal Alexandra Theatre

work that, when the show transferred to New York in September, the producers thought better of yoking them together and turned it into two separate one-act musicals, *The Land of Nod* and *The Songbirds*.

In bringing *Land of Nod* to the Princess to run in opposition to the Royal Alexandra's *Top O' Th' World*, the Syndicate began a practice that would go on for as long as the two theatres remained rivals: matching every show with something similar, but somehow "better"; if the Royal Alexandra had a big musical, the Princess had a bigger musical; if the Royal Alexandra had Shakespeare, the Princess had Shakespeare, but with a bigger star. This rivalry played out all over North America, wherever there were both Syndicate and independent theatres, and reached the height of its absurdity in New York in 1908. Minnie

An artist's idea of a setting in *Top O' Th' World*, with Kokomo, Kankakee the Eskimo, the friendly polar bear, the candyman and the Jack-in-the-box.

Maddern Fiske staged Molnar's drama *The Devil* (introducing American audiences to the young British actor George Arliss) and the Syndicate, on the very same night, opened the same play, with Edwin Stevens, a bigger and better-known star.

The Shuberts followed *Top O' Th' World* with a comedy hit, *The Road to Yesterday*, starring Minnie Dupree, one of the most talked-about new stars of the American stage, in her Canadian debut, guaranteed to draw the crowds. The play was a light fantasy in which a couple visit and observe themselves in past lives to find the causes of their 20th-century problems, and it was an audience and critical success.

The Road to Yesterday was followed with an "exotic" musical play – a lush costume piece – *The Blue Moon*, an imaginative romance/adventure tale of life in India under the Raj. And next came yet another fairy-tale, pantomime-inspired spectacular, Reginald de Koven's fantastical *Happyland*, or *The King of Elysia*. *Happyland*, set in the "land of the delights of love," was one of the Shuberts' biggest hits – in Boston, New York and for two full years on tour. Toronto audiences were fortunate to see it with its original stars, DeWolf Hopper (for whom it was written) and Marguerite Clark, two of the most popular players in operetta and musical comedy of the time.

Although these first shows were popular and successful, Lol Solman and Cawthra Mulock were, nonetheless, a little worried. They had no objection to musicals and light comedies adding colour and spice to a season – in-between the Shakespeare and the Ibsen – but they wanted the serious fare, as well. Solman sent a telegram to the Shuberts thanking them for their bookings to date, but politely asking when he might expect to welcome a top-notch dramatic company – Mrs. Fiske's, for example – to the Royal Alexandra. In response, he received a package of posters for his next scheduled attraction. On opening it, he was shocked to find that they advertised Klaw and Erlanger's Advanced Vaudeville. Without any warning, the Shuberts had settled their differences with the Syndicate and sold him out.

It was just business – a tactical move. The Shuberts had been too successful too quickly in their efforts to sign independent theatres to their alliance. There were too many theatres and too little product available to share among them; they could not make good on the promise of 25 to 40 weeks of first-class legitimate attractions per season for everybody. They had also been forced to admit that the Syndicate had been right about over-competition in limited markets; it made no sense to do as they had done with the Royal Alexandra and the Princess, pitting expensive musicals against one another in a small city. They had not, however – as they were at pains to explain to their unhappy allies – surrendered. They had just scaled things back a bit. It was only a truce, not the end of the fight. The Shuberts and the Syndicate had formed a new company, the United States

KLAW & ERLANGER'S ADVANCED VAUDEVILLE

STARS OF ALL NATIONS

Amusement Co., to work cooperatively in vaudeville enterprises – not legitimate theatre – and had assigned to that company 14 of "their" theatres. These were mostly newer theatres that had not yet established themselves as legitimate houses anyway – like the Royal Alexandra.

Lol Solman, however, had not given in to the Syndicate and would not lie down for the Shuberts, either. He rewrapped the vaudeville posters and sent them back. He then contacted a New York lawyer and ordered him – with the assent of his partners – to file a breach of contract suit against the Shubert brothers. He then sent a telegram to David Belasco – still a theatre outcast – asking his immediate, urgent help in putting together a resident stock company of American actors worthy of the Royal Alexandra . . . and then added a new set of instructions to his lawyer, to add the costs of organizing such a stock company to the claim for damages against the Shuberts. Solman, who knew "nothing about theatre" only a year before was suddenly a producer.

13

SMART ENOUGH
TO LEARN IT

As it happened, the Syndicate/Shubert truce lasted for only a little more than a year before the war began again. It was the first of many temporary lulls in the fighting, but for 15 months Lol Solman and the Royal Alexandra Theatre were on their own.

David Belasco responded to Solman's request for aid and sent him a stock company of solid actors, chosen from among members of his own company of players, headed by a competent actor/manager named Will H. Gregory. Solman christened Gregory's group "The Royal Alexandra Players" and rented a warehouse near the theatre, turning it into a shop in which he could build his own sets.

The Royal Alexandra Players remained in residence until February 1908 (when David Belasco needed them back at home), presenting 19 first-class productions, ranging from new comedies, such as James M. Barrie's *Quality Street*, to old warhorses — the tear-jerking *Camille* — to classics — R.B. Sheridan's *A School for Scandal*. In its last month the Players were able to secure the services of a major star from New York — Ida Conquest — to take the lead roles in the popular new plays *Old Heidelberg*, *The Girl With the Green Eyes* and *The Great Match*. *Old Heidelberg* was a sell-out and its Friday evening performance (it ran for only a week) was graced by the

Two programs for productions
by Lol Solman's Royal Alexandra
Players. It may only have been a
stock company, but its programs
were printed on silk.

Photos courtesy of the Toronto Public Library, Theatre
Collection.

presence of the Earl Grey, the seal of approval for the Royal Alexandra as an upper-class playhouse.

The Princess Theatre mounted what ought to have been overwhelming competition to Solman's efforts, the best in the Syndicate's arsenal of star-driven musicals and stage spectaculars, including Charles Frohman's famous production of James M. Barrie's *Peter Pan*, complete with its original London star, Maude Adams, arguably the most popular actress of the decade. But the creation of the Royal Alexandra Players had made Lol Solman a local hero. He was a Canadian St. George in battle with an American dragon, and patriotic sentiments were on his side (even though his stock company was made up of American actors, it had a Canadian name and a Canadian boss). The Players did good business in the face of the best competition the Princess could mount, helped along by the fact that Solman dropped his ticket prices (adding his calculations of resulting lost revenue to the damages in his lawsuit against the Shuberts).

When Belasco finally called the Royal Alexandra Players home to New York, Solman was ready. He had used the months of their residence in Toronto to build other relationships, make other deals and put together another stock company, all his own. The new company was made up principally of British actors — Torontonians then regarded British actors as, by definition, superior to American ones — and was called "The Royal Alexandra English Players." The company boasted one international star in its ranks, Letitia Marion Dallas, a famous Irish actress who performed under the stage name "Miss Darragh." The English Players could make an even stronger claim on patriotic support than had their predecessors, boasting the official patronage of William Mortimer Clark, the Lieutenant-Governor.

Solman used the English Players to fill in the gaps — and keep the theatre running — in-between the major touring productions he was able to negotiate with the few independent producers outside both the Syndicate and the Shubert camps. The Fiskes brought him the new dramas *Marta of the Lowlands* and *The Unbroken Road*, with the great Hungarian actress Bertha Kalich; the melodrama *Salvation Nell* and the drama *Rosmersholm* (the first professional production of an Ibsen play to be seen in Toronto), both starring the famous Minnie Maddern Fiske herself; and *Septimus* and *The Devil* with George Arliss. The dashing Canadian-born star James K. Hackett came with his swashbuckling production of *The Prisoner of Zenda*. David Belasco supplied his operetta *The Girl of the Golden West*, with star Blanche Bates; *The Music Master*, with Antoinette Perry; and the spectacular *The Warrens of Virginia*, with a cast including the young Toronto actress Gladys Smith, using for the first time her new stage name, "Mary Pickford." To cap it all, Solman secured the huge and highly regarded London, England–based Imperial Opera Co., which moved a company into the Royal Alexandra to stage 25 major productions in a row, the best of British operettas and musicals.

When the Syndicate/Shubert truce finally came to an end, the United States Amusement Co. collapsed – as did Klaw and Erlanger's Advanced Vaudeville – and the Theatre War resumed. The Shuberts returned, offering a new booking contract. Nothing had changed, except for the status of Lol Solman and the Royal Alexandra Theatre. They had gone it alone, kept their independence, kept the doors open and the marquee lights lit in the face of overwhelming competition and emerged with books still in the black. The Royal Alexandra was now an "established" legitimate theatre.

The Shuberts offered Solman programs for 1909 and 1910 that included the dramatic stars Sir Johnston Forbes-Robertson ("the greatest Hamlet of the age"), Alla Nazimova, Maxine Elliott and Laurette Taylor; the musical comedy headliners Eddie Foy, Blanche Ring and Marguerite Clark; and the matinee idols Guy Bates Post and William Faversham. For the summers, they proposed giving Toronto the best stock performers in their employ, the Percy Haswell Company. And Miss Haswell would not be presenting the usual low-budget, watered-down "standards" for which lesser stock companies were notorious. The Shubert brothers proposed using her, and the Royal Alexandra, to premiere first-class, new comedies and dramas they were

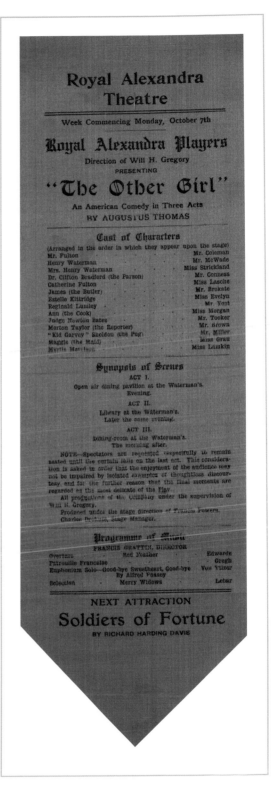

considering for Broadway and the road (today, we might call this "test-marketing," but the Shuberts presented the idea not as a test, but as a testament to the high regard they felt for the sophistication and taste of Royal Alexandra audiences).

As for Lol Solman himself, he had won his spurs. The Shuberts proposed that he go on their payroll as general manager for all Shubert theatre operations in Canada and as manager – in addition to the Royal Alexandra – of Montreal's Princess Theatre, a new acquisition in the Shubert circuit (for which Solman commissioned Frederick Challener to paint a sounding-board mural, *Orpheus Charming the Nymphs*, a sister mural to the Royal Alexandra's *Venus and Adonis*). They did request, however, that he drop that breach-of-contract lawsuit, which he did.

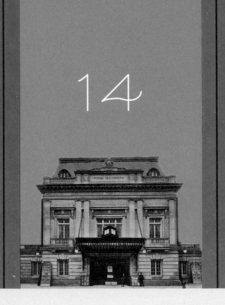

14

1912
A Death in the Family

ON THE NIGHT OF JULY 17, 1912, the Alexandra Company suffered its first loss with the death of 52-year-old partner Robert Alexander Smith. He was on his way home from the annual Lennox Picnic at Jackson's Point, a Conservative Party event thrown by North York MPP Herb Lennox, filled with political speeches, marching bands, sandwiches, potato salad and cherry pie and regarded by the party faithful as "the best picnic in the universe." He was driving home along Yonge St., just south of Richmond Hill, when his car crashed through a lantern-lit barrier and into a six-foot-deep ditch dug at the side of the road for the laying of a culvert. Smith was thrown from the open car and killed.

His body was driven back to Richmond Hill by his friend and partner in both the Royal Alexandra and the Island Ferry, Lol Solman, who had also been to the picnic and was driving home down Yonge St., right behind him.

Even allowing for the fact that people generally try to speak well of the dead, the comments of his friends, published the next day, indicate that Robert A. Smith was an extraordinarily well-regarded man:

THE TORONTO DAILY STAR

20TH YEAR. TORONTO, THURSDAY, JULY 18, 1912.—TWENTY-TWO PAGES. Last Edition.

WESTERN FARMING To Have an Elevator System STREET RAIL. CONFERENCE POSTPONED---RAILWAY

BUTLER OF TORONTO, WINS SECOND HEAT AT STOCKHOLM BY DEFAULT—DEFENCE COUNCIL WOULD COMMIT THE COLONIES TO FEDERATION—SCHWARTZ, N.Y. MURD

CALVERT AND BOVILLE EMPHATICALLY CONTRADICT TRAVERS' STATEMENT

Ex-Liberal Whip Heard of No Envelope, and Deputy Minister of Finance Did Not Get or Know of Any-one Getting $3,000.

HOTELMEN SAY PETER RYAN WAS THERE, BUT THERE WAS NO ROOM C IN HOTEL

Chief Justice Meredith Asks Whether, in View of McCarthy's Letter, There Shouldn't Have Been Strict Enquiry ---Investigation Adjourns for Two Months.

By a Staff Reporter.

Ottawa, July 18.—The enquiry into the Farmers Bank, continued here this morning by Sir William Meredith, brought out but little new evidence. It was expected that new ground would be broken, but the trend of the evidence in Toronto during the last two days of the investigation there made this practically impossible.

BISHOP BERNARD, of St. Hyacinthe, who joined Archbishop Bruchesi in pulling the ban on St. Marie College at St. John's, Que.

CITY GETS TRINITY SITE FOR $625,000

Terms, Subject to Ratification by Council, Were Arranged This Morning.

COLLEGE KEEPS BUILDING

Controllers Decide Not to Ask Sir James for Power to Raise Money.

WILL TAKE TIME TO FEDERATE BRITISH EMPIRE

Liberals Think Federating Process Will Be Long and Tedious.

UNIONISTS SAY IT MUST BE DONE SOON

Chronicle Says Britain Has Done More Than Her Share for Empire.

WAS IN NEED OF A TONIC

Standard Declares Borden Supplied It—No Announcement as to Naval Decision.

SCENE OF LAST NIGHT'S AUTO FATALITY

The telegraph pole on the left side is where the auto came to a stop, over a hundred feet from the obstruction, also shown. The machine was coming towards the reader. The supports to which the lanterns are attached are shown on the right side of this picture.

Above is shown a near view of the obstruction which Herbert McKenna, the chauffeur, attempted to avoid, resulting in the death of Mr. R. A. Smith and injuries to Mr. C. A. B. Brown and Mr. Victor Ross. The road is very narrow at this point. Lanterns can be seen hanging to the supports, on either end, on the left-hand side. The auto was going away from the reader.

GRAIN GROWERS MAY TAKE | FORMAL PROTEST IS

"He was the most generous man I have ever known. He was always helping his friends and his pocket was always at the disposal of anyone in trouble."

"No one ever went to Robert Smith with a request for assistance to come away empty-handed. He was forever kind, generous and genial. Thousands of Toronto people will mourn the loss of a true friend and advisor."

"R.A. Smith was a rich man when he died, I imagine he must have been worth at least a million dollars, and if he had cared for money he might have been worth ten times as much. But he always laughed at the man who piled up money. 'I have enough,' he would say, 'And there is plenty for my wife, if anything happens to me, so why should I become selfish?'"

TRAGIC DEATH OF A WELL-KNOWN TORONTO FINANCIER IN MOTOR CAR ACCIDENT

MR. R. A. SMITH MET INSTANT DEATH—J. LORNE CAMPBELL AND VICTOR ROSS INJURED

Party Were Returning From the Jackson's Point Picnic When Auto Crashed Into an Excavation Six Feet Deep Near Richmond Hill—C. A. B. Brown and the Chauffeur, H. McKenna, Escaped.

SMITH, CAMPBELL, AND ROSS THROWN CLEAR FROM AUTO—INJURED BROUGHT TO TORONTO

DEAD.

R. A. Smith, broker, of 487 Huron street.

INJURED.

J. Lorne Campbell, broker, 509 Huron street, deep scalp wound, fractured rib, and broken collar bone.

Victor Ross, financial editor of the Globe, right leg fractured above the knee, bruised about the right shoulder.

Herbert McKenna, chauffeur, bruised about the body.

ESCAPED UNINJURED.

C. A. B. Brown, Board of Education.

SCENE OF ACCIDENT.

Two-and-a-half miles south of Richmond Hill.

A prominent millionaire broker, instantly killed, two of his companions in a precarious condition, and the chauffeur of their car badly bruised, was the toll upon human life and limb when a party of motorists returning from the North York Lennox picnic, at Jackson's Point, crashed into a six-foot culvert excavation two-and-a-half miles south of Richmond Hill, a few minutes after midnight.

MR. R. A. SMITH, of Toronto, who was killed when a motor car was wrecked at Richmond Hill last night.

MR. VICTOR ROSS, one of the injured.

MR. J. LORNE CAMPBELL, whose leg was broken and head badly injured when thrown from the car.

FIGURES IN THE AUTOMOBILE TRAGEDY

LORNE CAMPBELL HAD COLLAR BONE BROKEN

Is in a Serious Condition, and Result May Prove Fatal—At St. Michael's.

MR. ROSS IN NO DANGER

MR. C. A. B. BROWN, member of the Board of Education, who escaped with a shaking up.

MANY TRIBUTES TO LATE MR. SMITH PAID BY FRIENDS

HAVE NOT DECIDED ON HOME LIFE ADDITION

The Plans Have Met With the Approval of the City Architect's Department.

TO RUN IT UP 298 FEET

HIGH COURT CLUB WON FOR THE CITY

When Case of Toronto v. Applebaum Was Called To-day, It Was All Over.

DUKE MAKES PRESENT TO THE HON. ROBERT ROGERS

C. A. B. BROWN SAYS HE HELD ON TO SEAT AND SO ESCAPED

Auto Going About Twenty-Five Miles an Hour When Accident Took Place.

HE ESCAPED ALL INJURY

Found Mr. Smith's Body in Ditch—Others Were Thrown Clear From the Car.

HERBERT McKENNA, The Chauffeur.

DR. CHOWN REMAINS GEN. SUPERINTENDENT

Even If He Decides to Become Head of the College at Vancouver.

FOR HIMSELF TO DECIDE

GOVERNMENT HOLDS BACK MONEY FOR THE GOOD ROADS SCHEME

TO PUT STANTON'S NAME ON THE HEGOCK MEMORIAL

EMERSON COATSWORTH, K.C., TO BE A PERMANENT JUDGE

Toronto's Ex-Mayor Has Shown Real Judicial Capacity Handling Division Court Work in Place of Judge Morson—Lawyers Speak Highly of His Work.

HANDLED THIRTY-SIX CASES IN HOUR AND A HALF METHODS COMPARED WITH JUDGE MORSON

EMERSON COATSWORTH, K.C., a leading judge in the Division Court, who is slated for a permanent judgeship.

CARS
For Liveries
AND
Real Estate Firms

1 Thomas Flyer, 80 h.p., 7-passenger for large fur owner.

RUSSELL MOTOR CAR CO.
100 Richmond St. West.

"The Orient's Best"
El-Hamur Cigarettes
15¢ PER BOX 25¢

Notice to Creditors and Others

The Union Trust Company
LIMITED
Capital (paid-up) $1,000,000   Reserve Fund $750,000

VISITORS TO ENGLAND

Our customers and friends are invited to make use of our London Office at 75 Lombard Street when visiting England.

J. M. McWHINNEY, General Manager.

The Army of Constipation
Is Growing Smaller Every Day.
CARTER'S LITTLE LIVER PILLS

PILES

Smith's shares in the Alexandra Company passed to his widow. His wife, his children and his grandchildren would continue to occupy the owners' box seats on Royal Alexandra opening nights for the next 51 years, until the dissolution of the partnership and sale of the theatre.

At the theatre, Percy Haswell had been onstage that night in a revival of Leo Ditrichstein's mistaken identity farce *Are You a Mason?*

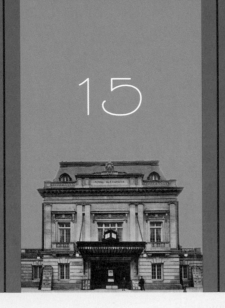

15

1915
The War Ends

THE GREAT THEATRE WAR came to an abrupt end -- at least as far as Toronto's part in it was concerned – on May 7, 1915. Around 2:30 that morning, the Princess Theatre burned down, leaving the Royal Alexandra as the city's sole remaining first-class legitimate theatre. Percy Haswell had been on the Royal Alex stage that night with the drama *East Lynne*, an adaptation of Mrs. Henry Woods' romantic novel, a best seller of the Victorian age, about an orphaned earl's daughter reduced to poverty by her late father's profligacy. The show at the Princess the evening of the fire had been *Daddy Long Legs* – in keeping with the tit-for-tat rivalry between the theatres, an adaptation of Jean Webster's equally best-selling novel about an even more impoverished orphan girl.

The loss of the Princess was the big news in the Toronto papers on May 7, but only because word had not yet come of another event – on that same morning – of far greater importance to the world, to Toronto and to the fortunes of the Theatrical Syndicate.

The Syndicate's creative head, Charles S. Frohman sailed at least once a year – usually in the spring – to England, where he had many theatre interests. In May 1915, he set out to attend the

The stage of the Princess Theatre, three days after the diasastrous fire of May 7, 1915. Note the charred wooden framing of the proscenium.

Photo courtesy of the City of Toronto Archives.

London opening – at his own theatre, the Duke of York's – of his latest West End production, a musical called *Rosy Rapture, The Pride of the Beauty Chorus*, starring the notorious Gaby Deslys (reputed to be the mistress of the King of Portugal) and the American singer Jack Norworth (forever famed as the composer of the song "Take Me Out to the Ball Game") and written by his close friend, James M. Barrie. Frohman never travelled alone and, on this occasion, his party was to include his latest protégé, a young actress named Rita Jolivet, and *Rosy Rapture's* composer, Jerome Kern. Kern, however, stayed up partying the night before and missed the boat. The boat was the luxurious Cunard liner RMS *Lusitania*.

Coincidentally, another passenger who missed the last sailing of the *Lusitania* – she was ill, and not, like Kern, hungover – was the fashion designer Lucile, Lady Duff-Gordon, creator of the *Merry Widow* hat. It would have been quite ironic if Lady Duff-Gordon had sailed on that voyage; three years earlier, she had been one of the few survivors of the *Titanic*.

A few days before Charles Frohman was to sail, the German embassy posted a notice in the east coast American newspapers, reminding still-neutral American travellers that Germany and Great Britain were at war and that ships, even passenger liners like the *Lusitania*, flying the British flag might be fired upon.

NOTICE!

TRAVELLERS intending to embark on the Atlantic voyage are reminded that a state of war exists between Germany and his allies and Great Britain and her allies; that the zone of war includes the waters adjacent to the British Isles; that, in accordance with formal notice given by the Imperial German Government, vessels flying the flag of Great Britain, or any of her allies, are liable to destruction in those waters and that travellers sailing in the war zone on the ships of Great Britain or her allies do so at their own risk.

IMPERIAL GERMAN EMBASSY
Washington, D.C.
April 22, 1915

The last photo ever taken of Charles S. Frohman, on the deck of the *Lusitania*, on his way to London to see his last musical, *Rosy Rapture, The Pride of the Beauty Chorus*.

Photo courtesy the New York Public Library, Billy Rose Theater Collection.

of both the Theatre Mechanics' Association — the union of stagehands — and "Chorus Equity," an association of dancers and extras (headed by the Canadian actress Marie Dressler), Actors' Equity shut down both Syndicate and Shubert theatres all over the continent. One of the few major theatres that remained open, unaffected by the strike, was the Royal Alexandra, where rates of pay and conditions of employment already met all the demands of the Standard Contract. Driven to the edge of bankruptcy, Abe Erlanger capitulated, signed, and the once all-powerful Theatrical Syndicate faded away. Erlanger would remain a force in the business — as a theatre-owner, a producer, a director and a booking agent — and a thorn in the Shubert side until his death in 1930, but the Napoleonic crown passed from his brow to that of Lee Shubert.

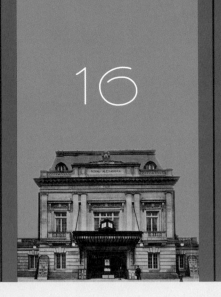

1918
The Plague Year

IN THE WINTER OF 1918, just a few months before the end of the First World War, a new strain of influenza appeared somewhere in Asia – probably in China – and spread quickly westward. It first caught the attention of European health officials in Spain, from where it seemed to spread to the north and east and onto the battlefields of the war. Mistakenly believing Spain to have been the point of origin, the world press dubbed the new disease "the Spanish 'Flu." The first of the warring forces to notice and report on its virulence and deadly nature – and to correctly diagnose it as the cause of the frightening, and increasing, number of fatal cases of "pneumonia" among its troops – was the Imperial German Army. The press of the Allied nations greeted the news from Germany with delight. When it was discovered that the 'flu had taken an entire German division out of action on the eastern front, the papers quipped that at long last the Spanish – who had remained neutral throughout the war and, notoriously, grown rich on trading with both sides – were finally contributing something worthwhile to the Allied effort. What they did not know, because the news was blocked by their own governments' censors, was that what was happening in the German army was also happening in the British, French, American and Italian armies.

The people of Thebes appeal to their king and their gods to lift the plague from their city in Sir John Martin-Harvey's production of *Oedipus Rex* at the Royal Alexandra. Martin-Harvey employed dozens of Toronto amateurs as extras for his crowd scenes.

Photo courtesy of the Toronto Public Library. Theatre Collection.

It's interesting today to look back at the Toronto newspapers of the late summer and early fall of 1918. It was the custom then to publish death notices – with photos, when possible – of local soldiers who had fallen in the war in the last 24 hours. What one can't help but notice, with the wisdom of hindsight, is how many of these notices at that time listed the cause of death as "pneumonia"; and how those pneumonia deaths increased in number every day until, by October, they outnumbered the deaths from bullets or bombs. It's probable that most, if not all, of these pneumonia deaths were the 'flu. Most of those who died in 1918 did actually die of pneumonia, a secondary infection caused by the disease. Calling it pneumonia, however, hid from the public the fact that the Spanish Influenza pandemic was a public health catastrophe to surpass even the great Black Death of the Middle Ages. Worldwide, it may have killed as many as 100 million people.

The 'flu came to Toronto in October and the city was completely unprepared. At the beginning of the month, with the number of cases still apparently manageable, the newspapers ran stories quoting local medical experts who reassured the public that there was nothing to fear, that this so-called Spanish Influenza was nothing new, nothing but a severe form of "the grippe," with which we were all familiar, and promising that its "germ" would soon be identified and a cure would quickly follow. Patent medicine companies advertised that the cure was already here, that the 'flu could easily be prevented by any of an array of balms, liniments and breakfast cereals – or, if you already had it, wrung out of your body with purgatives and laxatives. Then the papers began publishing the death numbers from the city's hospitals and the news that those hospitals were opening annexes in warehouses – places to put more beds and places to house temporary morgues – and the patent medicine ads all but vanished.

On Friday, October 18, the city acted and posted notices closing all places of amusement, all places where people might gather (and this would include, although they were not mentioned in the notices, Toronto's churches) for the duration of the epidemic. The decree took effect on Saturday, October 19, allowing one more performance of the hit musical comedy *The Kiss Burglar* at the Royal Alexandra, before the doors had to be locked. The theatre innocently advertised that final performance of October 19, urging audiences to hurry to buy tickets: "ITS JOY KILLS THE 'FLU.' YOUR LAST CHANCE TO LAUGH."

And then, as quickly as it began, it was over. In late October, deaths went into sharp decline, as did new influenza cases. By November 1, all agreed that the crisis had passed. The Royal Alexandra re-opened on November 4 with the Guy Bolton/P.G. Wodehouse musical *Ask Dad*, in its pre-Broadway tryout. A week later, on November 11, the war ended and Toronto celebrated a double victory: the Germans were beaten; the 'flu was conquered.

The trains had kept on running thoughout the emergency, but few people travelled. It was clear to almost all by then that there was danger in crowds and confined spaces. By the end of November, however, all worry seemed gone for good and Cawthra Mulock made a long-planned and long-delayed business trip to New York. He told Lol Solman that he planned to see a few

DEATH CALLS BIG FINANCIER

Cawthra Mulock, Industrial Captain, Dies in New York

After a brief illness from influenza, Mr. Cawthra Mulock, second son of Chief Justice Sir William Mulock, K.C.M.G., died yesterday in New York city. His death removes a prominent member of the financial and industrial world.

The late Mr. Mulock was a member of the Cawthra family, the founder of which came to Upper Canada when Toronto had few inhabitants. Born in 1884, he was educated at Upper Canada College and later spent some time at the University of Toronto. In June of 1903 he was married to Adele Baldwin, the fourth daughter of Chief Justice Sir Glenholme Falconbridge.

In 1905 he was elected a member of the Toronto Stock Exchange. He rapidly became connected with many corporations and enterprises. He became a director of the Penny Bank of Toronto, the Confederation Life Association, Guardian Trust Company, the Imperial Bank of Canada, Vice-President of the National Trust Company, and head of the Canada Bread Company.

The late Mr. Mulock also showed ability in connection with the National Iron Works. It is located on Ashbridge's Bay and was one of the first in the locality. It was established in 1910 and its product is said to rank with the first in Canada.

From the time he went into the financial world to personally take care of the $8,000,000 fortune which came to him from Mrs. Cawthra-Murray, he actively supported movements of a public character and contributed to charities. When the Board of Governors of the Toronto General Hospital decided to change the location, Mr. Mulock was one of the first to place his name upon the subscription list.

Mr. Mulock's capital was responsible for the erection of the Royal Alexandra Theatre. He was a member of the National Horse Show Association and the Advisory Board of the Civic Art Guild.

While much of his time was taken up with business, he had traveled extensively. His one recreation was motoring.

The late Mr. Mulock was a member of the firm of Cawthra Mulock & Co. He was an Anglican, and a Liberal.

The funeral will take place on Tuesday afternoon at 3 o'clock from his late residence, at 528 Jarvis street.

FINANCIER DEAD

MR. CAWTHRA MULOCK,
Toronto financial and industrial leader, who died in New York.

EXPRESS RATES TO BE RAISED

Toronto Board of Trade Will Fight Proposed Advances

The sweeping changes proposed by the three railway express companies with respect to the new schedule of express rates which will be submitted for ratification at the approaching sitting of the Dominion Railway Board at Toronto, will be vigorously opposed by local shippers.

Mr. T. Marshall, Traffic Manager of the Toronto Board of Trade, last night stated that the matter will be taken up this week by the Transportation Committee of the Board, which is in receipt of a copy of the new schedule of rates, and which will not increase uniformly between all points but will advance on a sliding scale varying from a minimum of about thirty to a maximum of one hundred per cent.

The largest percentage of increase will be on shipments to Toronto, and the lowest to Vancouver. The rate of increase is not, however, based on

---

shows while there, perhaps make some bookings for the coming months at the Royal Alexandra. A day after his arrival, however, he took ill. The hotel doctor diagnosed influenza and had him taken to hospital. Two days later, on December 1, he died. Mulock was only 33 and had been in the pink of health, but that was the odd pattern of the Spanish Influenza; most of the millions who died had, a few days before, been healthy young adults.

Sir William Mulock took the train to New York to claim his son's body and bring it home. The funeral took place at Cawthra and Adèle's Jarvis St. home on December 3. Those who died of the 'flu were buried as quickly as possible.

Following her husband's death, Adèle Mulock closed the house on Jarvis and she and her three young children left Toronto for Cannes, France, where she spent most of the rest of her life. Lol Solman assumed the presidency of the Alexandra Co. and Cawthra Mulock's shares were turned over, with the rest of his estate, to the administration of the Royal Trust Co.

Cawthra and Adèle's son, Cawthra Falconbridge Mulock, came home to take up residence in Ontario more than 50 years after his father's death. Although he had visited Canada, he lived most of his adult life in England, where he became a well-known painter. In the late 1950s, he purchased a tract of woodland near Newmarket and built a beautiful house there – Falconfield – for his retirement. He and his British-born wife, Julyan, however, did not move in permanently until 1973, when their children finished school. On her husband's death in 1998, Julyan Mulock gave the house and the 120 hectares of forest surrounding it to the Federation of Ontario Naturalists. It is now the Cawthra Mulock Nature Reserve.

The Jarvis St. mansion Cawthra and Adèle Mulock built in 1903 is now long-gone, but the neighbourhood remembers the family with two high-rise apartment buildings on what was once its property – the Cawthra Apartments at 100 Gloucester and the Mulock Apartments at 105 Isabella – and Cawthra Park, beside the Church St. Community Centre, at 519 Church.

THE SOLMAN ERA

Lᴏʟ Sᴏʟᴍᴀɴ ᴅɪᴅ ɴᴏᴛ ᴄʟᴏsᴇ ᴛʜᴇ ᴛʜᴇᴀᴛʀᴇ for Cawthra Mulock's funeral; he felt that his partner would not have wanted that. That night, the Royal Alexandra staged the musical *Take It from Me*, remembered today — if at all — for one song: "I Like to Linger in the Lingerie."

Lol Solman did not like either musicals or "spectacle." Long before, when he and Cawthra Mulock had first talked about building a theatre, they had agreed that the Royal Alexandra would be devoted to "entertainment from a cultural standpoint" and "I Like to Linger in the Lingerie," "Glad Girlies" and "Tinkling Tunes" did not qualify. Solman was happiest when his theatre hosted — as it did — Robert Bruce Mantell as Hamlet, E.H. Sothern and Julia Marlowe as Orsino and Viola, or Sir John Martin-Harvey as Oedipus Rex. He was, however, both a businessman and a realist and recognized the clear fact that what filled theatre seats and kept the books in the black were musicals, spectacles and comedies, and that it was the income from these that gave him the luxury of occasionally doing as he pleased. Back in 1908, the Royal Alexandra had been delighted to book a week of Minnie Maddern Fiske and George Arliss in Ibsen's *Rosmersholm*. This was definitely "entertainment from a

Lol Solman at his desk in the original manager's office — now the box office — of the Royal Alexandra, sometime around 1930.
Photo courtesy of the Archives of the City of Toronto.

cultural standpoint," but the empty seats in the theatre prompted *The Telegram*'s critic to write (in eerie premonition of *Take It from Me*?) that Toronto audiences clearly preferred "lingerie to literature" in their theatrical entertainment.

Fortunately, the Shubert brothers loved musicals. It was on musicals and spectacles (and spectacular musicals) that their reputation and success had been built, and, with the death of the Syndicate, they had a ready supply of the biggest and the best. In the years following the First World War they would send Lol Solman a steady stream of legendary musical money-makers and legendary stars: the Shuberts own *The Passing Show of 1918*, with Fred and Adele Astaire; Al Jolson's *Sinbad* and *Bombo*; Marilyn Miller's hit *Sally*; Victor Herbert's *Babes in Toyland*; Beatrice Lillie and Gertrude Lawrence in *Charlot's Revue*; Donald Brian and Jeanette MacDonald in *Yes, Yes, Yvette*; Eddie Cantor's *Make It Snappy*; and company after company of the perennial favourites, the shows that refused to ever die, *Rose Marie*, *The Desert Song*, *Blossom Time*, *The Student Prince* and *Chu Chin Chow*.

The last in that list was the biggest show ever to play the Royal Alexandra — biggest in terms of size, the grandfather of

the megamusicals of the 1980s. There were three hundred performers in the original touring cast of 1919 (the show had avoided the Actors' Equity strike when its producers, the Shubert-
allied company Comstock and Gest, became the first to sign the
Standard Contract); an animal menagerie that included three
camels, eight donkeys and three yaks; a 30-piece orchestra; and a
small army of stagehands and dressers to handle the elaborate
scenery and costume changes. The original London production
had opened in 1916 and ran for five full years, playing to more
than 3 million people, setting a British stage record that would
not be equalled for 40 years. It also set a record in earning more
than a million dollars for its author, Oscar Asche (who, nevertheless, died broke; he lost it all, he said, on the greyhounds).

With the exception of *Charlot's Revue*, these great musicals
were all American; even *Chu Chin Chow*, a British musical, toured
North America with an American cast, under American management. There was as yet no Canadian made first-class professional theatre – things had not changed since Toronto historian
(and actor, composer and playwright) Jessie Middleton wrote
just before the war, "There is no Canadian Drama. It is merely a
branch of the American Theatre, and, let it be said, a most profitable one." But it was not, yet, Canadian production that Lol
Solman and those who sought that "entertainment from a cultural standpoint" craved; it was British. American musicals were
"entertainment," but Britain was still seen by English-speaking
Canadians as the home of "culture." That British culture was
their protection against an otherwise inevitable dissolution in
the vast American melting pot. It had always been Solman and
Mulock's hope that the Royal Alexandra would attract the great
stars of the London stage. From time to time, it did, but visits by
British shows and performers had been few and far between
before the war – it was simply too far to travel, and far too
expensive – and had stopped entirely during the war.

Just before the war, Sir Johnston Forbes-Robertson, making
his final Canadian tour with *Caesar and Cleopatra*, *Hamlet* and *The
Merchant of Venice*, had lamented the fact that there was not "a

Robert Bruce Mantell

NEW DRESSES FOR "CHU CHIN CHOW"
Very Suitable to the Sultry Climate of Old Bagdad.

chain of theatres, under Canadian control, from Halifax to Victoria." How much more attractive (and more profitable) that would make Canada to British managers.

In 1919, a Montreal-based company called Trans-Canada Theatres Ltd. set about doing what Forbes-Robertson had suggested, with the purchase of Toronto's Grand Opera House and all the rest of Ambrose Small's chain of theatres. The principals of this company were the anglophilic Montreal businessmen Henry Joseph, Henry Beauclerk, Sir William J. Shaughnessy and Sir William's father, Sir Thomas George Lord Shaughnessy, founder and former president of the Canadian Pacific Railway. Their silent partner in Toronto — silent because his participation was not strictly compatible with his employment (and contracts) with the Shuberts — was Lol Solman.

Trans-Canada Theatres never acquired enough theatres to actually stretch from Halifax to Victoria, but they made up for the spareness of their circuit by organizing round trip bookings, with touring British companies playing each theatre on the circuit twice, once on the road from Halifax to the west and once again on the road back east to Halifax (and the ship to take them home to England). This was not a common practice. As long as there was enough product on the road to allow them some booking flexibility, theatre owners balked at the idea of committing themselves, far in advance to return performances of unknown shows. The vaudeville impresario Alexander Pantages was notorious for booking one-way Canadian tours that would take performers from Halifax to Vancouver and leave them there. If they wanted to come back east, they would have to either pay their own ways or accept new Vancouver-to-Halifax contracts at lower wages — and if the first leg of the journey had not been a success, there would be no second contract.

The Shuberts may not have been aware of the extent of Solman's involvement in the management of Trans-Canada Theatres Ltd., but they certainly had no objection to his booking shows for the Royal Alexandra through it. Indeed, it gave them a cost-free opportunity to gauge audience reactions to British

productions that might, in future, interest them for American re-mounts.

The first of the Trans-Canada bookings to play the Royal Alexandra was the musical *The Maid of the Mountains*, a sell-out despite having no "name" stars. After the long dry spell of the war, Torontonians were, indeed, eager to hear British accents onstage, even if from the lips of actors they had never heard of.

The Maid of the Mountains was followed by the first real stars of the British stage Toronto audiences had seen since Forbes-Robertson, Sir John Martin-Harvey and his wife, Nina de Silva, with their repertory company. For the trip west, Martin-Harvey performed Maeterlinck's *The Burgomaster of Stilemonde* and the classic, actor's tour-de-force drama of life on the stage, *Garrick*; for the second engagement, on the trip back east, he repeated those productions and added two more: the sword-and-costume adventure tale of the English Civil War *The Breed of the Treshams* and his signature piece, a stage adaptation of Dickens' *A Tale of Two Cities* titled *The Only Way*, in which he spoke the famous lines (not in the novel) "'Tis a far, far better thing that I do now than I have ever done before," still well-remembered — even quoted — by people who have never otherwise heard of either *The Only Way* or Sir John Martin-Harvey.

The British imports of Trans-Canada Theatres were roaring box-office successes across the country, but, alas, the costs of bringing the shows over and touring them were too high to be covered even by full houses in every city played. Trans-Canada went bankrupt in 1923. The company's assets — including the former Ambrose Small theatres — were purchased by Famous Players Canadian Corp., a motion picture distributor, and converted to use as cinemas.

On Trans-Canada's collapse, the company's recording secretary — a young man named Ernest Rawley — moved to Toronto to work for Famous Players, and lost his job when that company decided to stop allowing its theatres to be used for live performances. Lol Solman rescued him from the movies, putting him on contract as the Royal Alexandra's publicist and, incidentally, hiring him to find ways to keep the British shows

Matheson Lang

coming. Rawley managed this by setting up a new silent part-
nership between Solman and Montreal impresario Bert Lang –
All-Canada Tours Ltd. All-Canada assumed the management of
Sir John Martin-Harvey's popular tours and brought the Royal
Alexandra the renowned British repertory companies of
Seymour Hicks and Ellaline Terriss and (Canadian-born)
Matheson Lang. It also gave Toronto its first real British pan-
tomimes (not homemade imitations), with some of the most
important stars of that peculiar genre – George Robey, Wee
Georgie Hood and Dan Leno. For musical entertainment "from
a cultural standpoint," four tours of London's D'Oyly Carte
Opera Co. performed, doing the complete Gilbert and Sullivan
operetta canon by the fourth. Without a large enough circuit of
Canadian theatres into which to book, however, All-Canada
Tours could not sustain itself; in 1930 it too went bankrupt.

Dan Leno

Everyone in the touring theatre business in the 1920s faced a serious, new problem - and one that got steadily worse as the decade progressed. Both the theatres and the actors were disappearing. People blamed the automobile, the rise of the middle-class, the failure of public education, too many immigrants, loss of gentility, postwar moral degeneration, jazz music, radio and moving pictures for what was happening; but it was mostly the moving pictures.

For actors, the post–First World War growth of the cinema meant liberation from the road. For the first time in history, it became possible for an actor to make a decent living without having to spend most of his life in transit from one nameless town to another, shivering in railroad cars, sleeping in fleabag hotels and eating bad food in surly boarding houses. He could settle down in one place and stay there, and the work was easier. As much as actors might then – as they still do today – say that the theatre was their spiritual home and the temple of their true art, what a pleasant, easygoing place winter-free Hollywood, California, was to make one's temporal home in 1925.

For theatre owners and managers, the growth of motion picture production meant an endless supply of low-cost product, a near-infinity of choice and the freedom to make their own schedules — if a cinema found itself with a hit, it could hold it over and run it as long as it remained profitable. A legitimate theatre was bound to the schedules set by some booking agent a thousand miles away and would often see its hits close far too early, to be replaced by turkeys to which it was contractually bound for a full week, even if there were no audience. Theatre owners who converted to motion pictures had to reduce their ticket prices, of course, but the huge reduction in their staffing and operating costs — and the increase in their audiences — more than made up for that.

As theatre owners across North America abandoned their stages and installed screens — or were bought out, as the Ambrose Small/Trans-Canada theatres were — by motion picture distributors, the opportunities for touring theatre companies shrank. As touring players abandoned the stage for the movies, there was less and less product available for the few theatre owners who still tried to hang on. In the end, whatever the cause and whichever the effect, the road began to dry up. It would never disappear entirely, but it became less and less important as a source of revenue as the legitimate theatre business became concentrated in, and sat down in, New York City. Where once a long continental tour had been every producer's goal, by the late twenties the hope had become a long run on Broadway with, perhaps, a short out-of-town tryout prior to New York, and, perhaps, a limited tour after the Broadway closing, limited to the few remaining cities that had good theatres and had established reputations as "good theatre towns," where a producer could still hope for a reasonable profit. Across the continent, the "regional" towns starved for quality live theatre.

One bright spot in all this is that the continued existence of hold-outs like Lol Solman gave new opportunities to the development of local theatre companies, and it was in the 1920s that a professional Canadian theatre began to emerge. The American-born actor Vaughan Glaser established a permanent stock company, training and employing local actors, at the Uptown Theatre. At the Royal Alexandra, Solman gave his stage to Capt. Merton Plunkett, of Orillia, and his ex-all-soldier troupe, The Dumbells, who would produce 12 original musical revues over seven years, never failing to fill the theatre with patriotic audiences enthusiastic for the novelty of professional theatre that had been entirely "made in Canada."

In the 1920s Lol Solman himself got into the motion picture business when the Shuberts formed a partnership with Marcus Loew, builder of Toronto's double-decker, vaudeville and motion picture Elgin and Winter Garden Theatre. They asked Solman to assume the post of vice-president of Loew's Canadian operations. He did not, however, approve of showing films at the Royal Alexandra. There were exceptions, of course, if the film was something that might be considered in some way special and not beneath the dignity of a fine first-class legitimate theatre. In 1909, Solman permitted the exhibition of documentary films by Lyman Howe featuring motion pictures of the Wright brothers' first flight; in 1912, he screened *The Delhi Durbar: With Our King and Queen Through India*, a two-and-a-half-hour film documenting the 1911 Asian trip of King George and Queen Mary (and this was very, very special: it was a colour film, and accompanied by a live chorus of 24, a 20-piece brass band and three pipers). In 1915, the Royal Alexandra showed film footage of the Great War — *On the Battlefields of France* — and hosted the Canadian premiere (with the audience in formal dress) of D.W. Griffith's epic *The Birth of a Nation* (although this film was actually booked in by Solman's assistant, W.J. Breen, while Lol was in hospital with appendicitis; he must also have been ill in 1918, when Breen, at the behest of the Shuberts, showed both William Farnum's *Les Misérables* and sex-symbol Theda Bara's *Cleopatra*). In 1927, in another special event, Solman exhibited A.D. "Cowboy" Kean's *Policing the Plains*, the very first Canadian-made feature film.

In 1930, the Shuberts arranged and paid for the installation of a sound system, for talking pictures, in the Royal Alexandra. Solman told them that he would give up and quit before he would allow his theatre to be used to show "talkies," but, in the end, he gave his consent to the first sound motion picture they proposed, Lewis Milestone's Academy Award-winner, *All Quiet on the Western Front*. It was a very good film, and had the advantage of having been written by Maxwell Anderson and George Abbott, two respectable writers for the legitimate stage whom Solman knew well.

In January 1931, Lol Solman allowed another commercial motion picture in, swearing it would be the last for a long time. The first year of the Great Depression, 1930, had been difficult for everyone, including the Shuberts. That fall, there was nothing available on the road and Solman found himself facing the prospect of shutting the theatre for three or four months — and he held the firm belief that any theatre that went dark in mid-season might as well just close down for good. The Uptown's Vaughan Glaser had just retired (and the Uptown gone entirely to motion pictures), but Solman talked him into putting together a new company — Toronto actors who had worked with him at the Uptown — and directing two plays at the Royal

Alexandra in November, Lol Solman producing. Over Christmas, he and Ernest Rawley kept the lights on by producing their own pantomime, *Sinbad the Sailor*, with Capt. Plunkett, several of the Dumbells and a local cast. Solman had arranged an appearance by the British actors Maurice Colbourne and Barry Jones in Shaw's *The Apple Cart* for February, but January was empty and Solman, sadly, filled it with a three-week engagement of the new American war film *Hell's Angels*. It was to have been four weeks, but the print was held for examination at the border; the censors were concerned by the word "Hell" in the title. But then, it was back to first-class legit with the kind of plays the theatre was meant to do. The *Globe and Mail* theatre critic Herbert Whittaker, on the occasion of the 50th anniversary of the Royal Alexandra, wrote of such episodes, "A lady may sometimes take in paying guests, but that does not make her a boardinghouse keeper."

In February, with the crisis passed, Lol Solman relaxed enough to realize that he was seriously ill. On February 20, he

The Dumbells, a troupe of soldiers formed to entertain the troops at Vimy, re-formed after the war and toured Canada for seven years, never failing to draw crowds to the Royal Alexandra.

Photo courtesy of the Archives of Ontario.

The suave Maurice Colbourne was one of the few British actor-managers willing to tour Canada. He brought his repertory of Shaw comedies to the Royal Alexandra through the 1930s.

entered Wellesley Hospital with pneumonia. The papers published cheery reports telling the public that he was getting better daily, but he died on March 24, missing the opening of Madge Kennedy in A.A. Milne's sentimental comedy *Michael and Mary* at the Royal Alexandra, a play he probably would have liked.

Lol Solman's funeral was held at St. Andrew's Presbyterian, the "Salvation" corner of the old Crossroads of the Four 'Nations. Two hundred cars followed the coffin to Mt. Pleasant Cemetery, said to be the biggest procession of automobiles the city had ever seen. William J. Breen, his assistant since 1910, took over as manager of the Royal Alexandra at what promised to be a very difficult time; in October 1931, the Shuberts filed for bankruptcy protection.

Solman's death left only one member of the original partnership, Stephen Haas, still living. Haas had by this time, however, retired to live in his country home, Strathmore, near Cobourg, and put his shares along with Cawthra Mulock's and Solman's under the management of the Royal Trust Co. On behalf of the Trust, the young lawyer Gordon Perry assumed the position of president of the Alexandra Co.

18

THE IMPOSSIBLE YEARS

THE 1930S, THE DECADE OF THE GREAT DEPRESSION, were the worst years in the history of North American theatre. Back in the time when Cawthra Mulock built the Royal Alexandra there had been more than three hundred touring companies more or less permanently on the road. When William J. Breen took over management of the theatre in 1931, there were only two dozen left. At the height of the Golden Age, there were fifteen hundred legitimate theatres in North America; by late 1931, more than one thousand of these had closed their doors — most of them, forever. In 1932, the Royal Alexandra was the only first-class legitimate theatre still operating in Canada.

It became impossible for a theatre manager to plan a season. A contract was no guarantee that a show, a producer, an acting company would still be in business by the engagement date. For his season of 1935, Breen had booked 19 shows from New York; only five of these actually made it to Toronto. There was a joke on Broadway: "The most popular new play these days is the one called *Cancelled*. You see its name on theatre marquees everywhere."

William Breen made an effort to repeat what Lol Solman had done during the theatre's crisis of 1908, setting up his own resident company, the Toronto Repertory Theatre Co, under the

A view from the stage in the 1930s. The glass front of the followspot booth, top centre, is closed in, re-fitted for the projection of motion pictures.

actor and director Cameron Matthews. He produced two plays, *The Pursuit of Happiness* and *Charley's Aunt* at the Royal Alexandra before losses forced him to shut the company down.

As much as possible, Breen – like Lol Solman before him – resisted the easy temptation of booking in films to tide himself over between shows. As with Solman, there were exceptions made for exceptional films, such as Noel Coward's *Cavalcade*, a celebration of the British Empire, in 1933, which Breen made into a special event, the invited opening-night audience – which included the elderly Sir William Mulock – in top hat, white tie and tails. Like Solman, Breen did not much care for the talkies, even though his young son, Robert, became a famous motion-picture child star. He exhibited *Grand Hotel*, *Lost Horizon* and *Dinner at Eight*, but none of Bobby Breen's popular films of the 1930s – not *Let's Sing Again*, or *Rainbow on the River*, or *Make a Wish*, or *Johnny Doughboy* – ever made it to the Royal Alexandra screen. Breen stuck to his first-class legitimate theatre mandate even though he was forced to darken the theatre for 22 weeks in 1932, 21 in 1933, a terrible 41 in 1934 and a barely supportable 32 in 1935. In New York, Lee Shubert, his company in receivership, asked, "Where is the miracle that will save theatre?"

Shubert helped answer his own question. Throughout the twenties, the Shuberts had often been criticized – with their lavish and endless stream of spectacles and musicals – as being "too commercial" and more concerned with mass appeal (and box-office receipts) than with the art of the stage. Even their Canadian manager, Lol Solman, worried about that. But, in the depths of the Depression, they proved their critics wrong. Although the Shubert Corporation was bankrupt, and de-listed from the New York Stock Exchange, Lee and Jacob Shubert were still, personally, wealthy men. Throughout the thirties, they continued to produce, using their own money. To protect their productions from the creditors of the Shubert Corp., they often hid their involvement, shunning the spotlight and listing others as producers. The famous *Ziegfeld Follies* productions of the 1930s billed "Mrs. Florenz Ziegfeld" as producer, but Mrs. Ziegfeld (the actress and singer Billie Burke) had been left broke and deeply in debt on her bankrupt husband's death in 1931; the actual, uncredited producer of the *Follies* was Lee Shubert. More important, however, was the Shuberts' continuing investment in other people's shows; throughout the Depression, they spent millions, with little expectation of return, in keeping Broadway alive. In 1933 alone, at least half the shows in New York had made it to the stage thanks to Shubert financing.

And then, against the advice of his friends and the objections of his bankers, Lee Shubert bought back and re-opened his bankrupt company.

That Broadway stayed open was of vital importance to the Royal Alexandra. First, because Broadway, even if wounded, could still send him a few touring shows and new, Broadway-bound tryouts; second, because foreign attractions, on their way to Broadway, could easily stop in first in Toronto for a few days, even if they were not touring anywhere else. Thanks to his relationship with the Shuberts and their own need for product, it

Alfred Lunt and Lynn Fontanne made their first appearance at the Royal Alexandra in *The Taming of the Shrew* in 1935.

Ethel Barrymore starred in the 1938 production *Whiteoaks*, based on the novel by Canadian author Mazo de la Roche.

was also possible for Breen to hire Ernest Rawley and send him to England to negotiate directly with British companies, offering them runs in Toronto followed by New York; Breen was able to become, in a small way, a Broadway booking agent. It was as such that he brought the Royal Alexandra – and New York – the English Light Opera Co., the Sir Barry Jackson Repertory Theatre Co. (with stars Donald Wolfit and Peggy Surtees), the Lady George Cholmondley Co., Maurice Colbourne and Barry Jones' Repertory Co. (introducing North American audiences to the young Jessica Tandy in their production of *Charles the King*), the Stratford-upon-Avon Shakespeare Festival Co., the Sir John Martin-Harvey Co. and, from Dublin, the famed Abbey Players.

The Shuberts could not reciprocate with anything like the quantity of what they had been able to put on the road in the twenties, but they made up for it in quality, mounting short, New York-Boston-Toronto-Philadelphia tours that would bring the Royal Alexandra the Walter Hampden Repertory Co.; their own production of *Victoria Regina*, with Helen Hayes; Maurice Evans in *King Richard II*; Kaufman and Hart's hit comedy *You Can't Take It with You*; the Katharine Cornell Repertory Co. with *The Barretts of Wimpole St.*, *Candida* and *Romeo and Juliet*; the first Ibsen Toronto had seen in a long time, Ruth Gordon in *A Doll's House* and Alla Nazimova in *Ghosts*; the great Ethel Barrymore in a dramatization of the Canadian novel *Whiteoaks*; Clifton Webb and Estelle Winwood in Wilde's *The Importance of Being Earnest*; Gertrude Lawrence in *Susan and God*; Walter Huston and Fay Bainter in *Dodsworth*; Orson Welles' controversial, modern-dress production of *Julius Caesar* (which closed in Toronto, its tour abruptly cancelled as other scheduled theatres went permanently dark); the musicals *The Green Pastures*, *As Thousands Cheer*, *Pins and Needles* and *At Home Abroad*, with Beatrice Lillie and Ethel Waters; the Theatre Guild productions of Eugene O'Neill's *Ah, Wilderness*, with George M. Cohan, and *The Taming of the Shrew*, with Alfred Lunt, Lynn Fontanne and Sidney Greenstreet; Cedric Hardwicke in *The Amazing Dr. Clitterhouse*; Cornelia Otis Skinner's one-woman shows (inexpensive to tour and enormously popular) *Edna, His*

GILBERT MILLER
presents
HELEN HAYES
in THE CROWNING ACHIEVEMENT
OF HER DISTINGUISHED CAREER
"Victoria Regina"
BY LAURENCE HOUSMAN
STAGED BY MR. MILLER
ENTIRE PRODUCTION DESIGNED BY REX WHISTLER

Wife and *The Six Wives of Henry VIII*; and the Toronto homecoming of one of the city's most famous actors, ever, Raymond Massey in *The Shining Hour* and *Abe Lincoln in Illinois.*

The runs were short – some as few as three days – as producers cut costs and the dark spells in between were often very long, but the Royal Alexandra managed the impossible; it not only survived the Dirty Thirties – the only legitimate theatre in Canada that did so – but managed to bring Toronto some of the best and most memorable theatre the city had ever seen. In 1939, William Breen felt good enough about future prospects to spend some money fixing the house up. The new King George VI and Queen Elizabeth scheduled a royal visit to Canada – the first ever by a reigning monarch – and Breen had high hopes they would come to visit the country's last royal theatre. He spent three weeks polishing the woodwork, repainting the auditorium and the dressing rooms, hanging a brand-new crimson act curtain (with the Royal Coat of Arms in gold) and re-covering the walls

London, Ontario-born Richard B. Harrison took the lead role of "de Lawd" in an epic production of *The Green Pastures* in 1933.

of the ladies' retiring room (with green and ecru silk tapestry) and the tearoom (in orchid-coloured silk). To Breen's disappointment, the King and Queen got no nearer the Royal Alexandra than Union Station, but the theatre looked wonderful.

After the refurbishing, and with no royal visitors to show around after all, William Breen decided that 29 years had been enough for him and he retired, handing the manager's master key and his account books to the publicist and booking agent, Ernest Rawley.

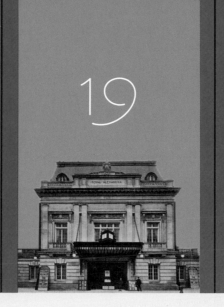

19

THE FORTIES

WHEN ERNIE RAWLEY took over management of the Royal Alexandra, the Depression was almost over, but that meant little to the state of the theatre business. The damage had been done. Hundreds of great theatres were gone; the road had all but vanished. To make matters even worse, the Second World War meant the end of any hope of further imports from England. Rawley had two choices if he wanted to keep the theatre open at least a few months a year: find local product or show more movies. He did both. Like his predecessors, Solman and Breen, he tried to keep the Royal Alexandra's film screenings of high quality and to make them "theatrical" events. His great motion picture fallback was Disney's *Fantasia*, which he premiered in 1941 as a black-tie evening; the special screenings of *Fantasia* at the Royal Alexandra became an annual event in Toronto — all the way until 1953 — on a par with the Christmas pantomime, the Santa Claus Parade, *The Nutcracker* ballet, the Orange Parade and the Canadian National Exhibition.

Ernie Rawley fell into show business in Montreal when he answered a newspaper ad seeking a stenographer for Lord Shaughnessy's Trans-Canada Theatres Ltd. He was only 15 or 16 or 17 at the time — depending on which account you read — had

One Week Beginning MONDAY NIGHT, APRIL 22
Katharine CORNELL
and THE PLAYWRIGHTS' COMPANY present
No Time for Comedy
by S. N. BEHRMAN
with FRANCIS LEDERER
MARGALO GILLMORE · JOHN WILLIAMS
Staged by GUTHRIE McCLINTIC
Settings by JO MIELZINER

MAIL ORDERS NOW!
Eves.: Orch. $2.50, $3.00; 1st Balc.
$1.50, $2.00, $2.50; 2nd Balc. $1.00,
Mats. (Wed. - Sat.); Orch. $2.00,
$2.50; 1st Balc. $1.50, $2.00; 2nd
Balc. $1.00. Enclose stamped, re-
turn envelope.

dropped out of high school and just finished a business course in which he learned to type and take shorthand. He became Trans-Canada's "recording secretary" and, in time, assistant to its booking manager, from whom he learned all there was to know about the complex arts of contracting, booking, routing and scheduling touring theatre companies across Canada. In 1923, when Trans-Canada went into receivership, he remained as the company's sole employee, handling all its business by himself until 1925, when Famous Players took over.

For a while, Famous Players continued using the Trans-Canada theatres for live performances – in addition to motion pictures – and brought Rawley to Toronto to manage the bookings. The first person he met when he arrived at his new office was the receptionist, Frances Ross, whom he married three years later. Around the time of the wedding, he lost his job; Famous Players decided that live theatre had no future and converted all of its houses to motion picture use only, effectively killing what was left of the road in Canada.

Ernie Rawley set out on his own as a freelance impresario, booking agent and publicist, finding steady work in all three capacities with Lol Solman and William Breen at the Royal Alexandra and, at the same time, booking and producing concert attractions for Massey Hall. It was thanks to Rawley's work that Breen was able to secure the tours of the Abbey Players and the Barry Jackson and Maurice Colbourne/Barry Jones repertory companies during the darkest days of the Depression; and, for Breen, Rawley himself produced the Canadian-cast pantomimes *Sinbad the Sailor* and *Robinson Crusoe*. It was after the latter, in 1934, a money-loser, that Ernie Rawley decided to give up the theatre and find a steady job in some business with a future, one that could offer a regular paycheque. He became an insurance salesman.

On his first day of making sales calls, with an experienced agent along as his prompter, Rawley's route took him past the Royal Alexandra Theatre. He asked the other agent to stop and wait a moment while he ran quickly inside, just to say hello to some friends who were working there that day. One thing led to another until, as he recalled in an interview in 1957, "It must have been at least a couple of hours before I remembered the poor guy waiting in the car. But when I ran out to apologize, he just grinned and said, 'You don't want to sell insurance,' and drove off." Rawley went back to his shaky business and, when William Breen offered him the management of the Royal Alexandra, accepted without hesitation.

It was Rawley's stated goal that the Royal Alexandra would never again go dark for half the year, not even just for the summer. To this end, he put together, as Lol Solman had done in 1907, his own stock company, headed by Broadway veterans Frank McCoy and Ethel Britton, actors-turned-producers, who, in turn, hired a veteran Broadway director, Robert Henderson, to assemble and direct a base company of Canadian actors who could be supplemented, as in the old days, with the occasional imported British or American star.

Rawley began 1940 with a line-up he and Breen had already put together, bringing Maurice Colbourne, Barry Jones and Jessica Tandy back from England (it would be their final appearance at the Royal Alexandra as the war closed the sea lanes); a Shubert musical, *Three After Three*, by Hoagy Carmichael and Johnny Mercer, with film stars Mitzi Green, Simone Simon and Stepin' Fetchit; the Shubert revue *The Streets of Paris*, with Carmen Miranda; a touring production of the Broadway hit *The Little Foxes*, starring Tallulah Bankhead and Dan Duryea; the drama *Ladies in Retirement*, with Flora Robson and Estelle Winwood; Maurice Evans' great production of *Hamlet*; and, in a fundraiser for the Canadian Red Cross, Katharine Cornell in *No Time for Comedy*. It was a splendid season of first-class productions, with great stars, but it ended in April, with nothing left on the horizon before the fall. In June, then, Rawley dropped ticket prices from their winter high of $2 down to $1 and launched his stock company. At that time, the Royal Alexandra had not had a summer season for 16 years and, in the opinion of everyone he had asked – and many he had not asked – summer stock was dead, and a waste of his time and money; no one went to the theatre

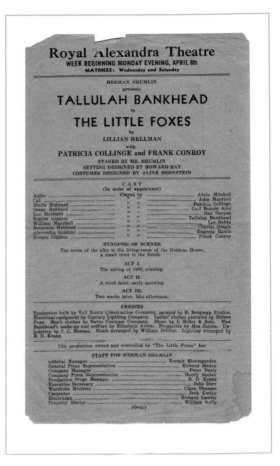

in the summer anymore. To make it more difficult, Henderson could find no New York stars to import – no one willing to take the chance of bombing in Toronto with a company of unknown Canadians. He and Rawley, however, felt ready to take the chance themselves; he had put together a solid group of actors, including such former stalwarts of the Vaughan Glaser troupe as Earle Grey, who would go on to become a pioneer of television drama. Toronto surprised the critics; people did come. Eight excellent contemporary dramas and comedies later, with a local cast and no American stars, Rawley had kept his theatre open all summer long and emerged with books in the black.

So good was the summer of 1940 that, the next summer – and all the summers of the forties after – Rawley and Henderson's stock company did attract stars: Gloria Swanson, Ethel Barrymore, Tallulah Bankhead (who did Noel Coward's *Private Lives* for Ernie Rawley before she starred in the same play in New York), Fay Wray, José Ferrer, Lenore Ulric (who starred in *Rain* on Broadway and repeated her role for Royal Alexandra summer stock), Conrad Nagel, Ana Sten, Mary Boland, and, from Britain via Hollywood, C. Aubrey Smith in Galsworthy's *Old English*. Rawley was bringing Toronto a summer stock series as good as what, a few years before, most North American theatres would have been happy to have in their regular seasons. By 1944, he felt so confident in the public response to Robert Henderson's company that he broke one of the great taboos of summer stock to stage a July week of *Hamlet*, with Broadway and film actor Tom Rutherfurd. This was something just not done; Shakespearean tragedy was considered far too heavy fare for a summer audience and believed to need, at the best of times, a name actor – a Forbes-Robertson or John Gielgud or Maurice Evans – to have any hope of success. *Hamlet*, however, sold out that week and Ernie Rawley brought it back for a second in July and a third in September.

The drying up of the road that had begun in the 1930s continued – and, if possible, got even worse – in the forties. The Second World War made touring by English companies impossible and –

with rationing — had a serious dampening effect on Broadway touring, as well. The days of the big musical seemed over and done. The Shuberts' endless road tours of the old operetta standards — *Blossom Time, Rose Marie* and *The Student Prince* — went on and on, but seemed to get a little lighter, less elaborate and more tattered with each pass through the Royal Alexandra, but there were fewer and fewer new musicals able to move anywhere outside Broadway. There were some, of course — the revues *Hellzapoppin'* and Katherine Dunham's colourful *Tropical Revue* were big hits on the road in 1942 and 1944; the new Gershwin folk opera *Porgy and Bess* packed the house in 1943; and Al Jolson came to town with his very last stage musical, *Hold On to Your Hats*, in 1941, just before the United States entered the war (in the audience on one of the five nights of Jolson's show were the young newlyweds Ed and Anne Mirvish, who would soon become very important people in the theatre's story) — but, to fill the gap, Ernie Rawley had to produce his own musicals. *Ritzin' the Blitz, The Merry Widow, Anything Goes, The Vagabond King, The Desert Song, New Moon* and *The Chocolate Soldier* all played the Royal Alexandra during the war, with Canadian casts, giving — along with the seasons of summer stock — immense stimulus to the growth of a professional theatre community in Toronto.

The difficulties of touring meant a trimming of the fat from what did travel out from Broadway during the forties and the road, while slim, boasted unprecedented quality with such fabled productions as Tallulah Bankhead's *The Little Foxes; The Philadelphia Story*, with Katherine Hepburn and Van Heflin; Alfred Lunt and Lynn Fontanne in *There Shall Be No Tonight*; Orson Welles' productions of *Native Son* and *Othello* (with Paul Robeson, José Ferrer and Uta Hagen); Ethel Barrymore in the *Corn Is Green; The Three Sisters*, with Katharine Cornell, Judith Anderson and Ruth Gordon; John Barton in *Tobacco Road*; Diana Barrymore in *Rebecca*; Walter Hampden and Cecilia Loftus in *Arsenic and Old Lace*; and Clifton Webb's *The Man Who Came to Dinner*.

Costs and wartime travel restrictions limited these tours to a few theatres in a few cities only, and their producers chose very

The *Globe and Mail*, August 21, 1943: Hector Charlesworth's column praises the efforts of Ernest Rawley's stock company.

Ernie Rawley's production of
Ritzin' the Blitz, in 1942, was a
wartime morale-builder, making
light of the bombing of London
and raising funds for the Red Cross.

carefully where to send them — only the best theatres in the "best theatre towns," the cities that had an established reputation for the love of good live theatre. That this group still included Toronto and the Royal Alexandra owed much to the efforts of Ernie Rawley.

THE FIFTIES

ERNEST RAWLEY WAS A MAN of wide-ranging tastes in entertainment — he once said that he liked anything on a stage, from Shakespeare to pie-in-the-face comedy, as long as it was well performed — and he did not limit himself to the legitimate theatre's usual repertoire. In the twenties and thirties, his clients as a publicist and booking agent had included Toronto's Massey Hall, and he had developed a taste for opera and ballet. Both had certainly been presented at the Royal Alexandra before Rawley became manager, but he would make them a regular feature of his seasons from the late 1940s through the 1950s.

The Royal Conservatory Opera School was established in 1946 and began presenting public performances of opera excerpts at Hart House Theatre and the Eaton's Auditorium soon thereafter. Rawley booked them into the Royal Alexandra in 1950 — a company of one hundred — to stage three complete operas, *Rigoletto, Don Giovanni* and *La Bohème,* and again in 1951, as "Opera Festival Toronto," with *The Marriage of Figaro, Faust* and *Madame Butterfly* and made their appearance an annual event for eleven seasons. On their 12th season at the Royal Alexandra, the company adopted the new name, by which it's still known today, the Canadian Opera Company.

Ernie Rawley at the door of the
Royal Alexandra, at the time of the
theatre's 50th anniversary in 1957.
Photo courtesy of the *Toronto Star*.

Ballet, however, was Rawley's passion – outside good drama.
There had been very little ballet performance at the Royal
Alexandra in its early years – the Ballets Russes in 1912, the great
Anna Pavlova in 1916 – and dance had been absent since Ruth St.
Dennis made a two-night appearance in 1927. During the war,
Rawley negotiated tours with the American impresario Sol
Hurok, bringing in the Ballet Russe de Monte Carlo, with

Alexandra Danilova, and the Ballet Theatre, with Alicia Markova. In 1949, he staged an event known as *The Canadian Ballet Festival*, involving every professional dance company in the country – the Ballet Club of Toronto, the Hamilton Ballet, the Mildred Wickson Ballet, Neo-Dance Theatre, the Ottawa Ballet, Vancouver's Panto-Pacific Ballet, the Ruth Sorel Ballet of Montreal, the Winnipeg Ballet, Toronto Ballet and the Volkoff Canadian Ballet Co. Following the war, in the 1950s, he imported the London Festival Ballet, with Anton Dolin, and the Sadler's Wells Ballet Co., with Margot Fonteyn and Moira Shearer. And then, in 1953, he turned his theatre over to a promising new company headed by a British-born dancer named Celia Franca, the National Ballet of Canada. The Royal Alexandra would be a home stage for the National Ballet for the rest of Ernie Rawley's tenure as manager, all the way to 1963.

By and large, the late 1940s and the 1950s were good years for

The Canadian Opera Company to be. The sixth annual Opera Festival on the Royal Alexandra stage in 1955, with *La Traviata*. The cast for this production included Jon Vickers, Jan Rubes and Andrew McMillan.

Photo courtesy of the Toronto Public Library, Theatre Collection.

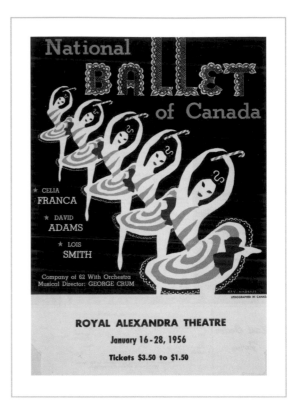

the theatre. Broadway once again began pumping out musicals and the Royal Alexandra treated its audiences to an astonishing deluge of new shows: *Oklahoma!*, *Carousel*, Harold Arlen's *Bloomer Girl*, *Annie Get Your Gun*, *High Button Shoes*, *Finian's Rainbow*, Beatrice Lillie in *Inside USA* (with a cast of 107), *Brigadoon*, *Kiss Me Kate*, *Paint Your Wagon*, *Call Me Madam*, *Guys and Dolls*, *South Pacific*, *The Pajama Game*, *The King and I*, *Can-Can* and *The Music Man*. Rawley also staged, along the way, two memorable Canadian-made musicals, Mavor Moore's *Sunshine Town* — a production of Dora Mavor Moore's New Play Society, starring Robert Goulet — and an amateur production from Ottawa (one that began, at any rate, as an amateur production), the musical satire *My Fur Lady*. It was *My Fur Lady* that was onstage on the occasion of the theatre's 50th anniversary, in August 1957. *My Fur Lady* was a fitting symbol for 50 years of success. It was the first show, ever, at the Royal Alexandra to sell out completely — every seat for every scheduled performance — before its opening (this would not happen again for ten years, when another Canadian musical — *Anne of Green Gables* — opened the season of 1967).

My Fur Lady Marks 50 Years For Royal Alexandra

MANAGER ERNEST RAWLEY AND THE ROYAL ALEX
—Star Photo by Howard Anderson

HELEN HAYES   KATHARINE HEPBURN   TALLULAH BANKHEAD
—Photo by Vandamm

SIR HARRY LAUDER
—Photo by White Studio

BEATRICE LILLIE
—Photo by Eileen Darby

Schubert Musical Was Opener For 1907 'Top Layer of Society'

By DOUGLAS BLANCHARD

The Royal Alexandra theatre celebrates its 50th anniversary Aug. 26 when it opens for the fall season with "My Fur Lady." That's the all-Canadian satire which made such a hit at Stratford. It is the latest of several thousand Royal Alex presentations that have brought practically every stage celebrity of the English-speaking world here since "the world's most up-to-date theatre" opened in 1907 with a lavish musical comedy straight from Broadway.

Hard at work behind the scenes will be Reuben Elliott, 84, master prop man. That's what he was doing at the first performance, and what he's been doing ever since. Master carpenter will be Jack Koster, 76, who also grew up with the Royal Alex. They have seen thousands of different shows at close range and neither of them would give a plugged nickle for TV or movies.

"Every performance has been a miracle of communication between audience and actors. It works both ways. And you'll never get anything like it on a screen," they agreed after talking over old times yesterday. They still love the atmosphere of the theatre even when it's dark for the summer.

SCHUBERT OPENING

"When Cawthra Mulock decided to build the most modern theatre in the world he chose what was then the busiest location in Toronto," they said. The lieutenant-governor's residence was right across the street (there were no freight cars then). The grounds of Upper Canada college surrounded the theatre site. We had the whole top layer of society at the opening performance, including the leaders of Church and state. Sir William Mulock was one of our warmest supporters and he delighted to come backstage and see the actors. There were more than 100 in the cast that first night. It was a Schubert musical comedy called "Top O' The World" and it starred Anna Laughlin.

Although architect Peter Lyle took the New Amsterdam theatre in New York as his general model, he introduced several features that were first in the world. An air-conditioning system using tons of ice (shovelled into tanks down under) fed frigid air through vents under the seats and a fan drew it to the roof. Trouble was it cooled the wrong end as well as going against the laws of gravity. It was not until the forties that modern air-conditioning systems were introduced pulling the air down from the ceiling.

It was the first fully fireproof theatre in the world with floors three feet thick of solid concrete. It was specially designed for acoustic effects and it replaced the former standard system of squares and right angles with gentle curves and an intimate effect suitable for a combination theatre. The audience marvelled at tapestries from France and marble from Italy. Seating capacity has stayed at the 1,500 mark.

General manager Ernest Rawley's office has walls covered with pictures of the great stars of past and present. Old-timers like Harry Lauder and Sarah Bernhardt seem to haunt the place like ghosts.

"There have been scores of great moments," he said. "I'll never forget the time Margot Fonteyn gave one of her greatest performances in Swan Lake — dancing that was technically and emotionally perfect. And the time the full house stood up as one person for George Formby. And the times when Al Jolson used to throw the program aside and say we haven't really got started — then he would then sing his heart out into the early hours of the morning.

PRE-MOVIE ARLISS

The old-timers talk for hours about Walter Hampden in Arsenic and Old Lace, Macbeth and Richelieu. Of how George Arliss wowed them in Disraeli long before he went on the screen. Of the Wandering Jew and Andrew Lang. Of Sir John Martin Harvey in the Old Way and the Burgomaster.

They assure you the best Hamlet ever was Sir Johnston Forbes-Robinson. They tell you that Lucille Ball did better acting on the stage of the Royal Alex than she's ever done on TV since. And how they were doing the Wizard of Oz half a century ago with stage settings that would make the highly touted TV technicians of today gasp with amazement (they even had a hurricane in the theatre).

"And when Robert B. Mantell put on a show (he would change the title every day for a week) we often had over 100 drops to handle," said the old hands. I tell you few boys today know what to do with sets in TV. And who is there in Hollywood to compare to Sarah Bernhardt and a whole generation of stars that put soul into acting. Even Marie Dressler did better on stage. And back in the days when theatres were the only way to spend an evening out people really used their imagination. They got enjoyment the like of which you can never buy with expensive mechanical gadgets."

And how about the future? Mr. Rawley is confident. Said he: "Competition from TV is tough. But it is making the shows better. Anything on tour today is topnotch, it has to be. We can no longer consider ourselves a mass entertainment medium. But there is a steady quality audience that appreciates the best. The legitimate theatre has been called that fabulous invalid because it has survived so many crises: movies, radio, sports and now TV.

Listed for the coming season are a wide variety of attractions including the Ziegfeld Follies (which are also celebrating their 50th anniversary), the Great Kalanag with his extravaganza of musical magic, Opera Festival (Carousel, Merry Widow, Die Fledermouse), Tunnel of Love, Separate Tables, National Ballet, Middle of the Night (Edward G. Robinson), Spring Thaw (the Mavor Moore-Lorne Greene touring version), etc.

Said Mr. Rawley: "Aside from the great state institutions of Europe, the Royal Alex is one of the few theatres in the world that have remained under one ownership with one policy all during the years. In 1907 the Mulock family laid down the policy of entertainment from the cultural standpoint, bringing the great stars of the British and American stage to Toronto audiences. Today the Mulock estate maintains that policy. It's up to the public to show its support."

GERTRUDE LAWRENCE

LEONIDE MASSINE
—Photo by Maurice Seymour

ETHEL BARRYMORE
—Photo by Vandamm

VETERANS R. ELLIOTT AND J. KOSTER
—Star Photo by Howard Anderson

MARGOT FONTEYN   MADELEINE CARROLL

DANTE THE MAGICIAN

MAE WEST
—Photo by Lucas and Monroe Studio

MAURICE EVANS
—Photo by John Dryer

GLORIA SWANSON
—Photo by De Sola

ALFRED LUNT AND LYNN FONTANNE
—Photo by Vandamm

G. MUSGROVE, J. ANDERSON, K. CORNELL
—Photo by Vandamm

In 1953, Ernie Rawley proudly reported back to Gordon Perry and the Royal Trust Co. that the Royal Alexandra had broken a record. It had been open and running, never once dark, for 72 continuous weeks. There was no other North American theatre outside of New York that had ever done such a thing.

The theatre on its 50th birthday. The three-sheet posters advertise *My Fur Lady*, the first show in the history of the theatre to sell out its entire run before opening.
Photo from the collection of Ed Mirvish.

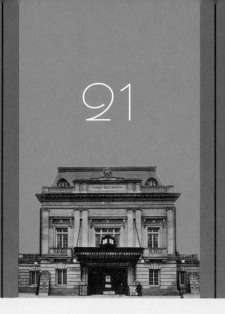

21

FOR SALE

STEPHEN HAAS, the last of the original partners of the Alexandra
Co., died on March 29, 1943, his shares transferred by his estate to
the administration of Gordon Perry for the Royal Trust Co. At
that point, the Royal Alexandra Theatre was, technically, for
sale. No one — none of the heirs of the founders — pressed for
any immediate action. Some, however, began to think about it
in 1960, when a new theatre opened in Toronto and took away
the opera, the ballet and — it seemed at the time — all the big,
profitable musicals.

That theatre was the O'Keefe Centre for the Performing Arts,
a "multi-purpose entertainment venue" seating 3,200. It opened
on October 1, 1960, with the pre-Broadway tryout of *Camelot*, starring Julie Andrews, Richard Burton and Robert Goulet. In 1961,
the Canadian Opera Co. moved in permanently, to be followed
by the National Ballet in 1964. Who could blame them? The
O'Keefe offered a huge stage for opera, lots of workshop space
(which the Royal Alexandra lacked) and a potential 1,700 more
tickets that might be sold for each performance. It was so cav-
ernous, of course, that its stage productions would require
sound amplification, but that, at the time, seemed to make it

The brand-new O'Keefe Centre in 1963. The opening of this gigantic auditorium, with more than twice the seating capacity of the Royal Alexandra, was a serious challenge to the pre-eminence of the older theatre. Photo courtesy of the *Toronto Star*.

even more modern and appealingly state-of-the-technical art.

The management of the O'Keefe realized fairly quickly that their huge house was best suited for extravagant spectacles and did not do well with smaller, more intimate shows, designed for a smaller, more traditional theatre. They made a deal with Ernie Rawley; rather than compete with one another, they would share a joint subscription season; the big, elaborate musicals would play the O'Keefe and the dramas and comedies would come to the Royal Alexandra. It seemed, under the circumstances, a good arrangement for everyone, but the loss of the big musicals weighed heavily on the Royal. In 1961, the joint-subscription arrangement gave Rawley two disastrously depressing and unpopular plays – *Toys in the Attic* and *A Taste of Honey* – that he would not otherwise have booked and an equally shunned production of *The Threepenny Opera* starring ex-striptease artiste Gypsy Rose Lee, a musical that had been judged too small-scale for O'Keefe Centre (Miss Lee, while she might have not have

been a critical or financial success, had the kindness to tell newspaper reporters that she much preferred the Royal Alexandra to
the O'Keefe, that it was "the most beautiful, delightful theatre I
know. It would break my heart if anything happened to it."

In 1962, Rawley recorded the first really bad money-losing
year the Royal Alexandra had suffered since the Depression.
The heirs of founders and the trustees of the estates decided
that the time had come to sell. Ernie Rawley publicly suggested that the theatre be purchased by some level of government.
He had seen and participated in the creation of a national opera
company and a national ballet. Now was the time, he said, for
Canada to also have a national theatre, where there would be a
permanent company of actors – and a school like that of the
National Ballet – in which non-profit plays and musicals of high
quality could be developed and sent out on tour across the
country. No one in the city, provincial or federal governments
seemed warm to this idea.

The theatre for sale, manager
Ernie Rawley takes a long last look
at the stage as he worries about
its future.

Photo courtesy of the *Toronto Star*.

Rawley and Gordon Perry did, however, succeed in extracting a promise from the heirs and trustees of the Alexandra Co.: they agreed not to sell immediately to the highest bidder, but to try to find a buyer who would promise to at least attempt to continue operating the Royal Alexandra as a theatre. If they could find such a person, they agreed that they would accept his bid even if it were significantly lower than others. There was a limit, however, to how low they would go. After some argument, they agreed on the figure of $215,000 — still a lot of money in 1962, but nowhere near the actual value of the land and building. They would not, they warned, wait for long for such a buyer; there were interested parties ready to pay a good deal more if they would be at liberty to tear the building down.

Ernie Rawley was weighing his options for early retirement when an unexpected job offer came from New York. In the late 1950s, U.S. courts had declared the Shubert Organization a trust — a monopoly as powerful in its control of touring theatre as the Theatrical Syndicate had once been — and ordered it to give up its booking agency. Bookings had then been split between two companies, the Legitimate Independent Theatres of North America (of which Rawley was an officer) and the Independent Booking Office. There were then only about 30 legitimate theatres still operating outside New York, and having two booking agencies to serve them seemed a little wasteful so, in 1962, the two merged to form one organization and offered Rawley the job of general manager, with an office on Broadway. He accepted. He and Florence planned to move to New York within three months. He hoped only that he would have the chance, before he left Toronto, to hand his keys over to someone he could trust to keep the Royal Alexandra running.

22

DEUS EX MACHINA
An Honest Buyer

In January 1963, with Jean Kerr's comedy *Mary Mary* on the stage of the Royal Alexandra, Ernie Rawley made the announcement that the theatre was to be sold within six weeks. He was to leave for New York at the end of February and the trustees wanted a deal closed by then. There were several purchase offers on the table, most of them well above the $215,000 asking price. Rumour had it that the highest bid — in excess of $300,000 — had come from Toronto Hydro, which planned to build offices on the site, Union Gas was another bidder, also with plans for an office building; and there was a third interested party, an unnamed property developer who had no immediate plans for the theatre, other than tearing it down and using the site as a parking lot while he thought about the possibilities.

On February 13, with only two weeks to go, Rawley revealed in a *Globe and Mail* interview that there was another bidder, Edwin Mirvish, owner of the Toronto discount store Honest Ed's. How much Mirvish had put on the table Rawley would not say, but he did tell the paper, "I know Mr. Mirvish wants to keep it as a theatre. He is very interested in the theatre and particularly in the Royal Alexandra."

January 1963. *Mary Mary* is on the stage and the Royal Alexandra faces the wrecker's ball. Is it the end of the road? Or will an unexpected saviour descend, *deus ex machina*, from the flies?

Ed Mirvish's offer was the lowest of all received – the minimum acceptable $215,000 – but he was the only one willing to keep the theatre open, as a theatre. Rawley and Gordon Perry reminded the trustees of their agreement to give preference to a buyer, even if the low-bidder, who would keep the Royal Alexandra going. They argued the case for Ed Mirvish – and for the moral obligation of the heirs of Mulock, Haas, Smith and Solman to save this cultural landmark – for two days, and they won. On February 15, the trustees accepted Mirvish's cheque for $215,000 and the Royal Alexandra Theatre was his. The old Alexandra Co. was dissolved. The stagehands' union threw a grand party for Ernie Rawley and he left for New York (where he continued to keep a close eye on the fortunes of the Royal Alexandra for the next 20 years).

The stagehands' union, IATSE Local 58, bids farewell to Ernest Rawley in a party on the stage of the Royal Alexandra. In the front, centre-left, are Ed Mirvish, Ernie Rawley (in glasses and dark suit) and Frances Rawley (with cane).

Photo courtesy of the *Globe and Mail*.

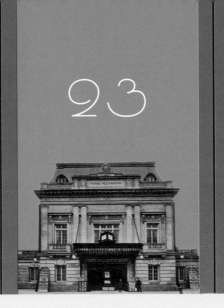

23

MR. MIRVISH

In 1963, ED MIRVISH knew no more about the theatre business than had Lol Solman in 1907. He had been inside the Royal Alexandra only three times in his life – once with his father, who took him to see Al Jolson in *Big Boy* in 1927, and once with his wife, Anne, whom he took to see Jolson, again, in *Hold On to Your Hats* in 1941 (Jolson, Ed liked to tell people, had been his introduction to show business in more ways than one; in 1914, his circumcision had been performed by the entertainer's father, Rabbi Moshe Reuben Yoelson, of the Talmud Torah Synagogue in Washington, D.C.), and once in 1957, to take his son, David, to see the magic show *Sim Sala Bim*. He had grown up in the two rooms occupied by the family over his father's Dundas St. grocery store, just a few blocks from the Standard Theatre, a Yiddish-language house at Dundas and Spadina, but he had never seen a show there. As a boy, working in his father's store, he had many times been given free passes to the Standard in exchange for putting the theatre's posters in the shop window, but he had never been able to use them; he had to work on Fridays and Saturdays and had no time for playgoing. In the late 1950s, the old Standard – then called the Victory Burlesque – went up for sale and Ed had briefly considered buying it. He paid "a man named Hack,"

who knew a lot about theatres, to have a look at the Victory and give him an opinion. Mr. Hack advised that the place wasn't worth it; it would cost far too much to fix it up; but, he suggested, "If you want to buy a theatre, and if the Royal Alexandra ever comes up for sale, you should try for it. It's a sweetheart."

Ed was born in Colonial Beach, Virginia, an oceanfront resort town near Washington, D.C., on July 24, 1914. His parents were recent immigrants – his father, David, from Vilnius, Lithuania; his mother, Anna, from Austrian Galicia. On his birth, his parents named him Yehuda; his cousin, Frances, Americanized this to Edwin. When he was two, his family moved to Washington, where his father opened a small grocery store.

In 1923, the Mirvish family moved to Toronto, where David had been offered a job as a salesman for Virtue Ltd., publishers of the two-volume *Encyclopedia of Freemasonry*. While he was himself an enthusiastic Mason, David Mirvish did not find many others in Toronto who shared sufficiently in that enthusiasm to pay the $42 price for the encyclopedia. Unable to make ends meet, he turned to selling Fuller Brushes door-to-door and then, in 1925, rented a small store at 788 Dundas St. West in which he opened D. Mirvish Groceries. The property included a four-room apartment. David, Anna and the baby, Lorraine, shared one room; Ed and his younger brother, Robert, another; the other two rooms were sublet. For many years, the tenant was a Rabbi Dinkin, who slept in one room and used the other as a Hebrew school. There was one bathroom shared by all, including Rabbi Dinkin's students, and Ed later said that it was his dream to one day live in a house in which he would not have to wait in line for his turn to use the washroom.

Catastrophe struck the family in 1929, when David Mirvish took ill and was bedridden for six months, leaving his wife and young son to look after the struggling, technically bankrupt store. In 1930, David died. Ed was then 15. He dropped out of high school – his formal education at an end – to assume the role of provider for his mother, his brother and his sister.

To all Fathers of the Bride, a Warning

By HERBERT WHITTAKER

With the sale of the Royal Alexandra Theatre, Toronto finds itself in a position rather like that of the father of the bride. Despite assurances that she will be taken care of in the manner to which she has been accustomed, for the father there is still some sense of loss, and a nervous condition mingling with the feelings of pride and happiness.

An old theatre represents the accumulation of happy memories, and the names which have graced the Royal Alexandra would dignify most European theatres, names like Lunt and Fontanne, Sir Harry Lauder, Anna Pavlova, the Barrymores, Sir John Martin-Harvey, Mrs. Fiske, Sir George Arliss, Sir Johnston Forbes-Robertson, Tallulah Bankhead, Dame Edith Evans, Katharine Cornell and Dame Margot Fonteyn, Sir John Gielgud, Sir Ralph Richardson and Gertrude Lawrence.

There has been much concern expressed since we reported that the Royal Alexandra was on the block. Ways, means and money have been discussed. But people couldn't believe that it would be sold and for a while it looked as if the theatre might slip through our fingers. The announcement that Ernest Rawley was leaving his long-held post of manager brought that threat closer to home.

Several groups of citizens, mindful of the danger and the need, have since moved to save it. The situation was eased when the board of directors refused an offer which would led to the destruction of the 56-year-old edifice. Yesterday's decision carries with it a guarantee that the Royal Alexandra will continue to function as a theatre. Mr. Rawley has declared himself satisfied.

Why this great concern about an old theatre? Do we need the Royal Alexandra? What's wrong with O'Keefe Centre? And doesn't that St. Lawrence development take care of any future need? It is a good time to answer some of these questions.

SHOWBUSINESS

tions, so that we may have a clearer idea of the importance of the sale of a building which, of its very nature, has become a public building, a monument to past culture and a promise of future joys.

It is not simply a matter of sentiment which makes us appreciate the Royal Alex (beloved buildings also acquire nicknames) and our need of it. It is a remarkably well-built theatre, in excellent condition, with acoustics which bring forth from the actors who play there the same kind of satisfaction that musicians express about Massey Hall. Other towns may well envy us the possession of both.

It is not possible to build such edifices as well today. The old builders had information and experience which was lost during the years when the only theatres built were motion picture palaces, designed for a different function. Intimacy has no value to a cinema.

The Royal Alex was built for the best possible communication between actors and audiences and that, I must stress, means communication without aid of microphones. It makes possible a direct empathy.

One has only to see a play in the larger O'Keefe Centre to realize the difference. The School for Scandal was enchanting to those of us who were seated close, despite the fact that its starry cast did resort to microphones. But to many who saw it, the impact was considerably less.

"If these are the best actors of England and this Sheridan comedy a rare classic," such playgoers have a right to say, "we don't think they are so great. They didn't do all that much for us."

Of course not. The point is that O'Keefe Centre is a comfortable, spacious and most effective home for musical comedies, for opera, for ballet and even for great solo performers. It is slow death for legitimate theatre.

It is important that we recognize this fact, for we cannot expect others to concern themselves.

We cannot blame Alexander Cohen, who hooks the O'Keefe attractions, for bringing The School For Scandal to the Centre. He was sincere in saying that only a house as big as this would supply the financial returns to make such an importation profitable. And if, in a few years, the Toronto audience for such attractions vanishes — which it will do — we cannot expect Mr. Cohen to feel any guilt.

We must take the responsibility ourselves, and the precautions. When O'Keefe Centre itself was built, for instance, another impresario, Sol Hurok, had agreed to transfer his ballet attractions to it, away from the unsuitable Maple Leaf Gardens. But the larger house, with the larger grosses, still fascinates Mr. Hurok, despite diminishing attendance. Why should he care? Diminishing that audience may be but it will last out Mr. Hurok's time and serve his purpose. Let Toronto worry about what happens afterward.

And Toronto must worry about it. We need the Royal Alexandra if we are to enjoy properly the straight plays which come to this town, as well as to house the National Ballet and such other top Canadian attractions as the Canadian Players and the forthcoming Spring Thaw. We need it as much as we need O'Keefe Centre for the larger spectacles, the Crest for our own productions, Massey Hall for concerts and the Maple Leaf Gardens for hockey.

If we came close to losing the Royal Alex this time, let it be a warning how easily the things of proved value can slip away from us. We are grateful to the new ownership of the Royal Alexandra and we wish it therefore the very best of happiness and good fortune, with every hope it will serve Toronto with integrity and taste, and the theatre in general with the dignity and affection it deserves.

Ed worked to keep the grocery store running for five more years before he finally accepted the futility of the effort and gave up. The clamouring creditors seized the stock, and Ed took a job, at $13 a week, in the produce department of Power Supermarkets, a new grocery chain run by Leon Weinstein, a former neighbour and creditor of D. Mirvish Groceries. By 1940, he had risen to the post of produce manager for the chain and was making $22 a week (and working, often, from 7 AM until 1 AM, six days a week; it would have been seven days, but for the *Lord's Day Act*, which forced Power's to close on Sundays). Somehow, in the course of all this, he managed to find a modest social life. He met girls and went on dates. One of the dates — a blind one — was with a talented artist and singer named Anne Maklin, from Hamilton, Ontario; he fell in love with her, and she with him, and they married in June 1941.

Four months later, on his way home from work, Ed passed a small shop at Bloor and Bathurst with a "For Rent" sign in the window. It was a good location and the rent was low. He talked it over with Anne and she suggested that they take it and open a dress shop. She had clerked in a dress shop in Hamilton and knew the business, and Toronto was then filling up with young women, come from the farms and small towns of Ontario to

take work in the new, wartime factories. Anne and Ed had a total capital of $175 – wedding present money – but they cashed in her life insurance policy and made a down payment on a stock of women's clothes. Anne designed a sign – "Sport Bar" – and Ed cut the letters out of a sheet of plywood. He also built a counter and set up some shelves, and they were in business. He kept the (18-hour) day job at Power and Anne ran the store, handling both the buying and selling. On Sundays, they would go downtown to Eaton's department store to check out the windows, seeing what fashions Eaton's was selling and, sometimes, making sketches of the displays to duplicate the design ideas for their own shop window. Within six months Ed realized that he no longer needed the produce manager's $22 a week; the Sport Bar was a winner.

In 1944, the block of stores in which the Sport Bar was situated came up for sale – the whole block – and Ed and Anne Mirvish took another gamble, borrowed the money and bought the property. They knocked down the walls between the shops and opened a new, higher-end ladies' wear store, more than four times the size of the Sport Bar, "Anne and Eddy's." They also bought a new house in a nice, middle-class neighbourhood, for they were expecting a baby.

Anne and Eddy's was a success, but Ed Mirvish quickly tired of the ladies' wear business. With Anne at home with the baby, he found himself having to take her role in the store, and he did not enjoy it. As Anne explained it, "Ed didn't realize that dresses weren't like groceries. Dresses were a service item that needed selling to the customers. I liked waiting on people, chatting with them, making suggestions, helping them to find things and trying to please them, but Ed wasn't inclined that way." Ed's inclination was to find a way of running a store in which customers would serve themselves; he would stock the shelves and the customers would choose what they wanted while he stood at the cash register. When a Woolworth's store in Hamilton burned out, Ed drove down and bought its entire stock, bringing it home and storing it in his basement. That was the beginning; he continued buying up odd lots of merchandise at fire sales and bankruptcy sales and from jobbers of miscellaneous odds and ends, storing all in his basement. In 1948, the basement was full. There were thousands of items that, Ed calculated, had cost him an average of a quarter of a cent each; if he could sell the lot at an average of a penny each, the whole exercise would have been well worth the effort. He closed down Anne and Eddy's, stacked his eccentric array of merchandise on orange crates, hung up a sign he had painted himself — NAME YOUR OWN PRICE! NO REASONABLE OFFER REFUSED! — and put an ad in the newspapers:

Our Building is a dump!
Our Service is rotten!
Our Fixtures are orange crates!
But!!!
Our Prices are the lowest in town!
Serve yourself and save a lot of money!

In a spirit of self-mocking fun, he called the new store "Honest Ed's." It was his cautious plan to open on Saturdays only; if he could clear $100 a week, he would be happy. He did, of course, far better than that. The store hours were soon extended to two days a week, then three, then four, then six.

Ed had invented a new concept in retailing, the discount department store. Torontonians took to it, and to him. The lopsided store, its constantly changing merchandise, its unashamedly corny advertising, its giveaways and loss leaders and its colourful, screwball promotions made Ed famous, loved and rich — rich enough to pay $215,000 cash for the Royal Alexandra Theatre.

Ed Mirvish had actually been interested in the Royal Alexandra for quite some time before he bought it. He had always remembered the advice of Mr. Hack. When the word first got out that the theatre might be for sale, at the urging of Anne, he had twice sent an agent, the lawyer Bert Stitt, down to Gordon Perry's office to discuss a purchase. He had insisted, however, on anonymity. The agent was not to reveal on whose behalf he was making the approach. The reason was that Mirvish feared Perry and the trustees, as representatives of Toronto's dignified WASP establishment, would not entertain an offer from a parvenu Jewish shopkeeper who called himself "Honest Ed," staged marathon dance contests and wrote such advertising slogans as, "Honest Ed's going bald, but his prices are hair-raising." When Perry refused to deal with the agent, Ed Mirvish, reluctantly, revealed himself. Perry's response was, "Ed, why didn't you say it was you? I'm happy to talk to you."

24

A FACELIFT

FOR THE REST OF HIS LIFE, Ed Mirvish insisted that the only reason he bought the Royal Alexandra was that it was a bargain — and, at $215,000, it was that — but he had accompanied his cheque with a pledge to continue running it as a legitimate theatre. The trustees had not demanded a "forever" to go with the pledge; they only asked for a five-year commitment. If, after five years, the theatre was not paying its own way, Ed would be free to do with it as he pleased, even tear it down. He and Anne, however, were determined to prove that they could not only make a go of it, but make a go of it for a full 52 weeks a year. Later, after many more than five years, he would admit that if he knew then what he eventually learned about the theatre business — "as long as the theatre's shut and the lights are off, your losses are manageable; but as soon as you open the doors, there's no limit to what it can cost you" — he would never have begun. But to begin, Anne convinced him that, if they were to keep it running, the Royal Alexandra needed some fixing up.

It's often been suggested the theatre was a derelict shambles in 1963 and had been losing money for years. The truth is that it was actually in relatively good shape — Solman, Breen and Rawley had looked after it very well — and it had (almost) always

Laying carpet, reupholstering the seats and raising the new chandelier. Ed Mirvish finds a moment to sit down.

Photo courtesy of the *Globe and Mail*.

shown a profit. The year 1962, a very bad year, aside, any losses on the books had been, in Rawley's words "pocket money," and had been balanced out in succeeding seasons. The theatre had not, however, had a good, general clean-up and fresh coat of paint since 1939, and the big chandelier over the auditorium needed replacing, and some of the old silk wall-coverings were faded, dirty and a little frayed. The Mirvishes also noted that the seats were lumpy and uncomfortable and a little too closely crowded together, and the intermission line-ups at the washrooms reminded Ed uncomfortably of the family apartment, shared with Rabbi Dinkin's Hebrew School, on Dundas St.

Ed and Anne closed the Royal Alexandra for three months and hired an interior designer, Herbert Irvine – the man responsible for the Eaton's store windows they used to copy for the Sport Bar – and an architect, Hugh Allward – the man who had posed as Cupid for Frederick Challener's mural, 58 years before.

If they were going to change the wallpaper and reupholster

the seats, Ed let it be known that he preferred to see both done in red and Irvine agreed with him. Red was the best colour, the proper colour, for a theatre interior. It was warm and inviting, regal and festive and, the designer pointed out, gave a rosy glow to the people in the audience, making them look and feel better. Ed always told people who asked that he chose the red flocked "French Baroque" wallpaper that still covers the walls of the auditorium because he found a good supply of roll-ends from a local jobber at a bargain price. The truth, however, is that Irvine chose it as perfect for the Edwardian look of the theatre, and it was imported from Europe and anything but cheap.

Irvine and Allward removed all the seats in the theatre, padded them with foam rubber and recovered them in red velvet. When they put them back, they altered the arrangement slightly, permanently removing seats, where they could, to give a little more leg and arm room. They pulled up the old carpeting and installed new, running it – more than a mile of it – up the

Ed Mirvish may be wondering if he's done the right thing as he surveys the work in progress in the empty theatre.

stairs, all the way to the gallery. They cleaned the mural and repainted the proscenium, the ceilings and the box and balcony fronts. They repainted and restored the tearoom and hung a new, red velvet act curtain and new crystal chandeliers and wall sconces. They refurnished the lobbies with antiques – marble-topped Louis XVI tables and commodes. Outside, they cleaned the stonework and replaced the old marquee with a newer, wider, grander and better-lit one. Off the tearoom, on either side, Allward built new washrooms to relieve the intermission crunch, building out on the second floor terraces, carefully selecting the new exterior brick to match the old so closely that few today – or even in 1963 – could tell that there had been any alteration to the building's façade. For all those three months, the auditorium was filled with scaffolding as Allward and Irvine overlooked no detail. Irvine even commissioned the design of new "period" uniforms for the ushers, with maroon jackets, gold epaulettes, ruffled shirts, black satin knee-breeches and buckled shoes (uniforms

The old marquee — in place since 1907 — comes down. Note what it looked like across the street from the Royal Alexandra in 1963. The neighbourhood had suffered a sad decline.

Photo courtesy of the Toronto Public Library. Theatre Collection.

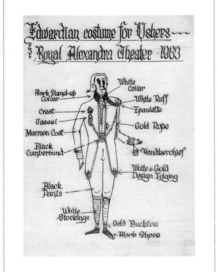

that the ushers, to a man, balked at wearing until Ed talked them into it; "Let's just try it out and see what happens," he said, "If no one likes them, we won't keep them"; everyone did like them, but they proved impossible to maintain and were abandoned).

The items Ed removed from the theatre — the marquee and the seats — he moved up to an old factory building he owned at Bloor and Brunswick streets. In 1964, this would become the 100-seat Poor Alex Theatre, a performance venue for amateur groups and small-scale professional, experimental drama.

The auditorium scaffolding came down on Sunday, September 8, 1963, and Ed and Anne Mirvish opened the doors to seven hundred guests, invited in to have a look at what had been

In his new livery, an usher awaits his audience in the empty gallery.

done before the official re-opening the next evening. Ernie Rawley, who had known the theatre inside and out since 1925, was among those on the tour and he had to admit that the Royal Alexandra was now, "More beautiful than ever." Lady Eaton, widow of the famous department store's Sir John Craig Eaton, afterward wrote to Ed and Anne, "I can honestly say that there is nothing in Vienna, Rome, Milan, Paris, London, New York or Chicago that begins to compare with the charm that is the Royal Alexandra." And the *Globe and Mail* critic Herbert Whittaker enthused that the renovations had made the Royal Alexandra, "I swear, the most theatrical-looking theatre this side of the Paris Opera House or Covent Garden." Although the Mirvishes had spent more than twice the purchase price of the theatre on its renovation, Anne Mirvish denied that they had done all that much. "It was all here already," she said. "We just revived it."

25

LEARNING THE ROPES

THE OPENING NIGHT OF THE "NEW" ROYAL ALEXANDRA THEATRE, on September 9, 1963, was as grand an occasion as the theatre had ever known. Anne Mirvish arrived on the arm of William Earl Rowe, the Lieutenant-Governor, while Ed escorted Lady Eaton to the same box seat she had occupied 56 years before, on the opening night of *Top O' Th' World*. The mayor was there, as were the Broadway actors Lou Jacobi and June Havoc and producers James Nederlander and Gerald Schoenfeld – up from New York for the occasion – and the cream of Toronto's still-small professional theatre community. Tom Patterson, founder of the Stratford Festival, drove up to say, "This is the most exciting night I've had since 1953." The ushers wore their elegant livery and rolled a red carpet to the King St. curb. Even the free house programs were special that night, with thick, red-flocked covers embossed with the Royal Coat of Arms, in gold.

The play for the evening was *Never Too Late*, a comedy by Sumner Arthur Long, directed by George Abbott, with film and television stars William Bendix (who, like Ed Mirvish, had worked in his family's grocery store until the Depression closed it), Nancy Carroll and Will Hutchins. The critics were mixed.

Opening night, 1963. The audience arrives under the 1,363 light bulbs of the new marquee.

Photo courtesy of the *Toronto Star*.

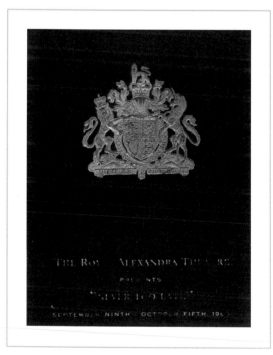

The usually unforgiving Nathan Cohen, at the *Toronto Star*, described *Never Too Late* as "an animated and agreeable drollery." The usually kinder Herbert Whittaker, at the *Globe and Mail*, wrote that the refurbished theatre was more exciting than the comedy re-opening it, but obligingly provided a good quote for the newspaper ads: "Keeps the audience laughing unabatedly for a whole evening." The good quotes and the good publicity around the renovations kept the houses full and *Never Too Late* closed with a decent profit, good enough to wash away all the red ink from 1962. When Ed Mirvish confessed to William Bendix that he really knew nothing about the theatre business, Bendix replied, "Oh, you're doing all right."

With things again up and running, Ed sent his accountants, William Walton and Henry Kates, down to the Royal Alexandra to help him get a better grasp of this business he knew nothing about. Kates was to hang around the box office, observe, learn and report back; on his own initiative, he also drove to the

Stratford Festival on weekends to see plays and attend public lectures on theatre by the playwright and administrator Tom Hendry (a fellow accountant).

Some of what Hank Kates reported back puzzled and upset Ed. There was, for example, no accounting in the box office. Tickets – preprinted and arranged in a slotted cabinet – were sold over the counter for cash and no record kept. The cash would be turned over to the theatre's treasurer, counted and deposited in the bank, but there was no way to match the cash with the actual tickets sold – nothing to prevent a dishonest box-office clerk from giving tickets away, or discounting them and selling to scalpers, or simply pocketing a small percentage of the day's receipts. To Ed and Hank, the answer was simple: install a cash register. This idea, however, was vigorously opposed by both the theatre's manager, Edwin DeRocher (Ernie Rawley's former assistant) and its long time treasurer, Bill Reynolds. This, they argued, was the *theatre*, not a common shop; theatres did not have cash registers. Ed installed the cash register.

Equally puzzling was Kates' discovery that the theatre maintained an escrow account. All money received for tickets for future performances – advance sales – was held in escrow and neither counted nor available for use until several days after the curtain went down on the performance in question. This, DeRocher and Reynolds explained, was a long-established theatre custom; the money was put aside until they were sure it would not have to be refunded. Ed argued that if he had to refund money, he certainly would – from his own pocket, if necessary – but that, in the meantime, he saw no reason why the advance sale money should not be available for use. This argument Ed also finally won, but not until he fired the treasurer.

Refunds were another subject of dispute. Under DeRocher, Rawley and Breen before them, the Royal Alexandra regularly refunded money, after the fact, to ticket buyers who complained that they did not enjoy a show. To Ed, this seemed an invitation to bankruptcy. If a customer at the Sport Bar returned a dress,

First-nighter Anne Mirvish, in the days when people still dressed up for the theatre.

The paint still wet, William Bendix (left) and Ed Mirvish have a look around the theatre just before the opening of *Never Too Late*.
Photo courtesy of the *Globe and Mail*.

September 9, 1963. Toronto actors Tom Kneebone, Marilyn Gardner and Barbara Hamilton arrive for the opening night performance of *Never Too Late*.
Photo courtesy of the *Toronto Star*.

he at least got the dress back and could return it to the rack, but when the curtain fell on a theatre performance, it was over, forever. He could not re-sell a ticket to last night's show. He did not, however, want the Royal Alexandra to be the *only* theatre that did not offer refunds. Was this tradition? Was it expected of theatres everywhere? He called around and talked to theatre managers in New York and London and made the startling discovery that no one else had such a refund policy. The Royal Alexandra was the only theatre, anywhere, that sold its tickets on approval. The O'Keefe Centre had also done so for a while, when it first opened, but only because it was copying the Royal Alexandra. Ed changed the policy; all ticket sales were now final.

Mirvish and DeRocher clashed frequently. In 1964, the latter resigned to take a job in the U.S. and Ed assumed the manager's

A beginner at the game in 1964, Gino Empry handled the Royal Alexandra's publicity and press relations for the next 25 years. The cigarette and the telephone were seldom far from his face.

Photo courtesy of the *Toronto Star*.

office himself, bringing in a friend he had known since their Dundas St. childhood, Yale Simpson, as his assistant manager. Yale's theatre experience consisted entirely of having once played a small role in his high school's production of *Macbeth*, but he could handle the daily nuts and bolts — building maintenance, concessions, box-office and front-of-house management

of the theatre. Ed would vacate the manager's office for Yale in 1969. For artistic matters, theatrical matters, Ed relied upon the advice and active participation of Anne and their son, David, and his brother, Robert.

When the theatre's publicist, complaining that she was being asked to work under amateurs, followed DeRocher out the door, Ed replaced her with a part-time freelancer, someone he found more amenable to trying out new ways of doing things, a brash and flamboyant young would-be publicist and entertainers' agent named Gino Empry, who would stay with the Royal Alexandra for the next 25 years and become something of a Toronto legend himself. Gino was then just starting out. The Royal Alexandra was his first client; he was an amateur, too.

Ed's younger brother, Robert, was then living in New York, where he had established himself as a novelist and short-story writer. Ed made him his booking agent; he would go see the new Broadway shows, pick what he liked and negotiate the deals to bring them to Toronto. Bob Mirvish didn't have an office, but would handle the Royal Alexandra's New York business over

At the old stage door, used as an office by the stage crew, with (left to right) head electrician Sam Black, crew chief Vic Eggleston, stagehand Rick Ashby, Ed Mirvish and head of props Buddy Lloyd.

Photo from the collection of the Royal Alexandra Theatre.

lunches at Sardi's Restaurant. British producer Paul Elliott, who would bring dozens of plays and musicals to Toronto — from Ray Cooney farces to such memorable productions as Glenda Jackson's *Hedda Gabler* and Michael Redgrave's *Voyage 'Round My Father* — had many such lunches, sitting around a table at Sardi's with Bob Mirvish, Ernie Rawley and Vic Egglestone, the Royal Alexandra's carpenter and backstage crew chief, who would fly down to talk over the technical details. "I don't recall there ever being a contract, or anything in writing," he says. "Just lunch, a conversation and a handshake."

Miraculously, it all worked. There were a few stumbles along the way as everyone learned and gained experience, but the Royal Alexandra paid its own way, and more, and stayed open. At the end of the five-year trial period, and release from his purchase obligation to keep it running, there was no question in Ed's mind about the future of the theatre. "Theatre," he said, "isn't a business; it's a disease. But I've caught it."

THE RESTAURANT
BUSINESS

WHILE THE ROYAL ALEXANDRA THEATRE was not derelict in 1963, its neighbourhood was. The old Four 'Nations had become grey and grimy. Where Government House and its park had once stood were railway marshalling yards. The former King St. campus of Upper Canada College was filled with ugly brick factories and warehouses. The building beside the theatre housed a printing plant, its machinery thudding through the night. Just to the west, on the west side of Duncan St., was a brass foundry. It was not a pleasant place to linger or walk, and there was nowhere to eat a pre-theatre or post-show meal. Ed Mirvish felt it vital for the future of the theatre that something be done to make the neighbourhood brighter, more attractive, more interesting and more people-friendly. He then knew no more about the restaurant business than he did about the theatre business, but reasoned that having a restaurant beside the Royal Alexandra might be a good way to begin a transformation of, at least, his block. In 1964, he bought the building next door – the printing plant – at King and Duncan. It cost him more than twice what the theatre had, but he felt it to be a good investment; a restaurant there would draw people into the area (and past the theatre) and the theatre would keep the restaurant supplied with customers.

In the beginning, Ed had a vision for his restaurant. He planned to model it on a famous Boston eatery called Durgin-Park, where the customers sat on benches at long, communal tables and ate simple, New England family fare – clam chowder and boiled corned beef and cabbage. That idea, perhaps fortunately, faded away as he began thinking in more theatrical terms. He consulted with a number of experts – restaurant architects and designers – but, when no one could come up with any ideas that excited him, proceeded on his own, playing around with whims and relying on instinct. He began buying odds and ends, bits of this and that he fancied to fit in with new visions growing in his mind – or, just as often, inspiring new visions of their own. He bought a set of huge brass doors from a bank that had gone under the wrecker's ball; he bought a warehouse-full of old, Tiffany-style lamps; he bought job-lots of stained-glass windows, mismatched tables and chairs, antique pickle jars and coin banks; he bought a collection of chamber pots (one of which had once been used – there was a document to prove it – by the Prince of Wales), an assortment of 19th-century copies of Greek statues, a wooden cigar-store Indian, music boxes and penny arcade games, bronze Chinese incense burners, old oil paintings, ornamental urns depicting the victories of Napoleon and Louis XV cabinets to put them on. And then he put them all together in one magnificent, eccentric, three-dimensional collage that he called "Ed's Warehouse," a restaurant that served only roast beef (but cut in three different ways).

The original Warehouse, opened on January 20, 1965, sat only 180. As the line-ups stretched down the block, Ed opened a second dining room in 1966, and a third in 1967, and a fourth in 1968. By 1969, he could seat 1300 customers in the Warehouse, but it still wasn't enough; he bought the brass foundry across the street and opened a new restaurant complex, Old Ed's, along the same lines as the Warehouse (but with more on the menu). By the time he was finished, Old Ed's and the Warehouse Restaurants could serve three thousand meals at a single sitting.

The restaurants are gone now. The last, Old Ed's, closed in 2000. It was their success, however, that made them redundant. The Warehouse restaurants sparked a wave of urban renewal that would have been unimaginable in 1964 as other entrepreneurs took advantage of the changing neighbourhood, converting once-dingy industrial buildings into upscale offices, shops and even more restaurants, the biggest concentration of good places to eat in Toronto. With King Street transformed, the Mirvish restaurants were no longer necessary; they had more than served their purpose and Ed began shutting them down, renting the spaces they had occupied to others. Although he lost his own favourite places to have lunch and host opening night parties for the Royal Alexandra, he said that he had never really wanted to be in the restaurant business anyway. Like the dress shops in the forties, restaurants required too much customer service for his taste.

27

MUSICALS AND MORE

FROM THE DAY HE BEGAN RUNNING THE ROYAL ALEXANDRA, Ed Mirvish chafed against the deal by which he shared a subscription season with the O'Keefe Centre, with the big touring musicals going to the big theatre and the smaller straight plays and comedies coming to him. In 1965 he announced that the arrangement was over and the Royal Alexandra would go it alone.

Ernie Rawley, who had made the original deal, flew up to Toronto to talk Ed out of this rash decision. Rawley argued that the Royal could not hope to compete with a 3,200-seat theatre; modern touring musicals cost too much money to stage and could not afford to play the smaller house. Two weeks in the O'Keefe would send them away with a profit; two weeks in the Royal Alexandra, with a loss. Given the choice, Rawley feared that even producers of smaller, straight plays would choose the O'Keefe and its higher potential gross, leaving the Royal Alexandra dark and dead. Besides, he argued, the arrangement had brought Ed some splendid dramas and comedies — *Barefoot in the Park* with Myrna Loy, *Any Wednesday* with Larry Parks, *Traveller without Luggage* with Ben Gazzara and *Here Today* with Tallulah Bankhead and Estelle Winwood — all within the past year. The

Spring Thaw '65. The popular revues were an annual event at the Royal Alexandra from 1963 through 1980. The ornate wrought-iron decorations around the entrance came down shortly after this photo was taken; too many people bumped their heads or snagged their clothing.

Photo courtesy of the Toronto Public Library, Theatre Collection.

deal had not even precluded musicals at the Royal Alexandra. Broadway would still send smaller-scale shows, better-suited to the more intimate theatre, such as 1964's David Merrick production of *Stop the World, I Want to Get Off*, with Anthony Newley. And there was always local production. Ed, himself, had begun to produce summer musicals, borrowing the old summer stock idea, with local casts and imported stars – *The Sound of Music, My Fair Lady, Annie Get Your Gun* (with Elaine Stritch), *Brigadoon, Can-Can, Finian's Rainbow, Gypsy* and *Guys and Dolls* (with Hal Linden), all Royal Alexandra Theatre productions in 1964 and '65 – not to mention the popular, locally made *Spring Thaw* revues that were already becoming a Royal Alexandra tradition. Ed gave way to Rawley this once and agreed to continue sharing with the O'Keefe, for a while, but he had already formulated a radical, new idea of his own for bringing big, new musicals to the Royal (without having to produce them himself).

Ed had already discussed his new idea with Broadway producer David Merrick earlier that year. Merrick had a big, new musical – *Hello, Dolly!* – which he was planning to bring into the O'Keefe Centre for two weeks. That meant a maximum audience of about 50,000; there could be no more, because the O'Keefe was too tightly booked to give the show any more than two weeks before it would have to move out. If, however, Merrick would bring *Hello, Dolly!* into the Royal Alexandra, Ed was convinced that it could run for three months, to almost three times the audience it would have at the O'Keefe. So sure was he that he was right that he was willing to give Merrick a written guarantee of $100,000 a week. And money aside, he pointed out, the show would look and sound so much better in the Royal Alexandra: "The difference between the Royal and the O'Keefe is like the difference between mink and muskrat." Merrick, however, decided to play it safe and went to the O'Keefe.

Ed Mirvish continued in the sharing arrangement with the O'Keefe for another three years, but the rupture finally came in 1968. Despite (or, perhaps, because of) its huge size, the O'Keefe had been losing money and its owner, the O'Keefe Brewing Co. (it was in those days known as "the house that beer built"), sold the property to the City of Toronto. To Ed, this was insupportable. While he risked all to run his theatre as a business, as it had been run since 1907, the O'Keefe – which he could not help but regard as a major rival – was now to be a publicly subsidized theatre. Toronto City Council made the decision to end the shared subscription and Ed turned to New York producers Morton Gottlieb and Manny Azenberg to help him build a new, independent subscription series for the Royal Alexandra alone. He did not, however, have to go head-to-head against the O'Keefe immediately. His brother, Bob, called from New York to let him know that he had been having conversations with some people interested in bringing a new musical to Toronto, not on tour for two weeks, but for a long run, perhaps even a sit-down production.

The show in question was *Hair*, Broadway's biggest hit, and

Hair's curtain call, December 29, 1969. The show would set a longevity record for Toronto, and the Royal Alexandra Theatre.

Photo courtesy of the *Toronto Star*.

the suggestion being made was that if a local producer would come in as a partner, the New York producers would stage a Toronto "franchise" production. Like Ed, they believed the possibility was there for a big musical to run in Toronto for several months, and they liked the Royal Alexandra. Ed did not want to be the local producer, however. It was too much like selling dresses, he said; too much service. But he called someone who would be interested, John F. Bassett, Jr., of the *Toronto Telegram* and CFTO Television, and Bassett was enchanted. *Hair* had then been running for 12 months on Broadway and new productions were scheduled in London, Paris, Munich, Stockholm and Copenhagen. Could it do 12 months in Toronto?

It could. *Hair* opened at the Royal Alexandra Theatre on December 29, 1969 — with a Canadian cast — and ran all the way to January 4, 1971, returning for an extra month in the summer of 1971. No stage production had ever run so long at the Royal Alexandra — or anywhere else in Toronto. Anne Mirvish went to see the show every night and joined the cast — and half the audience — dancing onstage for the finale. *Hair* made $3 million and proved that David Merrick should have listened when Ed Mirvish came to talk to him about the possibilities of a three-month run for *Hello, Dolly!*

Following *Hair*, the theatre celebrated its 65th anniversary with a gala party, organized by Anne Mirvish, the theatre event of the season. And then, Ed did go head-to-head with the O'Keefe. In 1971 and '72, he bid directly against the Centre to snatch away the contracts for the musicals *Applause* with Lauren Bacall, *Company* with Elaine Stritch and George Chakiris, *Carousel* with John Raitt, *Irene* with Debbie Reynolds, *The Rothschilds* with Theodore Bikel and *Purlie* with Robert Guillaume; and the

The audience clambers to the stage — invited or not — to dance with the cast of *Hair* in the grand finale.

Photo courtesy of the *Toronto Star*.

Honest Ed beats O'Keefe for top N.Y. shows

By JEREMY BROWN
Star staff writer

Honest Ed Mirvish today revealed his Royal Alexandra theatre has outbid O'Keefe Centre for some of Broadway's top shows.

He likened his battle with the O'Keefe, which is owned by Metro Toronto, with the war in Viet Nam.

"Nobody wins in any war except the munitions maker," Mirvish said, "and in this case it's the New York producers."

The Royal Alexandra, which has half as many seats as the O'Keefe—1,500 compared to 3,200—has lined up:

The Doll's House with Claire Bloom, Sept. 13-Oct. 2; Sleuth, Oct. 11-30; Company, Nov. 1-20; Applause with Lauren Bacall, Nov. 29-Dec. 18; School for Wives with Brian Bedford, Dec. 27-Jan. 15; and the musical Purlie, Jan. 21-Feb. 12.

A show business source said that unless Mirvish charged $15 a seat he would lose $50,000 a week with Applause, even with full houses for that show's three-week run.

Mirvish wouldn't say how much he is paying for Applause but admitted it could be described as a "loss leader."

He said his 9,000 subscribers will get first crack at tickets at normal prices, but he is considering charging higher prices for the transient trade.

Mirvish has complained bitterly that he has to compete with a publicly owned facility which he believes can pay whatever it wants for a show.

Hugh Walker, O'Keefe's managing director, was in New York today looking for new shows and was not available for comment.

How did Honest Ed get the shows? With money, and because his brother Robert, lives, in New York and spends most of his time wheeling and dealing with producers. O'Keefe has no permanent representative in New York.

Ed Mirvish's "loss leader" in his first independent subscription season, Lauren Bacall onstage in the musical *Applause*, 1971.
Photo courtesy of the Toronto Public Library. Theatre Collection.

O'Keefe-coveted, big-star straight plays *A Doll's House* with Claire Bloom, *Captain Brassbound's Conversion* with Ingrid Bergman, *The Day After the Fair* with Deborah Kerr and *Promenade All* with Hume Cronyn, Eli Wallach and Ann Jackson.

It was a little disingenuous of Ed to complain to *Toronto Star* reporter Jeremy Brown that the O'Keefe "can pay whatever it wants for a show," for he had outbid the Centre, paying more than its budget could bear, on all these shows. It was equally disingenuous for Mr. Brown, however, to suggest that, in the era

The original cast of *Godspell*, in 1972. The young unknowns of the company are, standing in the rear, Eugene Levy, Victor Garber and Martin Short; seated in rear, Rudy Webb and Gerry Salsberg; foreground, Jayne Eastwood, Valda Aviks, Avril Chown, Andrea Martin and Gilda Radner.

Photo courtesy of the Toronto Public Library, Theatre Collection.

of telephones and airplanes, Ed's success was due to his brother's living in New York. A few days after this article appeared, Hugh Walker, of the O'Keefe Centre, did make a comment, suggesting that Ed was paying "incredible prices" and would certainly lose money. Ed responded, "I don't lose money in theatre."

Note the number of subscribers the Royal Alexandra salvaged as its own after breaking with the O'Keefe: 9000; in a few short years, this figure would rise to 52,000.

While he battled the O'Keefe, and while people were still humming "Let the Sunshine In," Ed Mirvish talked to New York producer Edgar Lansbury about another possible sit-down production along the lines of *Hair*. The new show was *Godspell*, a hit on Broadway for the past year. It was a much smaller show than *Hair* – with a single set and a cast of only ten – and, some felt, too small even for the Royal Alexandra. Because it was smaller, simpler, cheaper and potentially less aggravating, Ed Mirvish did come on board as a co-producer, but he scheduled the show for only three months, over the summer of 1972. He had then just secured Theodore Bikel in *The Rothschilds* for September and needed *Godspell* off his stage by then. The cast was entirely local, no one anyone had ever heard of, most of them just kids in their first paid jobs on a stage.

Godspell began performances on May 26, 1972, and ran through the summer to September 3rd, when Ed had to take it down to make room for Theo Bikel. But it was still a sell-out and he could not bear to close it, so he rented another theatre, the small Bayview Playhouse, and put it there. It ran at the Bayview until August 12th, 1973, breaking *Hair's* longevity record. *Godspell's* new record would stand until 1986, when the megamusical was reborn with *Cats*. Ed later lamented that he hadn't kept *Godspell* at the Royal Alexandra and sent *The Rothschilds* to the Bayview.

The experiences of *Hair* and *Godspell* taught Ed, Anne and – especially – David Mirvish that they no longer had to think quite so much in terms of short runs by British or American touring companies, or of British and American stars. Toronto had become a theatre centre in its own right, and capable of mounting and supporting its own productions, with its own stars.

8

RISKS AND REWARDS

PRODUCING ONE'S OWN SHOWS, unfortunately, does not always lead to successes like *Godspell* and there were other ventures through the years that sometimes made Ed Mirvish question the idea. In 1966, he had high hopes for a Canadian farce, *Like Father, Like Fun*, by Vancouver writer Eric Nicol. The show had been a winter hit at the Vancouver Playhouse and a friend — Dave Broadfoot, a star of the *Spring Thaw* revues — saw it and telephoned Ed, recommending it for the Royal Alexandra. Ed read the script, read the enthusiastic Vancouver reviews and bought the play. He staged it in Toronto in July and August, and then toured it to Montreal. The Toronto critics did not like *Like Father, Like Fun* — the *Toronto Star*'s Nathan Cohen called it "the worst show to be performed at the Royal Alexandra since the end of World War Two . . . and very probably in the theatre's entire history" — but audiences laughed in all the right places and it did a good business, good enough that Ed thought he might take it to Broadway.

Nathan Cohen, when he learned what was on Ed's mind, called him to urge against the idea. Keep touring it across Canada; it will do well in Charlottetown, Winnipeg and Calgary, but don't even think of New York. Nevertheless, Ed did take it to Broadway, where it opened at the Brooks Atkinson Theatre in

69

Donald O'Connor, Anne and
Ed Mirvish check their watches,
counting down to the gala opening
of *Say Hello to Harvey*.

Photo from the Royal Alexandra Theatre Collection.

October 1967 (under a new title: *A Minor Adjustment*). It was a disaster; the New York critics panned it and the play closed after only three performances, losing its entire investment.

And then there was *Say Hello to Harvey*. This one seemed a sure thing, a guaranteed success, a proven winner. It was a musical, based on Mary Chase's Pulitzer Prize–winning comedy *Harvey*, about the tipsy Elwood Dowd and his imaginary friend, a six-foot-tall invisible rabbit. Mary Chase herself had written the script, music was by the highly successful composer Leslie Bricusse and the stars were to be Donald O'Connor and Patricia Routledge. Ed agreed to co-produce the show with Michael McAloney, with whom he'd worked on the Royal Alexandra's summer musicals in 1963 and '64. The plan was to try it out in Toronto and then – if it was a hit, as it was sure to be – go to New York. They opened in September 1981 and closed in October. The critics savaged the production and it was only by virtue of its being a part of the 1981 season subscription series, with tickets pre-sold, that it lasted even those four weeks. This time, Ed heeded what the critics had said and did not proceed with the Broadway plans.

Despite the occasional bad luck, David Mirvish was convinced that the Royal Alexandra's future lay in producing its own shows. There had been some wonderful short-run plays and musicals brought in by touring companies through the sixties and seventies, but some duds as well, and David feared that he saw a general decline in the quality of touring shows for the future. Ed was not so sure. In 1982, he had purchased and restored London, England's historic theatre The Old Vic and begun producing plays there, in house. While The Old Vic, under Mirvish direction, won fists-full of prestigious awards (and a CBE for Ed, for services to British theatre), it was losing money. David, however, made a convincing argument. In 1986, Ed handed management over to his son and stepped — not all the way, not quite yet, but slightly   into the background and David launched a new company, Alexandra Productions, and began a new era in the life of the Royal Alexandra as a producing theatre.

David Mirvish began Alexandra Productions — later renamed Mirvish Productions — with only two employees, the Toronto-based independent producers Ernest Schwarz and Brian Sewell, who had impressed him in their mounting of a major commercial success with *Cloud Nine, The Desert Song* and *Kismet* (the latter at the Royal Alexandra). Ernie and Brian's job was to both find new projects for original production and to forge co-production alliances with the large non-profit regional theatres — the Shaw and Stratford festivals, the Manitoba Theatre Centre, the Citadel Theatre and others — and the many smaller, subsidized theatre companies that had sprung up all over the country since the early 1970s.

These co-production agreements would allow the non-profits to stage productions they might not otherwise have been able to afford, with those productions then transferring to the Royal Alexandra.

David, in the meantime, would scout for possible high-quality

David Mirvish, left, and Ed
Mirvish, right, escort Diana,
Princess of Wales, into the Royal
Alexandra for a performance of
Les Misérables. The Princess sat
in the orchestra and not in a box.

co-productions, tours and transfers from Britain, Europe and the U.S., but would cast his net widely and no longer rely on the New York booking agents or standard touring productions. And so, in its first three seasons, Mirvish Productions brought Toronto the Royal National Theatre's *Animal Farm*; a co-production with the Stratford Festival of *The Mikado* (which they would transfer to Broadway); the first-ever North American engagement of the Berliner Ensemble, with Brecht's *The Threepenny Opera* and *The Caucasian Chalk Circle*; original productions of *HMS Pinafore* (a Dora Award-winner) and *Damn Yankees*; the English Shakespeare Company's unforgettable stagings of *Henry IV* and *Henry V*; *Pride and Prejudice* in co-production with the Citadel Theatre; and the sell-out *Sweet Bird of Youth*, with Joanne Woodward and Charles Durning, in co-production with the famous American regional theatre, the Williamstown Festival.

In 1988, this activity caught the attention of British producer Cameron Mackintosh, with whom Ed had already staged seven successful productions. Mackintosh then had a major hit in London and on Broadway with the new musical *Les Misérables*. He had been thinking about mounting a North American tour, with a short run in Toronto, but began to wonder if, possibly, Mirvish Productions might assemble a Canadian company and co-produce a sit-down staging of the musical that could play Toronto as long as public interest warranted. David Mirvish accepted the proposal and, on March 15, 1989, the Canadian production of *Les Misérables* opened at the Royal Alexandra. It would run for the next 14 months, go on a four-month-long Mirvish-sponsored national tour (and spawn a second, French-language company) and then return to the Royal for an additional 13 months. *Godspell*'s record was broken and *Les Misérables* proved the most financially successful production in the theatre's history — so successful that David and Ed felt the confidence to build a second theatre, the Princess of Wales, a sister to the Royal Alexandra, a block away. The Princess of Wales would house another co-production with Cameron Mackintosh, *Miss Saigon*, and a future musical co-production with Disney Theatricals, the long-running *The Lion King*.

Ed, Anne and David Mirvish and the original cast of *Les Misérables* celebrate a record-breaking 750th performance — 750 for the adults and 100 for the children, who were rotated every three months.

ROYAL ALEXANDRA THEATRE

Performance

JUNE/AUGUST 2000

BENNY ANDERSSON AND BJÖRN ULVAEUS'

MAMMA MIA!

THE SMASH HIT MUSICAL BASED ON THE SONGS OF ABBA®

David Mirvish's point — and abilities — proven, Ed Mirvish handed him the reins of the Royal Alexandra and retired from the theatre in 1990. David would continue the policies and practices he had begun in 1986, breaking the *Les Misérables* records almost immediately with a two-straight-year run of his co-production of the musical *Crazy for You* (with a Canadian cast), a production with Roger Horchow and Elizabeth Williams, and again with the five-year run — beyond anyone's wildest dreams in the days of *Hair* and *Godspell* — of *Mamma Mia!*, a North American premiere of London producer Judy Craymer's European hit that would take many in its original Canadian cast to the *second* North American engagement, on Broadway.

Today, David Mirvish continues as the head of Mirvish Productions, with Brian Sewell and David Mucci — who, as an actor, holds the record for the most appearances on the Royal Alexandra stage by a single performer — as his executive producer and general manager. And a new generation stands ready in the wings; all David and Audrey Mirvish's three children have expressed their interest in the family businesses and the eldest, Rachel, is now on her father's staff.

THE SHOW GOES ON

On August 26, 2007, the Royal Alexandra Theatre celebrated its anniversary — 100 years to the day since Anna Laughlin put on her rabbit-skin coat to play Kokomo in *Top O' Th' World*.

The theatre hosted an open house for three thousand guests — roughly one for every show that's played its stage. Sadly absent was Ed Mirvish, who died on July 11, just a few weeks short of his 93rd birthday, but he was surely there in spirit, along with Cawthra Mulock, Lol Solman, William Breen, Ernie Rawley, Yale Simpson and all the hundreds of others who loved the theatre and worked to keep it alive, through the bad times and the good.

The old Princess is gone now, as are the Grand Opera House, the Majestic, the Star and Shea's — all the great theatres of 1907 — and only the Royal Alexandra remains. It's now a Canadian National Historic Landmark, one of the last — and the best-preserved — of the fine theatres of the Edwardian era still with us. But it is no museum piece; visitors who walked across the venerable stage on the anniversary — walking where Al Jolson had often stood, and Mary Pickford, Bea Lillie, Helen Hayes, the Barrymores, Katharine Cornell, John Gielgud, Donald Wolfit and Johnston Forbes-Robertson — had to step around the ongoing

construction work, preparing that stage for the first production of its 101st season, and the yet unknown stars whose names will be whispered along with those of the illustrious past at some other open house, long in the future.

THE ROYAL ALEXANDRA AT 100
A Photo Essay by Edward Burtynsky

Welcome inside the Royal Alexandra on its 100th anniversary. The wallpaper and seat colours have changed since 1907 and the lighting is new, but little else. Cawthra Mulock would still feel at home.

Photo by Edward Burtynsky.

A view of the stage from the first balcony. The wide-angle lens emphasizes
the functions of the proscenium in classic theatre design — a funnel to
draw the eye in to the stage and a horn to project sound out into the
auditorium. Photo by Edward Burtynsky.

In the lobby, the stairs to the upper levels. The newel post, railings and balusters are of hand-carved cherrywood and the wall panelling and trim are of Circassian walnut. Photo by Edward Burtynsky.

Orchestra-level seating. The seat frames, arm-rests and decorative end caps are original — unchanged in 100 years. The wire frames visible on the seat bottoms at the left are designed to hold the gentlemen's hats that gentlemen no longer wear. Photo by Edward Burtynsky.

At the very top of the theatre, in the fly loft, the 19th and 21st centuries
meet in the ancient hempen rope and belaying pin system on the left
and the modern cotton and polyester lines and rope-locks on the right.
Photo by Edward Burtynsky.

In the close confines of the fly loft — with a warning sign to remind us
just how close they are — the leftovers and graffiti of bygone shows.

Photo by Edward Burtynsky.

A century's performers have left their autographed photos on the walls of the stage door entrance, the fading sepias of 1907 side-by-side the colour prints of today. Photo by Edward Burtynsky.

The secret side — the inside — of the stage door, a place few from the audience will ever see. Outside, the world goes on; in here, time stands still. Photo by Edward Burtynsky.

Under the photos, the walls are papered with the luggage tags of touring companies from the days when actors' lives were on the road and the aristocrats of theatre were those who could boast they were "born in a trunk." Photo by Edward Burtynsky.

From the stage, an actor's-eye view of the house, as seen by performers
from the night of August 26, 1907, until tonight. Photo by Edward Burtynsky.

THE FACES ON THE WALL

WALK THROUGH THE OLD STAGE ENTRANCE or up and down the stairwells or through the lobbies of the Royal Alexandra and you'll find the walls lined with photographs — hundreds of photographs; no one knows exactly how many — of the actors and actresses who have played the theatre's stage over the past 100 years. There are the famous and the infamous, the immortal and the forgotten, but each one has a story to tell. Here are just a few, passed on a random stroll.

Johnston Forbes-Robertson and Gertrude Elliott

SIR JOHNSTON FORBES-ROBERTSON AND GERTRUDE ELLIOTT GO together on the wall because they were not only husband and wife, but also, respectively, the leading man and leading lady of the Forbes-Robertson Repertory Co. Sir Johnston is seen in this photo in costume for his role in Jerome K. Jerome's drama *The Passing of the Third Floor Back*; Lady Gertrude is dressed for her role in Shaw's *Caesar and Cleopatra* (a play written for her husband).

Johnston Forbes-Robertson was born in London, in 1853, of ancient, royal Scots blood — he claimed to trace his direct descent from Donnchad mac Crínáin, the 11th-century King of Scots who entered theatre history as "King Duncan" in Shakespeare's *Macbeth*. His ambition was to become an artist and he was admitted to the Royal Academy, to study painting, in 1870. Although he did become an accomplished portrait painter, the need to earn a living led him to acting, for which he had a natural talent (although he wrote, near the end of his career, "Never at any time have I gone on the stage without longing for the moment the curtain would come down on the last act. Rarely, very rarely have I enjoyed myself in acting.").

Whether or not he enjoyed it, Forbes-Robertson did well on the stage. Sir Henry Irving invited him to join his famous company as second lead and, when Irving went off on tour, to take it over as manager and leading man. As such, in 1897, at the age of 44, Forbes-Robertson played the role of Hamlet at Irving's Lyceum Theatre. No one seemed to notice that he was a bit old for the part and he was a sensation, the toast of London. Irving had made his own reputation as Hamlet, but when he saw Forbes-Robertson in the role he announced that he could never play the part again. He also told Forbes-Robertson that it was time for him to strike out on his own, with his own company, which he did.

The company Johnston Forbes-Robertson put together included the young American actress Gertrude Elliott, sister of the already famous Maxine Elliott. He and Miss Elliott married in 1900 and, together, first toured North America in 1904.

The Forbes-Robertson Co. made its first appearance at the Royal Alexandra Theatre in May 1910, with *The Passing of the Third Floor Back*, the story of a saintly and mysterious stranger who moves into the third-floor back bedroom of a depressing Bloomsbury boarding house and transforms the lives of his sad fellow-boarders. It was the artistic event of the season. The show was to play from Monday, May 2, through Saturday, May 7. On the morning of Friday, May 6, Royal Alexandra manager Lol Solman reported that evening's performance and both the Saturday matinee and evening performances sold out, with total box-office receipts for the week the highest in the theatre's three-year history. And then, his assistant, W.J. Breen, arrived in the theatre with the news that King Edward VII was dead.

Solman feared that Johnston Forbes-Robertson would cancel both the Friday and Saturday performances as soon as he learned of the King's death; he and the King had been personal friends for years, ever since Edward's days as the wild-partying (and theatregoing) Prince of Wales. But what, he wondered, if Forbes-Robertson did not know until after the show?

Forbes-Robertson was staying at the King Edward Hotel. It was his habit to walk straight from the hotel to the theatre every evening, 45 minutes before curtain. Solman sent Breen and two ushers out with pockets-full of money to buy up every newspaper on every newsstand and in every shop window along King St. between the hotel and the theatre. Solman himself went to the hotel to walk with Forbes-Robertson, keep him in conversation, and prevent his talking to anyone else along the way.

The plan almost worked. The stage manager had called "places, everyone" and Forbes-Robertson was walking from his dressing room to his stage position when he passed two stagehands discussing the death of King Edward. He refused to go on.

No one knows what Lol Solman said to convince him to change his mind. Perhaps Forbes-Robertson was too much the professional to cancel a performance just as the curtain was to go up; perhaps he feared looking foolish if he cancelled so late in the day; but he relented and the Friday show went on as scheduled. He did, however, cancel both Saturday shows (all that record-breaking money had to be refunded) and force Solman to promise to close the theatre for the full week of the King's funeral if he ever wanted to see Sir Johnston Forbes-Robertson at the Royal Alexandra again.

Marilyn Miller

THE PHOTOGRAPH OF MARILYN MILLER is inscribed to Lol Solman and was presented to him at the close of the run of the musical *Sally* at the Royal Alexandra in 1923.

If you were born between 1920 and 1935, or thereabouts, and your name is Marilyn, chances are very good that you were named for Marilyn Miller. Her name was Mary and her mother's name was Lynn. She put the two together to make Marylynn as a new name for herself when she was offered an important part in the *Ziegfeld Follies of 1918*, but Ziegfeld thought it looked odd and suggested she change the spelling to Marilyn. That was, according to the legend, the invention of a brand-new, never-before-used woman's name.

That story may or may not be true, but it is an odd fact that the name "Marilyn" very suddenly became extremely popular around 1920 and, by 1930, was one of the top ten names for newborn girls in North America. One of

those we do know, for certain, who was named for Miss Miller was the film actress Marilyn Monroe; her real name was Norma Jean and a Hollywood casting director suggested the change to "Marilyn," because she reminded him so strongly of Marilyn Miller. That was in 1946, and the original Marilyn was then, sadly, ten years dead.

Marilyn Miller's stage career began when she was only four years old. She was a tap-dancer — "Mademoiselle Sugarlump" — in her family's vaudeville act. Vaudeville took her from her hometown of Dayton, Ohio, all the way to London, where Lee Shubert saw her in a show in 1914 and brought her back to the U.S. to appear — she was only 16 at the time — in the 1914 and 1915 editions of the Shubert revue *The Passing Show*. In 1918, she starred in the Shubert musical *Fancy Free* — which played the Royal Alexandra in February of that year — and then went on to the *Ziegfeld Follies*.

The Jerome Kern/Victor Herbert/Guy Bolton/Buddy DeSylva musical *Sally* — about a dishwasher who's mistaken for a famous ballerina, but proves that she can sing and dance up a storm when put on the stage — made her famous all over North America, the epitome of cute, blonde wholesomeness and the highest-paid actress in musical theatre.

Royal Alexandra audiences in 1923 greeted her with enthusiasm as (almost) a daughter-come-home, as she was then newly wed to Toronto-born silent film actor Jack Pickford, younger brother of Mary Pickford. That marriage, unfortunately, ended in divorce in 1927. In 1934, she married a stage manager and sometimes chorus dancer named Chet O'Brien. If you had children in the 1970s or '80s (or were yourself a child then), you may remember Chet as Mr. Macintosh, the soft-shoe-dancing fruit-stand owner on *Sesame Street*.

Marilyn Miller died in 1936, of complications following simple surgery to relieve a sinus condition.

Tallulah Bankhead

MARILYN MILLER MAY HAVE INSPIRED millions to call their daughters "Marilyn," but there was only one Tallulah — or two, actually. Tallulah Bankhead was named for her grandmother, who was, in turn, named for the wild Tallulah River in Georgia (the location of the motion picture *Deliverance*), which, allegedly, took its name from the Cherokee for "thundering waters." In the 1940s, she sued the manufacturers of Prell Shampoo for appropriating her name in magazine ads and radio commercials in which a shampoo tube with female legs sang

> *I'm Tallulah the tube of Prell*
> *And I've got something to tell.*
> *Your hair can be radiant and dandruff-free!*
> *All you've got to do is take me home,*
> *And squeeze me!*

At first, Prell argued that the name was chosen randomly, for its "t" to go with "tube," but finally gave up and settled. Everyone knew that there was only one Tallulah.

She was both blessed and cursed by a peculiar quirk of memory. On the blessing side, she could learn her parts in plays within a day; she needed only to read a script through twice to memorize the whole thing — all the parts. On the curse side, she could not remember the names of people in the real world; she recognized faces, but could not match them with names. She took to calling everyone "darling" and, all her life, people would make fun of her for what they thought an absurd affectation, not realizing that it was a mask behind which she hid an embarrassing disability.

Tallulah Bankhead was born in 1903 into a wealthy and politically prominent Huntsville, Alabama, family – her grandfather was a U.S. senator and her father was speaker of the American House of Representatives – and was educated in a convent school. She began her show-business career at the age of 16, entering her photo in a magazine contest and winning a walk-on part in a silent film.

The motion picture was shot in New York, and Tallulah remained there (with an aunt as chaperone) to try her luck on the stage. After five years, with little to show for them, she sailed to England, taking, she said, the advice of an astrologer who told her, "Your future lies across the water. Go if you have to swim."

In London, in 1923, she won a prominent part in *The Dancers*, a new play by Gerald duMaurier, and suddenly found herself famous, although as much for her personality and lifestyle as for her acting abilities. Tallulah embodied the "flapper" ideal – young, beautiful, fashionable, witty, outspoken and liberated. She smoked, she drank, she partied and she unashamedly flaunted a glamorously scandalous love life – a parade of handsome actors, young millionaires and sons of the peerage – inspiring a cultlike fan following of young, working-class women who dressed like her, cut their hair like hers and called everyone "dahling." Her fans were known to line up for tickets 48 hours in advance of an opening and to cheer wildly when she came on stage, chanting "Tallulah, Tallulah, Tallulah Hallelujah." The newspapers called them "Tallulah's gallery girls."

In 1931, Paramount Pictures offered her a contract and she returned to the U.S. She made three films for Paramount and three more for MGM, but she didn't like California or the movies and, in 1933, moved back to New York, and the stage, where she finally found real American stardom in 1935, in Somerset Maugham's drama *Rain*. In 1939, Tallulah Bankhead entered the company of the legends of theatre with her stunning performance as the ruthless, calculating Regina Giddens in Lillian Hellman's *The Little Foxes* – in which she made the first of her five appearances at the Royal Alexandra in April 1940.

She returned to Toronto in 1946 to star with the Royal Alexandra's own stock company in Noel Coward's *Private Lives* and again in 1947 with a tour of Jean Cocteau's *The Eagle Has Two Heads* – a play most memorable for the fact that, during rehearsals, she fired a young actor named Marlon Brando whose "attitude" she disliked. She was back in 1950 with a touring production of *Private Lives* (from which the photo on our wall comes – Tallulah as Amanda and Donald Cook as Elyot). We saw her for the last time in 1963, co-starring with her real-life best friend Estelle Winwood in the comedy *Here Today*, her next-to-last stage performance. Tallulah Bankhead died in 1968.

The Dumbells

M.603.1

THE NAME HAS NOTHING TO DO WITH COMIC STUPIDITY, but is a reference to the insignia of the Third Division of the Canadian Corps during the First World War, a pair of crossed dumbells, symbolizing strength.

During the war, the YMCA organized about 30 small amateur groups — called "concert parties" — of soldier volunteers to stage morale-boosting entertainments for Canadian troops on the front lines. One of these was the Dumbells, led by YMCA entertainment director Merton W. Plunkett, of Orillia, Ontario (assigned the rank of captain by the army) and his brother, Corporal Al Plunkett. Originally there were ten in the company: Ted Charters, Ross Hamilton (a female impersonator known as "Marjorie"), Allan Murray ("Marie from Montreal"), piano player Jack Ayre, Bill Tennent, Bert Langley, Frank Brayford, Leonard Young and the Plunkett brothers. They gave their first show — humorous sketches and popular and comic songs — in the trenches around Passchendaele in August 1917, and their second that same month, at Vimy Ridge.

The Dumbells were constantly on the move, up and down the frontlines of Belgium and France, playing in difficult and dangerous situations, carrying a knock-down stage, an old and battered upright piano, burlap curtains and footlights made from biscuit tins. At first, they made everything they needed themselves with whatever was at hand, but, as their fame grew, theatres and individual actors in Britain began sending them gift baskets of old costumes, props and wigs.

The army did not plan on any of the concert parties becoming permanent; all the players were scheduled to be returned to active service — Leonard Young had been with an earlier group, the Princess Pat's Light Infantry Comedy Company, and returned to the front lines, where he lost a leg, before joining the Dumbells. But the Dumbells proved such a hit that the Third Division's commander, Major-General L.J. Lipsett, made their assignment an indefinite one and allowed Mert Plunkett to expand the group to 16, and then 20, absorbing members of other concert parties.

In 1918, in a public relations move, the army sent the Dumbells to London to perform in England's largest vaudeville theatre, the Coliseum, where they played to full houses for four weeks.

On their return home to Canada in 1919, Merton and Al Plunkett wrote an original musical revue for the now-civilian Dumbells, *Biff, Bing, Bang*. They borrowed $18,000 to put it onstage, rehearsed at the Orillia Opera House, tried out in Owen Sound and opened at the Grand Theatre in London, Ontario, then transferring for a successful 16-week run at Toronto's Grand Opera House.

In May 1921, they took *Biff, Bing, Bang* to the Ambassador Theater in New York, the first Canadian musical revue to appear on Broadway. It ran for three months. Jack Ayre became the first Canadian to conduct an orchestra on Broadway and Al Jolson, who came to see the show, tried to steal the troupe's crooner, Al Plunkett, offering him a permanent position (which he declined) with his Winter Garden Co.

The Dumbells came home to tour Canada with their original shows *Carry On* in 1922, *Cheerio* in 1923 and *Ace High* in 1924. In 1925, Lol Solman, became their tour manager and, from then on, the Royal Alexandra Theatre was the Dumbells' home base. They would stage 15 shows at the Royal, from *Oh, Yes* in 1925 to *The Dumbells*, their farewell concert in 1933.

John Martin-Harvey

JOHN MARTIN-HARVEY's father was a yacht designer and boat-builder who brought his son up to follow in his footsteps. However, he chanced to build a yacht for and become friends with the dramatist W.S. Gilbert, of Gilbert and Sullivan, who introduced his boy to the wicked stage.

Like the similarly hyphenated Sir Johnston Forbes-Robertson, Martin-Harvey was a member of Sir Henry Irving's Royal Lyceum Theatre Company, where he played minor parts in Irving's productions. Also with Irving's company at that time was Angelita Helena Maria de Silva Ferro, daughter of the Chilean consul in London, who became Mrs. Martin-Harvey, but performed with her husband under the name Miss N. de Silva.

In 1899, Irving gave Martin-Harvey the chance to take a leading role in a play, *The Only Way*, an adaptation of Charles Dickens' *A Tale of Two Cities*, and that part made him famous. He continued performing the role of Sidney Carton in *The Only Way* up until his retirement from the stage in the late 1930s. He claimed to have played the part three thousand times before he finally gave it up.

After Irving's death in 1905, he and Miss de Silva formed their own repertory company

Mr. Martin Harvey.
Lieutenant Peresby (The Rat)

Fred Roe.
23 June 1905

and made many tours in both Great Britain and North America. He was of tremendous importance to the Royal Alexandra Theatre. In the 1920s, the road began to dry up and the old repertory companies all but disappeared. Martin-Harvey, "the last of the great actor-managers," continued to bring old-fashioned 19th-century-style British rep across the ocean — in his latter years, under the tour management of the Royal Alexandra's Ernest Rawley — when few others thought it still worth the cost and effort.

Martin-Harvey was a matinee idol across Canada and he never failed to fill theatres all over the country with signature productions as diverse as the historical romances *Scaramouche* and *The Breed of the Treshams*, the classic Greek tragedy *Oedipus Rex*, Shaw's *The Devil's Disciple* and the modern, symbolist drama *Pelléas et Mélisande*. One of his many Canadian admirers was the writer-to-be Robertson Davies, who saw him perform at the Grand Theatre in London, Ontario, and made him the model for his character Sir John Tresize in the novel *World of Wonders*.

Elsa Ryan, Bertha Kalich and Philip Merivale

HERE WE HAVE AN INGÉNUE OF EARLY MUSICAL COMEDY, a great European tragedienne and a romantic leading man from the British stage. What they have in common that groups them all together on a stairwell wall is that all three brought the censors down upon the Royal Alexandra.

Elsa Ryan starred in the musical comedy *The Blue Mouse*, by Clyde Fitch, which came to the Royal in March 1909. *The Blue Mouse* was about a nightclub singer and this suspicious fact, along with Fitch's reputation for occasionally touching on – by the standards of the time – "sophisticated" subjects, attracted the attention of the Reverend Mr. J.M. Wilkinson.

Wilkinson had no official or legal authority, but had appointed himself as a guardian of public morals and exercised considerable influence in this role. When the titillating word spread that he had concerns about the suitability of *The Blue Mouse*, there was a run on the box office and the show opened to a capacity audience. When Wilkinson showed up, with a police officer in tow, there were no tickets to be had. He insisted, however, on being seated and he and his escort were given folding chairs, placed in a side aisle, beside an exit. The next day, the newspapers gleefully reported that the Rev. Wilkinson and a morality squad officer identified as "Inspector Stephen" had violated the Toronto fire code by blocking an aisle, and had been unable to find anything offensive in *The Blue Mouse*.

The Hungarian-born Bertha Kalich was one of the first great international stars to play the Royal Alexandra. She had been a member of Minnie Maddern Fiske's famous repertory

Elsa Ryan

Bertha Kalich

company and appeared on the Toronto stage in 1908 in the drama *Marta of the Lowlands* and in 1909 in *The Unbroken Road*, to great applause. She came back in 1911 in a dramatization of Tolstoy's *The Kreutzer Sonata*.

By then, the Rev. Mr. Wilkinson had been replaced by a group of clergymen and prominent citizens – also completely unofficial – known as "the Committee of Forty." The committee read the play in advance of its opening and went to the police with a list of complaints. Staff Inspector George Kennedy brought those complaints to Royal Alexandra manager Lol Solman, ordering him to delete a line referring to a child's illegitimacy, remove a scene in which two characters fought over a bottle of carbolic acid and, most seriously, drop the curtain before the final scene, in which the lead character (Miss Kalich) shoots her husband dead. "No more may murder be done promiscuously on Toronto stages. Hereafter it is to be done behind dropped curtains, so that it will not shock the nervous and the sensitive."

Solman did as bidden. In the final scene, as Kalich picked up a revolver, he dropped the curtain. The shots rang out and he then raised the curtain for the cast bows. Bertha Kalich was furious and swore never to appear on a Toronto stage again, but she forgot in time and returned in 1919 and again in 1926, coincidentally, the year of the far more serious Merivale affair.

That was in September 1926. Philip Merivale (pictured here in costume for the 1931 production of *Death Takes a Holiday*) was starring in a "sophisticated comedy" called *Scotch Mist*. This work was interesting in that its author, Patrick Hastings, was a British MP and cabinet minister. The play had been a hit in London, where it starred Tallulah Bankhead, but the censor thought it a bit risqué for Toronto. It dealt far too lightly with the serious subject of marital infidelity.

By then, Toronto had an official censor, with legal authority, H.M. Wodson, of the Board of Police Commissioners. Mr. Wodson read *Scotch Mist* and wrote Solman a lecturing letter with a list of lines of dialogue he wanted cut. "A theatre manager," he wrote, "must think not only of his

THE ROYAL ALEXANDRA THEATRE

box-office receipts, but of the law of the land and the standards of the community. . . . As is well known, most of the plays coming to Toronto have been seen in the cities to the south of us, seen by tens of thousands of people . . . [but] I do not mean by this to suggest that because a play has satisfied playgoers in the U.S.A, it should be accepted here without question . . . we have not yet accepted the ideals of Broadway, where in the name of entertainment the prostitute is glorified and sexual abnormality lionized."

Solman gave the censor's letter to *Scotch Mist*'s stage manager and forgot the matter. The cuts were not made; the stage manager may have assumed the letter misaddressed, as there were neither any prostitutes nor identifiably sexually abnormal characters in *Scotch Mist,* nor had the play yet been performed on Broadway or anywhere else in the U.S. Under the law, however, the theatre was responsible for what happened on its stage and a warrant was issued for Lol Solman's arrest on the charge of "operating an immoral show."

Fortunately, nothing came of it. Solman wrote an official letter of apology, admitting his negligence, and charges were dropped. Years later, he still complained that the whole affair had been provoked by the *Scotch Mist* stage manager to generate publicity and promote ticket sales, both of which it did.

Philip Merivale

William Gillette

WILLIAM GILLETTE once said of himself, "I'm a pretty fair stage carpenter and not altogether bad as an actor, after I have written myself a good part that suits me." He did write a few good parts that suited him, but none better remembered than that of the great detective Sherlock Holmes.

Gillette was not the first actor to play Sherlock Holmes, but he was, in a sense, the character's creator. Sir Arthur Conan Doyle may have written the original novels and stories, but it was William Gillette who gave Holmes the voice, look and physical presence by which the world came to know him. It was Gillette who first dressed Holmes in a deerstalker cap and Inverness cape, with a magnifying glass in his pocket and a curved-stem calabash pipe in his hand (liking the way the pipe enhanced his profile). And it was Gillette, not Conan Doyle, who wrote the line "Elementary, my dear fellow." Every actor to play the role since has, consciously or not, copied some aspect of William Gillette's characterization.

The original idea of turning the Holmes stories into a full-length play was Arthur Conan Doyle's own, and he wrote the first attempt – five acts – himself, but could find no one to stage it. His agent sent a copy of the script to the American producer Charles S. Frohman, who pronounced it "impossible" as a drama, but suggested that his friend, actor and writer William Gillette, might be able to do something with it.

With Conan Doyle's permission, Gillette set about rewriting, working in hotel rooms while on tour with his play *Secret Service*. He finished the job one afternoon in San Francisco, in November 1898, and left the manuscripts – both his and Conan Doyle's original – in his room when he went to the theatre. He came back to find the hotel had burned down, but he was able to rewrite the whole thing, from memory, by Christmas. Two months later, he travelled to England, met Conan

Doyle and presented him with the finished play; for the meeting, Gillette dressed in a deerstalker cap and Inverness cape. Conan Doyle approved the look.

Sherlock Holmes had its world premiere in Buffalo, New York, in October 1899, and opened on Broadway in November for a seven-month run. The London production opened at Henry Irving's Lyceum Theatre in September 1901 — with a 12-year-old named Charlie Chaplin playing the role of a newsboy — and ran for another seven months there (including a royal command performance before King Edward and Queen Alexandra). Sir Arthur Conan Doyle attended the London premiere and wrote to Gillette, "My only complaint is that you made the poor hero of the anemic printed page a very limp object as compared with the glamour of your own personality, which you infuse into his stage presentment."

For the next 34 years, hardly a season passed without William Gillette performing his Sherlock Holmes at least once, somewhere. In 1913, he announced his retirement and the "farewell" of Holmes — he was then 58 and felt he was getting too old for the part — but he was back on the road in 1915. He retired again in 1923, but only for a few weeks. The absolutely final tour began in 1929 and was still going on in 1932, when he brought the play to the Royal Alexandra Theatre. His definitely final performance as Holmes was in 1935 — when he was 79 — in a radio adaptation by Orson Welles. Welles said at the time, "It is not enough to say that William Gillette resembles Sherlock Holmes; Sherlock Holmes looks exactly like William Gillette."

William Gillette's skills as a carpenter are still there for everyone to see in the eccentric, 24 room medieval fantasy castle Seven Sisters — financed by the millions he made from *Sherlock Holmes* — he designed and built for himself near East Haddam, Connecticut, at the time of his 1913 "retirement." The castle sits on a 115-acre estate, surrounded by a three-mile-long private railway, and features an ingenious system of mirrors — of Gillette's design — that enabled him to view all public areas from his bedroom, to facilitate, he said, "making grand entrances at opportune moments." The castle is now a state park and open to the public.

Marion Lorne

THIS PHOTO OF MARION LORNE is a special favourite, for it is the prodigal child among the faces on the Royal Alexandra's walls. It was stolen in 1986 and then mysteriously and anonymously returned (by, according to the note, a friend of the contrite thief) 20 years later. Miss Lorne is seen here as Veta in Mary Chase's comedy *Harvey*, in which she co-starred with Joe E. Brown at the Royal Alexandra in 1947 and again in 1949.

The character she played in *Harvey* was that of a nervous and befuddled society matron, and that character became her stock-in-trade throughout the 1950s — as Mrs. Gurney, the stuttering English teacher on the television series *Mr. Peepers* — and 1960s — as the clumsy and forgetful Aunt Clara in the sitcom *Bewitched*. Few who saw her on television — or in *Harvey* — probably realized that the American-born actress had once been a major figure in London theatre and, in the words of Alfred Hitchcock (who cast her in her first film), "more than an actress in England; she was an institution."

Marion Lorne started out in theatre in a stock company in Connecticut and made her Broadway debut in the comedy *Mrs.*

Temple's Telegram in 1905. She had a very successful New York career until 1914, when she appeared on Broadway in a comedy called *Don't Weaken*, written by a young British playwright named Walter C. Hackett. It was a dreadful failure, closing after five performances, but Miss Lorne married Mr. Hackett and went home with him to London, where she starred in a half-dozen of his plays — comedies — and became one of London's best-known comic actresses.

In 1930, she and her husband opened their own theatre, the Whitehall, in London's West End. Under Marion Lorne's management, it became the city's leading venue for comedy and home to the famous — and quite risqué — wartime *Whitehall Follies*, starring the dancer Phyllis Dixey, "the Queen of Striptease."

Walter Hackett died in 1942 and Marion Lorne ran the Whitehall on her own until 1944, when she decided to retire and move back to North America. She might never have worked again, but director Antoinette Perry offered her the role in that touring production of *Harvey*, keeping her busy for two years, after which came the offer of the film *Strangers on a Train* from Alfred Hitchcock, and the television series, and she kept on performing right up until the day she died, in 1968, at the age of 85, right after filming episode #137 of *Bewitched*.

Joe E. Brown

"Harvey"

THE PULITZER PRIZE PLAY

Sir Harry Lauder

THE IMPISH-LOOKING LITTLE MAN IN THE KILT IS SIR HARRY LAUDER who, during the years of the First World War, was said to be the highest-paid stage performer in the world. Although he appeared many times in pantomime and revue, he was not, properly speaking, of the legitimate stage; a singer and stand-up comedian, he belonged to vaudeville and music hall.

He was born in Scotland, into a large family reduced to poverty on the death of his father. He went to work in a textile mill at 14, and in a coal mine at 16. At 18, he won an amateur-night contest in a music hall and, encouraged by family and friends, embarked on a career as an Irish-dialect singer and comedian (Scots audiences thinking this funnier than Scottish-dialect comedy).

By the early 1890s, he was a music-hall star and a favourite — and friend — of the Prince of Wales (before he became King Edward VII), who presented him with the walking stick that became his trademark. It was during the First World War, however, that he reached the heights, as an army recruiter and salesman of war bonds, all across the British Empire.

Lauder made the war effort his personal, patriotic crusade. He assembled, at his own expense, a pipe band that he marched up and down and back and forth across Scotland in a recruiting drive in which he, personally, was said to have signed 12,000 young men to the colours. The success of his variety shows selling war bonds and raising funds for the Red Cross, Belgian war relief and his own "Harry Lauder Million Pound Fund" for disabled veterans was unprecedented; in one 1916 engagement at the Royal Alexandra — one of his nine appearances here — he is said to have raised a staggering $750,000 in audience pledges. There was one sour note in that Canadian tour of 1916, when the newspapers revealed that Lauder was being paid an unheard-of $5000 per performance for his fund-raising efforts, many felt him to be taking advantage of the tradegy of war; but any doubts were washed away in a flood of tears when his only son, John, an officer of the Argyle and Sutherland Highlanders, was killed in action in France. Lauder received the telegram news of his son's death just a few hours before a show, but went on, as scheduled, laughing, joking and singing comic songs, betraying no signs of his grief, until the curtain came down and he collapsed backstage.

Harry Lauder was knighted by King George V in 1919, in recognition of his services to the Empire during the war

Al Jolson

HE CALLED HIMSELF "THE WORLD'S GREATEST ENTERTAINER" AND, for 30 years, even those who were appalled by the ego that lay behind that claim had to admit that it might have been the truth. Al Jolson holds a special place in the history of the Royal Alexandra, for he proclaimed it his favourite theatre: "It's the only theatre I know," he said, "that makes my voice sound even better than I think it does."

He was born Asa Yoelson — or, perhaps, Hesselsohn — in a Lithuanian village in 1884 or '85 or '86 — no one's sure of the exact year — the son of a rabbinical student. His father came to the United States in 1890, leaving the family at home until he could establish himself. When he became rabbi of the Talmud Torah Synagogue in Washington, D.C., in 1894, he sent for his wife and sons.

Rabbi Yoelson's wish was that both his sons, Asa and Hirsch, would follow in his footsteps and he gave the boys singing lessons, training them to be cantors in the synagogue. Asa, however, wanted to be called "Al" and Hirsch, "Harry," and both preferred ragtime to liturgical music. They ran away from home in 1899 and joined a travelling circus. By 1901, both were working as singers and dancers in vaudeville, burlesque and minstrel shows.

Al Jolson's big break came in 1911, when he was offered a part in the Broadway musical revue *La Belle Paree*. Florenz Ziegfeld then offered him a chance to audition for *The Follies*, but he turned it down, saying that he didn't audition for anyone. He was not yet, however, well known outside New York when he first came to the Royal Alexandra in January, 1913, in the musical *The Whirl of Society*. The star of that show was Gaby Deslys and it was her name that drew the crowds — she was said to have been the mistress of King Manuel, of Portugal, whose extravagant gifts to her (pearls and diamonds) had played a part in his overthrow in a revolution in 1910. Jolson was then better known in Toronto as a one-time bellboy at the Iroquois Hotel, but he stole the show so thoroughly that the audience all but forgot there was anyone else on the stage.

He returned to Toronto later in 1913 as the star of *Honeymoon Express*, in 1915 with *Dancing Around* and in 1916 with *Robinson Crusoe, Jr.* — by which time his name was on the marquee and posters, and in the newspaper ads above the title (and in bigger type) than the name of the show. The show itself became irrelevant, because it was Jolson people came to see. He became notorious for throwing away the scripts and ad-libbing and for adding new musical numbers — unknown to the authors, the orchestra or the rest of the cast — at will. From time to time, he would even stop shows entirely, dismissing his fellow players and sending them back to their dressing rooms as he kept the stage, alone, for a solo concert.

Not only did he get away with this behaviour, audiences loved him for it. When he stopped a performance of the musical *Bombo* on Broadway to sing a few new songs he liked that were not in the show, the house stood, stamped, cheered and chanted his name, bringing him back for 37 curtain calls. The critic Robert Benchley wrote of him:

> *"To sit and feel the lift of Jolson's personality is to know what the coiners of the word 'personality' meant. Unimpressive as the comparison may be to Mr. Jolson, we should say that John the Baptist was the last man to possess such a power. There is something supernatural back of it, or we miss our guess. When Jolson enters, it is as if an electric current had been run along the wires under the seats where the hats are stuck. The house comes to tumultuous attention. He speaks, rolls his eyes, compresses his lips, and it is all over. You are a life-member of the Al Jolson Association. He trembles his underlip, and your heart breaks with a loud snap. He sings, and you totter out to send a night letter to your mother. Such a giving-off of vitality, personality, charm, and whatever all those words are."*

Oddly enough, for all the self-confidence Al Jolson displayed onstage, the thought of performing before a live audience terrified him. There were evenings on which the stage manager had to push him, quivering with fear, onto the stage and, all his life, the theatres in which he performed kept buckets in his dressing room and in the wings should his extreme stage-fright lead him — as it often did — to vomit.

Jolson brought nine shows to the Royal Alexandra stage. The last was *Hold On to Your Hats*, in 1941. It was his final show; he closed it, on the road, right after its Toronto engagement. Although only 55 (or 56, or 57), he felt worn out and no longer able to summon up the energy for the kind of performance people had come to expect of him. He died, of a heart attack, in 1950.

Fred and Adele Astaire

EVERYONE REMEMBERS FRED ASTAIRE FROM THE MOVIES, BUT WHO WAS ADELE?

She was his older sister — by almost two years — and dancing partner throughout his stage career, before he ever thought of motion pictures. They came from Omaha, Nebraska, and started out together as vaudeville performers in 1903, when Adele was six and Fred had just turned five.

They didn't make it to Broadway until 1917, when they won roles in the musical *Over the Top*. They came to the Royal Alexandra with their second big New York production, *The Passing Show of 1918* (which, despite its title, did not reach Toronto until 1919).

During their teenaged vaudeville years, the Astaires had become close friends with George and Ira Gershwin and all had vowed that, someday, they would work together. They kept that promise in 1924, when Fred and Adele starred in the first full-length Gershwin musical, *Lady Be Good* (in which they played a vaudeville brother and sister dance team). They followed that hit with another — the Gershwins' *Funny Face*, in which Adele sang the song *S'Wonderful* — and another, the Howard Dietz/Arthur Schwartz musical *The Band Wagon*.

While many would later talk of Fred Astaire as one of the greatest dancers of the

20th century, it was Adele who was the star of their days as a duo. This may have been principally to do with the fact that she was pretty while Fred was a little odd-looking; gregarious while Fred was withdrawn; chatty and witty while Fred was shy; fun-loving while Fred was "serious" (Adele's nickname for him was "Moaning Minnie"); and could sing rings around her brother. Although she always insisted that Fred was the creative genius in the partnership, everyone assumed that she was the creator of the unique Astaire style and that Fred just tagged along.

In 1932, right after *Band Wagon*, Adele married Lord Charles Cavendish, younger son of the Duke of Devonshire, and retired from the stage, going off to live a fairy-tale life at Lismore Castle, in Ireland. Despite having had his first solo hit that year, right after the wedding, in Cole Porter's *Gay Divorce*, Fred feared that he lacked the confidence to continue performing without her – not, at any rate, live, onstage. They had had offers from Hollywood, and Fred went west to take a screen test, which he famously failed; his auditioner's note read, "Balding. Can't sing. Can't act. Can dance a little." Nevertheless, Hollywood took a chance on him, teamed him with a young dancer named Ginger Rogers and put the two of them in a musical film called *Flying Down to Rio*, beginning a legendary screen career.

After Fred hit it big in Hollywood, Adele thought she might give the movies a try, as well. In 1937, she began working on a film with dancer Jack Buchanan and singer Maurice Chevalier. After two days' work, however, she viewed the rushes and withdrew from the project. "Oh boy," she said, "if my brother sees this, I'm gone."

In later years, the playwright P.G. Wodehouse wrote of the end of the Fred and Adele Astaire duo, "Fred struggled on without her for a while, but finally threw his hand in and disappeared. There is a rumour that he turned up in Hollywood. It was the best the poor chap could hope for after losing his brilliant sister."

Paul Robeson

PAUL ROBESON WAS A CHARACTER who would have been unbelievable in a novel or play. He first came to fame as a high school football star and, later, as a football player for Rutgers University and a member of both the 1917 and 1918 All-American teams. His Rutgers coach proclaimed him the greatest player ever seen on the gridiron. He was also his class valedictorian at Rutgers, a member of the Phi Beta Kappa academic honour society and holder of varsity letters in basketball, baseball and track and field. He could also read 20 languages and speak, with fluency, 12.

Robeson studied law at Columbia University – paying his way through school by working part-time as an actor (making his Broadway debut in 1921, while a law student), concert singer and professional football player. He was a practising attorney in New York City when he starred, on the side, in Eugene O'Neill's *All God's Chillun Got Wings* (a play about a remarkable black man who becomes a lawyer). He then moved to England, where he starred in the London productions of O'Neill's *The Emperor Jones*, an enormously successful and critically acclaimed *Othello* (with Judith Evans as his Desdemona) and the musical *Show Boat*. He returned to the U.S. in 1932 to do *Show Boat* on Broadway and to make the 1936 film version of the musical, from the soundtrack of which his "Ol' Man River" became one of the best-selling records of the decade. He then toured Europe and the Soviet Union as a singer, performing American folk songs and spirituals to wildly enthusiastic audiences.

Robeson went back to England at the start of the war and was spending most of his time entertaining troops, singing on the radio and performing in patriotic concerts when, in 1943, his friend, actor José Ferrer, talked him into braving the Atlantic crossing and coming home to mount his *Othello* on Broadway. Ferrer directed and co-starred as Iago, with his wife, Uta Hagen taking the role of Desdemona. The play ran for 296 performances in New York, almost twice the performance record of any Shakespearean play ever produced on Broadway, and then went on tour, where it broke all records for any touring Shakespearean play, as well.

Othello came to the Royal Alexandra in September 1944, and many who saw it thought it the theatre event of the decade. Many others, however, went away disappointed. Paul Robeson had never before performed on a Canadian stage and hundreds came to the theatre knowing him only from BBC Radio concerts and records — especially that recording of "Ol' Man River" — in the mistaken assumption that *Othello* was a musical.

Those disappointed fans finally got a chance to hear Robeson sing, live, in 1952. He had been accused of being a Communist sympathizer and subversive by the U.S. Congress and his passport had been revoked; he was forbidden to leave the United States. To protest and dramatize his situation, he rented a flatbed truck, parked it on the U.S. side of the Niagara River, and used it as a stage from which to sing (with amplification) to an estimated 40,000 Ontario fans on the other side of the river. When the travel ban was lifted in 1956 (after he won a lawsuit against the U.S. State Department), his first trip abroad was to Toronto, where he performed a concert at Massey Hall.

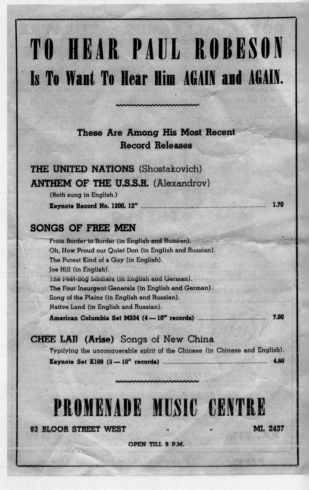

Evelyn Nesbit

In 1913, the Shubert Organization producers Comstock and Gest put together a touring show called *Mariette*. It was not exactly a play, or a musical, or even a revue. They called it a "musical divertissement" and its sole reason for being was the display of the former Broadway chorus girl Evelyn Nesbit. Comstock and Gest felt confident that the show would sell out everywhere, that people would flock just for a glimpse of Miss Nesbit, beautiful principal figure in a spectacular, high-society murder. Unfortunately, they were wrong and *Mariette* fared very poorly; its week at the Royal Alexandra lost money, Torontonians apparently feeling they had better things to do with their money than pay to gape at an infamous adultress.

Evelyn Nesbit started her theatre career in 1901, in the chorus of the musical *Floradora*, when she was only 16. It was there, singing and dancing in the number "Tell me, pretty maiden, are there any more at home like you?" as one of the six identically sized "Floradora girls" (all were 5 feet, 4 inches tall and required, on pain of dismissal, to maintain a weight of exactly 130 pounds), that she caught the eye of the architect and collector of chorus girls Stanford White.

White had many connections in theatre and the arts and used his influence to find steady work for Evelyn, most notably as a model for his friend, the illustrator Charles Dana Gibson. Evelyn was the original model for "the Gibson girl," the ideal of Edwardian feminine beauty. The author Lucy Maud Montgomery had a Gibson drawing of Evelyn Nesbit, clipped from a magazine, pinned to the wall above the desk at which she wrote *Anne of Green Gables*. But Evelyn was no Anne Shirley.

Through Gibson, Evelyn met the young artist and sometime actor John Barrymore, by whom, at 17, she became pregnant. Barrymore proposed marriage, but Stanford White advised against the match and drove Evelyn to New Jersey, where he enrolled her in a private boarding school and arranged for an operation, for "appendicitis." The school, incidentally, was run by a Mrs. DeMille, whose son, the future film director Cecil B. DeMille, later recalled being bribed by John Barrymore to smuggle in his letters to Evelyn.

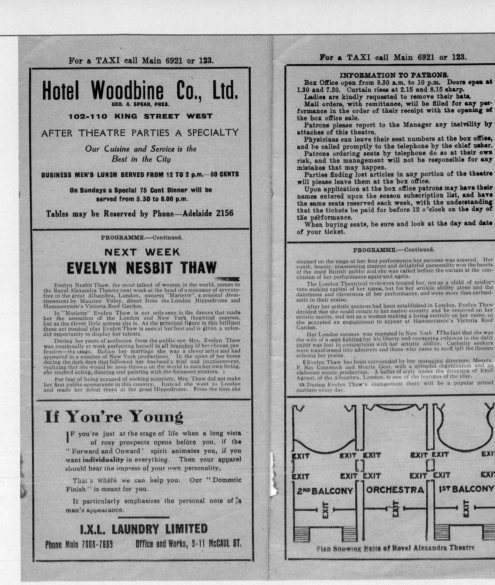
Upon her graduation from Mrs. DeMille's academy, Evelyn moved back to New York, where she met and, in 1905, married a wealthy young playboy named Harry Thaw, heir to a fortune in coal, steel and railroad shares. In 1906, however, she left Thaw and asked him for a divorce. The enraged Thaw believed – possibly correctly – that Evelyn had gone back to Stanford White. A few nights after her departure, Thaw saw the architect in the theatre, in the audience of the revue *Mam'zelle Champagne*, made his way over to his seat and shot him three times, in the head.

Harry Thaw went through two long murder trials, the first ending in a hung jury, despite the fact that hundreds of people saw him shoot Stanford White. He was finally acquitted on the claim of temporary insanity. He divorced Evelyn, but she got none of his money. With White's influence gone, she had trouble finding work. His friends, even Gibson, wanted nothing to do with her. She put together a vaudeville act in partnership with a dancer named Jack Clifford – whom she later married – and it was this act that Comstock and Gest picked up and made the basis for *Mariette*. They billed her as Evelyn Nesbit Thaw and referred to her in all publicity as "Mrs. Thaw," just to make sure everyone knew that this really was *the* Evelyn Nesbit, the woman whose husband had killed her lover, all the while issuing protestations that *Mariette* was, in any way, intended to exploit the terrible tragedy.

Katharine Cornell

THE PICTURE ON THE WALL is of a scene in *Romeo and Juliet*. The Juliet is Katharine Cornell and the Romeo, Basil Rathbone. It's too bad we have no other photos of that production, for the role of the nurse was played by Edith Evans, Mercutio was Brian Aherne and Juliet's doomed cousin Tybalt was played by a 17-year-old novice named Orson Welles. Many years later, after a long and distinguished film career, Basil Rathbone looked back on this *Romeo and Juliet* — which played the Royal Alexandra in December 1934 — as the high point of his life as an actor and the one performance for which he would like to be remembered.

The most remarkable thing about that *Romeo*, however, was that it came to Toronto at all. This was in 1934 and theatres were closing everywhere, converting to motion pictures — the Royal Alexandra would soon be the only remaining legitimate theatre in Canada — and no one was touring, anywhere. No one, that is, but the repertory company headed by Katharine Cornell and her husband, director Guthrie McClintic.

Miss Cornell could easily have stayed safely in New York, or gone to Hollywood and made movies. The powerful critic Alexander Woollcott had proclaimed her "the first lady of theatre" and she was, along with Helen Hayes and Ethel Barrymore, a reigning star of Broadway, but she loved working in repertory and loved the challenge of the road. She would go wherever there was an audience that wanted to see her and her 1934 tour of *Romeo and Juliet*, *The Barretts of Wimpole Street* and Shaw's *Candida* took her, McClintic, Rathbone, Welles, Aherne and Edith Evans on a 21,000-mile, 77-city journey, from Georgia to California and back again, with very little in her pocket at the end to show for the effort. "We opened up the road," she said. "We made *The Barretts* and *Candida* pay for Shakespeare. *The Barretts* never played to an empty house. The receipts would be something like $33,000, then about $28,000 for *Candida* and, for *Juliet* about $18,000 to $19,000, so that we came back having more than broken even. We really felt prideful."

One legendary Christmas, the Katharine Cornell troupe was on its way to Seattle, by rail, when a flood forced a detour and long delay. The actors arrived after 11:00 on the evening they had been scheduled to open. They took their trunks to the theatre and were shocked to find a full house still there, waiting for the past three hours for the show to begin. Miss Cornell apologized to the audience, the actors dressed and the curtain rose on *The Barretts of Wimpole Street* at 1:00 in the morning.

Katharine Cornell was from Buffalo, New York. Her father was a doctor, who gave up medicine to do something more interesting and became manager of Buffalo's Star Theatre. Her wealthy grandfather, who acted with a local amateur company, owned a mansion in which he built a fully equipped theatre, in the attic. Acting, she wrote, was in her blood:

> "The feeling for it was absolutely born in me. My first memories, however, are not of actors but of the theatre — a stage; the curve of a proscenium; a curtain with something wonderful behind it, which might lift at any moment. That was in my grandfather Cornell's house in Buffalo. I never got to act there, of course. I was just a very small child sitting on the steps watching rehearsals.
>
> "My father was an exceptionally fine amateur player — my aunt was too. Even at our summer home in Cobourg, Ontario — a grand old-fashioned house — there was a long gallery at the back near the garden where they used to put on plays.
>
> "I think it was the advent of Maude Adams' Peter Pan in my father's theatre, in 1907, that first made me know that I wanted to devote my life to the stage. I had looked forward to Maude Adams with such eagerness that, when the time came, it was sheer agony. At first I hid my face in the curtains of the box because I couldn't bear to look. Then, afterward, utter enchantment."

Katharine Cornell continued touring until her husband's death in 1961, when she left the stage, feeling that acting, without him as her director, would be too difficult for her. "I continued in the theatre buoyed up mostly by his enthusiasm for it. He was one of those people who fascinated you always. You were never bored; sometimes upset, but never bored."

Altogether, she appeared 14 times at the Royal Alexandra, with a stellar array of co-stars, attracted to tour for the chance of working with her, that included — in addition to Basil Rathbone, Brian Aherne, Edith Evans and Orson Welles — Tyrone Power, Christopher Plummer, Marian Seldes, Anthony Quayle, Philip Merivale, Jean-Pierre Aumont, Judith Anderson, Ruth Gordon and Edmund Gwenn. Equally interesting are the many stars-to-be who broke into the theatre in minor roles in one of her companies. In 1988, David Mirvish produced the drama *A Man For All Seasons* in London, with Charlton Heston in the role of Sir Thomas More. Heston told him he hoped the show would do well enough in Britain that it might be considered for a tour to the Royal Alexandra, where he had made his professional debut as a spear-carrier in Katharine Cornell's 1947 production of *Antony and Cleopatra*.

Todd Duncan

His name was actually Robert Todd Duncan. He was born in Danville, Kentucky, on February 2, 1903. He had a dual career in opera and in teaching. He studied music at Butler University and took his master's degree in music education at Columbia University and, subsequently, began a distinguished 50-year career as a teacher of vocal performance at Howard University. He made his professional debut in 1933, starring in a New York production of Mascagni's *Cavalleria Rusticana* with an all-black company, the Aeolian Opera, and followed that with a successful European tour as a concert artist. In 1945, he made American stage history when he sang the roles of Tonio in *I Pagliacci* and Escamillo in *Carmen* with the New York City Opera Company; it was the first time a black singer had ever performed with a major American opera company and, not only that, the first case — these were "white" roles — of colour-blind casting on the American stage.

Todd Duncan was a serious, classical musician who had no interest in or time for popular music. When George Gershwin called him one day in 1934 to ask if he might be interested in a role in a proposed new musical called *Porgy and*

Bess, he declined. He had heard of Gershwin, vaguely, but thought him just a piano player in some jazz band. When friends talked him into meeting Gershwin and reading his score, and he did so, he expressed surprise at learning that George Gershwin actually composed music.

Todd Duncan took the part, the role of Porgy, for the premiere performance of *Porgy and Bess*, in Boston, in 1935. The show then ran for almost a year on Broadway before going on its first – the first of many – North American tours, ending up at the prestigious National Theatre, in Washington, D.C., where Duncan refused to perform until the management agreed to end, forever, the practice of racial segregation in audience seating.

Porgy and Bess did not reach Toronto until March 1943. Despite the fact that the musical and its stars were by then world famous and the Canadian premiere a momentous event, Royal Alexandra manager Ernie Rawley could not find hotel accommodations for the cast. It was not, local hotel managers explained to him, that they were racist, but only that they feared their many American customers might take offence at seeing black people in the lobbies and on the elevators.

Rawley contacted Toronto churches and arranged private housing for the *Porgy* cast. Todd Duncan and the company arrived at Union Station on the evening of March 6 and Rawley went to the station to meet them and arrange the dozen cabs to take them to the homes of their scattered hosts, all over the city. The players exited the train onto an open platform and into a freezing rain. When he saw them standing there, soaked and shivering, Rawley lost his notoriously short temper. He marched the company across the street and into the lobby of the Royal York Hotel, where he demanded to see the manager and publicly shamed him into giving rooms to everyone.

After *Porgy and Bess*, Todd Duncan starred in two other Broadway shows, Vernon Duke's *Cabin in the Sky* and Kurt Weill's *Lost in the Stars*, before going back to teaching and to touring the world in concert. He died in 1998, at the age of 95.

Debbie Reynolds
and John Gielgud

IT'S DIFFICULT TO IMAGINE THE PAIRING OF
DEBBIE REYNOLDS, bubbly star of fluffy
Hollywood musicals, and Sir John Gielgud,
the dignified British Shakespearean, but they
once performed together on the stage of the
Royal Alexandra, although few in the audience knew about it at the time. It happened
in November 1972, in a revival of the 1920s
musical *Irene*.

Irene had played the Royal Alexandra three
times before, twice in 1921 and once in 1923. It
had done well on Broadway, but the touring
production was seen as a vehicle devised principally to promote the would-be star Dale
Winter, wife (widow, actually) of the Chicago
gangster Big Jim Colosimo, who was believed
to have been shot down by Al Capone,
although no one ever proved it. Dale had taken
singing lessons from Enrico Caruso, but that
didn't help much and *Irene* died and remained
forgotten until 1971, when playwright Hugh
Wheeler rewrote it and producers Harry Rigby
and Jerome Minskoff restaged it, hoping to take
advantage of the craze for vintage musicals
sparked by *No, No, Nanette*.

Sir John Gielgud was the producers' curi-
ous choice as director — he had done opera,
but had never directed a musical — and
Debbie Reynolds was the star. The show had

its pre-Broadway tryout at the Royal Alexandra and disaster struck when Debbie Reynolds, with a full house in attendance, lost her voice; she was unable to speak above a whisper. There was an understudy, but she had not yet rehearsed. Ed Mirvish claimed the dubious credit for what happened; he suggested that Miss Reynolds go on, act and dance, and that Gielgud stand in the wings and read her lines.

Ed may have been inspired by Debbie Reynolds' role in the film *Singin' in the Rain*, in which she stood backstage and provided the speaking and singing voice for an inept silent film star to mime before a live audience. It worked in the movie, but not in real life. The Toronto audience was furious at hearing Miss Reynolds' songs recited by "some man." Half the audience walked out at intermission, and the theatre had to refund almost everyone's money. Ed Mirvish always expressed puzzlement at the failure of his idea. He had given the theatre an historic moment, the first (and last) musical performance by one of the 20th century's greatest classical actors.

1907

08/26-09/07
Top O' Th' World
By Mark Swan and James O'Dea, lyrics by
James O'Dea, music by Manuel Klein and
Anne Caldwell
Producer/Director: Shuberts/Frank Smithson
Cast: Harry Fairleigh and Anna Laughlin

09/09-09/14
The Road to Yesterday
By Beulah Dix and Evelyn G. Sutherland
Producer/Director: Shuberts/J.C. Huffman
Cast: Minnie Dupree, White Whittlesley and
William Beery

09/16-09/21
The Blue Moon
By Harold Ellis/Paul Rubens/
Percy Greenbank/Howard Talbot
Producer: Shuberts
Cast: James T. Powers, Frank Farrington
and Marion Jacques ("the Blue Moon")

09/23-09/28
Happyland, or The King of Elysia
By Frederick Ranken, music by Reginald de
Koven
Producer: Shuberts
Cast: De Wolf Hopper and Marguerite Clark

09/23-10/28
Mrs. Dane's Defence
By Henry Arthur Jones
Producer/Director: The Royal Alexandra
Players/Will H. Gregory
Cast: Grace Mae Lamkin, Robert Conness,
Herbert A. Yost, Elfreda Lasche and others

10/07-10/12
The Other Girl
By Augustus Thomas
Producer/Director: The Royal Alexandra
Players/Will H. Gregory

10/14-10/19
Soldiers of Fortune
By Augustus Thomas, from the novel by
Richard Harding Davis
Producer/Director: The Royal Alexandra
Players/Will H. Gregory

10/21-10/26
The Cowboy and the Lady
By Clyde Fitch
Producer/Director: The Royal Alexandra
Players/Will H. Gregory

10/28-11/02
At the Whitehorse Tavern
By Hans Muller and Erik Charell
Producer/Director: The Royal Alexandra
Players/Will H. Gregory

11/04-11/09
The Second in Command
By Robert Marshall
Producer/Director: The Royal Alexandra
Players/Will H. Gregory

11/11-11/16
The Dancing Girl
By Henry Arthur Jones
Producer/Director: The Royal Alexandra
Players/Will H. Gregory

11/18-11/23
A Good Fellow
By Francis Powers
Producer/Director: The Royal Alexandra
Players/Will H. Gregory

11/18-11/23
Miss Hobbs
By Jerome K. Jerome
Producer/Director: The Royal Alexandra
Players/Will H. Gregory

11/25-11/30
Quality Street
By James M. Barrie

Producer/Director: The Royal Alexandra
Players/Will H. Gregory

12/02-12/07
The Henrietta
By Bronson Howard
Producer/Director: The Royal Alexandra
Players/Will H. Gregory

12/09-12/14
The Masqueraders
By Henry Arthur Jones
Producer/Director: The Royal Alexandra
Players/Will H. Gregory

12/16-12/21
Camille
By Alexandre Dumas
Producer/Director: The Royal Alexandra
Players/Will H. Gregory

12/23-12/28
All the Comforts of Home
By William Gillette
Producer/Director: The Royal Alexandra
Players/Will H. Gregory

12/30-01/04/08
A School for Scandal
By R.B. Sheridan
Producer/Director: The Royal Alexandra
Players/Will H. Gregory

1908

01/06-01/11
The Christian
By Hall Caine
Producer/Director: The Royal Alexandra
Players/Will H. Gregory

01/13-01/18
The Girl with the Green Eyes
By Clyde Fitch
Producer/Director: The Royal Alexandra
Players/Will H. Gregory
Cast: Ida Conquest and The Royal
Alexandra Players company

01/20-01/25
Old Heidelberg
By Wilhelm Meyer-Foerster
Producer/Director: The Royal Alexandra
Players/Will H. Gregory
Cast: Ida Conquest and The Royal
Alexandra Players company

01/27–02/01
The Great Match
By Clyde Fitch
Producer/Director: The Royal Alexandra
Players/Will H. Gregory
Ida Conquest and The Royal Alexandra
Players company

02/03–02/08
Marta of the Lowlands
By Angel Guimera
Produced and directed by Harrison Grey
Fiske
Cast: Bertha Kalich, Henry Kelker, Hardee
Kirtland, Robert McWade, Edith Taliaferro
and others

02/10–02/15
Diplomacy
By Victorien Sardou
Producer/Director: The Royal Alexandra
English Players/William Sauter
Cast: William Sauter, Miss Darragh, Jane
Marbury and others

02/17
Brother Officers
By Leo Trevor
Producer/Director: The Toronto Garrison
Dramatic Co.
Cast: Beverley Robinson, Miss Ridout,
Isabel Johnston, Mabel Jackson, Lt. Col.
Septimus Denison, Lt. John Hinds and
Lt. Long-Innis

02/18–02/22
She Stoops to Conquer
By Oliver Goldsmith
Producer/Director: The Royal Alexandra
English Players/William Sauter
Cast: Ivan Simpson, William Sauter and
others

02/24–02/29
Girl of the Golden West
By David Belasco, music by William Furst
Producer/Director: David Belasco
Cast: Blanche Bates, Harriet Sterling,
Charles Millward, Cuyler Hastings, John F.
Webber, Thomas Delmar and others

03/02–03/07
The Liars
By Henry Arthur Jones
Producer/Director: The Royal Alexandra
English Players/William Sauter

03/09–03/14
London Assurance
By Dion Boucicault
Producer/Director: The Royal Alexandra
English Players/William Sauter

03/23–03/28
The Magistrate
By Arthur Wing Pinero
Producer/Director: The Royal Alexandra
English Players/William Sauter

03/30–04/04
The Idler
By Haddon Chambers
Producer/Director: The Royal Alexandra
English Players/William Sauter

04/06–04/11
The Private Secretary
By Gustav Von Moser
Producer/Director: The Royal Alexandra
English Players/William Sauter

04/13–04/18
Our Boys
By H.J. Byron
Producer/Director: The Royal Alexandra
English Players/William Sauter

04/20–04/25
The Lottery of Love
By Augustin Daly
Producer/Director: The Royal Alexandra
English Players/William Sauter

04/27–05/02
Rosmersholm
By H. Ibsen
Producer/Director: Harrison Grey Fiske
Cast: Minnie Maddern Fiske, Bruce MacRae,
Fuller Melish and George Arliss

05/04–05/05
Minstrel Show
Toronto Rowing Club

05/07–05/09
Three Little Maids
By Paul Rubens
Producer/Director: Toronto Men's Press
Club/R.S. Piggott

05/11–05/16
San Toy
By Edward Morton, Harry Greenbank,
Adrian Ross, music by Sidney Jones
Producer/Director: The Imperial Opera
Co./Edward A. Weil
Cast: Elgie Bowen, Adelaide Manola,
W.L. Romaine, Edward Earle, Harry Girard
and others

05/18–05/23
Dolly Varden
By Stanislaus Stange, music by Julian
Edwards, based on Dickens' *Barnaby Rudge*
Producer/Director: The Imperial Opera Co./
Edward A. Weil

05/25–05/30
A Country Girl
By J.T. Tanner, Paul Rubens and Adrian
Ross/music by Lionel Monckton
Producer/Director: The Imperial Opera Co./
Edward A. Weil

06/01–06/06
A Runaway Girl
By Seymour Hicks, Harry Nicholls/music by
Ivan Caryll and Lionel Monckton
Producer/Director: The Imperial Opera Co./
Edward A. Weil

06/08–06/13
The Geisha
By Owen Hall, music by Sidney Jones
Producer/Director: The Imperial Opera Co./
Edward A. Weil

06/15–06/20
San Toy
By Edward Morton, Harry Greenbank,
Adrian Ross, music by Sidney Jones
Producer/Director: The Imperial Opera Co./
Edward A. Weil

06/22–06/27
The Mikado
By Gilbert and Sullivan
Producer/Director: The Imperial Opera Co./
Edward A. Weil

08/29–09/04
Robin Hood
By Harry B. Smith, music by Reginald de
Koven
Producer/Director: The Imperial Opera Co./
Edward A. Weil

09/05–09/18
Floradora
By Owen Hall, music by Leslie Stuart
Producer/Director: The Imperial Opera Co./
Frank W. Stammers

09/19–09/25
The Circus Girl
By J.T. Tanner and W. Palings, music by
Ivan Caryll and Lionel Monckton
Producer/Director: The Imperial Opera Co./
Frank W. Stammers

09/26–10/02
El Capitan
By Charles Klein, music by John Philip
Sousa
Producer/Director: The Imperial Opera Co./
Frank W. Stammers

10/03–10/09
The Belle of New York
By Hugh Morton, music by Gustave Kerker

Producer/Director: The Imperial Opera Co./
Frank W. Stammers

10/10-10/16
The Wizard of the Nile
By Harry B. Smith, music by Victor Herbert
Producer/Director: The Imperial Opera Co./
Frank W. Stammers

10/17-10/23
The Gay Parisienne
By George Dance, music by Ivan Caryll
Producer/Director: The Imperial Opera Co./
Frank W. Stammers

10/24-10/30
The Wedding Day
By Stanislaus Stange, music by Julian
Edwards
Producer/Director: The Imperial Opera Co./
Frank W. Stammers

10/31-11/06
The Chimes of Normandy
By Robert Planquette
Producer/Director: The Imperial Opera Co./
Frank W. Stammers

"THE CHIMES OF NORMANDY".

11/07-11/13
The Mikado
By Gilbert and Sullivan
Producer/Director: The Imperial Opera Co./
Frank W. Stammers

11/14-11/20
The Bohemian Girl
By Alfred Bunn, music by Michael William
Balfe
Producer/Director: The Imperial Opera Co./
Frank W. Stammers

11/21-11/27
Sergeant Kitty
By A. Baldwin Stone
Producer/Director: The Imperial Opera Co./
Frank W. Stammers

11/28-12/04
Robin Hood
By Harry B. Smith,
music by Reginald de Koven
Producer/Director: The Imperial Opera Co./
Frank W. Stammers

12/05-12/11
Rob Roy
By Harry B. Smith,
music by Reginald de Koven
Producer/Director: The Imperial Opera Co./
Frank W. Stammers

12/12-12/18
Fantana
By Robert B. Smith and Sam Shubert,
music by Raymond Hubbell
Producer/Director: The Imperial Opera
Co./Frank W. Stammers

12/19-12/24
HMS Pinafore
By Gilbert and Sullivan
Producer/Director: The Imperial Opera Co./
Frank W. Stammers

12/19-12/24
Santa Claus
By Harry Rowe Shelley
Producer/Director: The Imperial Opera Co./
Frank W. Stammers

12/25-01/01/09
Jack and the Beanstalk
Producer/Director: The Imperial Opera Co./
Frank W. Stammers

01/04-01/09
Mr. Crewe's Career
By Marion Fairfax, from the novel
by Winston Churchill
Producer/Director: Comstock & Gest
Cast: Tully Marshall, Fritz Williams,
William Lewers, Molly Pearson and others

01/11-01/16
The Warrens of Virginia
By William C. De Mille
Producer/Director: David Belasco
Cast: Mary Pickford, Frank Keenan, Violet
Rand, Charlotte Walker, Richard Story,
Blanche Yurka, William McVay and others

01/18-01/23
The Man and His Mate
By H.R. Durant
Producer/Director: L.L. Sire
Cast: Hilda Spong, Herbert Percy, Mary
Mallon, William Bonnell, Frank Wunderlee
and Adelaide Cummings

01/25-01/30
The Devil
By F. Molnar
Producer/Director: Harrison Grey Fiske
Cast: George Arliss and Grace Elliston

02/01-02/06
The Rejuvenation of Aunt Mary
By Anne Warner
Cast: May Robson, Lila Blow, Nina Savikke,
Harry Cowley and Jack Storey

02/08-02/20
The Prisoner of Zenda (Anthony Hope),
John Glayde's Honor (Alfred Sutro),
Don Caesar's Return (Victor Mapes),
The Crisis (Winston Churchill)
Producer/Director: The Hackett Amusement
Co./James K. Hackett
Cast: James K. Hackett, Fred W. Strong,
Guy Coombs, Fred A. Sullivan, Arthur
Hoops, J.C. Mathews, Beatrice Beckley,
Nina Morris and Alison Skipwith

02/22-02/27
Canton and Company
By J. Hartley Manners and Arthur D. Eddy
Producer: Shuberts
Cast: Laurette Taylor, George Fawcett,
Jane Peytton, A.H. van Buren, Jack Webster
and others

03/01-03/06
Brown of Harvard
By Rida Johnson Young
Producer: Shuberts
Cast: James Young, Catharine Calvert
and others

03/08-03/13
The Blue Mouse
By Clyde Fitch, from the German of
Alexander Engel and Julius Horst
Producer/Director: Clyde Fitch
Cast: Elsa Ryan, Robert Demster,
Birdie Luttrell, Effie Warner and others

03/15-03/20
Salvation Nell
By Edward Sheldon
Producer/Director: Harrison Grey Fiske
Cast: Minnie Maddern Fiske and
Holbrook Blinn

03/22-03/27
Girls
By Clyde Fitch
Producer/Director: Shuberts
Cast: Eleanor Burrill, Ethel Strickland, Elvira Bates and others

03/29-04/03
The Unbroken Road
By Thomas Dickinson
Producer/Director: Harrison Grey Fiske
Cast: Bertha Kalich, Eugene Ormonde, Riley Chamberlain, Florence Arnold, Blanche Weaver and others

04/05-04/10
Mrs. Wiggs of the Cabbage Patch
By Anne Crawford Flexner
and Alice Hegan Rice
Producer/Director: Liebler & Co./
George C. Tyler
Cast: Blanche Chapman, Lottie Alter, Helen Lowel, Florence Busby, Helen Raymond and others

04/12-04/17
The World and His Wife
By Charles F. Nirdlinger
Producer/Director: Felix Isman
Cast: William Faversham, Julie Opp, Olive Oliver, Lionel Belmore and others

04/19-04/24
The Mimic World
By Edgar Smith and Addison Burkhardt, music by Carl Rehman and Seymour Furth
Producer/Director: Shuberts and Lew Fields
Cast: Gertrude Hoffman, Charles King, Elizabeth Brice, Gladys Moore and others

04/26-05/01
Beverly of Graustark
By George Barr McCutcheon
Producer/Director: A.G. Delameter and William Morris/Oscar Eagle
Cast: Jessie Busley, Mrs. Charles G. Craig, Douglas J. Wood, Francis Justice, Horace Vinton and others

05/03-06/05
Lyman Howe Pictures
Motion pictures

06/18-06/19
Uncle Tom's Cabin
By Hector Charlesworth, Douglas Hallam, James P. Haverson and J.A. McNeil
Producer/Director: The Toronto Press Club

06/21-06/26
The Music Master
By Charles Klein

Producer/Director: David Belasco
Cast: David Warfield, Antoinette Perry, William Elliott and others

08/20-09/04
Mr. Hamlet of Broadway
By Edgar Smith and Edward Madden, music by Ben Jerome
Producer/Director: Shuberts
Cast: Eddie Foy

09/06-09/11
The Man from Home
By Booth Tarkington
and Harry Leon Wilson
Producer/Director: Liebler & Co.
Cast: Henry Hall

09/13-09/18
The Wolf
By Eugene Walter
Cast: Carl Anthony

09/20-09/25
The Debtors
By Margaret Mayo
Producer/Director: Allison-Ziegler Co./Joseph W. Herbert
Cast: Digby Bell, Kathleen Clifford and others

09/27-10/02
The Bachelor
By Clyde Fitch
Producer/Director: Shuberts/Clyde Fitch
Cast: Charles Cherry, Percy Lyndall, Ralph Morgan and others

10/04-10/09
The Witching Hour
By Augustus Thomas
Producer/Director: Shuberts
Cast: Howard Gould

10/11-10/16
Foreign Exchange
By Booth Tarkington and Harry L. Wilson
Producer/Director: Liebler & Co.
Cast: Percy Haswell, Ruth Holt Boucicault, E.M. Holland, Vincent Serrano and others

10/18-10/23
The Bridge
By Rupert Hughes
Producer/Director: Harrison Grey Fiske
Cast: Guy Bates Post, Charles Tisdale, Merle Maddern, Emmett C. King, Douglas J. Wood, Alfred Paget and others

10/25-10/30
Septimus
By Philip Littell

Producer/Director: Harrison Grey Fiske
Cast: George Arliss, Emily Stevens and others

11/01-11/06
A Man's World
By Rachel Crothers
Producer/Director: Shuberts
Cast: Mary Mannering, Charles Richman, Master Mark Short and Clara Oaks

11/08-11/13
The Passion Flower
By Brandon Tynan
Producer/Director: Shuberts
Cast: Alla Nazimova, Brandon Tynan, Harry Kolker, Ernest Glendinning and others

11/15-11/20
Going Some
By Rex Beach and Paul Armstrong
Producer/Director: Shuberts
Cast: Walter Jones, Lawrence Wheat and Aubrey Beattie

11/22-11/27
National Grand Opera Co., with Aida, Lucia di Lammermoor, Il Trovatore, La Traviata, Carmen, Rigoletto, Cavalleria Rusticana, I Pagliacci
Producer/Director: L.Raybaut and G. Agelini

11/29-12/04
The Battle
By Cleveland Moffatt
Producer/Director: Liebler & Co.
Cast: Wilton Lackaye, Thomas McGrane and others

12/06-12/08
Billy
By Robert B. Kegerreis
Producer/Director: Shuberts
Cast: Edgar Atchison-Ely, Jane Marbury, Marion Chapman and others

12/09-12/11
The Return of Eve
By Lee Wilson Dodd
Producer/Director: Shuberts
Cast: Bertha Galland

12/13-12/18
The Rose of Algeria
By Glen MacDonough/Victor Herbert
Producer/Director: Lew Fields/Ned Wayburn
Cast: Eugene Cowles, George Leon Moore, Maitland Davies, William Gaston and others

12/20-12/25
The King of Cadonia
By Frederic Lonsdale, Adrian Rose/Jerome Kern and Sydney Jones

Producer/Director: Shuberts
Cast: Marguerite Clark, William Norris,
Clara Palmer, William Danforth, Zelda Sears
and others

12/25-01/01
Jack and the Beanstalk
Producer/Director: The Imperial Opera Co./
Frank W. Stammers
Cast: William Sellery and others

12/27-01/01/10
The Blue Mouse
By Clyde Fitch
Producer/Director: Shuberts
Cast: Mabel Barrison, Harry Conor
and a cast of 23

1910

01/03-01/08
Marcelle
By Frank Pixley/Gustav Luders
Producer/Director: Shuberts
Cast: Louise Gunning, Jess Dandy, Charles
King, Norma Borwn, Florence Rother,
Nellie King and others

01/10-01/12
Deborah of Tod's
By Mrs. Henry de la Pastero
Producer/Director: Maxine Elliott and Co.
Cast: Maxine Elliott, O.B. Clarence,
Irene Kelly, Arthur Byron and others

01/13-01/15
The Inferior Sex
By Frank Stayton
Producer/Director: Maxine Elliott and Co.
Cast: Maxine Elliott, O.B. Clarence,
Irene Kelly, Arthur Byron and others

01/17-01/22
Hammerstein Opera & Manhattan Opera
Comique: Lucia di Lammermoor, Faust,
La Mascotte, Mignon, The Chimes of
Normandy, Carmen
Producer/Director: Arthur Hammerstein

01/24-01/29
The White Sister
By F. Marion Crawford
Producer/Director: Liebler & Co.
Cast: William Farnum, James O'Neill,
Viola Allen and others

01/31-02/05
The Dawn of a Tomorrow
By Frances Hodgson Burnett
Producer/Director: Liebler & Co./Hugh Ford
Cast: Eleanor Robson, Fuller Melish,
William Sauter and others

02/07-02/12
Dick Whittington
Producer/Director: Shuberts
Cast: Frank Byron, Harry Clarke, Louise
Dresser, the Bird Ballet and others

02/14-02/19
Is Matrimony a Failure?
By Leo Ditrichstein
Producer/Director: David Belasco
Cast: Frank Worthing, James Bradbury,
Anne Sutherland, William Norris, Jane
Cowl, Blanche Yurka and others

02/21-02/26
The Belle of Brittany
By Leedhan Bantock, P.J. Barrow, Percy
Greenbank/Howard Talbot and Marie Horn
Producer/Director: Shuberts
Cast: Elsa Ryan, Frank Daniels, Frank
Hushford, Christine Nelson and others

02/28-03/05
The Fighting Hope
By W.J. Hurlbut
Producer/Director: David Belasco
Cast: Blanche Bates, Milton Sills,
John W. Cope, Wedgewood Nowell
and Loretta Jones

03/07-03/12
A Certain Party
By Edward W. Townsend
and Frank Ward O'Malley
Producer/Director: Liebler & Co./Hugh Ford
Cast: Mabel Hite, Mike Donlin, John T.
Kelly, Amy Ames, Viola Knott, Madge
Richardson and Beatrice Moreland

James O'Neill

03/14-03/19
The Beauty Spot
By Joseph W. Herbert/Reginald de Koven
Cast: Jefferson De Angelis, Viola Gillette,
George J. McFarlane, Isabel D'Armond
and others

03/21-03/26
Cameo Kirby
By Booth Tarkington and Harry Leon
Wilson
Producer/Director: Liebler & Co./Hugh Ford
Cast: Dustin Farnum, Eugene O'Rourke,
Gordon Johnstone, Edwin Brandt
and others

03/28-04/02
Havana
By George Grossmith Jr. and Graham
Hill/Leslie Stuart
Producer/Director: Shuberts
Cast: James T. Powers, Percy Ames,
Edith Decker and Erminie Clarke

04/04-04/09
Earl Grey Competition in Drama
Margaret Eaton School of Expression

04/11-04/16
Herod
By Stephen Phillips
Cast: William Faversham

04/18-04/23
One of the Family
By C.T. Dazey
Cast: Muriel Starr and Charles Richman

04/25
Actors' Fund Benefit

04/25-04/30
The Christian
By Hall Caine
Cast: Maude Fealy, James Durkin, John
Drumier, Theodore Marston, Mat Anderson
and others

05/02-05/06
The Passing of the Third Floor Back
By Jerome K. Jerome
Producer/Director: Shad Frost
and Percy Burton
Cast: Johnston Forbes-Robertson, Allen
Thomas, David Powell, Montagu Rutherford,
Kate Carylon, Evelyn Weeden, A.G. Poulton,
Alexande Cassy, Haidee Wright and others

05/09-05/14
The Easiest Way
By Eugene Walter
Producer/Director: David Belasco
Cast: Frances Starr and Joseph Kilgour

05/23-05/28
San Carlo Grand Opera Co.: La Forza del
Destino, Carmen, Il Trovatore, La Bohème,
Lucia di Lammermoor, Cavalleria Rusticana
Conductors: Agide Jacchia and Roberto
Francini

05/30-06/04
Sothern and Marlowe Repertory Co.:
Romeo and Juliet, The Merchant of Venice,
As You Like It, The Taming of the Shrew,
Hamlet
By Wm. Shakespeare
Producer/Director: The Sothern and
Marlowe Repertory Co.
Cast: E.H. Sothern and Julia Marlowe

06/06-06/11
The Marriage of Kitty
By Cosmo Gordon Lennox
Producer/Director: Percy Haswell Stock
Co./Percy Haswell and Allen Fawcett
Cast: Percy Haswell

06/13-06/18
Leah Kleschna
By C.M.S. McClellan
Producer/Director: Percy Haswell Stock
Co./Percy Haswell and Allen Fawcett
Cast: Percy Haswell

06/20-06/25
As You Like It
By Wm. Shakespeare
Producer/Director: Percy Haswell Stock
Co./Percy Haswell and Allen Fawcett
Cast: Percy Haswell

06/27-07/02
The Blue Mouse
By Clyde Fitch
Producer/Director: Percy Haswell Stock
Co./Percy Haswell and Allen Fawcett
Cast: Percy Haswell

07/04-07/09
Her Own Way
By Clyde Fitch
Producer/Director: Percy Haswell Stock
Co./Percy Haswell and Allen Fawcett
Cast: Percy Haswell

07/11-07/16
The Fighter
By Hilliard Booth
Producer/Director: Percy Haswell Stock
Co./Percy Haswell and Allen Fawcett
Cast: Percy Haswell and George Fawcett

07/18-07/23
A Night Off
Producer/Director: Percy Haswell Stock
Co./Percy Haswell and Allen Fawcett
Cast: Percy Haswell

07/25-07/30
School
By Tom Robertson
Producer/Director: Percy Haswell Stock
Co./Percy Haswell and Allen Fawcett
Cast: Percy Haswell

08/01-08/06
The Light Above
By Edwin Milton Boyle
Producer/Director: Percy Haswell Stock
Co./Percy Haswell and Allen Fawcett
Cast: Percy Haswell

08/08-08/13
The Grasshopper
By Allen Fawcett
Producer/Director: Percy Haswell Stock
Co./Percy Haswell and Allen Fawcett
Cast: Percy Haswell

08/15-08/20
Divorçons
By Victorien Sardou
Producer/Director: Percy Haswell Stock
Co./Percy Haswell and Allen Fawcett
Cast: Percy Haswell

08/22-08/27
Arabian Nights
By Sidney Grundy
Producer/Director: Percy Haswell Stock
Co./Percy Haswell and Allen Fawcett
Cast: Percy Haswell

08/28-09/03
Mother
By Jules Eckert Goodman
Producer/Director: William S. Brady
Cast: Emma Dunn, Frederick Perry, Minette
Barret, Marion Chapman and others

09/05-09/10
The Aborn English Grand Opera Co.:
Carmen, Lucia di Lammermoor, The
Bohemian Girl, Il Trovatore, Faust
Producer/Director: Milton and
Sargent Aborn

09/12-09/17
The Lottery Man
By Rida Johnson Young
Producer/Director: Shuberts
Cast: Cyril Scott, Helen Lowell and others

09/19-09/24
The Nigger
By Edward Sheldon
Producer/Director: Shuberts and
William A. Brady
Cast: William Cullington, Maud Durand,
Guy Bates Post, J.M. Colville, Florence
Rockwell and others

09/26-10/01
The Passing of the Third Floor Back
By Jerome K. Jerome
Producer/Director:
Shad Frost and Percy Burton
Cast: Johnston Forbes-Robertson and others

10/03-10/08
The Naked Truth
By George Poston and W.B. Maxwell
Producer/Director: William A. Brady
Cast: Henry E. Dixie and Herbert Standing

10/10-10/15
The Midnight Sons
By Glen McDonough/Raymond Hubbell
Producer/Director: Lew Fields/Ned Wayburn
Cast: Theodore Burns, Kitty Francis,
the English Pony Ballet and others

10/17-10/22
Mr. Preedy and the Countess
By R.C. Carton
Producer/Director:
Shuberts and Daniel V. Arthur
Cast: Lynn Fontanne, Arthur B. Murray
and others

10/24-10/29
The Yankee Girl
By George Hobart/Silvio Hein
Producer/Director: Lew Fields
and Frederick McKay
Cast: Blanche Ring, Harry Gilfoil and others

10/31-11/05
New Theatre Co. of New York:
The Thunderbolt (Arthur Wing Pinero),
The Merry Wives of Windsor
Producer/Director: The New Theatre
Co./Winthrop Ames and George Foster Platt
Cast: Louis Calvert, Edith Wynn Matthison,
Rose Coghlan, Leah Bateman-Hunter
and others

11/07-11/12
When All Has Been Said
By Bayard Veiller
Producer/Director: Liebler & Co.
Cast: Emily Stevens, Eugene Ormonde,
Thomas Tobin and others

11/14-11/19
Up and Down Broadway
By Edgar Smith, William Jerome,
Jean Schwartz
Producer/Director: Shuberts/William Wilson
Cast: Eddie Foy, Emma Carus and
Barney Bernard

11/21-11/26
The Merry Widow
By Franz Lehar/Victor Leon, Leo Stein
Producer/Director: H.W. Savage
Cast: Charles Meakins and Mabel Wilber

11/28-12/03
A Bridal Trip
By Harry B. Smith/Robert Planquette
Producer/Director:
The Grace van Studdiford Opera Co.
Cast: Grace van Studdiford and
Maude Odell

12/05-12/10
The Little Damozel
By Monkton Hoffe
Producer/Director:
Henry W. Savage/Edward Fitzgerald
Cast: Cyril Keightly, George Graham,
Henry Wenman, Henry Vogel and others

12/12-12/17
The Bohemian Girl
By Alfred Bunn/Michael W. Balfe
Producer/Director:
Aborn English Grand Opera Co.
Cast: Blanche Duffield, Charles E.
Gallagher, Bertha Shaley and
James Stevens

12/26-12/31
The Dawn of a Tomorrow
By Frances Hodgson Burnett
Producer/Director: Liebler & Co.
Cast: Gertrude Elliott, Scott Gatty
and Fuller Melish

1911

01/02-01/07
Judith Zaraine
By C.M.S. McClellan
Producer/Director: Liebler & Co.
Cast: Lena Ashwell, Charles Waldron,
John E. Kellerd, Gordon Johnstone,
Edward Lamgton and others

01/09-01/14
Sauce for the Goose
By Geraldine Bonner and Hutchison Boyd
Producer/Director: William A. Brady
Cast: Grace George, Herbert Perry,
Frederick Perry and Keith Wakeman

01/16-01/21
Tillie's Nightmare
By Edgar Smith
Producer/Director: Lew Fields
Cast: Marie Dressler and a cast of 79

Marie Dressler

01/23-01/28
The Fourth Estate
By Joseph Medill Patterson
and Harriet Ford
Producer/Director: Liebler & Co.
Cast: Joseph Woodburn, Charles Balsar,
George Thompson, Selene Johnson and
Harriet Ross

01/30-02/04
The Edward Terry Repertory Co.: Sweet
Lavender (Pinero), The Magistrate (Pinero),
The Toymaker of Nurenberg (Austin
Strong), Liberty Hall (R.C. Carton), Bardell

vs. Pickwick, Flanders' Widow (Sydney
Valentine and M-E. Francis)
Producer/Director: The Edward Terry
Repertory Co.
Cast: Edward Terry and others

02/06-02/11
The Jolly Bachelors
By Glen MacDonaugh/Raymond Hubbell
Producer/Director: Lew Fields/Ned Wayburn
Cast: Stella Mayhew, Nat Fields, Lucy
Weston, Al Leech, Billie Taylor and others

02/13-02/18
The Encounter
By Pierre Berton
Producer/Director: Margaret Illington
Productions
Cast: Margaret Illington, Edward R.
Mawson, Sybil Hammersley and others

02/20-02/25
The New Prince of Pilsen
By Frank Pixley/Gustav Luders
Producer/Director: H.W. Savage/
George W. Marion
Cast: Wallace Beery, Frances Cameron
and Jess Dandy

02/27-03/04
Daddy Dufard
By Albert Chevalier and Lechmere Worrall
Producer/Director: Liebler & Co.
Cast: Albert Chevalier, Leslie Kenyon,
Violet Henning, Mary E. Barker and others

03/06-03/11
The Melting Pot
By Israel Zangwill
Producer/Director: Liebler & Co.
Cast: Walker Whiteside, Florence Fisher,
Louise Muldener, Hubert Wilke, Alice May,
Will D. Corbett and others

03/13-03/18
Two Women
By Rupert Hughes
Producer/Director: John Cort
Cast: Leslie Carter, E.J. Ratcliffe, Harrison
Hunter, Harry G. Carlton, Helen Tracy
and others

03/20-03/25
Madame Butterfly
By David Belasco/G. Puccini
Producer/Director: Aborn English Opera
Co., Milton and Sargent Aborn
Cast: Dora de Fillippe and Rose Vincent
(Cio-Cio San) and George Tennery
(Pinkerton)

03/27-04/01
The Fawn
By Edward Knoblauch
Cast: William Faversham, Julie Opp, Daisy
Bellmore, Elsie Oldham, Arthur Elliott
and others

04/03-04/08
The Kreutzer Sonata
By Jacob Gordin, after Tolstoy
Producer/Director: Shuberts
Cast: Bertha Kalich, Ida Goldsmith,
Lilian Kalich, Jennie Reiffarth, Kate Jepsom,
Frank Losee, Lyster Chambers and others

04/10-04/22
The Chocolate Soldier
By Stanislaus Stange/Oscar Strauss, based
on Shaw's *Arms and the Man*
Producer/Director: F.C. Whitney Opera Co.
Cast: Alice Yorke, Fritzi Von Busing,
Forrest Huff, Frances Kennedy, Fred Mace
and others

04/24-04/29
Green Stockings
By A.E.W. Mason and George Fleming
Producer/Director: Liebler & Co.
Cast: Margaret Anglin, H. Reeves Smith,
Maude Granger, Ruth Rose, Crosby Little,
Ruth Holt Boucicault, Henry Hull and others

05/01-05/06
The Kissing Girl
By Stanislaus Stange
Producer/Director: John P. Slocum and the
New Viennese Comic Opera/Stanislaus
Stange
Cast: Texas Guinan, Venita Fitzhugh,
"Mlle Vanity," Louis London and others

Texas Guinan

05/08-05/10
The Man Who Stood Still
By Jules Eckert Goodman
Cast: Louis Mann, Emily Ann Wellman
and others

05/11-05/13
The Cheater
By Louis Mann
Cast: Louis Mann, Emily Ann Wellman
and others

05/15-06/03
Lyman H. Howe Travel Festival
Motion pictures

06/05-06/10
The Cottage in the Air
By Edward Knoblauch
Producer/Director: Percy Haswell Stock Co.
Cast: Percy Haswell, Fred L. Tiden, Thomas
V. Emory, Angela Ogden, Booth Chaplin
and others

06/12-06/17
An American Widow
By Kellett Chambers
Producer/Director: Percy Haswell Stock Co.
Cast: Percy Haswell and others

06/19-06/24
Old Heidelberg
By Wilhelm Meyer-Foerster
Producer/Director: Percy Haswell Stock Co
Cast: Percy Haswell and others

06/26-07/01
Because She Loved Him So
By William Gillette
Producer/Director: Percy Haswell Stock Co.
Cast: Percy Haswell and others

07/03-07/08
The Great Unknown
By Augustin Daly
Producer/Director: Percy Haswell Stock Co.
Cast: Percy Haswell and others

07/10-07/15
Mrs. Temple's Telegram
By Frank Wyatt and William Morris
Producer/Director: Percy Haswell Stock Co.
Cast: Percy Haswell and others

07/17-07/22
A Woman's Way (Divorçons)
By Thompson Buchanan, adapted from
V. Sardou
Producer/Director: Percy Haswell Stock Co.
Cast: Percy Haswell and others
Guest: Lois Howell

07/24-07/29
The Man in the Box
By Harold McGrath
Producer/Director: Percy Haswell Stock Co.
Cast: Percy Haswell and others
Guest: Richard Bartholomew

07/31-08/05
Modern Marriage
By Harrison Rhodes
Producer/Director: Percy Haswell Stock Co.
Cast: Percy Haswell and others

08/07-08/12
The Three of Us
By Rachel Crothers
Producer/Director: Percy Haswell Stock Co.
Cast: Percy Haswell and others

08/14-08/19
Miss Hobbs
By Jerome K. Jerome
Producer/Director: Percy Haswell Stock Co.
Cast: Percy Haswell and others

08/21-09/02
Lyman H. Howe Pictures
Motion pictures

09/04-09/09
He Came from Milwaukee
By Mark Swan, Edward Madden/
Louis Hirsch, William Jerome, Melville Ellis
Producer/Director: Shuberts/Sydney Ellison
Cast: Sam Bernard, Nicholas Judels, George
Baldwin, Billy Gaston, Louise Mink, Anna
Wheaton and others

09/11-09/16
Overnight
By Philip Bartholmae
Producer/Director: William A. Brady
Cast: Thomas Emory, Sam Hardy,
Madge Kennedy and others

09/18-09/23
Rebellion
By Joseph Medill Patterson
Producer/Director: Liebler & Co.
Cast: Gertrude Elliott, George Farren,
George le Guerre, Fuller Melish and others

09/25-09/30
The Earl of Pawtucket
By Augustus Thomas
Producer/Director: John Cort
Cast: Lawrence D'Orsay, Katherine Emmet,
Henry J. Carvill and others

10/02-10/07
Aborn English Opera Co.: Thaïs,
Il Trovatore, Lucia di Lammermoor, Martha,
Tales of Hoffman
Producer/Director: Milton and Sargent Aborn
Cast: cast of 100

10/09-10/14
Robert B. Mantell Repertory Co.: Othello,
Hamlet, King Lear, The Merchant of Venice,
Macbeth, Julius Caesar, Richelieu

Producer/Director: Robert B. Mantell
Repertory Co.
Cast: Robert Bruce Mantell with Fritz
Leiber, John Crawley, John Burke,
L'Estrange Millman, Guy Lindsley,
Genevieve Hamper, Agnes Elliott Scott
and others

10/16-10/21
Pomander Walk
By Louis N. Parker
Producer/Director: Liebler & Co.
Cast: George Giddens, Lennox Paule,
Dorothy Parker, Cynthia Brooke, Maud
Milton, Reginald Dance, Marie Burke and
others

10/23-10/28
With Edged Tools
By Henry Seton Merriman
Producer/Director: Beck and Armitage
Cast: Hamilton Deane, Stanley Bedwell,
Marguerite Cellier, Richard Hicks
and others

10/30-11/04
Just to Get Married
By Cecily Hamilton
Producer/Director: William A. Brady
Cast: Grace George, F. Owen Baxter,
Lyn Harding, Emily Fitzroy, Jane Corcoran,
Mona Morgan and others

11/06-11/11
The Lady of Coventry
By Louis N. Parker
Producer/Director: Liebler & Co.
Cast: Viola Allen, Charles Waldron,
Henry Stanford and others

11/13-11/18
The Bohemian Girl
By Alfred Bunn/Michael W. Balfe
Producer/Director:
Milton and Sargent Aborn
Cast: Vera Allen, Helen Campbell, Herbert
Waterous, Jayne Herbert, Harold Blake,
Joseph Florian and others, in a cast of 150,
plus 20 horses

11/20-11/22
The Gamblers
By Charles Klein
Producer/Director: Authors' Producing
Co./Charles Klein
Cast: Jane Cowl, Charles Burbridge,
Orme Caldara, George Backus and others

11/23-11/25
The Piper
By Josephine Preston Peabody

Producer/Director: The New Theatre
Co./George Foster
Cast: Edith Wynn Matthison, William
Raymond, Albert Easdale, Warren Conlan
and others

11/27-12/02
HMS Pinafore
By Gilbert and Sullivan
Producer/Director:
Shuberts/Clarence Rogerson
Cast: De Wolf Hopper, Viola Gillette,
Eugene Cowls, George J. MacFarlane
and Alice Brady

De Wolf Hopper

12/04-12/09
Madame X
By Alexandre Bisson
Producer/Director: Henry W. Savage
Cast: Adeline Dunlap, Robert Paton Gibbs
and others

12/11-12/16
The Balkan Princess
By Paul Rubens
Producer/Director: Shuberts
Cast: Louise Gunning, Harold Crane
and a cast of 70

12/18-12/23
The Chocolate Soldier
By Stanislaus Stange/Oscar Strauss,
based on Shaw's *Arms and the Man*
Producer/Director: Whitney Opera Co.
Cast: Alice Yorke, Mildred Rogers, Juanita
Fletcher, Charles Bowers and others

12/25-12/30
The Opera Ball
By Sydney Rosenfeld/Richard Henberger
Producer/Director: Daniel V. Arthur
Cast: Marie Cahill, Harry Conor and others

1912

01/01-01/06
Tillie's Nightmare
By Edgar Smith
Producer/Director: Lew Fields
Cast: Marie Dressler, Eleanor Kent, Ethel
Fairbanks, W. de Grasse, May Howard,
Louise Nairn, George Gorman and others

01/08-01/20
The Blue Bird
By M. Maeterlinck
Producer/Director: Liebler & Co.
Cast: Burford Hampden (Tyltyl),
Ethel Downie (Mytyl) and others

01/22-01/27
Ballets Russes
Producer/Director: Comstock
& Gest/Theodore Kosloff
Cast: Gertrude Hoffman and a cast of 150

01/29-02/03
Excuse Me
By Rupert Hughes
Producer/Director: H.W. Savage
Cast: George W. Day, James Lacaye,
Geraldine O'Brien and others

02/05-02/10
Night Birds (Die Fledermaus)
By Johann Strauss
Producer/Director: Shuberts
Cast: Fritzi Scheff, George Anderson,
John E. Hazzard and a cast of 150

02/12-02/24
The Montreal Opera Co. Tosca, Faust,
La Bohème, Louise, Mme Butterfly,
Barber of Seville, Manon, Carmen,
Rigoletto, Mignon, Le Jongleur de Notre
Dame, Romeo et Juliette
Producer/Director:
Frank Meighan/Albert Clerk-Jeannotte

02/26-03/02
The Never Homes
By Glen MacDonough, Ray Goetz/
Baldwin Sloane
Producer/Director: Lew Fields
Cast: George W. Monroe, Helen Hayes,
Jess Dandy and a chorus of 60

03/04-03/09
Pomander Walk
By Louis N. Parker
Producer/Director: Liebler & Co.
Cast: George Giddens, Lennox Paule
and others

03/11-03/16
The Wedding Trip
By Fred de Gresac, Harry B. Smith/
Reginald de Koven
Producer/Director: Shuberts
Cast: Fritzi Von Busing, Edward Martinel
and others

03/18-03/23
Bunty Pulls the Strings
By Graham Moffat
Producer/Director: Shuberts
Cast: Ethelbert Hayes, Mollie McIntyre
and William Lennox

03/25-03/30
Hanky Panky
By Edgar Smith/E. Ray Goetz
and A. Baldwin Stone
Producer/Director: Lew Fields
Cast: Max Rogers, Bobby Norh,
Flora Parker and others

04/01-04/06
The Flirting Princess
By Will Hough, Frank Adams/
Joseph E. Howard, Harold Orlob
Producer/Director: Mort Singer
Cast: Harry Bulger and Helen Darling

04/08-04/13
Bunty Pulls the Strings
By Graham Moffat
Producer/Director: Shuberts
Cast: Ethelbert Hayes, Mollie McIntyre
and William Lennox

04/15-04/20
Baby Mine
By Margaret Mayo
Producer: William A. Brady
Cast: Marguerite Clark, Ernest Glendinning,
Agnes De Lane and Earle Mitchell

04/22-04/27
The Million
By George Beer and Marcel Guillemand
Producer/Director: Henry W. Savage
Cast: Taylor Holmes, Paul Kerr, Irene
Fenwick, Eulalie Jenson and others

04/29-05/04
Every Woman
By Walter Browne/G.W. Chadwick
Producer/Director: Henry W. Savage
Cast: Jane Oaker, Frederick Warde,
Marie Wainwright and a cast of 160

05/06-05/18
The Delhi Durbar
By Charles Urban
Colour motion picture

05/20-05/25
Lady Frederick
By W. Somerset Maugham
Producer/Director: Percy Haswell Stock Co.
Cast: Percy Haswell, Angela Ogden, Earle
Browne, Regan Hughston, Sumner Garde,
Charles Kennedy and James T. Galloway

05/27-06/01
The Jilt
By Dion Boucicault
Producer/Director: Percy Haswell Stock Co.
Cast: Percy Haswell and others

06/03-06/08
The Road to Yesterday
By Beulah Dix and Mrs. Greenleaf
Sutherland
Producer/Director: Percy Haswell Stock Co.
Cast: Percy Haswell and others

06/10-06/12
The Sothern and Marlowe Rep Co.:
Hamlet, Taming of the Shrew,
Romeo and Juliet, The Merchant of Venice
By Wm. Shakespeare
Producer/Director: Sothern and Marlowe
Repertory Co.
Cast: E.H. Sothern, Lenore Chippendale,
Rowland Buckstone, Frederick Lewis,
Sydney Mather and others

06/13-06/15
A Night Off
By Augustin Daly
Producer/Director: Percy Haswell Stock Co.
Cast: Percy Haswell and others

06/17-06/22
Love Watches
By Gladys Unger
Producer/Director: Percy Haswell Stock Co.
Cast: Percy Haswell and others

06/24-06/29
The Liars
By Henry Arthur Jones
Producer/Director: Percy Haswell Stock Co.
Cast: Percy Haswell and others

07/01-07/06
My Friend from India
By H.A. Du Souchet
Producer/Director: Percy Haswell Stock Co.
Cast: Percy Haswell and others

07/08-07/13
Are You a Mason?
By Leo Ditrichstein
Producer/Director: Percy Haswell Stock Co.
Cast: Percy Haswell and others

07/15-07/20
At the Whitehorse Tavern
By Hans Muller and Erik Charell
Producer/Director: Percy Haswell Stock Co.
Cast: Percy Haswell and others

07/22-07/27
Green Stockings
By A.E.W. Mason and George Fleming
Producer/Director: Percy Haswell Stock Co.
Cast: Percy Haswell and others

07/29-08/03
Dorothy Vernon of Haddon Hall
By Paul Kester
Producer/Director: Percy Haswell Stock Co.
Cast: Percy Haswell and others

08/05-08/10
All the Comforts of Home
By William Gillette
Producer/Director: Percy Haswell Stock Co.
Cast: Percy Haswell and others

08/12-08/17
The Country Mouse
By Arthur Law
Producer/Director: Percy Haswell Stock Co.
Cast: Percy Haswell and others

08/19-08/24
Making a Man of Him
Producer/Director: Percy Haswell Stock Co.
Cast: Percy Haswell and others

08/26-08/31
Master Will's Players
By Allen Fawcett
Producer/Director: Percy Haswell Stock Co.
Cast: Percy Haswell and others

08/26-08/31
The Marriage of Kitty
By Cosmo Gordon-Lennox
Producer/Director: Percy Haswell Stock Co.
Cast: Percy Haswell and others

09/02-09/07
The Kiss Waltz
By Edgar Smith/C.M. Ziehrev
Producer/Director: Valeska Suratt Operetta
Co./J.C. Huffman
Cast: Valeska Suratt, George Baldwin,
Ted Loraine and others

09/09-09/14
Overnight
By Philip Bartholmae
Producer/Director: William A. Brady
Cast: Thomas Emory, Clyde Hunnewell
and Ada Stirling

09/16-09/21
The Aborn English Grand Opera Co.: Tales
of Hoffman, Mme Butterfly, La Bohème,
Carmen, Lucia di Lammermoor, Lohengrin,
Hansel and Gretel, Il Trovatore
Producer/Director: Milton and
Sargent Aborn

09/23-09/28
Bunty Pulls the Strings
By Graham Moffat
Producer/Director: Shuberts
Cast: Molly Pearson, Edmund Beresford,
Vera Pole, Ethelbert Hayes and others

09/30-10/05
Bought and Paid For
By George Broadhurst
Producer/Director: William A. Brady
Cast: Frank Mills, William Harrigan
and others

10/07-10/12
Julius Caesar
By Wm. Shakespeare
Producer/Director: William Faversham
Cast: William Faversham (Antony), Tyrone
Power (Brutus), Fuller Melish (Caesar),
Kenneth Hunter (Octavius), Frank Keenan
(Cassius) and others

10/14-10/19
Excuse Me
By Rupert Hughes
Producer/Director: Henry W. Savage
Cast: Joseph Yanner, Thomas J. McMahon,
Edward Begley, Geraldine O'Brien, Vivian
Blackburn and others

10/21-10/26
The Merry Widow
By Franz Lehar/Victor Leon and Leo Stein
Producer/Director: Henry W. Savage
Cast: Charles Meakins, Mabel Wilber,
Vernon Dalhart and others

10/28-11/02
Everywoman
By Walter Browne
Producer/Director: Henry W. Savage
Cast: H. Cooper-Cliffe, Deirdre Doyle
and others

11/04-11/09
Miss Princess
By Frank Mandel, Will B.
Johnstone/Alexander Johnstone
Producer/Director: John Cort
Cast: Lisa Abarbanell, Ben Hendricks,
Isabel Francis, Charles P. Morrison,
Henrietta Lee and many others

11/11-11/16
Two Little Brides
By Arthur Anderson, James T. Powers,
Harold Atteridge/Gustav Kerker
Producer/Director: Shuberts
Cast: James T. Powers, Roy Purviance,
Charles H. Bowers, Gilbert Clayton
and many others

11/18-11/23
Carnival
By Compton MacKenzie
Producer/Director: William A. Brady
Cast: Compton MacKenzie,
Donald MacLaren, Frank Compton,
John Glendinning and many others

11/25-11/30
The Chimes of Normandy
By H.B. Farnie, Robert Reece,
Robert Planquette
Producer/Director: Aborn Opera
Comique Co.
Cast: William Woolf, Carrick Major
and others

12/02-12/07
The Bohemian Girl
By Alfred Bunn/Michael William Balfe
Producer/Director: The Aborn Opera
Comique Co.
Cast: James Stevens, Roy Pilcher,
Joseph Florian and others

12/09-12/14
Kindling
By Charles Kenyon
Producer/Director: Edward J. Bowes
Cast: Margaret Illington, Byron Beasley,
Ida Lewis, Florence Robinson and others

12/16-12/21
The Passing Show of 1912
By George Bronson-Howard,
Harold Atteridge/Louis A. Hirsch
Producer/Director: Shuberts and The Winter
Garden Co./Ned Wayburn
Cast: Texas Guinan, Louise Brunell, Trixie
Friganza, Loretta Healy and others

12/23-12/28
Little Women
By Marian de Forest
Producer/Director: William A. Brady/
Jesse Bonstelle and Bertram Harrison
Cast: Douglas Patterson, Jean Adair,
James Salisbury, Lola Donwin, Edna Walter,
Catherine Calhoun and others

12/30-01/04/13
A Marriage of Convenience
By Alexandre Dumas,
adapted by Sydney Grundy
Producer/Director: Lewis Waller
Cast: Reginald Dane, Lewis Waller
and others

1913

01/06-01/11
The Whirl of Society
By Harold Atteridge/Louis A.
Hirsch/Harrison Rhodes
Producer/Director: The Winter Garden
Company and Shuberts
Cast: Al Jolson, Fanny Brice, Gaby Deslys,
Lawrence D'Orsay and others

01/13-01/18
Ready Money
By James Montgomery
Producer/Director:
H.H. Frazee/Robert Milton
Cast: Hans Robert, Everett Butterfield,
Carl Harbaugh, Henry Miller Jr. and others

01/20-01/25
Robert B. Mantell Repertory Co.: Hamlet,
Macbeth, Richelieu, The Merchant of
Venice, Othello, King Lear, Richard III

ROBERT B. MANTELL
H. W. HANLEY, MANAGER
HAMLET

Producer/Director: William A. Brady
Cast: Robert Bruce Mantell with Allen
Thomas, Brigham Royce, Fritz Leiber,
Florence Rockwell, Genevieve Reynolds
and others

01/27-02/01
The Merry Countess
By Gladys Unger, Arthur Anderson/
Johann Strauss
Producer/Director: Shuberts/Melvlle Ellis
Cast: Fritzi Von Busing, Rex Fuehrer,
Maurice Farkoa, Roszika Dolly and others

02/03-02/08
The Mikado
By Gilbert and Sullivan
Producer/Director: Gilbert and Sullivan
Repertory Co., Shuberts
Cast: De Wolf Hopper with Blanche
Duffield, George J. MacFarlane, Eugene
Cowles, Kate Condon and Arthur Aldridge

02/10-03/01
Montreal Opera Co.: Il Trovatore, Romeo et
Juliette, Herodiade, La Bohème, Thaïs, Mme
Butterfly, Carmen, Barber of Seville, Tales
of Hoffman, Aida, Rigoletto, Lakme, Faust,
Le Chemineau, Louise, Tosca
Producer/Director: The Montreal Opera Co.

03/03-03/08
The Bird of Paradise
By Richard Walton Tully
Producer/Director:
Oliver Morosco/Richard Walton Tully
Cast: Pearl Rose, Lewis S. Stone, Guy Bates
Post, Margaret Langham and others

03/10-03/15
Top o'the Morning
By Anne Caldwell
Producer/Director:
Henry W. Savage/George Marion
Cast: Louise Farnum, Alice Claire Elliott,
T.Y. Daniell and others

03/17-03/22
Value Received
By Augustus MacHugh
Producer/Director:
William A. Brady/Cyril Scott
Cast: Marion Graham, Frances Carson,
Frank Patton and others

03/24-03/29
The Red Petticoat
Rida Johnson Young, Paul West/
Jerome Kern
Producer/Director: Shuberts

Cast: Helen Lowell, Louise Mink, Grace
Field, Frances Kennedy and others

03/31-04/05
The Blue Bird
By M. Maeterlinck
Producer/Director: Liebler & Co.
Cast: Buford Hampden, Charles Hampden,
Alice Butler, Editha Kelly and others

04/07
David Garrick
By Tom Robertson
Producer/Director:
Eaton Dramatic Club/E.A. Dalton

04/09-04/12
Twentieth Century Minstrels
Producer/Director: Lew Dockstader,
George Primrose
Cast: Lew Dockstader, George Primrose
and others

04/15-04/19
The Yeoman of the Guard
By Gilbert and Sullivan
Producer/Director: Canadian Conservatory
of Music

04/21-04/26
Sothern and Marlowe Repertory Co.:
Hamlet, As You Like It, The Merchant
of Venice, Twelfth Night, Much Ado About
Nothing, Romeo and Juliet, The Taming
of the Shrew
By Wm. Shakespeare
Producer/Director:
Sothern and Marlowe Repertory Co.
Cast: E.H. Sothern, Julia Marlowe, William
Harris, Milano Tilden, Frederick Lewis, John
S. O'Brien, Helen Singer, Lenore
Chippendale and others

04/28-05/03
Little Boy Blue
By A.E. Thomas, Edward A. Paulton/
Paul Rubens, Henry Bereny
Producer/Director: Henry W. Savage
Cast: Otis Harlan, Kathleen Clifford,
Maude Odell and others

05/05-05/10
Anna Russell's Old English Comedy Co.:
She Stoops to Conquer, The Rivals
By Goldsmith and Sheridan
Producer/Director: Anna Russell
Cast: Anna Russell, Thomas Fallon, Oswald
Yorke, George Giddens, Littledale Power
and others

05/12-05/17
The Road to Happiness
By Lawrence Whitman
Producer/Director: Shuberts
Cast: William Hodge, Wlliam McEvay
and Ida Vernon

05/19-05/24
Broadway to Paris
By George Bronson-Howard, Harold
Atteridge/Max Hoffman
Producer/Director:
Morris Gest/Ned Wayburn
Cast: Milbury Ryder, Ethel Hopkins, George
Austin Moore, Walter Haynes and others

05/26-05/31
Mrs. Dot
By Somerset Maugham
Producer/Director: Percy Haswell Stock Co.
Cast: Percy Haswell, Robert Cain, DeForest
F. Dawley, Effingham Pinto, Edward Hayes,
Walter Renfort, James T. Galloway,
Alexander Leftwich, James Randall, Florence
Short, Edna Hibbard and Julia Hanchett

06/02-06/07
A Butterfly on the Wheel
By Edward Hemmerde and Frances Neilson
Producer/Director: Percy Haswell Stock Co.
Cast: Percy Haswell and others

06/09-06/14
The Amazons
By Arthur Wing Pinero
Producer/Director: Percy Haswell Stock Co.
Cast: Percy Haswell and others

06/16-06/21
Sham
By Elmer Harris and Geraldine Bonner
Producer/Director: Percy Haswell Stock Co.
Cast: Percy Haswell and others

06/23-06/28
Green Stockings
By A.E.W. Mason
Producer/Director: Percy Haswell Stock Co.
Cast: Percy Haswell and others

06/30-07/05
The Glad Eye
By José Levy
Producer/Director: Percy Haswell Stock Co.
Cast: Percy Haswell and others

07/07-07/12
Divorçons
By Victorien Sardou
Producer/Director: Percy Haswell Stock Co.
Cast: Percy Haswell and others

07/14-07/26
Forty Minutes from Broadway
By George M. Cohan
Producer/Director: Percy Haswell Stock Co.
Cast: Percy Haswell and others

07/28-08/02
The Dawn of a Tomorrow
By Frances Hodgson Burnett
Producer/Director: Percy Haswell Stock Co.
Cast: Percy Haswell and others

08/04-08/09
Mrs. Leffingwell's Boots
By Augustus Thomas
Producer/Director: Percy Haswell Stock Co.
Cast: Percy Haswell and others

08/11-08/16
All-of-a-Sudden Peggy
By Ernest Denny
Producer/Director: Percy Haswell Stock Co.
Cast: Percy Haswell and others

08/18-08/23
The Runaway
By Michael Morton
Producer/Director: Percy Haswell Stock Co.
Cast: Percy Haswell and others

08/25-08/30
Sauce for the Goose
By Geraldine Bonner and Hutchison Boyd
Producer/Director: Percy Haswell Stock Co.
Cast: Percy Haswell and others

09/01-09/06
The Ham Tree
By George V. Hobart, William Jerome/Jean
Schwartz
Producer/Director: John Cort/Ned Wayburn
Cast: Paul La Croix, Jane Burby, Lulu Wells,
Lawrence Phillips and others, including
Ebenezer, the Minstrel Mule

09/08-09/13
The Blindness of Virtue
By Cosmo Hamilton
Producer/Director: The Company
of English Players/Cosmo Hamilton
Cast: Leo G. Carroll, Marguerite Collier
and others

09/15-09/20
Peg O'My Heart
By J. Hartley Manners

Producer/Director: Oliver Morosco
Cast: Elsa Ryan, Fanny Addison Putt,
Gilbert Douglas and others

09/22-09/27
Snow White and the Seven Dwarfs
By Jessie Braham White
Producer/Director: Winthrop Ames
Cast: Juliette Day, Sol Soloman, Roy
Cochrane, Olive Temple, Ada Deaves
and others

09/29-10/04
Oh, I Say
By Sydney Blow, Douglas Howe/
Jerome Kern
Producer/Director: Shuberts
Cast: Alice Yorke, Burt Clark, Walter Jones,
Joseph Phillips and others

10/06-10/11
The Firefly
By Otto Hauerbach/Rudolph Friml
Producer/Director: Arthur Hammerstein
Cast: Emme Trentini, William Woolf,
Roy Atwell and others

10/13-10/18
Within the Law
By Bayard Veiller
Producer/Director: Arch Selwyn:
The American Play Co.
Cast: Catherine Tower, DeWitt Jennings
and others

10/20-10/25
The Passing Show of 1912
By George Bronson-Howard,
Harold Atteridge/Louis A. Hirsch
Producer/Director: Shuberts,
The Winter Garden Co.
Cast: Trixie Friganza, Winona Wilkins,
George Moon, Gertrude Taylor
and many others

10/27-11/08
The Whip
By Cecil Raleigh and Henry Hamilton
Producer/Director: William A. Brady
and London Drury Lane Producing Co.
Cast: Hilda Honiss, Sara Raleigh, Alice
Esdin, Ethelbert Hayes, Eric Mayne, John L.
Shine, Herbert Sleeth and Myrtle Anson

11/10-11/15
Mariette
By Maurice Volny
Producer/Director: Comstock & Gest
Cast: Evelyn Nesbit Thaw, Jack Clifford,
Enrico Zanfretta, Arnaud Bros., Peppino,
Fouchere, Bernard and Weston, and the
Courtenay Sisters

11/17-11/22
Within the Law
By Bayard Veiller
Producer/Director:
Arch Selwyn/The American Play Co.
Cast: Marion Morton, James Lenhart,
George Leffingwell and others

11/24-11/29
Le Visiteur
By George Haud
Producer/Director: Comstock & Gest
Cast: Madame Polaire, M.E. Becman
and Mlle Clasis

11/24-11/29
International Vaudeville
Producer/Director: Comstock & Gest

12/01-12/06
Fanny's First Play
By G.B. Shaw
Producer/Director:
Shuberts/Granville Barker
Cast: Charles H. Croker-King, Claude Rains,
George Carr, Lewis Sealy and others

12/08-12/13
Honeymoon Express
By Jean Schwartz
Producer/Director:
Shuberts and The Winter Garden Co.
Cast: Al Jolson, Ray Samuels, Anna
Wheaton, Melville Ellis, Ada Lewis
and others

12/15-12/20
The Glad Eye
By José Levy
Producer/Director: Louis Meyer
Cast: Douglas Greet, Frederick Meads,
Katie Yeats and others

12/22-12/27
Omar, the Tent Maker
By Richard Walton Tully
Producer/Director: Oliver Morosco
Cast: Guy Bates Post, Jane Salisbury
and others, in a cast of 60

12/29-01/03/14
Romeo and Juliet, Othello, Julius Caesar
By Wm. Shakespeare
Producer/Director: William Faversham
Cast: William Faversham, Cecilia Loftus,
Julie Opp and others

1914

01/12-01/17
When Claudia Smiles
By Leo Ditrichstein/Anne Cladwell/
William Jerome/Jean Schwartz
Producer/Director: Frederic McKay
Cast: Blanche Ring, Harry Conor,
Charles J. Winninger and others

01/19-01/24
The Passing Show of 1913
By Harold Atteridge/Jean Schwartz
Producer/Director: Shuberts and
The Winter Garden Co.
Cast: Frank Conroy, Charles King,
Molly King, Sadie Burt, George Le Maire
and others

01/26-01/31
The National Opera Co. of Canada: Otello,
Mme Butterfly, Tosca, Samson et Dalila,
Lohengrin, Carmen, La Gioconda
Producer/Director: The National Opera Co.
of Canada

02/02-02/07
Twentieth Century Minstrels
Producer/Director: George Primrose,
Lew Dockstader
Cast: George Primrose, Lew Dockstader
and others

02/09-02/14
Her Own Money
By Mark Swan
Producer/Director: Shuberts
Cast: Julia Deane, Lionel Adams,
Maud Durand and others

02/16-02/21
Never Say Die
By William H. Post and William Collier
Producer/Director: Lew Fields
Cast: Nat C. Goodwin, Margaret Moreland
and others

02/23-02/28
Music Hall Variety
Producer/Director: William Morris
Cast: Alice Lloyd, Sidney Wood,
Frank Fogarty, Cowboy Minstrels,
Mel Craig, and the Doraine Sisters

03/02-03/07
Nobody's Daughter
By George Paston
Producer/Director: Lawson Butt
and A.E. Anson
Cast: Frank Kemble Cooper, Deirdre Doyle,
Essex Dane, Moya Mannering, Ada Deaves
and A.E. Anson

03/09-03/14
At Bay
By George Scarborough
Producer/Director: Shuberts
Cast: Ora Lee, Guy Standing, George
Howell, Chrystal Herne and others

03/16-03/21
Peg O'My Heart
By J. Hartley Manners
Producer/Director: Oliver Morosco
Cast: Elsa Ryan, Fanny Addison Pitt,
Roy Cochrane, Anna Hammond, Gilbert
Douglass, Lewis Broughton and others

03/23-03/28
When Dreams Come True
By Philip Bartholmae/Silvio Hein
Producer/Director: Philip Bartholmae
Cast: Joseph Santley, May Vokes,
Mignon McGibney and Dorothy Maynard

03/30-04/04
Bought and Paid For
By George Broadhurst
Producer/Director: William A. Brady
Cast: Kathleen MacDonell, Frank Mills,
Francis Coolin and Grace van Auker

04/06-04/20
Johnston Forbes-Robertson Repertory Co.:
Caesar and Cleopatra (Shaw), Hamlet,
The Merchant of Venice (Shakespeare),
The Light That Failed (George Fleming),
Of Mice and Men (Madeline Lucette Ryley),
The Passing of the Third Floor Back
(Jerome K. Jerome)

Producer/Director: Sir Johnston
Forbes-Robertson
Cast: Johnston Forbes-Robertson,
Gertrude Elliott and others

04/20-04/25
The Bird of Paradise
By Richard Walton Tully
Producer/Director: Oliver Morosco
Cast: Lenore Ulric, David Landau,
Robert Morris, William Desmond and others

04/27- 05/02
Pretty Mrs. Smith
By Oliver Morosco, Elmer Harris
Producer/Director: Oliver Morosco
Cast: Kitty Gordon, Dixie Blair,
Lenore Peters, Leila Bliss, Emily Miles,
Edward Martindell and others

05/04-05/09
E.H. Sothern Repertory Co.: Hamlet,
If I Were King, Lord Dundreary
Producer/Director:
E.H. Sothern Repertory Co.
Cast: E.H. Sothern, George W. Wilson,
Elizabeth Valentine, Alam Kruger and others

05/11-05/16
The Bonstelle Players: The Temperamental
Journey
By Leo Ditrichstein
Producer/Director: The Bonstelle
Players/Bertram Harrison
Cast: Edward H. Robins, Gavin Harris, Cyril
Raymond, Harriette Davis, Jane Wheatley,
Catharine Proctor and others

05/18-05/23
The Bonstelle Players: Merely Mary Ann
By Israel Zangwill
Producer/Director: The Bonstelle Players/
Bertram Harrison
Cast: Edward H. Robins and others

05/25-05/30
The Bonstelle Players: Little Miss Brown
By Philip Bartholmae
Producer/Director: The Bonstelle
Players/Bertram Harrison
Cast: Edward H. Robins and others

06/01-06/06
The Bonstelle Players: The Darling
of the Gods
By David Belasco and John Luther Long
Producer/Director: The Bonstelle
Players/Bertram Harrison
Cast: Edward H. Robins and others

06/08-06/13
The Bonstelle Players: Our Wives
By Helen Krafft and Frank Mandell
Producer/Director: The Bonstelle
Players/Bertram Harrison
Cast: Edward H. Robins and others

06/15-06/20
The Bonstelle Players: The Great Divide
By William Vaughn Moody
Producer/Director: The Bonstelle Players/
Bertram Harrison
Cast: Edward H. Robins and others

06/22-06/27
The Bonstelle Players: Bunty Pulls
the Strings
By Graham Moffat
Producer/Director: The Bonstelle Players/
Bertram Harrison
Cast: Edward H. Robins and others

06/29-07/04
The Bonstelle Players: Little Lord
Fauntleroy
By Frances Hodgson Burnett
Producer/Director: The Bonstelle Players/
Bertram Harrison
Cast: Edward H. Robins and others

07/06-07/11
The Bonstelle Players: Girl of the Golden
West
By David Belasco
Producer/Director: The Bonstelle Players/
Bertram Harrison
Cast: Edward H. Robins and others

07/13-07/18
The Bonstelle Players: Raffles
By E.W. Hornung and Eugene Presbery
Producer/Director: The Bonstelle Players/
Bertram Harrison
Cast: Edward H. Robins and others

07/20-07/25
The Bonstelle Players: Mary Jane's Pa
By Edith Ellis
Producer/Director: The Bonstelle
Players/Bertram Harrison
Cast: Edward H. Robins and others

07/27-08/01
The Bonstelle Players: The Witching Hour
By Augustus Thomas
Producer/Director: The Bonstelle
Players/Bertram Harrison
Cast: Edward H. Robins and others

08/03-08/08
The Bonstelle Players: Sherlock Holmes
By William Gillette
Producer/Director: The Bonstelle
Players/Bertram Harrison
Cast: Edward H. Robins and others

08/10-08/15
Paul J. Rainey's African Hunt Pictures
Producer/Director: Shuberts
Motion picture

08/17-08/22
The Chocolate Soldier
By Stanislaus Stange/Oscar Strauss,
based on Shaw's *Arms and the Man*

08/31-09/05
Peg O'My Heart
By J. Hartley Manners
Producer/Director: Oliver Morosco
Cast: Elsa Ryan, Vivian Gilbert, Alice Butler,
Agnes Heron Miller and others

09/07-09/12
The Whirl of the World
By Harold Atteridge/Sigmund Romberg
Producer/Director:
Shuberts and The Winter Garden Co.
Cast: George Moon, Daniel Morris, Edward
Cutler, Elisabeth Goodall and others

09/14-09/19
Too Many Cooks
By Frank Craven
Producer/Director: William A. Brady
Cast: Clarence Oliver, Inez Plummer
and others

09/21-09/26
San Carlo Grand Opera Co.: Carmen,
La Traviata, Faust, Cavalleria Rusticana,
I Pagliacci, Rigoletto, Il Trovatore,
Lucia di Lammermoor
Producer/Director: San Carlo Grand Opera
Co./Fortune Gallo

09/28-10/03
The Blue Bird
By Maurice Maeterlinck
Producer/Director: Liebler & Co.
Cast: Jack Davis, Harriet Mendel and others

10/05-10/10
The Marie Tempest Repertory Co.: At the
Barn (Anthony P. Wharton), The Marriage
of Kitty (Cosmo Gordon-Lennox),
Mary Goes First (Henry Arthur Jones),
Art and Opportunity (Harold Chapin)
Producer/Director: Shuberts

Cast: Marie Tempest, Kenyon Tusgrave,
Landerdale Maitland, W. Graham Brown,
John Alexander, Kate Serjeantson, Barbara
Fenn, Lillian Cavanaugh and others

10/12-10/17
Within the Law
By Bayard Veiller
Producer/Director: Arch Selwyn and
The American Play Co.
Cast: Marion Morton, James B. Leinhart,
Rockcliffe Fellows, Catherine Tower, George
B. Leffingwell and others

10/19-10/24
HMS Pinafore
By Gilbert and Sullivan
Producer/Director: Shuberts
Cast: Bertram Peacock, Vernon Dalhart,
Ruby Cutter Savage, Marie Hogan
and others

10/26-10/31
The Belle of Bond Street
By Owen Hall, Harold Atteridge/
Ivan Caryll and Lionel Monkton
Producer/Director: Shuberts
Cast: Sam Barnard, Cyril Chadwick,
Florence Nugent Jerome, Mollie King
and others

11/02-11/07
The Robert B. Mantell Repertory Co.:
King John, Macbeth, Hamlet, King Lear,
Romeo and Juliet, The Merchant of Venice,
Richelieu (Bulwer-Lytton)
Producer/Director:
Robert B. Mantell Repertory Co.
Cast: Robert Bruce Mantell, Virginia
Bronson, Genevieve Hamper, Edward
Lewers, John Burke, Fritz Lieber, Genevieve
Reynolds, Florence Auer, Ethel Mantell
and others

11/09-11/14
The Midnight Girl
By Adolph Philipp and Edward Paulton
Producer/Director: Shuberts
Cast: George MacFarlane, Margaret
Romaine, Marie Flynn, Dolly Castles
and others

11/16-11/21
High Jinks
By Otto Hauerbach, Rudolph Friml
Producer/Director: Arthur Hammerstein
Cast: Stella Mayhew, Eugene O'Rourke,
Billie Taylor and others

11/30-12/05
The Appeal
By C.M. Brune
Cast: Joseph Kent, Henley Edwards,
Cyphers Weaver, Enid Morel and others

12/07-12/12
A Mix-Up
By Parker Hord
Producer/Director: Shuberts
Cast: Marie Dressler, Evelyn Vaughan,
Bert Lytell and others

12/14-12/19
Kitty MacKay
By Catherine Chisholm Cushing
Producer/Director: William Elliott
Cast: Irene Haisman, Reginald Denny
and Agnes Kelly

12/21-12/26
The Story of the Rosary
By Walter Howard/Annie Saker
Producer/Director: Comstock & Gest
Cast: Annie Saker, George Desmond,
Albert Paumier and others

12/28-01/02
The Things That Count
By Laurence Eyre
Producer/Director: William A. Brady
Cast: Florine Arnold, George Paige
and others

12/29-01/03
Romeo and Juliet, Othello, Julius Caesar
By Wm. Shakespeare
Producer/Director: William Faversham
Cast: William Faversham, Cecilia Loftus,
Julie Opp and others

1915
....

01/04-01/09
The Gilbert and Sullivan Opera Co.:
Iolanthe, The Sorcerer, Trial by Jury,
The Mikado, HMS Pinafore
By Gilbert and Sullivan
Producer/Director: William A. Brady
Cast: De Wolf Hopper, Arthur Aldridge,
Herbert Waterous, John Willard,
Arthur Cunningham, Gladys Campbell,
Jayne Herbert and others

01/11-01/16
The Third Party
By Mark Swan
Producer/Director: F. Ray Comstock
Cast: Taylor Holmes, Walter Jones
and others

01/18-01/23
Omar, the Tent-Maker
By Richard Walton Tully
Producer/Director: Tully and Buckland
Cast: Guy Bates Post, John Hunter Booth,
John Waller, Louise Waller, Edith Holt and
others, in a cast of 60

01/25-01/30
A Pair of Sixes
By Edward Peple
Producer/Director: H.H. Frazee
Cast: Mark Smith, Ralph Herta, Ethel
Jackson and Marion Ballou

02/08-02/13
The Golden Age
By Joseph Nevin Doyle, under the auspices
of the IODE and HH the Duke of Connaught
Cast: Tandy McKenzie, Edith St. George,
Roy McKellar and others

02/22-02/27
The Bird of Paradise
By Richard Walton Tully
Producer/Director: Oliver Morosco
Cast: Lenore Ulric, William Desmond,
Mary Grey, David Hartford, Laura Adams
and others

03/01-03/06
The Percy Haswell Stock Co.:
Trifling with Tomorrow
By Frank Mandell
Producer/Director: Percy Haswell Stock Co.
Cast: Percy Haswell, Jack Amory, Madge
West and others

03/08-03/13
The Percy Haswell Stock Co:
A Scrap of Paper
By Victorien Sardou
Producer/Director: Percy Haswell Stock Co.
Cast: Percy Haswell and others

03/15-03/20
The Percy Haswell Stock Co:
What Happened to Jones?
By George Broadhurst
Producer/Director: Percy Haswell Stock Co.
Cast: Percy Haswell and others

03/22-03/27
The Percy Haswell Stock Co:
Madame Sherry
By Otto Hauerbach/Karl Hoschna
Producer/Director: Percy Haswell Stock Co.
Cast: Percy Haswell and others

03/29
Stephen Leacock
Lecture and reading in aid of
Belgian War Relief

03/29-04/04
The Percy Haswell Stock Co: Stop Thief
By Carlyle Moore
Producer/Director: Percy Haswell Stock Co.
Cast: Percy Haswell, Jack Amory, Madge
West and others

04/05-04/10
The Percy Haswell Stock Co: Mam'zelle
Producer/Director: Percy Haswell Stock Co.
Cast: Percy Haswell and others

04/12-04/17
The White Feather
By Lechmere Worral and J.E. Harold Terry
Producer/Director: William A. Brady
Cast: Roy Cochrane, Justine Cutting,
Louise Muldener, Paget Hunter and others

04/19-04/24
The Percy Haswell Stock Co:
Nearly Married
By Edgar Selwyn
Producer/Director: Percy Haswell Stock Co.
Cast: Percy Haswell, Jack Amory,
Madge West and others

04/26-05/01
The Percy Haswell Stock Co:
The Girl in the Taxi
By Stanislaus Stange
Producer/Director: Percy Haswell Stock Co.
Cast: Percy Haswell and others

05/03-05/08
The Percy Haswell Stock Co: East Lynne
By Mrs. Henry Wood
Producer/Director: Percy Haswell Stock Co.
Cast: Percy Haswell and others

05/10-05/15
The Percy Haswell Stock Co.:
A Celebrated Case
By Adolphe D'Ennery
Producer/Director: Percy Haswell Stock Co.
Cast: Percy Haswell and others

05/17-05/22
The Percy Haswell Stock Co:
The Two Orphans
By Adolphe D'Ennery
Producer/Director: Percy Haswell Stock Co.
Cast: Percy Haswell and others

05/24-05/29
The Percy Haswell Stock Co: Confusion
By Joseph Derrick
Producer/Director: Percy Haswell Stock Co.
Cast: Percy Haswell and others

05/31-06/05
The Percy Haswell Stock Co: Four One-Act
Plays: Betsy Manners (Allen Fawcett),
The Soldiers (Louise Carter-Brown),
Such Things (Lynn Osborne),
An Interrupted Divorce (Agnes Gavin)
Producer/Director: Percy Haswell Stock Co.
Cast: Percy Haswell and others

06/07-06/12
The Percy Haswell Stock Co:
Out of the Fold
By Langdon MacCormick
Producer/Director: Percy Haswell Stock Co.
Cast: Percy Haswell and others

06/21-06/26
The Robins Players: Seven Keys to Baldpate
By George M. Cohan
Producer/Director: The Robins Players
Cast: Edward H. Robins, Webb
Chamberlain, Emma Campbell,
Frank Crayne, Bertha Mann, Vivian Laidlaw,
Helen Travers and others

06/28-07/03
The Robins Players: Within the Law
By Bayard Veiller
Producer/Director: The Robins Players
Cast: Edward H. Robins and others

07/05-07/10
The Robins Players: The Fortune Hunter
By Winchell Smith
Producer/Director: The Robins Players
Cast: Edward H. Robins and others

07/12-07/17
The Robins Players: The Miracle Man
By George M. Cohan
Producer/Director: The Robins Players
Cast: Edward H. Robins and others

07/19-07/24
The Robins Players: The Argyle Case
By Harvey O'Higgins and Harriet Ford

Producer/Director: The Robins Players
Cast: Edward H. Robins and others

07/26-07/31
The Robins Players: The Misleading Lady
By Paul Dickey and Charles Goddard
Producer/Director: The Robins Players
Cast: Edward H. Robins and others

08/02-08/07
The Robins Players: The Marriage Game
By Anne Crawford Flexner
Producer/Director: The Robins Players
Cast: Edward H. Robins and others

08/09-08/14
The Robins Players: The Big Idea
By A.E. Thomas and Clayton Hamilton
Producer/Director: The Robins Players
Cast: Edward H. Robins and others

08/16-08/21
The Robins Players: A Woman's Way
By Thompson Buchanan
Producer/Director: The Robins Players
Cast: Edward H. Robins and others

08/23-08/28
The Robins Players: So Much for So Much
By Willard Mack
Producer/Director: The Robins Players
Cast: Edward H. Robins and others

08/30-09/04
The Bird of Paradise
By Richard Walton Tully
Producer/Director: Oliver Morosco
Cast: Laura Adams, Carlotta Monterey,
Hooper L. Atchley and many others

09/06-09/11
Trilby
By Paul Potter
Producer/Director: Joseph Brooks/Cecil King
Cast: Phyllis Neilson-Terry (Trilby O'Terrall)
and Lyn Harding (Svengali)

09/13-09/18
A Full House
By Fred Jackson
Producer/Director: H.H. Frazee
Cast: Walter Jones, Charles Gerrard,
Frances Savage, Adelaide Hibbard
and others

09/20-10/09
Birth of a Nation
Motion picture

10/11-10/16
Tonight's the Night
By Fred Thompson/Paul Rubens
Producer/Director: Shuberts/Edwin Emery
Cast: Laddie Cliff, Alfred Hemming, Wilfrid
Seagram, Philip Travers, Dorothy Maynard
and others

10/18-10/23
Peg O'My Heart
By J. Hartley Manners
Producer/Director: Oliver Morosco
Cast: Lisle Leigh, Lillian Kemble-Cooper,
Gordon Burby and others

10/25-10/30
The Peasant Girl
By Leo Stein, Harold Atteridge/
Rudolph Friml, Oscar Nedbal
Producer/Director:
Shuberts and Comstock & Gest
Cast: Edith Thayer, Frank Deshon, Almon
Knowles, Peggy Branson and others

11/01-11/06
The White Leather
By Lechmere Worral and J.E. Harold Terry
Producer/Director: William A. Brady
Cast: Arthur Elliott, Justine Cutting, Louise
Muldener, Paget Hunter and others

11/08-11/13
Dancing Around
By H. Atteridge/Sigmund Romberg
Producer/Director:
Shuberts, The Winter Garden Co.
Cast: Al Jolson, Lawrence D'Orsay,
Effie Graham and many others

11/15-11/20
San Carlo Grand Opera Co.: Aida,
Lucia di Lammermoor, Faust, Rigoletto,
Cavelleria Rusticana, I Pagliacci, Carmen,
Tales of Hoffman, Il Trovatore
Producer/Director:
San Carlo Grand Opera Co.

11/22-11/27
The Hawk
By François de Groisset
Producer/Director: William Faversham
Cast: William Faversham, Eva La Gallienne
and others

11/29-12/04
Experience
By George V. Hobart/Silvio Hein
Producer/Director:
William Elliott and Comstock & Gest
Cast: William Elliott, Maude Allan
and others

12/06-12/11
The Mikado
By Gilbert and Sullivan
Producer/Director:
IODE, Westminster Chapter

12/13-12/18
Maid in America
By Harold Atteridge/Sigmund Romberg
Producer/Director:
Shuberts and Winter Garden Co.
Cast: Florence Moore and others

12/20-12/25
On the Battlefields of France
Motion picture

12/27-01/01/16
The Man Who Married a Dumb Wife,
Androcles and the Lion
By Anatole France and G.B. Shaw
Producer/Director: Lillian McCarthy,
Granville Barker and Percy Burton
Cast: O.P. Heggie, Mary Forbes, Lionel
Braham, Charles Dodsworth, Reginald
Carrington and others

1916

01/03-01/08
The Girl Who Smiles
By Edward A. Paulton
Producer/Director: Ben Teal
Cast: Natalie Alt, George Baldwin,
William Danforth, Grace Leigh, Dottie King
and others

01/10-01/15
Two Is Company
By Edward A. Paulton
Producer/Director: Ben Teal
Cast: Amelia Stone, Armand Kalisz,
Edward A. Paulton and others

01/18-01/19
Pavlova Ballet Russe and Boston Grand
Opera: I Pagliacci, Coppelia, Madame
Butterfly, Snowflakes, La Bohème,
Spanish Ballet
Producer/Director: Max Rabinoff
Cast: Anna Pavlova, M. Valinsky, J.
Zalewsky, Ivan Clustine and Boston Grand
Opera Co.

01/20-01/22
Harry Lauder
Producer/Director: William Morris
Cast: Harry Lauder and His Highland Boys,
Al Golem Troupe

01/24-01/29
The Quinneys
By Horace Annesley Vachell
Producer/Director: Frederick Harrison
Cast: Cathleen Nesbitt, Frederick Ross,
Margaret Watson, Pegg Rush, Arthur
Grenville and others

01/31-02/05
Omar, the Tent-Maker
By Richard Walton Tully
Producer/Director: Tully and Buckland
Cast: Guy Bates Post, Louise Grassler
and others, in a cast of 60

02/07-02/12
The Night Before
By Harry Lauder
Producer/Director:
William Morris and Harry Lauder
Cast: Jimmy Prevan, Jessie Villars,
Carrie Glenn and others

02/14-02/19
The Dynasts
By Thomas Hardy
Producer/Director: Frank Lascelles
Cast: Mrs. Cawthra Mulock, Mrs. T. Eaton
and others, in a cast of 200

02/21-02/26
The Quinneys
By Horace Annesley Vachell
Producer/Director: Frederick Harrison
Cast: Clifford Brooke, Lucy Beaumont,
Henry Gribble and others

02/28-03/04
A Pair of Sixes
By Edward Peple
Producer/Director: H.H. Frazee
Cast: Maude Eburn, Harry Stubbs, Mary
Beban, James T. Galloway and others

03/03
Theatrical Mechanics Association
Benefit

03/06-03/11
Nobody Home (Mr. Popple)
By Paul A. Rubens and Guy Bolton/
Jerome Kern
Producer/Director: F. Ray Comstock
and Elizabeth Marbury
Cast: Zoe Barnett, Alison McBain, Lawrence
Grossmith, Marion Davis and others

03/13-03/18
The Great Pursuit (The Idler)
By C. Haddon Chambers
Producer/Director:
Joseph Brooks/Fred G. Latham
Cast: Jeanne Eagels, Montagu Love, Phyllis
Neilson-Terry, Marie Tempest and others

Marie Tempest

03/20-03/25
The White Feather
By Lechmere Worral
Producer/Director: William A. Brady
Cast: Albert Brown, Arthur Elliott,
Stapleton Kent, Paget Hunter,
Olive Temple and others

03/27-04/01
Twin Beds
By Salisbury Fields and Margaret Mayo
Producer/Director: Selwyn and Co.
Cast: Lois Bolton, John Welsh,
Claire Weldon and others

04/03-04/08
Talk, Talk, Talk
By A.G. Duggan/J. Ernest Lawrence
Producer/Director: The 50,000 Club
Cast: Marguerite Walsh and
Charles H. Downey

04/10-04/15
The Only Girl
By Henry Blossom/Victor Herbert
Producer/Director:
Joe Weber/Fred G. Latham
Cast: Wilda Bennett, Vivian Wessell
and others

04/17-04/22
The Two Virtues
By Alfred Sutro
Cast: E.H. Sothern, Blanche Yurka,
Alexandra Carlisle, Haidee Wright
and others

04/24-04/29
A Pair of Queens
By O.A. Hauerbach, A. Seymour Brown
and Harry Lewis
Producer/Director: H.H. Frazee
Cast: Maude Eburn, Joseph Santley,
Kathleen Clifford and others

05/01-05/06
The Robins Players: Under Cover
By Roi Cooper Megrue
Producer/Director: The Robins Players
Cast: Edward H. Robins and the Robins
Players: Frances Neilson, Thomas E.
Jackson, Thomas McKnight, Karl Sheahan,
Emma Campbell, Vivian Laidlaw, Jack
Amory, Helen Travers and others

05/08-05/13
The Robins Players: Believe Me, Xantippe
By Fred Ballard
Producer/Director:
The Robins Players/Frances Neilson
Edward H. Robins and the Robins Players

05/15-05/20
The Robins Players: Widow by Proxy
By Catherine Chisholm Suching
Producer/Director:
The Robins Players/Karl Sheahan
Cast: Edward H. Robins and the Robins
Players

05/22-05/27
The Robins Players: Seven Keys to Baldpate
By George M. Cohan
Producer/Director:
The Robins Players/E.H. Robins
Cast: Edward H. Robins and the Robins
Players

05/29-06/03
The Robins Players: Inside the Lines
By Earl D. Biggars
Producer/Director:
The Robins Players/E.H. Robins
Cast: Edward H. Robins and
the Robins Players

06/05-06/10
The Robins Players: Mrs. Bumpstead-Leigh
By Henry James Smith
Producer/Director: The Robins Players
Cast: Edward H. Robins and
the Robins Players

06/12-06/17
The Robins Players: Kick In
By Willard Meek
Producer/Director: The Robins Players
Cast: Edward H. Robins and
the Robins Players

06/19-06/24
The Robins Players: We Are Seven
By Eleanor Gates
Producer/Director: The Robins Players
Cast: Edward H. Robins and
the Robins Players

06/26-07/01
The Robins Players: Rolling Stones
By Edgar Selwyn
Producer/Director: The Robins Players
Cast: Edward H. Robins and
the Robins Players

07/03-07/08
The Robins Players: Girls
By Clyde Fitch
Producer/Director: The Robins Players
Cast: Edward H. Robins and
the Robins Players

07/10-07/15
The Robins Players: Nearly Married
By Edgar Selwyn
Producer/Director: The Robins Players
Cast: Edward H. Robins and
the Robins Players

07/17-07/22
The Robins Players: Smith
By Somerset Maugham
Producer/Director: The Robins Players
Cast: Edward H. Robins and
the Robins Players

07/24-07/29
The Robins Players: The Tongues of Men
By Edward Childs Carpenter
Producer/Director: The Robins Players
Cast: Edward H. Robins and
the Robins Players

07/31-08/05
The Robins Players: The Conspiracy
By Robert Baker and John Emerson
Producer/Director: The Robins Players
Cast: Edward H. Robins and
the Robins Players

08/07-08/12
The Robins Players: The Commuters
By James Forbes
Producer/Director: The Robins Players
Cast: Edward H. Robins and
the Robins Players

08/14-08/19
The Robins Players: My Lady's Garter
By Lee Morrison
Producer/Director: The Robins Players
Cast: Jack Amory and the Robins Players

08/21-08/26
The Robins Players: Beverley's Balance
(The Woman in the Case)
By Paul Kester
Producer/Director: The Robins Players
Cast: Jack Amory and the Robins Players

08/28-09/02
The Bird of Paradise
By Richard Walton Tully
Producer/Director: Oliver Morosco
Cast: June Janin, David Landau, Ethel
Remey, Arthur Maitland, Laura Adams
and others

09/04-09/16
On Trial
By Elmer Reizenstein (Elmer Rice)
Producer/Director: Cohan & Harris
Cast: Frances McGrath, Rowland G.
Edwards, Jack Amory and others

09/18-09/23
A Pair of Silk Stockings
By Cyril Harcourt
Producer/Director: Shuberts
Cast: Langdon Bruce, A.E. Winnington
Barnes, Ida Stratham and others

09/25-09/30
Along Came Ruth
By Holman Day
Producer/Director: James B. Beury
Cast: Frances McGrath, Jack Amory,
Vivian Laidlaw, Clyde North and others

10/02-10/04
San Carlo Grand Opera Co.: Carmen,
Martha, Rigoletto, Aida
Producer/Director: San Carlo Grand
Opera Co.

10/05-10/07
Maud Allen Dance Co.
Producer/Director: Maud Allen

10/09-10/14
Somebody's Luggage
By Mark Swan
Producer/Director: Shuberts
Cast: James T. Powers, Grace Hamilton
and others

10/16-10/21
A King of Nowhere
By J. and L. DuRocher MacPherson
Producer/Director:
The Garrick Co./Jesse Bonstelle
Cast: Sidney Greenstreet, Lou Tellegen,
Mercedes Desmore, Wilda Marie Moore
and others

10/23-10/28
Robinson Crusoe, Jr.
By Harold Atteridge/Sigmund Romberg
Producer/Director:
Shuberts and The Winter Garden Co.
Cast: Al Jolson, Lawrence D'Orsay
and others

10/30-11/18
His Brother's Keeper
By Robert Porter
Producer/Director:
Robert Edeson & Associates
Cast: Robert Edeson, Stella Archer,
Ann MacDonald and others

11/06-11/11
Hobson's Choice
By Harold Brighouse
Producer/Director: Shuberts/B. Iden Payne
Cast: Margaret Nybloc, Jane Ross, Edward
Naimby, Helen Beaumont, Eddie Phelan
and others

11/13-11/18
The Robert B. Mantell Rep. Co.: Richard III,
King Lear, Macbeth, Othello, Richelieu,
Hamlet, The Merchant of Venice
Producer/Director: William A. Brady
Cast: Robert Bruce Mantell, Genevieve
Hamper, Fritz Leiber, John L. Burke,
Lila Dell Frost, John Ray and others

11/20-11/25
Just a Woman
By Eugene Waller
Producer/Director: Shuberts
Cast: Mabel Brownell, Grace Studdiford,
Ernest Anderson and others

11/27-11/29
Boston Grand Opera Co.: Andrea Chenier,
Faust, Mme Butterfly, Tosca
Producer/Director: Max Rabinoff

11/30-12/01
The Lodger (Who Is He?)
By Horace A. Vachell
Producer/Director:
Ernest Shuter/Lionel Atwill
Cast: Lionel Atwill, Phyllis Ralph, Beryl
Mercer, Harry Ashford and others

12/04-12/09
The Girl from Brazil
By Edgar Smith, Matthew Woodward/Robert
Winterberg and S. Romberg
Producer/Director: Shuberts
Cast: Frances Demarest, Dorothy Maynard,
Maude Odell, Nora White, George Hansell
and others, in a cast of 50

12/11-12/16
HMS Pinafore
By Gilbert and Sullivan
Producer/Director:
Working Circle of the 180th Auxiliary
Cast: Flo Higgins, Gladys Jones,
Harold Hollingshead, J.P. Bastedo,
Galdstone Brown and others

12/18-12/23
The Merry Wives of Windsor
By Wm. Shakespeare
Producer/Director:
James K. Hackett/Thomas A. Wise
Cast: Thomas A. Wise, Constance Collier,
Isabel Irving, W. Lawson Butt, Auriol Lee,
Vera Fuller-Melish, Robert Mantell Jr.
and others

12/25-12/30
The Masquerader
By John Hunter Booth
Producer/Director: Richard Walton Tully
Cast: Guy Bates Post, Louis Calvert,
Thais Lawson and others

1917

01/01-01/06
The Only Girl
By Henry Blossom/Victor Herbert
Producer/Director: Joe Weber
Cast: Adelle Hassan, Laura Arnold,
Emmanuel Turner and others

01/08-01/13
A Daughter of the Gods
Motion picture

01/15-01/20
Very Good, Eddie
By Guy Bolton, Philip Bartholmae/
Jerome Kern
Producer/Director: Elizabeth Marbury and
F. Ray Comstock
Cast: Ada Lewis, Georgie Mack. Arthur
Aylesworth, Helen Raymond, Mignon
McGibney and others

01/22-01/27
The Passing Show of 1916
By Harold Atteridge/Sigmund Romberg
Producer/Director:
Shuberts/ The Winter Garden Co.
Cast: Ed Wynn, Fred Walton, Augusta Dean,
the Ford Sisters, the Five Violin Sisters
and others

01/29-02/03
Flora-Bella
By Cosmo Hamilton, Dorothy Donnelly
Producer/Director: John Cort
Cast: Linda Abarbanell, Irving Brooks
and others

02/05-02/10
The Girl Who Smiles
By Edward A. Paulton
Producer/Director: Ben Teal
Cast: Beth Groves-Young, Fred Frear,
Willis Claire, Geraldine Malone and others

02/12-02/17
The Flame
By Richard Walton Tully
Producer/Director: Richard Walton Tully
Cast: Marion Coakley, June Hawthorne,
Francis Verdi and others

02/19-02/24
His Majesty Bunker Bean
By Lee Wilson Dodd
Producer/Director: William H. Currie
Cast: Taylor Holmes, Maude Hannaford,
Charles Abbe and others

02/26-03/03
The Cinderella Man
By Edward Childs Carpenter
Producer/Director: Oliver Morosco
Cast: Phoebe Foster, Frank Bacon, Frank
Gillmore, Florence Pendleton and others

03/05-03/10
Birth of a Nation
Motion picture

03/12-03/17
Pierrot the Prodigal (L'Enfant Prodigue)
By Michel Carre and Andre Wormser
Producer/Director:
Winthrop Ames and Walter Knight
Cast: Paul Clerget, Gabrielle Perrier,
Marjorie Patterson, Margot Kelly and
Charles Dubuis

03/19-03/24
Stocks and Stockings
By Charles Edwin Summers
Cast: George Parsons, Stanley Harrison,
Peggy Cameron, Georgia Lawrence
and others

03/26-03/31
Aborn Grand Opera Co.: Il Trovatore,
Rigoletto, Samson and Delilah, Tales of
Hoffman, Jewels of the Madonna, Faust,
Carmen, Cavalleria Rusticana, I Pagliacci,
Lucia di Lammermoor, Madama Butterfly

Producer/Director: Milton and
Sargeant Aborn

04/09-04/14
The Flame
By Richard Walton Tully
Producer/Director: Richard Walton Tully
Cast: June Hawthorne, Marion Coakley,
Godfrey Matthews, Francis Verdi, Harriet
Sterling and others

04/16-04/21
Mother Carey's Chickens
By Kate Douglas Wiggin
and Rachel Crothers
Producer/Director: Ralph Cummings
Cast: Marion Barney, Antoinette Walker,
Constance Molineaux, Doris Eaton, Lorne
Parker, Wallace Owen, Charles Eaton
and others

04/23-04/28
Follow Me
By R.B. Smith/S. Romberg
Producer/Director: Shuberts
Cast: Anna Held, Sylvia Jason, Charles
McNaughton, Harry Lewis, George Lydecker
and others

04/30-05/05
The Robins Players: Hit the Trail Holiday
By George M. Cohan
Producer/Director:
The Robins Players, James B. Beury
Cast: Edward H. Robins, Jack Amory,
Eugene Frazier, Baker Moore, Ethel
Intropodi, Virginia Fox Brooks and others

05/07-05/12
The Robins Players: Rich Man, Poor Man
By George Broadhurst
Producer/Director:
The Robins Players, James B. Beury
Cast: Edward H. Robins and others

05/14-05/19
The Robins Players: Broadway Jones
By George M. Cohan
Producer/Director:
The Robins Players, James B. Beury
Cast: Edward H. Robins and others

05/21-05/26
The Robins Players: On Trial
By Elmer Reizenstein (Elmer Rice)
Producer/Director:
The Robins Players, James B. Beury
Cast: Edward H. Robins and others

05/28-06/02
The Robins Players: The Claim
By Charles Kenyon and Frank Dare
Producer/Director:
The Robins Players, James B. Beury
Cast: Florence Roberts, Edward H. Robins
and others

06/04-06/09
The Robins Players: Romance
By Edward Sheldon
Producer/Director:
The Robins Players, James B. Beury
Cast: Edward H. Robins and others

06/11-06/16
The Robins Players: The Man Who Owns
Broadway
By George M. Cohan
Producer/Director:
The Robins Players, James B. Beury
Cast: Edward H. Robins and others

06/18-06/23
The Robins Players: Mile a Minute Kenyon
By Owen Davis
Producer/Director:
The Robins Players, James B. Beury
Cast: Edward H. Robins and others

06/25-06/30
The Robins Players: Annabel Lee
By Earle Brown
Producer/Director:
The Robins Players, James B. Beury
Cast: Edward H. Robins and others

07/02-07/07
The Robins Players: The Cinderella Man
By Edward Childs Carpenter
Producer/Director: The Robins Players,
James B. Beury
Cast: Edward H. Robins and others

07/09-07/14
The Robins Players: Arms and the Girl
By Grant Stewart and Robert Baker
Producer/Director:
The Robins Players, James B. Beury
Cast: Edward H. Robins and others

07/16-07/21
The Robins Players: Never Say Die
By William H. Post
Producer/Director:
The Robins Players, James B. Beury
Cast: Edward H. Robins and others

07/23-07/28
The Robins Players: House of Glass
By Max Marcin

Producer/Director:
The Robins Players, James B. Beury
Cast: Edward H. Robins and others

07/30-08/04
The Robins Players: The Dummy
By Harvey J. O'Higgins
Producer/Director:
The Robins Players, James B. Beury
Cast: Edward H. Robins and others

08/06-08/11
The Robins Players: Rio Grande
By Augustus Thomas
Producer/Director:
The Robins Players, James B. Beury
Cast: Edward H. Robins and others

08/13-08/18
The Robins Players: A Full House
By Fred Jackson
Producer/Director:
The Robins Players, James B. Beury
Cast: Edward H. Robins and others

08/20-08/25
The Robins Players: Shirley Kaye
By Hubert Footner
Producer/Director:
The Robins Players, James B. Beury
Cast: Edward H. Robins and others

08/27-09/01
The Bird of Paradise
By Richard Walton Tully
Producer/Director: Oliver Morosco
Cast: Marion Hutchins, John Harrington
and others

09/03-09/08
The Flame
By Richard Walton Tully
Producer/Director: Richard Walton Tully
Cast: June Hawthorne, Godfrey Mathews,
James Seeley and others

09/10-09/15
You're in Love
By Rudolph Friml, Otto Harbach
Producer/Director: Arthur Hammerstein
Cast: Marie Flynn, Garner Crane, Carl
McCullough, May Thompson and others

09/17-09/22
Canary Cottage
By Oliver Morosco, Elmer Harris,
Earl Carroll
Producer/Director: Oliver Morosco
Cast: Dorothy Webb, Charles Ruggles,
the Ergotti Lilliputians and others

09/24-09/29
The Sky Pilot
By Frank Mandell, George Brennan
Cast: Brandon Tynan, Ernest Anderson,
Regina Wallace and others

10/01-10/06
Love o'Mike
By Thomas Sydney/Jerome Kern/
Harry B. Smith
Producer/Director:
Elizabeth Marbury and Lee Shubert
Cast: Sydney Stone, Spalding Hall,
Shep Kamp, Kirk Bride and others

10/08-10/13
Johnny Get Your Gun
By Dorothy Donnelly, Edmund Burke
Producer/Director: John Cort
Cast: Louis Dennison, Lorraine Frost,
Theodore Babcock, Louise Mackintosh
and others

10/15-10/20
Experience
By George V. Hobart
Producer/Director: Elliott, Comstock & Gest
Cast: Dorothy Newell, Jean Downs, Marie
Horne, Raymond van Sickle, William Betts
and others

10/22-10/27
Show of Wonders
By Harold Atteridge/S. Romberg
Producer/Director: J.J. Shubert
Cast: Marilyn Miller, George Monroe,
Eugene Howard, Willie Howard, Adele
Ardsley, Jack Coogan and others

10/29-11/03
Nothing But the Truth
By James Montgomery Flagg
Producer/Director:
G.M. Anderson and L. Lawrence Weber
Cast: William Collier, Ned Sparks, Betty
Wales and others

11/05-11/10
Her Soldier Boy
By Rida Johnson Young/Emmerich Kalman
Producer/Director: Shuberts
Cast: Clifton Crawford, Forrest Huff,
Mabel Weeks, Cyril Chadwick and others

11/12-11/17
The Passing Show of 1917
By Harold Atteridge/S. Romberg
Producer/Director: Shuberts/J.C. Huffman
Cast: De Wolf Hopper, Irene Franklin,
Jefferson De Angelis, Helen Carrington
and others

11/19-11/24
The Thirteenth Chair
By Bayard Vellier
Producer/Director: William Harris Jr.
Cast: Blanche Hall, Marie Goff,
Joseph Garry and others

11/26-11/28
Boston Grand Opera Co.: Lucia di
Lammermoor, Rigoletto, Madame Butterfly,
Tales of Hoffman
Producer/Director: Max Rabinoff

11/29-12/01
Harry Lauder
Producer/Director: William Morris
Cast: Harry Lauder, Arnaut Bros.,
Cleo Gascoyne and others

12/03-12/08
Very Good, Eddie
By Guy Bolton, Philip Bartholmae/
Jerome Kern
Producer/Director:
Elizabeth Marbury and F. Ray Comstock
Cast: Georgie Mack, Denman Maley, Harry
Myers, Helen Raymond, Olive Reeves-Smith
and others

12/11-12/15
Good Gracious, Annabelle
By Clare Kummer
Producer/Director: Arthur Hopkins
Cast: Isabelle Lowe, Robert Middlemass,
Ralph Binker, Lydia Dickson and others

12/17-12/22
A Successful Calamity
By Clare Kummer
Producer/Director: Arthur Hopkins
Cast: William Gillette, William Devereux,
Charles Lane and others

12/24-12/29
Oh, Boy
P.G. Wodehouse, Guy Bolton/Jerome Kern
Producer/Director: F. Ray Comstock and
William Elliott/Edward Royce
Cast: Helen Shipman, Charles Compton,
Adelaide Hibbard and others

12/31-01/05/18
Old Lady 31
By Rachel Crothers
Producer/Director: Lee Kugel
Cast: Emma Dunn, Ray L. Royce,
Louis Fierce, Marie Pecheur, Lottie Church
and others

1918

01/07-01/12
The Wanderer
By Maurice V. Samuels
Producer/Director:
Comstock, Elliott & Gest/David Belasco
Cast: Nance O'Neil, James O'Neill, Charles
Dalton and a cast of 200, plus 120 sheep

01/14-01/19
Katinka
By Otto Harbach/Rudolph Friml
Producer/Director: Arthur Hammerstein
Cast: Howard Langford, Eva Lynn,
Clara Palmer and others

01/22-01/26
Upstairs and Down
By Frederic and Fanny Hatton
Producer/Director:
Oliver Morosco/Robert Milton
Cast: Louis George Christie, Helen Sinnott,
Roberta Arnold, Frederic Tiden and others

01/28-02/02
Cleopatra
Motion picture

02/04-02/09
So Long, Letty
By Elmer Harris, Earl Carroll
Producer/Director: Oliver Morosco
Cast: Charlotte Greenwood, Sydney Grant,
May Boley and others

02/11-02/16
Fancy Free
By Dorothy Donnelly, Augustus Barratt
Producer/Director: Shuberts
Cast: Daisy Appleton, Marilyn Miller,
Hal Peel and others

02/19-02/23
Furs and Frills
By Edward Clark/Silvio Hein
Producer/Director: Arthur Hammerstein
Cast: Richard Carle, Burrell Barbaretto,
Fern Rogers and others

02/26-03/02
Doing Our Bit
By Harold Atteridge/S. Romberg,
Herman Timberg
Producer/Director: J.J. Shubert/J.C. Huffman
Cast: James J. Corbett, Frank Tinney,
Leanore Energie and others

03/05-03/09
Her Regiment
By William Le Baron/Victor Herbert
Producer/Director: Joe Weber
Cast: Donald Brian, Audrey Maple
and others

03/12-03/16
Les Misérables
Motion picture

03/18-03/23
Peter Ibbetson
By John Raphael,
based on the novel by George duMaurier
Producer/Director: Shuberts
Cast: John Barrymore, Constance Collier,
Laura Hope Crews and others

03/26-03/30
Nothing But the Truth
By James Montgomery Flagg
Producer/Director:
G.M. Anderson and L. Lawrence Weber
Cast: William Collier, Roy Fairchild,
Rapley Holmes, Ione Bright and others

04/01-04/06
Mary's Ankle
By May Tully
Producer/Director: A.H. Woods
Cast: Walter Jones, Alma Belwin and others

04/08-04/13
Edward H. Robins Players: Seven Chances
By Roi Megrue Cooper
Producer/Director:
Edward H. Robins Players
Cast: Edward H. Robins, Lynn Pratt,
Mortimer Weldon, Aimee Dalmores,
Helen Travers and others

04/15-04/20
Edward H. Robins Players: Broken Threads
By Ernest Wilkes
Cast: Edward H. Robins, M. Rello Webb,
Lynn Pratt, Mortimer Weldon, Aimee
Dalmores, Helen Travers and others

04/22-04/27
Edward H. Robins Players:
What's Your Husband Doing?
By George V. Hobart
Cast: Edward H. Robins and others

04/29-05/04
Edward H. Robins Players: This Way Out
By Frank Craven
Cast: Edward H. Robins and others

05/06-05/11
Edward H. Robins Players:
Here Comes the Bride
By Max Marcin and Roy Atwill
Cast: Edward H. Robins and others

05/10
La Derniere Classe
By M.R. Chauvelot
Producer/Director: Sir William Mulock

05/10
Bishop's Candlesticks (Les Misérables)
By Victor Hugo
Producer/Director: Sir William Mulock

05/10
L'Avare (Act III, Scene V)
By Molière
Producer/Director: Sir William Mulock

05/13-05/18
Edward H. Robins Players: The Gypsy Trail
By Robert Housom
Cast: Edward H. Robins, Lynn Pratt,
Mortimer Weldon, Helen Travers, Jack
Amory and others

05/20-05/25
Edward H. Robins Players:
Broadway and Buttermilk
By Willard Mack
Cast: Edward H. Robins and others

05/21-06/01
Edward H. Robins Players: Cheating
Cheaters
By Max Marcin
Cast: Edward H. Robins and others

06/03-06/15
Edward H. Robins Players: General Post
By J.E. Harold Terry
Cast: Edward H. Robins and others

06/17-06/29
Edward H. Robins Players: Mr. Barnum
By Harrison Rhodes and Thomas A. Wise
Cast: Edward H. Robins and others

07/01-07/06
Edward H. Robins Players: A Gentleman
from Mississippi
By Harrison Rhodes and Thomas A. Wise
Cast: Edward H. Robins and others

07/08-07/13
Edward H. Robins Players: Pals First
By Lee Wilson Dodd
Cast: Edward H. Robins and others

07/15-07/20
Edward H. Robins Players:
The Old Homestead
By Denman Thompson
Cast: Edward H. Robins and others

07/22-07/27
Edward H. Robins Players:
The Man from Mexico
By H.A. DuSouchet
Cast: Edward H. Robins and others

07/29-08/03
Edward H. Robins Players: General Post
By J.E. Harold Terry
Cast: Edward H. Robins and others

08/05-08/10
Edward H. Robins Players:
Johnny Get Your Gun
By Dorothy Donnelly
and Edmund Lawrence Burke
Cast: Edward H. Robins and others

08/12-08/17
Edward H. Robins Players:
Seven Keys to Baldpate
By George M. Cohan
Cast: Edward H. Robins and others

08/19-08/24
Edward H. Robins Players:
The Naughty Wife
By Fred Jackson
Cast: Edward H. Robins and others

08/26-08/31
The Bird of Paradise
By Richard Walton Tully
Producer/Director: Oliver Morosco
Cast: Florence Rockwell, George Lettingwell,
Albert Andrus, Brandon Evans and others

09/02-09/14
The Man Who Came Back
By Jules Eckert Goodman
Producer/Director: William A. Brady
Cast: Henry Hull, Clifford Demsey,
Maude Campbell and others

09/16-09/21
Fair and Warmer
By Avery Hopwood
Producer/Director: Selwyn and Co.
Cast: Sayer Midgley, Marie Colebrook,
Winthrop Chamberlain, Allan Mathers
and others

09/23-09/28
Rock-a-Bye Baby
By Margaret Mayo, Edgar Allan Woolf,
Herbert Reynolds/Jerome Kern
Producer/Director: Selwyn & Co.
Cast: Jefferson de Angelis, Walter
Lawrence, Louise Dresser, Edna Hibbard
and others

09/30-10/05
Eyes of Youth
By Max Marcin and Charles Guernon
Producer/Director:
Shuberts and A.H. Woods
Cast: Alma Tell, James Applebee, Gordon
Morris, Frederick Annesley and others

10/07-10/12
The Little Brother
By Milton Goldsmith and Benedict James
Producer/Director:
Shuberts and Walter Hast
Cast: Walker Whiteside, Tyrone Power,
Edith Latimer and others

10/14-10/19
The Kiss Burglar
By Glen MacDonough/Raymond Hubbell
Producer/Director: Coutts and Tennis
Cast: Patricia O'Hearn, Henry Coote,
Johnny Dale, Estelle Colbert and others

11/04-11/09
Ask Dad (Oh, My Dear)
By P.G. Wodehouse and Guy Bolton/
Louis A. Hirsch
Producer/Director:
F. Ray Comstock and William Elliott
Cast: Joseph Santley, Ivy Sawyer,
Roy Atwell, Juliette Day, Helen Barnes
and others

11/11-11/18
Oh Lady, Lady
By P.G. Wodehouse and Guy Bolton/Jerome
Kern
Producer/Director: Comstock & Elliott
Cast: Doris Predo, Harry Pauli, Grace
Daniels, May Elsie, Billy Gaston and others

11/18-11/23
Experience
By George V. Hobart
Producer/Director: Comstock & Gest
Cast: Guy Collins, May McManus,
Raymond Vansickle and others

11/25-11/30
The Very Idea
By William Le Baron
Producer/Director:
G.M. Anderson and L. Lawrence Weber

Cast: Mildred Post, Jack Hayden, Grace
Burns and others

12/02-12/07
Take It from Me
By William B. Johnstone/Will R. Anderson
Cast: Leona Thompson, Irving Mitchell,
Alice Hills, A. Douglas Leavitt and others

12/09-12/14
The Victory Girl
By Philip Bartholmae/Frank Towers
and Augustus Barratt
Producer/Director: Shuberts
Cast: Frank Fay, Justine Johnstone,
Violet Dale, Harry Conor, Alan Edwards,
Adele Ardsley and others

12/16-12/21
Oh, Look
By James Montgomery/Joseph
McCarthy/Harry Carroll
Producer/Director: Elliott, Comstock & Gest
Cast: The Dolly Sisters (Roszika "Rosie"
and Janci "Jenny"), Charles Lane,
Harry Fox and others

12/23-12/28
Parlor, Bedroom, and Bath
By C.W. Bell and Mark Swan
Producer/Director: A.H. Woods
Cast: Florence Moore, Joan Arthur, Beth
Merrill, Grace Fielkding, James Spottiswood
and others

12/30-01/04/19
The Wanderer
By Maurice V. Samuels
Producer/Director: Elliott, Comstock & Gest
Cast: Louise Orth, Frederick Lewis, Florence
Auer and others

1919

01/06-01/11
The Masquerader
By John Hunter Booth
Producer/Director: Richard Walton Tully
Cast: Guy Bates Post, Adele Ritchie,
Alice John and others

01/13-01/18
Oh, Boy
By P.G. Wodehouse and Guy Bolton/
Jerome Kern
Producer/Director: Comstock & Gest

Cast: Elaine Wilson, Edna May Oliver,
Charles Compton and others

01/20-01/25
Harry Lauder
Producer/Director: William Morris
Cast: Harry Lauder, Burt Melrose
and others

01/27-02/01
Everyman's Castle
By William Anthony McQuire
Producer/Director:
H.H. Frazee/Edward Ellsner
Cast: Robert Edeson, Wilton Lackaye,
Katherine Kaelred, Richard Taber and others

02/03-02/08
Robert B. Mantell Repertory Co.: Richelieu,
Hamlet, Romeo and Juliet, The Merchant of
Venice, Julius Caesar, Macbeth, Richard III
Producer/Director: Robert Bruce Mantell
Cast: Robert Bruce Mantell, Fritz Leiber,
John Burke, Frank Peters, Genevieve
Hamper, Marion Evenson and others

02/10-02/15
She Walked in Her Sleep
By Mark Swan
Producer/Director: George Broadhurst
Cast: Isabel Irving, Helen Lackaye,
Robert Ober, Arthur Aylesworth and others

02/17-02/22
Thirty Days
By A.E. Thomas and Clayton Hamilton
Producer/Director: H.H. Frazee
Cast: Frank McIntyre, Jessie Nagle,
Catherine Comegys and others

02/24-03/01
Maytime
By Rida Johnson Young and Cyrus Wood/
S. Romberg
Producer/Director: Shuberts
Cast: Peggy Wood, William Noriss, Melvyn
Stokes, Maude Odell and others

03/03-03/08
Business Before Pleasure
By Montague Glass
and Jules Eckert Goodman
Producer/Director: A.H. Woods
Cast: Jules Jordan, Harry First, Helen Gill,
Doris Kelly and others

03/10-03/15
Passing Show of 1918
By Harold Atteridge/Sigmund Romberg/
Jean Schwartz
Producer/Director: Shuberts

Cast: Fred Astaire, Adele Astaire,
Willie Howard, Irene Franklin and others

03/17-03/22
Leave It to Jane
By P.G. Wodehouse and Guy Bolton/
Jerome Kern
Producer/Director: Elliott, Comstock & Gest
Cast: Oscar Shaw, Carrie Reynolds
and others

03/24-03/29
See You Later
By P.G. Wodehouse and Guy Bolton/
Jean Schwartz
Producer/Director: Elliott, Comstock & Gest
Cast: T. Roy Barnes, Victor Moore, Frances
Cameron, Hattie Burke and others

03/31-04/05
Oh, Boy
By P.G. Wodehouse and Guy Bolton/
Jerome Kern
Producer/Director: Elliott, Comstock & Gest
Cast: Anna Wheaton, Hal Forde, Eileen
Wilson, Charles Compton, Edna May Oliver
and others

04/07-04/12
Seventeen
By Booth Tarkington
Producer/Director: Stuart Walker
Cast: Ruth Gordon, Gregory Kelly,
Lilian Ross and others

04/14-04/19
I Love You
By William Le Baron
Producer/Director: G.M. Anderson
Cast: John Westley, Gipsy O'Brien,
Ruth Terry and others

04/21-04/26
Lord and Lady Algy
By R.C. Carton
Cast: Maxine Elliott, William Faversham,
Mary Compton and others

Miss MAXINE ELLIOTT
GEO. J. APPLETON Manager

04/28-05/03
Chu Chin Chow
By Oscar Asche/Frederick Norton
Producer/Director: Elliott, Comstock & Gest
Cast: Lionel Braham, Marjorie Wood,
Eugene Cowles, Ritchie Ling and others,
in a cast of 300, with 3 camels, 8 donkeys
and 2 yaks

05/05-05/10
Tea for Three
By Roi Cooper Megrue
Producer/Director: Selwyn & Co.
Cast: Elsa Ryan, Norman Hackett,
Hayden Stevenson and others

05/12-05/17
Edward H. Robins Players: Someone
in the House
Producer/Director: Edward H. Robins
Players/Robert E. Homans
Cast: Edward H. Robins, Homer Barton,
Jack Amory and others

05/19-05/24
Edward H. Robins Players:
Rebecca of Sunnybrook Farm
By Kate Douglas Wiggin
and Charlotte Thompson
Cast: Edward H. Robins and others

05/26-05/31
Edward H. Robins Players:
Nothing But the Truth
By James Montgomery Flagg
Cast: Edward H. Robins, Homer Barton,
Jack Amory, Mary Emerson and others

06/02-06/07
Edward H. Robins Players: Polly with a Past
By Guy Bolton and George Middleton
Cast: Edward H. Robins, Homer Barton,
Jack Amory, Estelle Winwood and others

06/09-06/14
Edward H. Robins Players:
A Successful Calamity
By Clare Kummer
Cast: Edward H. Robins, Homer Barton,
Jack Amory, Estelle Winwood and others

06/16-06/21
Edward H. Robins Players: Hush
By Violet Pearns
Cast: Edward H. Robins, Homer Barton,
Jack Amory, Estelle Winwood,
Augusta Haviland and others

06/23-07/05
Edward H. Robins Players: Billeted
By E. Tennyson Jesse and H.M. Hartford
Cast: Edward H. Robins, Robert E. Homans,
Jack Amory, Estelle Winwood and others

07/12-07/19
Edward H. Robins Players: Yes or No
By Arthur Goodrich
Cast: Edward H. Robins, Robert E. Homans,
Jack Amory, Margaret Kent and others

07/21-07/26
Edward H. Robins Players:
A Very Good Young Man
By Martin Brown
Cast: Edward H. Robins and others

07/28-08/09
Edward H. Robins Players: Officer 666
By Augustin Machugh
Cast: Edward H. Robins, Robert E. Homans,
Jack Amory and others

08/11-08/16
Edward H. Robins Players: Call the Doctor
By Jean Archibald
Cast: Maude Fealy, Madeline Delmar,
Edward H. Robins and others

08/18-08/23
Edward H. Robins Players: Nothing But Lies
By Aaron Hoffman
Cast: Edward H. Robins, Robert E. Homans
and others

08/25-08/30
Edward H. Robins Players: Call the Doctor
By Jean Archibald
Cast: Maude Fealy, Madeline Delmar,
Edward H. Robins and others

09/01-09/06
Edward H. Robins Players: Nothing But
the Truth
By James Montgomery
Cast: Edward H. Robins, Robert E. Homans
and others

09/08-09/13
Edward H. Robins Players: Happiness
By John Hartley Manners
Cast: Edward H. Robins, Robert E. Homans,
Jack Amory and others

09/15-09/20
Edward H. Robins Players: Eyes of Youth
By Max Marcin and Charles Guernon
Cast: Edward H. Robins, Maude Fealy,
Jack Amory and others

09/22-09/27
The Master of Ballantrae
By Carl Mason, after R.L. Stevenson
Producer/Director:
Walter Hast/Hubert Druce
Cast: Walker Whiteside, Hubert Druce,
Arnold Lucy, William H. Sullivan,
Sydney Shields and others

09/29-10/04
Little Simplicity
By R.J. Young, Augustus Barratt
Producer/Director: Shuberts
Cast: Marjorie Gateson, Phil Pyley
and others

10/06-10/11
Up in Mabel's Room
By Otto Harbach and Wilson Collison
Producer/Director: A.H. Woods
Cast: Julie Ring, Sayer Midgley and others

10/13-10/18
Maytime
By R.J. Young/S. Romberg
Producer/Director: Shuberts/Edward Temple
Cast: William Norris, Grace Studdiford,
Carolyn Thomson, Melvyn Stokes
and others

10/20-10/25
Roads of Destiny
By Channing Pollock
Producer/Director: A.H. Woods
Cast: Florence Reed, Calvin Thomas
and others

10/27-11/01
The Riddle: Woman
By G. Jacobi
Producer/Director: Bertha Kalich
Cast: Bertha Kalich, Adele Klaer,
Charles Millward and others

11/03-11/08
Love for Sale
By Will B. Johnstone, Jack Wilson,
Thomas Johnstone and Harry Aurbacher
Producer/Director:
Progressive Amusement Co.
Cast: Kitty Gordon, Vera Beresford,
Jack Wilson and others

11/10-11/15
Gallo English Opera: The Mikado,
The Chimes of Normandy, HMS Pinafore
Producer/Director: Fortune Gallo
Cast: Jefferson De Angelis, Warren Proctor
and others

11/17-11/22
The Woman in Room 13
By Max Marcin and Samuel Shipman
Producer/Director: A.H. Woods
Cast: Robert Edeson, Catherine Tower,
Charles Waldron and others

11/24-11/29
Experience
By George V. Hobart/Silvio Hein
Producer/Director: Elliott, Comstock &
Gest/George V. Hobart
Cast: Maude Gage Fyles and
Donald Scanlan

12/01-12/06
Sothern and Marlowe Repertory Co.:
Twelfth Night, Hamlet, The Taming
of the Shrew
By Wm. Shakespeare
Producer/Director: Shuberts
Cast: E.H. Sothern, Julia Marlowe
and others

12/08-12/13
Business Before Pleasure
By Montague Glass
and Jules Eckert Goodman
Producer/Director:
A.H. Woods/George Marion
Cast: Jules Jordan, Harry First,
Lizzie Wilson and others

12/15-12/20
The Luck of the Navy
By Clifford Mills
Producer/Director:
Comstock & Gest/A.P. Kaye
Cast: Eleanor Street, Charles Croker-King,
A.P. Kaye, Patrick Ludlow and others

12/22-12/27
Oh, What a Girl
By Edgar Smith/Jacques Presburg
and Charles Jules
Producer/Director: Shuberts
Cast: Frank Fay, Sam Ash,
Elizabeth Moffat and others

12/29-01/03/20
At 9:45
By Owen Davis
Producer/Director: William S. Brady
Cast: Marie Goff, Kenneth MacKena
and others

1920

01/05-01/10
Friendly Enemies
By Aaron Hoffman and Samuel Shipman
Producer/Director: A.H. Woods
Cast: Henry J. Cooper, William H. Sloane,
Augusta Burmeister, Ray Wilson and
Natalie Manning

01/12-01/17
Chu Chin Chow
By Oscar Asche/Frederick Norton
Producer/Director: Comstock & Gest
Cast: Lionel Braham, Albert Hawson,
Eugene Cowles, Marjorie Wood and others

01/19-01/24
Tick, Tack, Toe
By Herman Timberg
Producer/Director: Herman Timberg
Cast: Jay Gould, Hattie Darling, Billie
Dreyer, Pearl Eaton, George Mayo
and Herbert Timberg

01/26-01/31
Monte Cristo, Jr.
By Harold Atteridge/S. Romberg.
Jean Schwartz
Producer/Director: Shuberts
Cast: Fanny Watson, Trixie Friganza
and others

02/02-02/07
Sir Harry Lauder
Producer/Director: William Morris
Cast: Harry Lauder

02/09-02/14
Take It from Me
By Will B. Johnstone/Will R. Anderson
Producer/Director: Joseph Gaites
Cast: Fred Hildebrand, Douglas Leavitt,
Zoe Barnett and the Gardiner Trio

02/16-02/21
Shubert Gaities of 1919
Producer/Director: Shuberts/Watson Barrett
Cast: Jack Norworth, Harry Watson,
Al Shayne, Janet Adair and a cast of 125

02/23-02/28
Good Morning, Judge
By Fred Thompson, Adrian Ross, Percy
Greenbank/Lionel Moncton and Howard
Talbot, based on Pinero

Producer/Director: Shuberts
Cast: Alice Handley, Dorothy Francis,
Budd Wann, Adele McHatten and others

03/01-03/06
Nothing But Love
By Frank Stammers/Harold Orlob
Producer/Director: Maddock and Hart
Cast: Ruby Norton, Andrew Tombes,
Sammy Lee and Betty Pierce

03/08-03/13
The Unknown Purple
By Roland West and Carlyle Moore
Producer/Director:
Roland West/Carlyle Moore
Cast: Arthur Le Vine, Herbert Ashton,
Vivian Allen and others

03/15-03/20
Passing Show of 1919
By Harold Atteridge/S. Romberg,
Jean Schwartz
Producer/Director: Shuberts/J.C. Huffman
Cast: Leeta Corder, Edward Cutler, Roy
Cummings, Helen Carrington, Jack Hall,
Marion Parks, Florence Cummings
and others

03/22-03/27
Oh, My Dear!
By P.G. Wodehouse, Guy Bolton/
Louis Hirsch
Producer/Director: Comstock & Elliott
Cast: Juliette Day, Douglas Stevenson,
Hal Forde, Joseph Allen and others

03/29-04/03
Too Many Husbands
By W. Somerset Maugham
Producer/Director: A.H. Woods
Cast: Estelle Winwood, Beatrice Miller, Ruth
Lispon, Marguerite St. John, Fritz William,
Lawrence Grossmith and others

04/05-04/10
Nightie Night
By Martha Stanley and Adelaide Matthews
Producer/Director:
Arthur Klauber and Selwyns
Cast: Francis Byrne, Dorothy Mortimer
and others

04/12-04/17
New York Metropolitan and Chicago Opera
Companies: Faust, Romeo et Juliette, Thaïs,
Cavalleria Rusticana, I Pagliacci, Carmen,
Tosca
Producer/Director: Victor Desautels

04/19-04/24
Martinique
By Laurence Eyre
Producer/Director:
Walter Hast/Laurence Eyre
Cast: Elsa Roem, Lumsden Hare, Liane
Bryon, Arthur Hohl, Ida Waterman
and many others

04/26-05/01
The Bird of Paradise
By Richard Walton Tully
Producer/Director: Oliver Morosco
Cast: Florence Rockwell, Brandon Evans,
Spring Byington and others

05/03-05/08
Frivolities of 1920
By William B. Friedlander
Producer/Director: G.M. Anderson
Cast: Richard Bold, Will Goodall, Doris
Lloyd, Carol Haydon, Jeanne Voltaire,
Ruby Hart and others

05/10-05/15
Edward H. Robins Players: Civilian Clothes
By Thompson Buchanan
Cast: E.H. Robins, Helen Holmes, Reina
Carruthers, Richie Ling, John Daly Murphy,
Ruth Gilmore, Romaine Callendar
and others

05/17-05/22
Edward H. Robins Players: Peter Ibbetson
By N. Raphael
Cast: Graham Velsey, Helen Holmes, Reina
Carruthers, Richie Ling, E.H. Robins and
others

05/24-05/29
Edward H. Robins Players: In Wrong
By Sydney Stone and Eleanor Maude Crane
Cast: E.H. Robins, Graham Velsey
and others

05/31-06/05
Edward H. Robins Players: Blind Man's Buff
By Henry Durrent
E.H. Robins, Helen Holmes, Romaine
Callendar, Jane Blake and others

06/07-06/12
Edward H. Robins Players: Cappy Ricks
By Edward E. Rose
Cast: E.H. Robins, Thomas A. Wise,
Austen Harrison and company

06/14-06/19
Edward H. Robins Players: Daddy
Dumplings
By George Bar McCutcheon and Earl
Carroll
Cast: E.H. Robins, Thomas A. Wise
and company

06/21-06/26
Edward H. Robins Players: Father and
the Boys
By George Ade
Cast: E.H. Robins, Thomas A. Wise and
company

06/28-07/03
Edward H. Robins Players: David Harum
By Edward E. Rose
Cast: E.H. Robins, Thomas A. Wise
and company

07/05-07/17
Edward H. Robins Players: Daddies
By John L. Hobble
Cast: E.H. Robins, Thomas A. Wise
and company

07/19-07/21
Edward H. Robins Players: Cappy Ricks
By Edward E. Rose
Cast: E.H. Robins and company

07/22-07/24
Edward H. Robins Players: Father
and the Boys
By George Ade
Cast: E.H. Robins and company

07/26-07/31
Edward H. Robins Players: Shore Leave
By Hubert Osborne
Cast: E.H. Robins, Thomas A. Jackson
and Mary Emmerson

08/02-08/07
Edward H. Robins Players:
Keep It to Yourself
By Mark Swan
Cast: E.H. Robins, Thomas A. Jackson
and company

08/09-08/14
Edward H. Robins Players:
A Prince There Was
By Robert Hilliard and Frank Westerton
Cast: E.H. Robins, Lorna Volare
and company

08/16-08/21
Edward H. Robins Players:
Keep Her Smiling
By John Hunter Booth
Cast: E.H. Robins, Harry P. Young
and company

08/23-08/28
Hello, Alexander
By Edgar Smith, Emily Young, Alfred
Bryan/Jean Schwartz
Producer/Director: Shuberts
Cast: James McIntyre, Thomas Heath
and others

09/03-09/11
Chu Chin Chow
By Oscar Asche/Frederick Norton
Producer/Director: Comstock & Gest
Cast: Lionel Braham, Thoral Lake, Clarence
Max, Albert Howson, Eugene Cowles,
Marjorie Wood, Adelaide Mesmer
and many others

09/13-09/18
Sinbad
By H. Atteridge/S. Romberg
Producer/Director: Shuberts
Cast: Al Jolson, Margaret Mack, Helen Ely,
Lawrence d'Orsay and others

09/20-09/25
Take It from Me
By Will B. Johnstone/Will R. Anderson
Producer/Director:
Joseph Gaites/Fred Bishop
Cast: Marjorie Sweet, Alice Hills, John A.
Hennings, Helen Gardiner and others

09/27-10/07
Dearie
By John F. Wilson/Malcolm Franklin
Producer/Director:
Dearie Co., Inc./Lee Morrison
Cast: Cosmo Bellew, Will Archie, Letty
Yorke, the Plantation Four and others

10/04-10/09
The Bird of Paradise
By Richard Walton Tully
Producer/Director: Richard Walton Tully
Cast: Florence Rockwell, Robert Brister
and others

10/11-10/16
The Prince and the Pauper
By Amelie Rives
Producer/Director: Shuberts
Cast: William Faversham, Ruth Findlay
and others

10/18-10/23
The Maid of the Mountains
By Frederick Lonsdale, Harry
Graham/Harold F. Simpson, F. Clifford
Harris, Valentine and James Tate
Producer/Director: Trans-Canada Theatres
Ltd. and Mr. Percy Hutchinson
Cast: Fred Wright, Mortimer White,
Edward D'Arcy, Paul Plunkett, Grenville
Hayes, Billy Abbott, Flora Le Breton
and others

10/25-10/30
His Honor, Abe Potash
By Montague Glass and Jules Eckert
Goodman
Producer/Director: A.H. Woods
Cast: Barney Bernard, Robert Cummings
and others

11/01-11/06
Greenwich Village Follies
By Philip Bartholmae, Arthur Swanstrom,
J. Murray Anderson/A. Baldwin Sloane
Producer/Director: John Murray Anderson
Cast: Al Lewis, James Watts, Al Herman,
Verna Gordon, Ted Lewis, the Hickey
Brothers and others

11/08-11/13
The Ruined Lady
By Frances Nordstrom
Producer/Director:
Grace George/Jesse Bonstelle
Cast: Grace George, Jean Oliver,
Ralph Glover, Neil Hamilton and others
(Humphrey Bogart, Co. Mgr.)

11/15-11/20
The Maid of the Mountains
By Frederick Lonsdale, Harry
Graham/Harold Simpson, F. Clifford Harris,
Valentine and James Tate
Producer/Director: Trans-Canada Theatres
Ltd. and Mr. Percy Hutchinson
Cast: Fred Wright, Mortimer White, Edward
D'Arcy, Paul Plunkett, Grenville Hayes, Billy
Abbott, Flora Le Breton and others

11/22-11/27
Walter Hampden Repertory Co.: Hamlet,
The Merchant of Venice, The Taming of
the Shrew
By Wm. Shakespeare
Producer/Director: Walter Hampden
Repertory Co./J. Harry Irvine
Cast: Walter Hampden, J. Harry Irvine,
Allan Thomas, William Sauter, Ernest
Rowan, Geneva Harrison and others

11/29-12/04
My Lady Friends
By Herbert W. Winslow, James
Montgomery, Frank Mandel
Producer/Director: H.H. Frazee
Cast: Jack Norworth, Everett Butterfield
and Jessie Nagle

12/06-12/11
Floradora
By Owen Hall/Leslie Stuart
Producer/Director: Shuberts
Cast: Walter Woolf, Norine Ussery, Imelda
La Mort and others

12/13-12/18
Linger Longer, Letty
By Anna Nichols, Bernard Grossman/
Alfred Goodman
Producer/Director: Oliver Morosco
Cast: Charlotte Greenwood, Robert Higgins,
Ida Stanhope and others

12/20-12/25
East Is West
By Samuel Shipman and John Hymer
Producer/Director: William Harris
Jr./Clifford Brooke
Cast: Helene Sinnott, William Bonelli, Lynn
Starling, Mary Emmerson and Vernon Kelso

12/27-01/01/21
The Blue Flame
By G.V. Hobart, John Willard,
Leta Vance Nicholson
Producer/Director: A.H. Woods
Cast: Theda Bara

1921

01/03-01/08
Irene
By James Montgomery, Joseph
McCarthy/Harry Tierney
Producer/Director: Vanderbilt Producing
Co./Edward Royce
Cast: Dale Winter, Raymond Crane
and others

01/10-01/15
Scandal
By Cosmo Hamilton
Producer/Director: Walter Hast
Cast: Charles Cherry, June Walker,
Henry Mowbray and others

01/17-01/21
Sir John Martin-Harvey Repertory Co.:
Garrick (Tom Robertson), The Burgomaster
of Stilemonde (Maeterlinck)
Producer/Director: Trans-Canada Theatres
Cast: John Martin Harvey, Fred Grove,
Gordon McLeod, Marie Linden, Mary Gray,
Miss N. de Silva and others

01/24-01/29
Maytime
By Rida Johnson Young/Sigmund Romberg
Producer/Director: Shuberts
Cast: Eileen Van Biene, Worthe Faulkner,
Otis Sheridan and others

01/31-02/05
Adam and Eva
By Guy Bolton, George Middleton
Producer/Director: Comstock & Gest/Robert
Milton
Cast: William Boyd, Molly NcIntyre,
Berton Churchill, Percy Waram and others

02/07-02/12
Aphrodite
By Pierre Frondale, George Hazelton/
Henry Fevrier, Anselm Goetzl
Producer/Director:
Comstock & Gest/E. Lyall Swete
Choreographed by Michel Fokine
Cast: Frederick Macklyn, Guy Hitner, W.
Clay Inman, Alfred Hemming, Patricia
O'Connor and others

02/14-02/19
The Beggar's Opera
By John Gay
Producer/Director: Ye Olde Masters
Producing Co./Nigel Playfair
Cast: Arthur Wynn, Percy Heming,
Lena Maitland, Sylvia Nolis, Nonny Lock
and others

02/21-02/26
Cinderella on Broadway
By Harold Atteridge/Bert Grant
Producer/Director:
Shuberts and The Winter Garden Co.
Cast: John T. Murray, Al Brendel, Vivien
Oakland, Flo Burt, the Glorias and others

02/28-03/05
Way Down East
Motion picture

03/21-03/26
Up in Mabel's Room
By Wilson Collier/Otto Harbach
Producer/Director: A.H. Woods
Cast: Sayer Midgley and Julie Ring

03/28-04/02
The Passing Show of 1920
By Harold Atteridge/Jean Schwartz
Producer/Director: Shuberts/J.C. Huffman
Cast: not recorded

04/04-04/09
The Beggar's Opera
By John Gay
Producer/Director: Ye Olde Masters
Producing Co./Nigel Playfair
Cast: Arthur Wynn, Percy Heming,
Lena Maitland, Sylvia Nolis, Nonny Lock
and others

04/11-04/23
Mecca
By Oscar Asche/Percy E. Fletcher
Producer/Director:
Comstock & Gest/E. Lyall Sweet
Cast: Richard Henry, Arthur Barron,
Lionel Braham, Hannah Toback, Kate
Mayhew and others

04/25-04/30
Sir John Martin-Harvey Repertory Co.:
The Only Way (Freeman Willis and
Frederick Langbridge), The Breed of
the Treshams (John Rutherford),
The Burgomaster of Stilemonde
(Maeterlinck), Garrick (Tom Robertson)
Producer/Director:
Trans-Canada Theatres Ltd.
Cast: John Martin Harvey, Fred Grove,
Gordon McLeod, Arthur Chesney, Mary
Gray, Miss N. de Silva and company

05/09-05/14
The Robins Players: The Charm School
By Alice Duer Miller and Robert Milton
Producer/Director: The Robins Players
Cast: E.H. Robins, Sam Hardy, Percival
Moore, Norval Keedwell, Thomas E.
Jackson, Graham Velsey, Miriam Sears,
Helen Stewart and others

05/16-05/21
The Robins Players: Experience
By George V. Hobart
Producer/Director: The Robins Players
Cast: E.H. Robins and company

05/23-05/28
The Robins Players: Adam and Eva
By Guy Bolton and George Middleton
Cast: E.H. Robins and company

05/30-06/04
The Robins Players: The Reason Why
By Mrs. Trimble Bradley and Grant Morris
Cast: E.H. Robins and company

06/06-06/11
The Robins Players: Good Gracious
Annabelle
By Clare Kummer
Cast: Miriam Sears and Faith Dorsey

06/13-06/18
The Robins Players: Scrambled Wives
By Adelaide Matthews and Martha Stanley
Producer/Director: The Robins
Players/Percival Moore
Cast: Miriam Sears, Faith Dorsey, Helen
Travers, Roland Young and others

06/20-06/25
The Robins Players: Wedding Bells
By Salisbury Field
Cast: Edward H. Robins, Helen Travers
and company

06/24
A Midsummer Night's Dream
By Wm. Shakespeare
Producer/Director: Mrs. George Nasmith
Cast: students of The Margaret Eaton
School

06/27-07/02
The Robins Players: No More Blondes
By Otto Harbach
Cast: Edward H. Robins and company

07/04-07/09
The Robins Players: The Hottentot
By William Collier and Victor Mapes
Cast: Edward H. Robins and company

07/11-07/16
The Robins Players: A Full House
By Fred Jackson
Cast: Edward H. Robins and company

07/18-07/23
The Robins Players: Captain Kidd
By Rida Johnson Young
Cast: Edward H. Robins and company

07/25-07/30
The Robins Players: Just Suppose
By Arthur Ellsworth Thomas
Cast: Edward H. Robins and company

08/01-08/06
The Robins Players: What's Your
Husband Doing?
By George V. Hobart
Cast: Edward H. Robins and company

08/08-08/13
The Robins Players: Just Suppose
By Arthur Ellsworth Thomas
Cast: Edward H. Robins and company

08/15-08/20
The Robins Players: Her Husband's Wife
By Arthur Ellsworth Thomas
Cast: Edward H. Robins and company

08/22-08/27
The Robins Players: Nightie Night
By Martha Stanley and Adelaide Matthews
Cast: Edward H. Robins and company

08/29-09/03
The Robins Players: The Hottentot
By William Collier and Victor Mapes
Cast: Edward H. Robins and company

09/05-09/10
Afgar
By Fred Thompson and Worton
David/Charles Cuvillier
Producer/Director:
Comstock & Gest/Frank Collins
Cast: Alice Delysia, W.H. Rawlins, Lupino
Lane, Bradford Kirkbridge and others

09/12-09/17
The Bird of Paradise
By Richard Walton Tully
Producer/Director: Richard Walton Tully
Cast: Ann Reader and others

09/19-09/24
The Skin Game
By John Galsworthy
Producer/Director: William A. Brady
Cast: Arthur C. Crosby, Matthew Bolton,
Reginald Dance and J. Lister Williams

09/26-10/01
Forever After
By Owen Davis
Producer/Director: William A. Brady
Cast: Alice Brady, Kenneth McKenna,
Burr Caruth and Alice Bromley Wilson

10/03-10/08
Artist's Life
By Peggy Wood and Samuel Merwin
Producer/Director: Shuberts/Stuart Walker
Cast: Peggy Wood, Arthur Albertson
and others

10/10-10/15
The Bat
By Mary Roberts Rinehart and Avery
Hopwood
Producer/Director: Wagenhals and
Kemper/Colin Kemper
Cast: Ursula Ellsworth, May Galyer,
Arthur O'Keefe and others

10/17-10/22
The Passing Show of 1921
Harold Atteridge/Jean Schwartz
Producer/Director: Shuberts/J.C. Huffman
Cast: Ina Hayward, Peggy Sisters, Jack Hall
and others

10/24-10/29
The Broken Wing
By Paul Dickey and Charles W. Goddard
Cast: Marguerite Risser, Thurston Hall
and Boris Korlin

10/31-11/05
The Walter Hampden Repertory Co.:
Hamlet, The Merchant of Venice, Romeo
and Juliet, The Taming of the Shrew,
Macbeth, The Servant in the House
(C. Rann Kennedy)
Cast: Walter Hampden, Ernest Rowan,
Allan Thomas, William Sauter, Mary Hall
and others

11/04
Just Suppose
By Arthur Ellsworth Thomas
Producer/Director: The Robins Organization
and the Canadian National Institute for
the Blind
Cast: Graham Velsey, Kathleen Wallace,
Walter Howe, Julia Hurley and Norman
Cope

11/07-11/12
The Bat
By Mary Roberts Rinehart and Avery
Hopwood
Producer/Director: Wagenhals and
Kemper/Colin Kemper
Cast: Ursula Ellsworth, May Galyer,
Arthur O'Keefe and others

11/14-11/19
Romance
By Edward Sheldon
Producer/Director: Lee Shubert
Cast: Ivan Sampson, Ben Lyon,
Phyliss Alden, A.E. Anson and others

11/21-11/26
Sir Harry Lauder
Cast: Harry Lauder and Henry Moore

11/28-12/03
Maytime
By Rida Johnson Young/S. Romberg
Producer/Director: Shuberts/Edward P.
Temple
Cast: John Wheeler, Grace Studdiford,
Philip Branson, Eileen Van Biene and others

12/05-12/10
The Hindu
By Gordon Kean
Producer/Director: Shuberts/John Harwood
Cast: Walker Whiteside, Arthur E. Sprague
and others

12/12-12/17
The Actor's Wife
By Emily Ann Wellman
Producer/Director: Shuberts
Cast: Emily Ann Wellman, Francesca Rotoli
and others

12/19-12/24
Shubert's International Vaudeville Revue
Producer/Director: Shuberts
Cast: Nana and Alexis, Hetty King, Hal
Forde, Giz Rice, Bert Clark and others

12/26-12/31
Irene
By James Montgomery, Joseph
McCarthy/Harry Tierney
Producer/Director: Vanderbilt Production
Co./Edward C. Royce
Cast: Howard Freeman, Booth Howard,
Harry Hoyt, Dale Winter and others

1922

01/02-01/07
Chuckles of 1921
Producer/Director: Shuberts
Cast: Clarke and McCullough and
Olga Mishka

01/09-01/14
Century Theatre Revue
Producer/Director: Shuberts
Cast: Jimmy Hussey and Century Theatre
Beauty Buds

01/16-01/21
Selwyn's Snapshots of 1921
By George Gershwin and others
Producer/Director: Shuberts,
The Selwyns and Lew M. Fields
Cast: Lew Fields, Moran and Wiser

01/23-01/28
Winter Garden Shubert Festival
Producer/Director: Shuberts
Cast: Nora Bayes, Fred Allen, Buddy Doyle
and others

01/30-02/04
Shubert's Vaudeville
Producer/Director: Shuberts
Cast: Hetty King, Anna Corday,
Equilli Brothers and others

02/06-02/11
Miss Lulu Bett
By Zona Gale
Producer/Director: Brock Pemberton
Cast: Carroll McComas, John Thorn
and others

02/13-02/18
Shuberts Vaudeville
Producer/Director: Shuberts
Cast: Alice Lloyd, Poodles the Clown,
Joe Jackson, Lipinski's Canine Ensure
and others

02/20-02/25
The Whirl of New York (Belle of New York)
By Hugh Morton, Edgar Smith/Gustav
Kerker, Al Goodman, Lew Pollack
Producer/Director: Shuberts
Cast: Florence Shubert, Purcelle Brothers,
Keno and Green, Bill Shay and others

02/27-03/04
Tickle Me
By Oscar Hammerstein II, Otto Harbach
and Frank Mandell/Herbert Strothart
Producer/Director: Arthur Hammerstein
Cast: Frank Tinney and Doris Arden

03/06-03/11
Just Suppose
By Arthur Ellsworth Thomas
Producer/Director: Trans-Canada
Theatres Ltd.
Cast: Graham Velsey, Kathleen Wallace,
Julia Hurley, Walter Howe and others

03/13-03/18
The Sothern and Marlowe Repertory Co.:
The Merchant of Venice, Twelfth Night,
Hamlet, The Taming of the Shrew
By Wm. Shakespeare
Cast: E.H. Sothern, Julia Marlowe, Frederick
Lewis, Sidney Mather, Lenore Chippendale,
Vernon Kelso and others

03/20-03/25
Smilin' Through
By Allan Langdon Martin
Producer/Director: The Selwyns/Jane Cowl
Cast: Jane Cowl, Lawrence Grant and others

03/27-04/01
The Man Who Came Back
By Jules Eckert Goodman
Producer/Director: William A. Brady
Cast: Arthur Ashley, Adda Gleason,
James Seeley and Philip Heege

04/10-04/15
San Carlo Grand Opera Co.: Rigoletto,
Aida, Mme Butterfly, Cavalleria Rusticana,
I Pagliacci, Faust, Lohengrin, Martha,
Il Trovatore
Producer/Director:
G.A. Altieri and Ernesto Knoch

04/24-04/29
The Circle
By Somerset Maugham
Producer/Director: Clifford Brooke
Cast: John Drew, Leslie Carter,
Ernest Lawford and others

05/01-05/06
The Robins Players: The Boomerang
By Winchell Smith and Victor Mapes
Cast: Edward H. Robins and the Robins
Players

05/08-05/13
The Robins Players: Ready Money
By James Montgomery
Cast: Edward H. Robins and the Robins
Players

05/15-05/20
The Robins Players: The Blue Pearl
By Anne Crawford Flexnor
Cast: Edward H. Robins and the Robins
Players

The Selwyns present
JANE COWL
in "Smilin' Through"
by ALLAN LANGDON MARTIN

05/22-05/27
The Robins Players: The Woman in Room 13
By Max Marcin and Samuel Shipman
Cast: Edward H. Robins and the Robins
Players

05/29-06/03
The Robins Players: The Brat
By Maude Fulton
Cast: Edward H. Robins and the Robins
Players

06/05-06/10
The Robins Players: Three Wise Fools
By Austin Strong
Cast: Thomas Wise, with Edward H. Robins
and the Robins Players

06/12-06/17
The Robins Players: Pomander Walk
By Louis N. Parker
Cast: Miriam Sears, Thomas Wise,
E.H. Robins and the Robins Players

06/19-06/24
The Robins Players: Pals First
By Lee Wilson Bodd
Cast: E.H. Robins and the Robins Players

06/26-07/01
The Robins Players: Cappy Ricks
By Edward E. Rose
Cast: E.H. Robins and the Robins Players

07/03-07/08
The Robins Players: Grumpy
By Horace Highes and T. Wigney Percival
Cast: E.H. Robins, Thomas Wise and the
Robins Players

07/10-07/15
The Robins Players: Tommy Comes to Town
By Roy Briant
Cast: E.H. Robins, Thomas Wise and the
Robins Players

07/17-07/22
The Robins Players: Main Street
By Harvey Higgins and Harriet Ford,
after Sinclair Lewis
Cast: E.H. Robins and the Robins Players

07/24-07/29
The Robins Players: How Much Do You
Love Me?
By Anne Morrison
Cast: E.H. Robins and the Robins Players

07/31-08/05
The Robins Players: Rollo's Wild Oat
By Clare Kummer
Cast: Roland Young, E.H. Robins and the
Robins Players

08/07-08/12
The Robins Players: Three Live Ghosts
By Guy Bolton and Max Marcin
Cast: Roland Young, E.H. Robins and the
Robins Players

08/14-08/19
The Robins Players: The Man in the Making
By James W. Elliott
Cast: E.H. Robins and the Robins Players

08/21
The Robins Players: The Night Cap
By Guy Bolton and Max Marcin
Cast: E.H. Robins and the Robins Players

08/28-09/02
The Blushing Bride
By Cyrus Wood/S. Romberg
Producer/Director: Shuberts/Frank Smithson
Cast: Cecil Lean, Cleo Mayfeld, Gertrude
Mudge and others

09/04-09/09
The Bat
By Mary Roberts Rinehart and Avery
Hopwood
Producer/Director: Wagenhals and Kemper
Cast: Julia Stuart, Norma Phillips,
Herbert Lieb and others

09/11-09/16
The Bird of Paradise
By Richard Walton Tully
Producer/Director: Richard Walton Tully
Cast: Ann Reader, Frederick Forrester
and others

09/18-09/23
Mother's Millions
By Howard McKent Barnes
Producer/Director: Augustus Pitou
Cast: May Robson, Russell Hicks and others

09/25-09/30
The Emperor Jones
Eugene O'Neill
Producer/Director: Adolph Klauber
Cast: Charles S. Gilpin and Andrew Malony

10/02-10/07
Make It Snappy
Producer/Director: Harold Atteridge,
Eddie Cantor/Jean Schwartz
Producer/Director: Shuberts/J.C. Huffman

Cast: Eddie Cantor, Lillian Fitzgerald, Helen
Carrington and others, including 75 Winter
Garden Beauties

10/09-10/14
Liliom
By F. Molnar
Producer/Director:
The Theatre Guild/Frank Reicher
Cast: Joseph Schildkraut, Eva Le Gallienne,
Elsie Bartlett and others

10/16-10/21
Greenwich Village Follies
Producer/Director: John Murray Anderson
Cast: Joe E. Brown, Ted Lewis, Eva Puck
and others

10/23-10/28
The Dover Road
By A.A. Milne
Producer/Director: Guthrie McClintic
Cast: Charles Cherry, Molly Pearson,
Kathleen Comegys, Reginald Mason
and others

10/30-11/04
Intimate Strangers
By Booth Tarkington
Producer/Director: Augustus Pitou
Cast: Elsa Ryan, Coates Gwynne,
Don Harrington and others

11/06-11/11
The Bat
By Mary Roberts Rinehart and Avery
Hopwood
Producer/Director: Wagenhals and Kemper
Cast: Kate Blanche, Marietta Craig,
Antoinette Crawford, Frederick M. Conklin
and others

11/13-11/18
Chu Chin Chow
By Oscar Asche/Frederick Norton
Producer/Director: Comstock & Gest
Cast: Lionel Braham, Virginia Howell,
Albert Fromm, Adelaide Mesmer and others

11/20-11/25
Bulldog Drummond
By "Sapper"
Producer/Director:
Charles Dillingham/Fred C. Latham
Cast: C. Croker-King, H.B. Warner,
George Sydenham and others

11/27-12/02
The Walter Hampden Repertory Co.:
Othello, Macbeth, The Servant in the House
(C. Rann Kennedy), Hamlet, Romeo and
Juliet, A New Way to Pay Old Debts
(P. Massinger)

Cast: Walter Hampden, William Sauter,
Mabel Moore and Ernest Rowan

12/04-12/09
Iolanthe
By Gilbert and Sullivan
Producer/Director: Canadian Operatic
Society/Reginald Stewart, George Stewart
Cast: W.R. Curry, Robert Lucas, Fred G.
Rogers, Kate Jackson, Jocelyn Clarke
and others

12/18-12/23
The Last Card
By Lillian Barrett
Producer/Director:
H.H. Frazee/Harrison Grey Fiske
Cast: Minnie Maddern Fiske and others

12/20-12/25
Tangerine
By Guy Bolton, Lawrence Langer, Philip
Bartholmae/Monte Carlo and Alma Sanders
Producer/Director: Carle Carlton
Cast: Julia Sanderson, Frank Crumit,
Frank Lalor, Beulah Berson and others

1923

01/01-01/06
Old Bill, MP
By Bruce Bairnsfeather
Producer/Director:
Sam H. Harris/Percival Knight
Cast: Olive Reeves-Smith, Charles
McNaughton, George Bancroft and others

01/08-01/13
To Love
Paul Geraldy
Cast: Grace George, Norman Trevor
and Robert Warwick

01/15-01/20
The Green Goddess
By William Archer
Producer/Director: Winthrop Ames
Cast: George Arliss, Ivan F. Simpson,
Elizabeth Risdon and others

01/22-01/27
Blossom Time
By Dorothy Donnelly/S. Romberg
Producer/Director: Shuberts
Cast: Joseph Mendelssohn, Raymond Metz,
Dallas Welford, Edith Thayer and others

01/29-02/03
The Monster
By Crane Wilbur
Producer/Director: Joseph M. Gaites
Cast: Crane Wilbur, Suzanne Coubet,
Howard Lang, Frank McCormick,
Walter Janes and Frederick Smith

02/05-02/10
Irene
By James Montgomery, Joseph
McCarthy/Harry Tierney
Producer/Director:
Vanderbilt Producing Co./Edward Royce
Cast: Dale Winter, Emma de Weale,
Mary Moore and others

02/12-02/17
The Goldfish
By Gladys Unger
Producer/Director: Shuberts/Stuart Walter
Cast: Marjorie Rambeau, George W.
Barbier, Thurlow Bergen, Jean Wardley
and others

02/19-02/24
The Cat and the Canary
By John Willard
Producer/Director:
Kilbourn Gordon/Ira Hards
Cast: Shirley Booth, Elsie Esmond,
Alma Kruger, W. Lee Tracy and others

02/26-03/03
Bombo
By Harold Atteridge/Sigmund Romberg
Producer/Director: Shuberts/J.C. Huffman
Cast: Al Jolson, Fritzi von Busing,
Forrest Huff, Mlle Fifi, the Bennett Sisters
and others

03/05-03/10
Jollies of 1923
Parkdale Canoe Club
Cast: Art Hatley and his Orchestra,
with Ted Fraser, W. Laing and others

03/12-03/17
The Passing Show of 1922
Producer/Director: Shuberts
Cast: Fred Allen, Willie Howard, Eugene
Howard, Sam Ash, Ethel Sutta and others

03/19-04/24
Land O'Romance
By Anna Nichols
Producer/Director: Augustus Pitou
Cast: Fiske O'Hara, Pat Clary and others

03/26-03/31
The Merry Widow
By Victor Leon, Leo Stein/Franz Lehar
Producer/Director: Henry W. Savage
Cast: Dorothy Francis, James Liddy
and others

04/02-04/07
The Russian Grand Opera Company: Boris
Godunoff, The Jewess (Jacques Halévy),
Eugene Onegin, A Night of Love,
Snegourotchka (Snow Maiden), Carmen,
Pique Dame (Tchaikovsky), The Demon
(Anton Rubenstein)
Producer/Director:
Sol Hurok presents Russian Grand Opera
Company, Eugene Fuerst conducting

04/04-04/09
Kempy
By J.C. Nugent, Elliott Nugent
Producer/Director: Richard G. Herndon
Cast: J.C. Nugent, Elliott Nugent,
Ruth Nugent and others

04/13
Theatrical Mutual Association Benefit
04/16-04/21
Molly Darling
By Otto Harbach, William Carey Duncan,
Phil Cook/Tom Johnstone
Producer/Director: Julian Mitchell
Cast: Jack Donahue, Mary Milburn,
Clarence Nordstom, Rose Kessner and others

04/23-04/28
Make It Snappy
By Harold Atteridge/Jean Schwart,
book by Eddie Cantor
Producer/Director: Shuberts/J.C. Huffman
Cast: Eddie Cantor, Lillian Fitzgerald, Helen
Carrington and others, including 75 Winter
Garden Beauties

04/30-05/05
Tom Jones
By Henry Fielding/Edward Gordon
Producer/Director: Canadian Operatic
Society/George and Reginald Stuart
Cast: Rupert Lucas, Brownlow Card,
Ellwood Genoa, Constance Stewart,
Dorothy Staley and others

05/07-05/12
Spice of 1922
By Jack Lait
Producer/Director: Ed L. Bloom
Cast: Ed Bendel, Flo Bert, Alice Ridnor,
Evelyn Downing and others

05/14-05/19
The Guilty One
By Michael Morton and Peter Traill
Producer/Director: A.H. Woods
Cast: Pauline Frederick, Charles Waldron
and others

05/21-05/26
Rob Roy, adapted from Sir Walter Scott
Producer/Director:
The Rob Roy Club/George Neil
Cast: G. Gordon Simpson, George Neil,
James Esplin, Florence Robinson, Pipe
Majors Murray and Fraser and others

05/28-06/02
His Holiness Pope Pius XI
Motion picture

06/04-06/09
Nice People
By Rachel Crothers
Producer/Director: The Royal Alexandra
Players/Norval Keedwell
Cast: Miriam Sears, Norval Keedwell,
Zola Talma, Earl House and Charles Halton

06/11-06/16
Captain Applejack
By Waller Hackett
Producer/Director: The Royal Alexandra
Players/Norval Keedwell
Cast: Miriam Sears, Norval Keedwell, Zola
Talma, Earl House, Charles Halton, George
Leffingwell, Edythe Tressider and others

06/18-06/23
39 East
By Rachel Crothers
Producer/Director: The Royal Alexandra
Players/Norval Keedwell
Cast: Miriam Sears, Norval Keedwell,
Zola Talma and Edythe Tressiter

06/25-06/30
It's a Boy
By William Anthony Maguire
Producer/Director: The Royal Alexandra
Players/Norval Keedwell
Cast: Miriam Sears, Norval Keedwell,
Charles Halton, George Leffingwell,
Everett Butterfield and others

07/02-07/07
The Dover Road
By A.A. Milne
Producer/Director: The Royal Alexandra
Players/Norval Keedwell
Cast: Miriam Sears, Norval Keedwell,
Charles Halton, George Leffingwell
and others

07/09-07/14
The Ghost Breaker
By Paul Dickey and Charles Goddard
Producer/Director: The Royal Alexandra
Players/Norval Keedwell
Cast: Miriam Sears, Norval Keedwell,
George Leffingwell and others

07/16-07/21
Spite Corner
By Frank Craven
Producer/Director: The Royal Alexandra
Players/Norval Keedwell
Cast: Charles Halton, George Leffingwell,
Zola Talma, Edythe Tressiter,
Grace Webster and others

07/23-07/28
The Misleading Lady
By Paul Dickey and Charles Goddard
Producer/Director: The Royal Alexandra
Players/Norval Keedwell
Cast: Miriam Sears, George Leffingwell,
D.C. Percival and others

07/30-08/04
Adam and Eva
By Guy Bolton and George Middleton
Producer/Director: The Royal Alexandra
Players/Norval Keedwell
Cast: Sam B. Hardy, Elmer Buffam,
Elsie Scott and members of the company

08/06-08/11
The Man in the Box
By Harold McGrath
Producer/Director: The Royal Alexandra
Players/Norval Keedwell
Cast: Sam B. Hardy, Miriam Sears

08/13-08/18
The Broken Wing
By Paul Dickey and Charles W. Goddard
Producer/Director: The Royal Alexandra
Players/Norval Keedwell
Cast: Edward Long, Norval Keedwell,
George Leffingwell, Miriam Sears
and others

08/20-08/25
Tea for Three
By Roi Cooper Megrue
Producer/Director: The Royal Alexandra
Players/Norval Keedwell
Cast: Miriam Sears, George Leffingwell
and others

08/27-09/01
Shuffle Along
By Eubie Blake and Noble Sissle

Cast: Noble Sissle, Eubie Blake, Lottie Gee,
Edith Spencer, the Four Harmony Kings
and others

09/03-09/08
The Bat
By Mary Roberts Rinehart and Avery
Hopwood
Producer/Director: Wagenhals and Kemper
Cast: Julia Stuart, Ursula Ellsworth, Rooney
Tanous, Charles Gotthold and others

09/10-09/15
How Come
By Eddie Hunter/Ben Harris
Producer/Director: Ben Harris
Cast: Eddie Hunter, Alberta Hunter,
Rastus Wilson, Nat Cash, Amon Davis,
George Cooper and others

09/17-09/22
Captain Briquet
By Rudolf Bessier and May Eddington
Producer/Director:
Shuberts/William Faversham
Cast: William Faversham, Hugh Buckler,
Emily Stevens, Edward Emery, Gilda Leary
and others

09/24-09/29
David Copperfield
By Andrew Halliday
Producer/Director:
All-Canada Tours/B.E. Lang
Cast: Fred Forrest, Bransby Williams,
Leslie Barrett, Minnie Waterford and others

10/01-10/06
Go-Go
Harry L. Cort, George E. Stoddard/C.
Luckyeth Roberts
Producer/Director: John Cort
Cast: Texas Guinan, Bernard Granville,
Don Barclay, Frank Doane, May Boley
and others

10/08-10/13
Good Morning, Dearie
By Anne Caldwell/Jerome Kern
Producer/Director: Edward Royce
Cast: Roland Hogue, Virginia Watson,
Edward Allen, Lou Powers and others

10/15-10/20
4 to 11
By Eleanor Robson and Harriet Ford
Producer/Director:
Winthrop Ames/Guthrie McClintic
Cast: Ann Davis, Merle Maddern, Olive
Valerie, Wright Kramer and others

10/22-10/27
Partners Again
By Montagu Glass and Jules Eckert
Goodman
Producer/Director:
The Selwyns and A.H. Wood
Cast: Barney Bernard, Alexander Carr,
Maurice Barret, Jennie Moscovitz
and others

10/29-11/03
Whispering Wires
By Kate McLaurine
Producer/Director: Shuberts
Cast: Louise Swanson, Helene Sullivan,
Robert Harrison and others

11/08-11/10
The Heart of Cellini
By Anthony Wharton
Producer/Director: B.C. Whitney
Cast: Lionel Atwill, Elsie MacKay,
Manart Kippen, Edward Forbes and others

11/12-11/17
Sally
By Guy Bolton, B.G. DeSylva/Jerome Kern
and Victor Herbert
Producer/Director:
Florenz Ziegfeld Jr./Edward Royce
Cast: Marilyn Miller, Leon Errol and others

11/19-11/23
The Theatre Guild Repertory Co.: He Who
Gets Slapped (Leonid Andreyev), The
Devil's Disciple (Shaw), Peer Gynt (Ibsen)
Producer/Director: The Theatre Guild
Repertory Co., Joseph M. Gaites/Philip
Moeller
Cast: Charles Croker-King, Basil Sidney,
Arthur Hughes, Florence Auer,
Erin O'Brien-Moore, Redfield Clarke,
Nanny Griffin, Asya Kass and others

11/26-12/01
The Bat
By Mary Roberts Rinehart
and Avery Hopwood
Producer/Director:
Lincoln A. Wagenhals and Colin Kemper
Cast: Julia Stuart, Zita Reith,
Ursula Ellsworth and others

12/03-12/08
You and I
By Philip Barry
Producer/Director: Richard Herndon
Cast: H.B. Warner, Lucille Watson
and others

12/10-12/15
The Gingham Girl
By Daniel Kusell, Neville Fleeson/
Albert von Tilzer
Producer/Director: Schwab and Kusell
Cast: Irma Marwick, Lorin Raker,
Wynne Gibson and others

12/17-12/22
David Copperfield
By Andrew Halliday
Producer/Director: All-Canada Tours
Cast: Fred Forrest, Bransby Williams,
Leslie Barrett, Minnie Waterford and others

12/24-12/29
The Maid of the Mountains
By Frederic Lonsdale and Harry
Gordon/Harold Frazier Simpson, F. Clifford
Harris, Valentine and James W. Tate
Producer/Director: Stanley T. Vermilyba
Cast: Ethel Walker, Mona Desmond,
Walter Greaza, Louis Templeton and others

12/31-01/05/24
Sir Harry Lauder
Producer/Director: William Morris
Cast: Harry Lauder

1924

01/07-01/26
The John Martin-Harvey Repertory Co.:
Hamlet, The Burgomaster of Stilemonde
(Maeterlinck), A Cigarette Maker's Romance
(Charles Hannan), Via Crucis (Hugo von
Hofmannsthal), Garrick (Tom Robertson),
The Taming of the Shrew, Oedipus Rex
(Sophocles), The Breed of the Treshams
(John Rutherford)
Producer/Director:
All-Canada Tours/B.E. Lang
Cast: Sir John Martin Harvey, N. de Silva,
Fred Grove, Gordon McLeod, Marie Linden,
Eugene Wellesley, Leonard Daniels
and others

01/28-02/02
The Greenwich Village Follies
Producer/Director: John Murray Anderson
Cast: Carl Randall, Ula Sharen, George
Rasely, John Sheehan, Ethel Davis
and others

02/04-02/09
So This Is London
By Arthur Goodrich
Producer/Director: George M. Cohan
Cast: Blossom O'Bryan, Ralph Locke, Allan
F. Moore, Reginald Canlington and others

02/11-02/16
I'll Say She Is
By Groucho Marx, Will B. Johnston/
Tom Johnston
Producer/Director: Joseph M.Gaites and
James B. Beury/Eugene Sanger and
Vaughan Godfrey
Cast: Groucho, Harpo, Chico, Zeppo Marx
with Lotta Miles, Florence Hedges, Marcelle
Hardie and others

02/18-02/23
Little Nellie Kelly
By George M. Cohan
Producer/Director: George M. Cohan
Cast: Norma Teriss, Arthur Cunningham,
Leslie Cole and others

02/25-03/01
Balieff's Chauve Souris
By Nikita Balieff
Producer/Director:
Comstock & Gest/Nikita Balieff
Cast: Nikita Balieff and others

03/03-03/08
Sancho Panza
By Melchior Lengyel/Hugo Felix
Producer/Director:
Russell Janney/Richard Boreslawsky
Cast: Otis Skinner with Robert Rosaire
(as Dapple, the Donkey), Marguerite
Forrest, Russ Whytal, Robert Tobson
and others

03/17-03/22
Polly Preferred
By Guy Bolton
Producer/Director:
Comstock & Gest/Winchell Smith
Cast: Genevieve Tobin, William Harrigan
and others

03/24-03/29
Lady of the Rose
By F.K. Lonsdale, Cyrus Wood/
Jean Gilbert, Alfred Goodman
Producer/Director: Shuberts
Cast: Walter Woolf, Harry K. Morton,
Nancy Gibbs, Detmar Poppen and others

03/31-04/05
The Sothern and Marlowe Repertory Co.:
Twelfth Night, Hamlet, Romeo and Juliet,
The Taming of the Shrew, The Merchant
of Venice
By Wm. Shakespeare
Cast: E.H. Sothern, Lenore Chippendale,
Florence Fair, Frederick Lewis, T.G. Bailey,
France Bendtsen, Frank Peters and others

04/07-04/12
The First Year
By Frank Craven
Producer/Director: John Golden
Cast: Scott Welsh, Patricia Diehearn, John
W. Ransome and others

04/14-04/19
Ziegfeld Follies
By Gene Buck/Victor Herbert, Louis Hirsch,
Dave Stamper
Producer/Director: Florenz Ziegfeld
Cast: The 16 Tiller Girls, William Collier,
Jimmy Hussey, 84 Ziegfeld Follies Beauties
and others

04/21-04/26
The White Sister
Motion picture

05/12-05/17
The Prince of Mah Jong
By Fraser Allen
Producer/Director: The Gyro Club of
Toronto/Fraser Allen
Cast: Betty Mariatt, Jeanne Haig, Margaret
Wilson, Doris Herring, Joseph Clarke,
Art Dunstan and others

05/19-05/24
So This Is London
By Arthur Goodrich
Producer/Director: The Metropolitan
Players/Lumsden Hare and George Cukor

Cast: Alan Bunce, Frank Conroy, Frances
Howard, Elsie Esmond and others

05/26-05/31
The Purple Mask
By Matheson Lang
Producer/Director: The Metropolitan
Players/Lumsden Hare and George Cukor
Cast: Alan Bunce, Frank Conroy, Frances
Howard, Elsie Esmond and others

06/02-06/07
A Tailor-Made Man
By Harry James Smith
Producer/Director: The Metropolitan
Players/Lumsden Hare and George Cukor
Cast: Alan Bunce, Frank Conroy, Frances
Howard, Elsie Esmond and others

06/09-06/21
Merton of the Movies
By George S. Kaufman and Marc Connelly
Producer/Director: The Metropolitan
Players/Lumsden Hare and George Cukor
Cast: Alan Bunce, Frank Conroy, Frances
Howard, Elsie Esmond and others

06/23-06/28
The Gold Diggers
By Avery Hopgood
Producer/Director: The Metropolitan
Players/Lumsden Hare and George Cukor
Cast: Frances Howard, Frank Conroy, Alan
Bunce, Elsie Esmond and others

06/30-07/05
So This Is London
By Arthur Goodrich
Producer/Director: The Metropolitan
Players/Lumsden Hare and George Cukor
Cast: Alan Bunce, Frank Conroy, Frances
Howard, Elsie Esmond and others

07/07-07/12
Kempy
By J.C. Nugent, Elliott Nugent
Producer/Director: The Metropolitan
Players/Lumsden Hare and George Cukor
Cast: J.C. Nugent, Ruth Nugent,
Alan Bunce, Frank Conroy and others

07/14-07/19
Restless Jim Mallon
By J.C. Nugent
Producer/Director: The Metropolitan
Players/Lumsden Hare and George Cukor
Cast: J.C. Nugent, Ruth Nugent, Alan Bunce
and others

07/21-07/26
Peg O' My Heart
By J. Hartley Manners

Producer/Director: The Metropolitan
Players/Lumsden Hare and George Cukor
Cast: Elsa Ryan, Alan Bunce, Edward
Douglas and others

07/28-08/07
In Love with Love
By Vincent Lawrence
Producer/Director: The Metropolitan
Players/Lumsden Hare and George Cukor
Cast: Elsa Ryan, Alan Bunce, Elmer Buffam
and others

08/04-08/09
The Old Soak
By Don Marquis
Producer/Director: The Metropolitan
Players/Lumsden Hare and George Cukor
Cast: Violet Dunn, Harold Thompson,
Elmer Buffam and others

09/08-09/13
The Robert B. Mantell Repertory Co.:
Richard III, King Lear, As You Like It,
Hamlet, Richelieu, Macbeth, The Merchant
of Venice, Romeo and Juliet
Cast: Robert Bruce Mantell, Vaughan
Deering, Edmond Dalby, Henry Buckler,
Genevieve Hamper and Agnes Elliott Scott

09/15-09/20
Romeo and Juliet
By Wm. Shakespeare
Producer/Director:
The Selwyns, with Adolph Klauber
Cast: Jane Cowl, Rollo Peters, Louis Hector
(Tybalt), Jesse Ralph (Nurse) and John
Crawley (Friar Lawrence)

09/22-09/27
Sweet Little Devil
By Frank Mandell, Laurence Schwab and
Buddy DeSylva/George Gershwin
Producer/Director: The Selwyns/Staged by
Edgar MacGregor; Musical Staging by
Sammy Lee; Miss Binney's ballet arranged
by Michel Fokine
Cast: Constance Binney, Ruth Warren,
William Wayne, Irving Beebe, Billie Taylor
and others

09/29-10/04
The Goose Hangs High
By Lewis Beach
Producer/Director:
Dramatists' Theatre Inc./James Forbes
Cast: George Alson, Lorna Elliott and others

10/06-10/11
The Passing Show of 1923
By Harold Atteridge/S. Romberg,
Jean Schwartz

Producer/Director: Shuberts
Cast: Georgie Price, Roy Cummings,
Margaret Breen, Jack Rice, Ladas May
and others

10/13-10/18
No Other Girl
By Aaron Hoffman, Bert Kalnar/Harry Ruby
Producer/Director:
A.J. Jones and Morris Green
Cast: Eddie Buzzell, Helen Ford and others

10/20-10/25
Blossom Time
By Donnelly/Romberg
Producer/Director: Shuberts
Cast: Edith Thayer, Bertram Peacock,
William Danforth and others

10/27-11/01
Bulldog Drummond
By "Sapper"
Producer/Director: Percy Hutchison
at the Queen's Theatre, London
Cast: Percy Hutchison, Frank Lacy
and others

11/03-11/08
The Outsider
By Dorothy Brandon
Producer/Director: William Harris Jr.
Cast: Lionel Atwill, Ann Davis, Whitford
Kane and others

11/10-11/15
Cheaper to Marry
By Samuel Shipman
Producer/Director: Richard
Herndon/Augustus Duncan
Cast: Harry Mestayer, Frank M. Thomas,
Mona Barons and others

11/17-11/22
Sitting Pretty
By P.G. Wodehouse, Guy Bolton/Jerome
Kern
Producer/Director: A.L. Jones and Norris
Green with Comstock & Gest
Cast: The Dolly Sisters, Frank McIntyre,
Paul Frawley and Fred Santley

11/24-11/29
Rob Roy
By Sir Walter Scott
Producer/Director:
The Rob Roy Club/George Heil
Cast: James Fray, F. Bryce, Evelyn M.
Braithwaite, James Esplin, Florence
Robertson and others

12/01-12/06
Charlot's Revue of 1924
Producer/Director: The Selwyns/Andre
Charlot
Cast: Beatrice Lillie, Gertrude Lawrence,
Herbert Mundin, Sam B. Hardy

12/08-12/13
Innocent Eyes
By Harold Atteridge/S. Romberg,
Jean Schwartz
Producer/Director: Shuberts
Cast: Vanessi, Lew Hearn, John V. Lowe,
Ruth Gillette and others

12/29-01/03/25
Tarnish
By Gilbert Emery
Producer/Director: John Cromwell
Cast: Frederic March, Edith Shayne,
Lou Ripley, Grace Connell, Edith Taliaferro
and others

1925

01/05-01/10
Blossom Time
By Donnelly/Romberg
Producer/Director: Shuberts/J.C. Huffman
Cast: Beulah Berson, Grace Ayeager, Sioux
Nedra, Ralph Soule, Knight MacGregor and
many others

01/12-01/17
Rose Marie
By Harbach, Hammerstein/Friml
Producer/Director:
Arthur Hammerstein/Paul Dickey
Cast: Arthur Cunningham, Betty Byron,
Alonzo Price, Henry White and others,
including a chorus of 52

01/19-01/24
Artists and Models of 1924
By J. Fred Coots, Harry Wagstaffe Gribble,
Sam Coslow, Clifford Grey/S. Romberg
Producer/Director: Shuberts
Cast: Buddy Doyle and others

01/26-01/31
Mr. Battling Butler
By Ballard McDonald/Walter Risemount
Producer/Director:
George Choos/Guy Bragdon
Cast: Charles Ruggles, Eugene McGregor,
Helen Eley, Lester Eilliott and others

02/02-02/07
Moonlight
By William B. Friedlander
Producer/Director: Lawrence Weber
Cast: Frank Crumit, Franker Woods,
Louis Simon and Julia Sanderson

02/09-02/14
Little Jesse James
By Harlan Thompson/Harry Archer
Producer/Director:
L. Lawrence Weber/Walter Brooks
Cast: Evan Valentine, John Milligan, Allan
Kearns, Madeleine Creye, Gladys Baxter,
George Spelvin and others

02/23-02/28
The Potters
By J.P. McEvoy
Producer/Director: Richard Herndon
Cast: Donald Meek, Eleanor Gordon,
Raymond Guion and Mary Sills

03/09-03/14
Parkdale Jollies of 1925
Producer/Director: Parkdale Canoe Club
Cast: Dorothy Walsh, Gwyneth Hitchman,
Jack Wise, George Young, Walter Lainy
and others

03/23-03/28
Greenwich Village Follies
Producer/Director: A.L. Jones Morris Green
Cast: Daphne Pollard, Tom Howard, Buster
West, Martha Graham and others

03/30-04/04
Rose Marie
By Harbach, Hammerstein/Friml
Producer/Director: Arthur Hammerstein
Cast: Irene Pavloska, Charles Silbert, Guy
Robertson, Beatrice Kay, Charles Meakins,
Phoebe Brun and others

04/06-04/18
White Cargo
By Leon Gordon
Producer/Director: Earl Carroll
Cast: Annette Margules, Allen Connor, Leon
Gordon, Wallis Clarke, Frederick Forrester
and James C. Carroll

04/20-04/25
The Dream Girl
By Rida Johnson Young, Harold
Atteridge/Victor Herbert
Producer/Director: Shuberts/J.C. Huffman
Cast: Fay Bainter, Walter Woolf, Vivara,
Ben Linn, Wyn Richmond and others

04/27-05/02
Balieff's Chauve Souris
By Nikita Balieff
Producer/Director:
Comstock & Gest/Nikita Balieff
Cast: Nikita Balieff and others

05/11-05/23
Oh, Yes
By M.W. Plunkett
Producer/Director:
The Dumbells Co. Ltd./M.W. Plunkett
Cast: The Dumbells: Al Plunkett, Ross
Hamilton, Red Newman, Jock Holland,
Stan Bennett, Pat Rafferty, Glen Allen
and Jimmy Devon

07/01-07/10
School for Scandal
By R.B. Sheridan
Producer/Director:
The Hugh Buckler Co./Hugh Buckler
Cast: Hugh Buckler, Violet Paget,
Lambert Larking, Violet Paget, Muriel Dean,
Edgar R. Warburton and others

07/11-07/18
Gay Lord Quex
By Arthur Wing Pinero
Producer/Director:
The Hugh Buckler Co./Hugh Buckler
Cast: Hugh Buckler, Lambert Larking, Inthia
Carpenter, Winnifred Hulse and others

07/20-07/25
Jane
By Harry Nicholls and Wim Lestocq
Producer/Director:
The Hugh Buckler Co./Hugh Buckler
Cast: Hugh Buckler, Lambert Larking
and others

07/27-08/01
Niobe
By Harry and Edward Paulton
Cast: Producer/Director:
The Hugh Buckler Co./Hugh Buckler
Hugh Buckler, Violet Paget and others

08/03-08/08
What Happened to Jones?
By George Broadhurst
Producer/Director:
The Hugh Buckler Co./Hugh Buckler
Cast: Hugh Buckler, Francis Compton
and others

08/10-08/15
So This Is London
Producer/Director: Arthur Goodrich
The Hugh Buckler Co./Hugh Buckler
Cast: Hugh Buckler, Violet Paget and others

12/27-01/01/27
Joy Bombs
By M.W. Plunkett
Producer/Director:
The Dumbells Co. Ltd./M.W. Plunkett
Cast: The Dumbells: Al Plunkett, Ross
Hamilton, Red Newman, Jock Holland, Stan
Bennett, Pat Rafferty, Glen Allen, Jimmy
Devon, Ben Allen and Morley Plunkett

1927

01/03-01/15
The Matheson Lang Repertory Co.:
The Chinese Bungalow (Marion Osmond
and James Corbet), The Wandering Jew
(E. Temple Thurston)
Producer/Director: All-Canada
Tours/Matheson Lang
Cast: Matheson Lang and company

01/17-01/29
The D'Oyly Carte Opera Co.:
The Mikado, The Gondoliers
By Gilbert and Sullivan
Producer/Director:
The D'Oyly Carte Opera/Harry Norris
Cast: Henry A. Lytton, Darrell Fancourt,
Bertha Lewis, Irene Hill and others

01/31-02/05
Green Fruit
By Gladys Unger, Clifford Grey/Maurice
Rubens, J. Fred Coots
Producer/Director: Shuberts
Cast: Mitzi, Ethel Intropodi, Eric Blore
and others

02/07-02/12
Big Boy
Harold Atteridge/Joseph Meyer
Producer/Director: Shuberts
Cast: Al Jolson, Colin Campbell, Viola
Gillette, Frankie Lane, George Andre
and others

02/14-02/19
The Honor of the Family
By Paul M. Potter
Producer/Director: The Charles Frohman Co.
Cast: Otis Skinner, Jessie Royce Landis
and others

02/21-02/26
Katja
By Frederick Lonsdale and Harry Graham

Producer/Director: Shuberts
Cast: Madeline Collins, Leonard Seeley,
Teddy Webb, Jack Sheehan and others

02/29-03/05
Parkdale Jollies of 1927
Producer/Director: The Hartford Production
Co. for the Parkdale Canoe Club

03/14-03/19
Old English
By John Galsworthy
Producer/Director: Winthrop Ames
Cast: George Arliss, Dora Lennox,
Ivan F. Simpson and others

03/21-03/26
The Scarlet Lily
By David Arnold Balch
Producer/Director:
Sanford E. Stanton/
E.J. Blunkart
Cast: Marguerite Risser, Donald Miles,
William Balfour and others

03/28-04/07
Yes, Yes, Yvette
By Frederic Isban/Irving Caesar/
Philip Charig
Producer/Director: H.H. Frazee
Cast: Donald Brian, Jeanette MacDonald
and others

04/04-04/06
Sir Harry Lauder
Producer/Director: William Morris
Cast: Sir Harry Lauder and others

04/07-04/09
The Quinneys
By Horace Annesley Vachell
Producer/Director: Theatre Guild of
Canada/William Podmore
Cast: William Podmore, Anne Carew,
George Le Guerre, Cecile Dixon and
Audrey Ridgwell

04/21-04/23
Denishawn Dance Co.
Cast: Ruth St.Dennis, Ted Shawn and others

04/26-04/30
The D'Oyly Carte Opera Co.: HMS Pinafore,
The Mikado, Yeoman of the Guard, The
Gondoliers
By Gilbert and Sullivan
Producer/Director: All-Canada Tours
Cast: Henry Lytton, Leo Sheffield, Winifred
Lawson, Bertha Lewis, Darrell Fancourt
and others

05/09-05/14
That's That
By M.W. Plunkett
Producer/Director:
The Dumbells Co., Ltd./M.W. Plunkett
Cast: The Dumbells: Al Plunkett,
Ross Hamilton, Glen Allen, Morley Plunkett,
Jock Holland and Pat Rafferty

05/16-05/21
What Every Woman Knows
By James M. Barrie
Producer/Director: William A. Brady
Cast: Helen Hayes, Kenneth MacKenna,
Selene Johnson, Lumsden Hare and others

Helen Hayes

05/23-05/28
George White's Scandals
By George White, William K. Wells,
B.G. DeSylva/Lew Brown, Ray Henderson
Producer/Director: George White
Cast: Sonia De Calva, Sammy Howard
and the Rasch Ballet

08/29-09/10
Oo La La!
By M.W. Plunkett
Producer/Director:
The Dumbells Co., Ltd./M.W. Plunkett
Cast: The Dumbells: Al Plunkett, Ross
Hamilton, Glen Allen, Morley Plunkett,
Jock Holland, Pat Rafferty, Red Newman,
Merton W. Plunkett, Jack McLellan,
Harry Binns, Fred Emney, Charley Jeeves
and Cameron Geddes

09/12-09/17
The Letter
By Somerset Maugham
Producer/Director: Messmore Kendall
Cast: Katherine Cornell, Allan Jeaves,
J.W. Austin, James Vincent, Sam Kim,
Mary Scott Seton and Lady Chong Goe

09/19-10/01
The American Light Opera Co.: The
Bohemian Girl (Alfred Bunn/Michael Balfe),
Martha (Von Flowtow), The Chocolate
Soldier (Stanislaus Stange/Oscar Strauss)
Producer/Director:
The American Light Opera Co.
Cast: George Shields, Theo Pennington,
Lulu Root, Carl Bundschu and others

10/03-10/08
Rose Marie
Otto Harbach, Oscar Hammerstein/R. Friml
Producer/Director: Arthur Hammerstein
Cast: Charles Meakins, Paul Donan,
Houstin Richards, Beulah Benson and others

10/10-10/15
The Vagabond King
By Brian Hooker and W.H. Post/Rudolf Friml
Producer/Director:
Russell Janney/Max Figman
Cast: Edward Neil, H. Cooper-Cliffe,
Carolyn Thomson. Alice Belmore Cliffe
and others

10/17-10/22
Oo La La!
By M.W. Plunkett
Producer/Director:
The Dumbells Co., Ltd./M.W. Plunkett
Cast: The Dumbells: Al Plunkett,
Ross Hamilton, Glen Allen, Morley Plunkett,
Jock Holland, Pat Rafferty, Red Newman,
Merton W. Plunkett, Jock McLellan, Harry
Binns, Fred Emney, Charley Jeeves and
Cameron Geddes

10/24-10/29
And So to Bed
By James Fagan
Producer/Director: James Fagan and
Lee Shubert/James Fagan
Cast. Jennie Rocht, Paul Nugent, Fred
O'Donovan (Samuel Pepys), Yvonne
Arnaud, Emlyn Williams (Pepys' Boy),
Gyles Isham, George Griffiths and others

10/31-11/05
The Jazz Singer
By Sam Raphaelson
Producer/Director:
Lewis & Gordon/Albert Lewis
Cast: George Jessel, Anna Lowenwirth,
Edward Arnold, Lea Taiz and others

11/07-11/12
The Fog
By John Willard
Cast: George Sydenham, Leslie King,
Dorothy Lyons and others

11/17-11/19
Mikhail Mordkin and his Russian Ballet:
Swan Lake, Ariadne, Carnival
Producer/Director: Mikhail Mordkin
Mikhail Mordkin and others

11/21-11/26
Junior League Revue

11/28-12/03
The White Eagle
By Brian Hooker and W.H. Post/R. Friml
Producer/Director: Russell Janney,
choreographed by Busby Berkely
Cast: Allan Prior, Lawrence D'Orsay,
Marion Keeler, Elsa Peterson, Forrest Huff,
Charles E. Gallagher and others

12/05-12/10
La Cianci and the New York Grand Opera
Co.: Aida, Cavalleria Rusticana, I Pagliacci,
Faust, Carmen, La Forza del Destino,
Il Trovatore, Otello
Producer/Director:
Vincent Cianci/Micael Feveisky, conducting

12/12-12/17
The Spider
By Fulton Oursler, Lowell Brentano
Producer/Director: Sam H. Harris
Cast: William Courtenay, Paul Harvey
and others

12/19-12/24
Policing the Plains
Motion picture

12/26 01/07/28
Aladdin
Producer/Director:
All-Canada Tours/B.L. Lang
Cast: Bertha Russell, Lillian Barnes, Dave
Lee, Fred Wolgast, Harry Gilmour and others

1928

01/09-01/14
Charley's Aunt
By Brandon Thomas
Producer/Director:
Mrs. Brandon Thomas/Cecil Barth
Cast: Jevan Brandon Thomas (playwright's
son), Gladys Miller, Ernest E. Norriss,
Douglas Brandford, Deirdre Doyle
and others

01/16-01/21
Scaramouche
By R. Sabatini
Producer/Director:
All-Canada Tours/B.E. Lang
Cast: John Martin-Harvey, Gordon McLeod,
Reginald Tibbett, Nina de Silva, Betty
Belloc and Marie Linden

01/23-01/28
Broadway
By Philip Dunning and George Abbott
Producer/Director: Jed Harris/Philip Dunning
and George Abbott
Cast: Frederick Howard, Helen Shea
and others

01/30-02/04
Oh, Kay
By P.G. Wodehouse, Guy Bolton/
George Gershwin
Producer/Director:
Aarons & Freedly, with Shuberts
Cast: Julia Sanderson, John E. Young,
Shepp Camp and others

02/06-02/11
My Maryland
By D. Donnelly/S. Romberg
Producer/Director: Shuberts
Cast: George Rymer, Lottice Howell, Ralph
Dunn, Little Miss Betty Brown and others

02/13-02/18
Hicks and Terriss Repertory Co.: Mr. What's
His Name (Seymour Hicks), Scrooge
(J.C. Buckstone)
Producer/Director: Hicks and Terriss
Repertory Co., All-Canada Tours
Cast: Ellaline Terriss, Gladys Tudor, Meg Le
Monnier, Betty Seymour Hicks and others

02/20-02/25
The Vagabond King
By W.H. Post and Brian Hooker/Rudolf Friml
Producer/Director:
Russell Janney/Richard Boleslavsky
Cast: Edward Nell Jr., Carolyn Thompson,
H. Cooper-Cliffe and Will H. Philbrick

02/27-03/03
The Desert Song
By Otto Harbach, Oscar Hammerstein II/
S. Romberg
Producer/Director: Schwab & Mandell
Cast: Robert Halliday, Ethel Louise Wright,
William O'Neal, Edmund Elton and others

03/05-03/10
Blossom Time
By D. Donnelly/S. Romberg
Producer/Director: Shuberts

Cast: Vera Aamazar, J.C. Gilbert,
Genevieve Neagle, Patrick Kelly and others

03/12-03/17
The Constant Wife
By Somerset Maugham
Producer/Director:
J.M. Welch Inc./William Postance
Cast: Margaret Teabeau, W. Boyd Davis,
Karl Edwards, Diane Tellegen, Norman
Hackett and others

03/26-03/31
John Martin-Harvey Repertory Co.:
The Burgomaster of Stilemonde
(Maeterlinck), A Cigarette-Maker's
Romance (Charles Hannon),
Scaramouche (R. Sabatini),
The Lyons Mail (Charles Reade)
Producer/Director: All-Canada Tours
Cast: John Martin-Harvey, Nina de Silva
and others

03/29-03/24
Gay Paree
By J. Fred Coots, Harold Atteridge, Mann
Holiner and Clifford Grey/Alberta Nichols
Producer/Director: Shuberts
Cast: Chic Sale, Irene Cornell and others

04/09-04/14
Lord Richard in the Pantry
By Sidney Blow and Douglas Hoare
Producer/Director: Mrs. Brandon Thomas
Cast: Jevan Brandon-Thomas, Richard
Cooper, Deirdre Doyle and others

04/16-04/21
The Merchant of Venice
By Wm. Shakespeare
Producer/Director: Winthrop Ames
Cast: George Graham, George Arliss,
Spring Byington (as Portia), David Leonard,
Sydney Booth and others

04/23-04/28
Yours Truly
By Clyde North/Raymond Hubbell
Producer/Director: Gene Buck
Cast: Leon Errol, the Tiller Girls and others

05/01-05/05
Hicks and Terriss Repertory Co.: The Man
in Dress Clothes, Mr. What's His Name
(Seymour Hicks)
Producer/Director: Hicks and Terriss
Repertory Co., All-Canada Tours
Cast: Ellaline Terriss, Gladys Tudor, Meg Le
Monnier, Betty Seymour Hicks and others

05/07-05/12
Balieff's Chauve Souris
By Nikita Balieff
Producer/Director:
Comstock & Gest/Nikita Balieff
Cast: Nikita Balieff (the maître de
chorégraphie for this edition was George
Balanchine, billed as "G. Bulanchin")

05/14-05/19
The Play's the Thing
F. Molnar, trans. P.G. Wodehouse
Producer/Director: Gilbert Miller
Cast: Holbrook Blinn, Hubert Druce
and others

05/21-05/26
Bubbling Over
By M.W. Plunkett
Producer/Director:
The Dumbells Co. Ltd./M.W. Plunkett
Cast: The Dumbells: Fred Emney,
Cameron Geddes, Harry Binns, Al Plunkett,
Pat Rafferty, Red Newman, Jock Holland,
Ross Hamilton, Glenn Allen, Charlie Jeeves,
Louis Crerar and Howard Fogg

05/28-06/02
The Road to Rome
By Robert Sherwood
Producer/Director: Charles L. Wagner
Cast: Richard Bird, Alice Brady, Lionel
Chambers, Douglas Wood and others

06/04-06/09
Saturday's Children
By Maxwell Anderson
Producer/Director: The Actors'
Theatre/Guthrie McClintic
Cast: Jean May, Hugh Banks,
T. Daniel Frawley and others

06/11-06/16
Broadway
By George Abbott and Philip Dunning
Producer/Director:
Jed Harris/George Abbott
Cast: John Carmody, Wally Ford,
Frank Shannon, Matt Briggs and others

08/27-09/08
Why Worry
By M.W. Plunkett
Producer/Director:
The Dumbells Co. Ltd./M.W. Plunkett
Cast: The Dumbells: Merton W. Plunkett,
Al Plunkett, Red Newman, Fred Emney,
Aileen Parker, Dorothy Stock, Teresa
Corrigan, Gracie Rae, Jessie Butt, Jock
Holland, Scotty Morrison, Morley Plunkett,

Harry Binns, Cameron Geddes, Howard
Fogg, Charlie Jeeves, Louis Crerar, Florence
Rowland, Grace Moore, Naomi MacIntosh,
Edna Grice, Merle Watson, Marjorie Pethic,
Iris Francis and Evelyn Clouthier

09/10-09/15
Bits and Pieces
Producer/Director: All-Canada Tours
Cast: George Robey, Marie Blanche,
the Hippodrome 8 and others

09/17-09/22
Good News
By Lawrence Schwab, B.G. DeSylva,
Lew Brown/Ray Henderson
Producer/Director: Laurence Schwab,
Frank Mandel/Edgar MacGregor
Cast: Don Lanning, Don Rowan, William
Wayne, Mildred Costello, Dolores Farris
and many others

09/24-09/28
When Crummles Played
By Nigel Playfair
Producer/Director:
Charles L. Wagner/Halliwell Hobbes
Cast: Halliwell Hobbes, Mylor Merriam,
Parker Mills, Nell Carter and many others

10/01-10/06
My Maryland
By D. Donnelly/S. Romberg
Producer/Director: Shuberts
Cast: Alexander Callum, Ruth Urban,
Lucette Parker and others

10/08-10/27
The D'Oyly Carte Opera Co.: The Mikado,
Ruddigore, Iolanthe, Trial by Jury,
The Pirates of Penzance, Patience
By Gilbert and Sullivan
Producer/Director: All-Canada Tours
Cast: Henry Lytton, Darrell Fancourt,
Blossom Gelsthorpe and others

10/29-11/03
The Trial of Mary Dugan
By Bayard Veiller
Producer/Director: A.H. Woods/Edwin Jones
Cast: John Spacey, Edith Broder, Edward
Emerson, John Costello and Louza Riane

11/05-11/10
Paris Bound
By Philip Barry
Producer/Director: Arthur Hopkins
Cast: Madge Kennedy, Don Cook,
Edward Fielding, Herbert Yost and others

11/12-11/17
Lovely Lady
By Gladys Unger, Cyrus Wood/Dave
Stamper and Harold Levey
Producer/Director: Shuberts/Milton Shubert
Cast: Emil de Tramont, Charles la Torre,
Anthony Sterling, Maryan Lynn, Frank
Greene, Mona Moray, Ruth Ames and
many others

11/19-11/24
Between Ourselves
Producer/Director: The Parkdale Canoe Club
Cast: George Robey, Jimmy Deans, Marie
Blanche, the Hippodrome 8 and others

12/03 12/08
And So To Bed
By James Fagan
Producer/Director: Shuberts/James Fagan
Cast: Walter Kingsford and others

12/10-12/15
The Silent House
By John Brandon and George Pickett
Producer/Director: Shuberts/Carl Hunt
Cast: Howard Lang, Dodd Mehan, Charles
McNaughton and others

12/25-12/29
The Trial of Mary Dugan
Bayard Veiller
Producer/Director: A.H. Woods/Edwin Jones
Cast: John Spacey, Edith Broder, Edward
Emerson, John Costello and Louza Riane

01/07-01/12
Bill of Divorcement
By Clemence Dane
Producer/Director: Gordon McLeod
Productions/Ivor Bernard
Cast: Lillian Christine, Oliver Walter
Heather McIntyre, Paul Sabina,
Gordon McLeod and others

01/14-01/19
The American Opera Co.: Faust, Carmen,
Mme Butterfly, Martha, Marriage of Figaro,
Legend of the Piper, I Pagliacci
Producer/Director: The American Opera
Co./Vladimir Rosing
Cast: John Moncrieff and others

01/28-02/02
Comédies Musicales Françaises: Un Bon
Garçon, Passionnemate, Trois Jeunes Filles
aux Folies Bergères
Producer/Director: J.A. Gauvin
Cast: Sonia Alny, Gina Barty, Jeanne de
Poumayrac, Yvette Herbeaux, Christian
Servatius, Georges Foix, Jose Daufy
and others

02/04-02/09
The Maurice Colbourne Repertory Co.:
John Bull's Other Island, Candida, You
Never Can Tell, Fanny's First Play, Dark
Lady of the Sonnets (Shaw)
Producer/Director: Maurice
Colbourne/Balliol Holloway
Cast: Maurice Colbourne, Lambert Larking,
Barry Jones, Barbara Wilcox, Rule Pyott,
Constance Pelissier, Haroldine Humphreys
and others

02/11-02/16
Blossom Time
By D. Donnelly/S. Romberg
Producer/Director: Shuberts
Cast: Genevieve Naegle, John Charles
Gilbert, Herman Lyle, Robert Lee Allen,
Nancy Sheridan, Mary Maher and others

02/18-02/23
The Maurice Colbourne Repertory Co.: John
Bull's Other Island, Candida, You Never
Can Tell, Dark Lady of the Sonnets (Shaw)
Producer/Director:
Maurice Colbourne/Balliol Holloway
Cast: Maurice Colbourne, Lambert Larking,
Barry Jones, Barbara Wilcox, Rule Pyott,
Constance Pelissier, Haroldine Humphreys
and others

02/25-03/09
The Stratford-Upon-Avon Festival Co.:
Taming of the Shrew, Hamlet, Julius Caesar,
The Merry Wives of Windsor, Henry IV
(Part 1), Midsummer Night's Dream,
The Merchant of Venice, Richard III
Producer/Director:
Comstock & Gest/W. Bridges Adam
Cast: Wilfred Alter, Mary Holder, George
Hayes, Dorothy Massingham and others

03/11-03/16
The Desert Song
By Otto Harbach, Oscar Hammerstein II
and Frank Mandell/Sigmund Romberg
Producer/Director: Schwab & Mandell
Cast: Bernard Granville, Bernice Claire,
Alexander Gray, Carlotta Miles and others

03/18-03/25
Luckee Girl (Un Bon Garçon)
By Gertrude Purcell/Maurice Yvain
Producer/Director: Shuberts
Cast: Billy House, Harry Puck, Leota Lane
and others

03/25-03/30
Here 'Tis
By M.W. Plunkett
Producer/Director:
The Dumbells Producing Co. Ltd.
Cast: The Dumbells: Al Plunkett, Fred
Emney, Charlie Jeeves, Scotty Morrison,
Red Newman, Morley Plunkett, Cameron
Geddes, Harry Binns, Jessie Butt, Aileen
Parker and the Dumbells Eight

04/01-04/06
Good News
By B.G. DeSylva, Laurence Schwab/Ray
Henderson
Producer/Director: Schwab & Mandell
Cast: Margaret Breen, Max Hoffman Jr.,
Katherine Morros, Will Ahern, Jerry Downes
and others

04/08-04/13
The D'Oyly Carte Opera Co.:
The Gondoliers, Trial by Jury, Pirates of
Penzance, Iolanthe, Ruddigore, Mikado
Producer/Director: All-Canada Tours

04/29-05/04
White Lilacs
By Harry B. Smith/Karl Hajos (Chopin)
Producer/Director:
Shuberts/George Marion
Cast: Charles Croker-King, De Wolf Hopper,
Mary Silveira, William Demarest (in the
chorus) and others

05/13-05/18
This Year of Grace
By Noel Coward
Producer/Director: Arch Selwyn
Cast: Beatrice Lillie, Marjorie Moss, Billy
Norton, Muriel Montrose and others

08/19-08/24
The New Moon
By Frank Mandel, Oscar Hammerstein II,
Laurence Schwab/Sigmund Romberg
Producer/Director:
Frank Mandel and Laurence Schwab
Cast: Charlotte Lansing, George Houston,
Roscoe Ails, Gaile Beverly and others

08/26-09/07
The Desert Song
By Otto Harbach, Oscar
Hammerstein/Sigmund Romberg
Producer/Director: Schwab & Mandel
Cast: Mary Chappelle, Louis Templeton
and others

09/09-09/14
Bird in Hand
By John Drinkwater
Producer/Director: Lee Shubert
Cast: Percy Rhodes, Douglas Jefferies, Eliott
Makeham, Richard Littledale, Freda Bruce
Lockhart, Olga Slade and others

09/16-09/21
Many Waters
By Moncton Heffe
Producer/Director:
Charles B. Cochrane and Arch Selwyn
Cast: Ernest Truex, Marda Vane and others

09/23-09/28
Journey's End
By R.C. Sherriff
Producer/Director: Gilbert Miller
Cast: Basil Gill, Desmond Roberts, Hugh
Williams and others

09/30-10/12
The John Martin-Harvey Repertory Co.:
The Only Way (Wills & Langbridge),
The Lowland Wolf (Angel Guimera)
Producer/Director: All-Canada Tours
Cast: John Martin-Harvey, Nina de Silva,
Eugene Wellesley, Alicia Travers,
George Thirwell, Walter Fitzgerald
and William Burchill

10/14-10/19
Balieff's Chauve Souris
By Nikita Balieff
Producer/Director: Comstock & Gest/Nikita
Balieff
Cast: Nikita Balieff and others

10/21-10/26
The Ringer
By Edgar Wallace
Producer/Director:
Gordon McLeod Productions
Cast: Gordon McLeod, Ernest Bodkin,
Lilian Christine, Margaret St. Barbe West
and others

10/28-11/02
The Maurice Colbourne Co.: The
Philanderer, Arms and the Man
By G.B. Shaw
Producer/Director:
Maurice Colbourne and Barry Jones

Cast: Maurice Colbourne, Barry Jones,
Lambert Larking, Margaret Rawlings,
Constance Pellisier and others

11/04-11/09
Come Eleven
By M.W. Plunkett
Producer/Director: The Dumbells Co.
Ltd./M.W. Plunkett
Cast: The Dumbells: Al Plunkett, Fred
Emney, Harry Binns, Betty Veronica,
Dora Marshall, Jessie Butt, Scotty
Morrison, Morley Plunkett, Howard Fogg,
Charlie Jeeves, Louis Crear, Frances
Corrigan and Theresa Corrigan

11/11-11/16
Hold Everything
By B.G. DeSylva, John McGowan,
Lew Brown/Ray Henderson
Producer/Director: Aarons & Freedley
Cast: Bert Lahr, Helen Gilligan, George
Murphy, Nina Olivette, Sally Sweet and
others

11/18-11/23
Jealousy
By Eugene Walter
Producer/Director:
A.H. Woods/Guthrie McClintic
Cast: Fay Bainter and Melvyn Douglas

11/25-11/30
The American Opera Co.: Faust, Carmen,
Mme Butterfly, Yolanda of Cyprus, Martha
Producer/Director:
American Opera Co./Vladimir Rosing

12/16-12/21
Thurston the Magician
Howard and Jane Thurston

12/23-01/04/30
Mother Goose
Producer/Director:
All-Canada Tours/Philip Rodway
Cast: Wee Georgie Hood, Dan Leno Jr., Red
Conquest, Florence Hunter, Maisie Weldon
and Hal Bryan

1930

01/06-01/11
Nina Rose
By Otto Harbach, Irving Caesar/
Sigmund Romberg
Producer/Director: Shuberts/J.C. Huffman,

choreographed by Busby Berkley
Cast: Guy Robertson, Berna Deane,
Leonard Creeley, Don Barclay,
Jack Sheehan and others

01/13-01/18
Blossom Time
By D. Donnelly/S. Romberg
Producer/Director: Shuberts
Cast: Knight MacGregor,
Genevieve Naegel and others

01/20-01/25
Rosemary
By Louis Parker and Murray Carson
Producer/Director: All-Canada Tours
Cast: John Martin-Harvey, Alicia Travers,
William Burchill, Mary Gray, George
Thirwell, Eugene Wellesley and others

01/27-02/01
She's No Lady
By Bruce Spalding and Anthony Baird
Producer/Director: H.H. Frazee Jr.
Cast: Robert Cummings, Lyle Overman,
Walter N. Greaza, Patricia Chapman
and others

02/03-02/08
The Maurice Colbourne Repertory Co.:
Arms and the Man, The Doctor's Dilemma,
John Bull's Other Island (Shaw)
Producer/Director: Maurice Colbourne
and Barry Jones/Maurice Colbourne
Cast: Maurice Colbourne, Barry Jones,
Lambert Larking, Margaret Rawlings
and others

02/10-02/15
Dear Old England
By H.F. Maltby
Producer/Director: E.F. Bostwick
Cast: Gladys Hanson, Edward Rigby
and others

02/17-02/22
Journey's End
By R.C. Sherriff
Producer/Director: Gilbert Miller
Cast: Henry Stephenson, Frederick Catling,
Richard Bird and others

02/24-03/01
Man and Superman
By G.B. Shaw
Producer/Director: Maurice Colbourne and
Barry Jones/Maurice Colbourne
Cast: Maurice Colbourne, Margaret
Rawlings, Esme Vernon, Barry Jones,
C. Haviland-Burke, Charles Emerson
and others

03/03-03/05
Harry Lauder
Producer/Director: William Morris
Cast: Harry Lauder, Arnaut Brothers,
Fleurette Joeffrie and others

03/06-03/08
Princess Agreneva-Slaviansky and
Her Royal Russian Chorus
Producer/Director: Morris Gest
Cast: 25 singers, dancers and musicians

03/10-03/15
Mlle Modiste
By Victor Herbert, Henry Blossom
Producer/Director: Shuberts
Cast: Fritzi Scheff, Detmar Poppen
and others

03/17-03/22
The New Moon
By Frank Mandel, Oscar Hammerstein II
and Laurence Schwab/S. Romberg
Producer/Director: F. Mandel and L. Schwab
Cast: Charlotte Lansing, George Houston,
Roscoe Ails, Gaile Beverly and others

03/24-02/29
Toronto Conservatory of Music: Hugh the
Drover, Hansel and Gretel
Producer/Director: National Council of
Education and the Toronto Conservatory
of Music, Ernest MacMillan conducting,
scenic design by Arthur Lismer

03/31-04/05
Naughty Marietta
By Rida J. Young/Victor Herbert
Producer/Director: Shuberts/Milton Aborn
Cast: Ilse Marvenga, Halfred Young, Herbert
Waterous, Clarence Harvey, Eulalie Young
and others

04/07-04/12
The Fortune Teller
By Harry Smith/Victor Herbert
Producer/Director: Shuberts
Cast: Eleanor Painter, Philip Conyers,
Jack Bosman and others

04/14-04/19
Bittersweet
By Noel Coward
Producer/Director:
Florenz Ziegfeld and Arch Selwyn
Cast: Evelyn Laye, Gerald Nodin,
Nancy Brown, Desmond Jones and others

04/21-04/26
Sari
By Emmerich Kalman
Producer/Director: George E. Wintz

Cast: Mitzi, Arthur Treacher, Boyd
Marshall, Maybeth Connolly, Jack Squires
and others

05/05-05/10
Babes in Toyland
By Glen McDonough/Victor Herbert
Producer/Director: Jolson Theatre Musical
Comedy Co. and Shuberts
Cast: Barry Lupino, Jane Waterous,
Marcella Swanson, Margaret Breen,
Barry Lupino Jr., Antoinette Lupino,
12 midgets and others

05/07-05/12
Jenny
By Edward Sheldon
and Margaret Ayer Barnes
Cast: Guy Standing, Jane Cowl and others

05/19-05/23
The Walter Hampden Repertory Co.:
Caponsachhi (Arthur Goodrich and
Rose Palmer), Richelieu (Arthur Goodrich),
Hamlet
Producer/Director: Walter Hampden
Cast: Walter Hampden and others

06/23-07/28
All Quiet on the Western Front
Motion picture

08/16-08/30
Splinters
Motion picture

09/01-09/06
Artists and Models of 1930
By Harold Stein and Ernie Golden
Producer/Director: Shuberts
Cast: Phil Baker, James Barton, Aileen
Stanley and others

09/08-09/13
Symphony In Two Flats
By Ivor Novello
Producer/Director:
Shuberts/G. Hamilton Gay
Cast: Ivor Novello, Anthony Hankey,
Frederic Oxley, Lillian Braithwaite,
Ethel Baird, Ann Trevor and others

09/15-09/18
Lincoln
Motion picture

09/22-10/04
Marigold
By L. Allen Harker and F.P. Pryor
Producer/Director: Simon Ord/Norman Page
Cast: Jean Clyde, Sophia Stewart,

Ellis Irving, Walter Roy, Lionel Gadsen
and others

10/20-10/25
Street Scene
By Elmer Rice
Producer/Director:
William A. Brady/Glenn Coulter
Cast: Norma Phillips, Mary Wall, Dorothy
Raymond, Alfred Webster and others

10/27-11/01
Nine 'til Six
By Aimee and Philip Stuart
Producer/Director: Shuberts and
Mrs. Charles B. Cochrane/Auriol Lee
Cast: Auriol Lee, Audrey Cameron,
Norah Balfour, Merle Tottenham, Lenore
Chippendale and others

11/03-11/08
The Street Singer
By Cyrus Wood, Edgar Smith
and Graham Johns/Nicholas Kempner
Producer/Director: Shuberts/Marcel Varnel
Cast: Archie Leach (Cary Grant), Queenie
Smith, George Hassell, Harry K. Morton,
Nick Long Jr., Audrey Mapel, Helen La
Vonne and others

Archie Leach (Cary Grant)

11/10-11/14
Dishonored Lady
By Edward Sheldon
and Margaret Ayer Barnes
Producer/Director:
Gilbert Miller/Guthrie McClintic
Cast: Katherine Cornell, Paul Harvey,
Fred L. Tiden, Ruth Fallows and
S. Herbert Braggiotti

05/05-05/07
Grand Hotel
Motion picture

10/03-10/12
The Merry Widow
By Victor Leon, Leo Stein/Franz Lehar
Producer/Director: Robert McLaughlin
Cast: Donald Brian, Vivian O'Brien,
Detmar Poppen and others

10/13-10/15
Sir Harry Lauder
Producer/Director: William Morris
Cast: Harry Lauder, the Kiltie Pipe Band
and others

10/17-10/22
The Chocolate Soldier
Stanislaus Stange/Oscar Strauss
Producer/Director:
The Knickerbocker Light Opera Company
Cast: Charles Purcell, Mary Atkins, John
Dunsmore and others

10/24-11/12
The Colbourne and Jones Co.: Too Good to
Be True (Shaw), The Queen's Husband
(Robert Sherwood), The Apple Cart (Shaw)
Producer/Director:
The Colbourne and Jones Co.
Cast: Barry Jones, Maurice Colbourne,
Bruce Belfrage and others

11/14-11/19
Rookery Nook
By Ben Travers
Producer/Director: Jack Minster
Cast: William Daunt, Jack Minster,
Madeline Gibson and others

11/21-11/26
Mourning Becomes Electra
By Eugene O'Neill
Producer/Director: The Theatre Guild/Philip
Moeller
Cast: Elizabeth Risdon, Leona Hogarth,
Lee Baker and others

11/28-12/03
Red Planet
By John Balderston and J.E. Hoare
Producer/Director:
Rowland Stebbins/Burk Symon
Cast: Bramwell Fletcher, Valerie Taylor,
Wallace Widdecombe and others

12/05-12/10
There's Always Juliet
By John Van Druten
Producer/Director: Shuberts

Cast: Violet Heming, Roger Pryor
and others

12/12-12/17
Cuckoo in the Nest
By Ben Travers
Producer/Director: Jack Minster
Cast: William Daunt, Jack Minster
and others

12/19-12/23
Rookery Nook
By Ben Travers
Producer/Director: Jack Minster
Cast: William Daunt, Jack Minster,
Madeline Gibson and others

12/26-12/31
Cuckoo in the Nest
By Ben Travers
Producer/Director: Jack Minster
Cast: William Daunt, Jack Minster
and others

1933

01/02-01/07
The Green Pack
By Edgar Wallace
Producer/Director: Percy Hutchison
Cast: Percy Hutchison, Frank Atherley,
Maude Cressall and others

01/16-01/18
The Student Prince
By Donnelly/Romberg
Producer/Director: Shuberts
Cast: Allen Jones, Gertrude King,
Charles Chesney and others

01/19-01/21
Blossom Time
By Donnelly/Romberg
Producer/Director: Shuberts
Cast: John Charles Gilbert, Allen Jones,
Kathryn Reece, Charles Chesney and others

02/06-02/18
The Abbey Theatre Players: Juno and
the Paycock (Sean O'Casey), Playboy
of the Western World (J.M. Synge), The
Whiteheaded Boy (Lennox Robinson),
Workhouse Ward (Lady Gregory), Kathleen
ni Houlihan (W.B. Yeats), The New Gossoon
(George Shields), The Far-off Hills (Lennox
Robinson), Riders to the Sea (J.M. Synge),

Spreading the News (Lady Gregory),
Autumn Fire (T.C. Murray)
Producer/Director: Abner and Wickes Inc.
Cast: Barry Fitzgerald, P.J. Carolan,
Eileen Crowe, Kate Curling, F.J. McCormick
and others

02/20-02/25
Cavalcade
Motion picture

03/13-03/18
The Cat and the Fiddle
By Otto Harbach/Jerome Kern
Producer/Director: Max Gordon
Cast: Bettina Hall, Arthur Treacher,
Michael Bartley, Odette Myrtil, Bobby
Jarvis and others

03/20-03/25
The Green Pastures
By Marc Connelly
Producer/Director:
Lawrence Rivers/Marc Connelly
Cast: Charles H. Moore, Nonie Simmons,
Richard B. Harrison ("de Lawd") and others

04/14-04/22
Springtime for Henry
By Benn Levy
Producer/Director: George Kondolph
Cast: Henry Hull, Gavin Muir, Edith
Atwater, Jane Buchanan and others

04/24-04/26
Counsellor at Law
By Elmer Rice
Producer/Director: Elmer Rice
Cast: Paul Muni, Anne Teeman and others

04/28-04/29
The Good Companions
Motion picture

08/23-09/02
Blossom Time
By Donnelly/Romberg

09/04-09/09
The Dumbells
M.W. Plunkett

10/02-10/07
Dinner at Eight
Motion picture

10/30-11/04
Music in the Air
By Oscar Hammerstein/Jerome Kern
Producer/Director: A.C. Blumenthal

Cast: Al Shean, Walter Slezak, Donald Brian, Alexis Obolensky, Nicholas Joy and others

11/06-11/11
The Late Christopher Bean
By Sidney Howard
Cast: Pauline Lord, Effie Shannon and others

11/13-11/18
Junior League Revue
Director/Producer: Jack Arthur
Cast: Boris Volkoff and ladies of the Junior League

11/23-11/25
Cornelia Otis Skinner: The Wives of Henry VIII, The Loves of Charles II, The Empress Eugenie
Cast: Cornelia Otis Skinner (solo)

11/27-12/02
San Carlo Opera Co: Aida, Faust, Hansel and Gretel, Carmen, Cavalleria Rusticana, I Pagliacci, Rigoletto, Mme Butterfly, Il Trovatore
Producer/Director:
Fortune Gallo/Arnoldo Lindi

12/04-12/09
Bittersweet
By Noel Coward
Producer/Director: Shuberts
Cast: Allan Jones, Margaret Carlisle, Leonard Creeley, Harry K. Morton and others

12/25-01/06/34
Robinson Crusoe
By Walter Johnson/Hy Dyson
Producer/Director:
Empire Theatricals Ltd./Walter Johnson
Cast: Constance Claxton, John E. Blight, Will Perry and others

1934

01/08-01/23
Women Kind
By John Housman and Lewis Galantiere
Producer/Director: Maurice Colbourne and Barry Jones/Maurice Colbourne
Cast: Rita Vale, Barry Jones, Maurice Colbourne, Lambert Larking and others

01/15-01/20
Dangerous Corner
J.B. Priestley
Cast: Gavin Muir, Jack Hartley, Warren Asche, Agnes George, Jane Wheatley and others

01/29-02/03
Biography
By S.N. Behrman
Producer/Director:
The Theatre Guild/Philip Moeller
Cast: Shepperd Strudwick, Ina Claire and others

02/05-02/10
The Shining Hour
By Keith Winter
Producer/Director:
Max Gordon/Raymond Massey
Cast: Gladys Cooper, Raymond Massey, Marjorie Fielding and others

03/06-03/10
Yoshe Kalb
By Maurice Schwartz
Producer/Director: Ed A. Relkin and S. Weintraub
Cast: Maurice Schwartz, Lazar Freed, Judith Arbarbanel and others

03/19-03/24
The Green Pastures
By Marc Connelly
Producer/Director: Laurence Rivers Inc.
Cast: Richard B. Harrison and others

04/02-04/07
Reunion in Vienna
By Robert Sherwood
Producer/Director: Maurice Colbourne and Barry Jones/Maurice Colbourne and Leonard Loan
Cast: Maurice Colbourne, Barry Jones, Mary Gildea, Fred Forrest, Lily Cahill, Sydney Mather, Lambert Larking and others

04/26-04/28
The Walter Hampden Repertory Co.:
Servant in the House (C. Rann Kennedy), Richelieu (Arthur Goodrich), Macbeth
Cast: Ernest Rowan, Mabel Moore, Walter Hampden, Mabel Moore and Edward Everett Hale

05/17-05/19
The Barretts of Wimpole Street (Rudolf Besier), Candida (Shaw)
Producer/Director: Katharine Cornell Repertory Co./Guthrie McClintic

Cast: Katharine Cornell, Edith Evans, Brian Aherne, Orson Welles, Basil Rathbone and others

11/05-11/10
The Abbey Theatre Players: Drama at Inish (Lennox Robinson), Well of the Saints (J.M. Synge), Hyacinth Halvey (Lady Gregory), The Courting of Mary Doyle (Edward McNulty), Grogan and the Ferret (George Shields), The Coiner (Bernard Duffy), Look at the Heffernans (Brinsley MacNamara), The Plough and the Stars (Sean O'Casey)
Producer/Director: Elbert A. Wickes
Cast: Barry Fitzgerald, P.J. Carolan, F.J. McCormick and others

11/19-11/24
Roberta
By Otto Harbach/Jerome Kern
Producer/Director:
Max Gordon/Hassard Short
Cast: Fay Templeton, Sidney Greenstreet and others

12/17-12/18
Romeo and Juliet
By Wm. Shakespeare
Producer/Director:
Katharine Cornell/Guthrie McClintic
Cast: Katharine Cornell, Basil Rathbone, Edith Evan, Brian Aherne, Orson Welles, Blanche Yurka and others

12/25-01/06
Robinson Crusoe
By Walter Johnson/Hy Dyson
Producer/Director:
Empire Theatricals Ltd./Walter Johnson
Cast: Constance Claxton, John E. Blight, Will Perry and others

Walter Hampden

12/25-12/29
Charley's Aunt
By Brandon Thomas
Producer/Director: Toronto Repertory
Theater Co./Cameron Matthews
Cast: Derek Fairman, Doris Lurey, Jack
Sheehan, Patricia Barclay and Sheila Marne

12/31-01/05/35
The Pursuit of Happiness
By Alan Child and Isabella Louden
Producer/Director: Toronto Repertory
Theater Co./Cameron Matthews
Cast: Cameron Matthews, Jack Sheehan,
Patricia Barclay, Sheila Marne, Fred Forrest
and others

1935

01/07-01/12
Laburnum Grove
By J.B. Priestley
Producer/Director: Gilbert Miller/Lewis Allen
Cast: Edmund Green, Margery Pickard
and others

01/21-01/23
Ruth Draper in Her Character Sketches
Producer/Director: Ruth Draper
Cast: Ruth Draper

01/24-01/26
L'Aiglon
By Edmond Rostand
Producer/Director: Lee Shubert
Cast: Merle Maddern, Eva Le Galliene,
Averell Harris, Helen Walpole and others

02/11-02/16
Petticoat Fever
By Mark Reed
Producer/Director:
Richard Aldrich/Alfred de Liagre
Cast: Dennis King, Ona Munson and others

02/18-02/23
The Distaff Side
By John Van Druten
Producer/Director:
Dwight Deere Wiman/Auriol Lee
Cast: Mildred Natwick, Sybil Thorndike,
Estelle Winwood and others

02/25-02/27
Ah, Wilderness
By Eugene O'Neill
Producer/Director:
The Theatre Guild/Philip Moeller
Cast: George M. Cohan, Elisha Cook Jr.,
Gene Lockhart, Ruth Gilbert, Catherine
Proctor and others

02/28-03/02
The Ziegfeld Follies
Producer/Director:
Mrs. Florenz Ziegfeld (Billie Burke)
Cast: Fannie Brice, Eve Arden and others

03/07-03/09
As Thousands Cheer
By Moss Hart and Irving Berlin
Producer/Director:
Sam H. Harris/Hassard Short
Cast: Ethel Waters, Porter Hall, Margaret
Irving, Jerome Cowan, Hal Forder and others

03/11-03/13
Mary of Scotland
By Maxwell Anderson
Producer/Director: The Theatre
Guild/Theresa Hilburn
Cast: Helen Hayes, Philip Merivale
and others

03/25-03/30
The D'Oyly Carte Opera Co.: Cox and Box,
HMS Pinafore, Iolanthe, The Gondoliers,
Yeoman of the Guard, Trial by Jury,
Pirates of Penzance, The Mikado
By Gilbert and Sullivan
Cast: Martyn Green, John Dean, Sydney
Granville, Charles Goulding, Leslie Rands,
Dorothy Gill, Eileen Moody and others

04/19-04/27
Dodsworth
By Sidney Howard, after Sinclair Lewis
Producer/Director: Max Gordon
Cast: Walter Huston, Fay Bainter, Nan
Sutherland, Frederik Worlock and others

05/06-05/11
Three Men on a Horse
By George Abbott and John Cecil Holme
Producer/Director:
Alex Yokel/George Abbott
Cast: Percy Kilbride, Sheldon Leonard,
Muriel Campbell, Mary Murphy, Gloria
Blondel and others

05/23-05/25
The Taming of the Shrew
By Wm. Shakespeare
Producer/Director:
The Theatre Guild/Henry Wagstaff Gribble
Cast: Alfred Lunt, Lynn Fontanne, Sidney
Greenstreet, Bretaigne Windust and others

09/23-09/28
Thumbs Up
Alan Baxter, H.I. Phillips, Harold
Atteridge/James Hanley, and Henry Sullivan
Producer/Director: John Murray Anderson
Cast: Eddie Dowling and others

10/14-10/19
Rose Marie
By Otto Harbach, Oscar
Hammerstein/Rudolf Friml
Producer/Director: Shuberts
Cast: Adele Ardsley, Roy Cropper,
Fred Hildebrand and others

10/16 (one matinee performance only)
Bittersweet
Noel Coward
Producer/Director: Shuberts
Cast: Adele Ardsley, Roy Creer,
Rollins Grimes, Sally Clifford and others

• • TWO SEASONS IN NEW YORK • •
ORIGINAL BROADWAY COMPANY INTACT

MAX GORDON
presents
WALTER HUSTON
in SINCLAIR LEWIS'
"DODSWORTH"
Dramatized by SIDNEY HOWARD
•
ROYAL ALEXANDRA 8 NIGHTS and 3 MATINEES
Starting FRI., APR. 19th. Ending SAT., APR. 27th
PRICES – Nights, $1.10, $1.65, $2.20, $2.75. Matinees Wednesday and
Saturday, $1.10, $1.65, $2.20 • Tax is Included • Mail Orders Filled.

10/21-10/26
A Midsummer Night's Dream
Motion picture

11/04-11/09
Blossom Time
D. Donnelly/S. Romberg
Producer/Director: Shuberts
Cast: Helen Arnold, Robert Lee Allen, John
Charles Gilbert, Marjorie Sweet and others

11/21-11/23
Ghosts
By Henrik Ibsen
Producer/Director: Alla Nazimova
Cast: Alla Nazimova, McKay Morris, Harry
Ellerbe, Ona Munson and Raymond O'Brien

11/25-11/30
Kind Lady
By Edward Chodorov
Producer/Director:
H.C. Potter and George Haight/H.C. Potter
Cast: Lucy Beaumont, Ralph McBane,
Constance Pellisier, Maria Paxton and others

12/09-12/14
Ruth Draper in Her Character Sketches
Cast: Ruth Draper

12/31-01/05/36
The Pursuit of Happiness
By Alan Child and Isabelle Louden
Producer/Director: Toronto Repertory
Theater Co./Cameron Matthews
Cast: Cameron Matthews, Jack Sheehan,
Patricia Barclay, Sheila Marne, Fred Forrest
and others

1936

02/10-02/15
Personal Appearance
By Lawrence Riley
Producer/Director: Brock
Pemberton/Antoinette Perry
Cast: Barbara Brown, Lora Rogers
and others

02/24-02/28
Three Men on a Horse
Producer/Director:
George Abbott and John Cecil Holm
Producer/Director:
Alex Yokel/George Abbott
Cast: Chester Clute, Sheldon Leonard,
Edward Nannery and others

03/30-04/04
At Home Abroad
By Howard Dietz and Arthur Schwartz
Producer/Director: Shuberts/Direction and
Design: Vincente Minelli
Cast: Beatrice Lillie, Ethel Waters, Vera
Allen and others

04/06-04/11
Personal Appearance
By Lawrence Riley
Producer/Director: Brock
Pemberton/Antoinette Perry
Cast: Barbara Brown, Lora Rogers
and others

04/13-04/18
The Great Ziegfeld
Motion picture

05/04-05/09
Winterset
By Maxwell Anderson
Producer/Director/Design: Guthrie McClintic
Cast: Burgess Meredith, Margo Still, Eva
Langbord (Margo Still was replaced by
understudy Eva Langbord, a Toronto
actress, midway through the run)

05/12-05/16
The Opera Guild of Toronto:
I Pagliacci, Cavalleria Rusticana, Tosca
Cast: Lawrence Power, Doris Godson
Gilmour, Gwendolyn Hale, Alice Strong
Rourke and others

09/14-09/19
The Night of January 16
By Ayn Rand
Producer/Director: A.H. Woods
Cast: Kate Bilniker, Curtis Cooksey,
Sarah Padden, Richard Carlson and others

09/21-09/26
Boy Meets Girl
By Sam and Bella Spewack
Producer/Director: George Abbott
Cast: Donald MacDonald, Clinton Sundberg,
Nigel Blake, Betty Field, Frank Fenton
and others

09/30-10/03
Hamlet
By Wm. Shakespeare
Producer/Director: Guthrie McClintic
Cast: John Gielgud, Judith Anderson, Lillian
Gish, Arthur Byron, John Emery and others

10/05-10/10
Romeo and Juliet
Motion picture

10/19-10/24
The Old Maid
By Zoe Atkins
Producer/Director: Stewart Chaney
Cast: Violet Heming, Mabel Taliaferro
and Ruth Hussey

10/26-10/31
The Great Waltz
By Moss Hart/Desmond Carter
Producer/Director:
Max Gordon/Hassard Short
Cast: Ruth Altman, Lee Whitney, Guy
Robertson, Robert Vernon, Gladys Clarke
and others

11/02-11/04
First Lady
By Katherine Dayton
and George S. Kaufman
Producer/Director:
Sam H. Harris/George S. Kaufman
Cast: Diantha Pattison, James Seeley, Helen
Brooks, Jane Cowl, Carrie Reynolds and
others

11/05-11/07
Hedda Gabler
By Henrik Ibsen
Producer/Director: Alla Nazimova
Cast: Alla Nazimova, Harry Ellerbe,
George Gaul, Eliot Cabot, Viola Frayne,
Leslie Bingham and Grace Mills

11/09-11/14
Lady Precious Stream
By Shih Hsiung
Producer/Director: Morris Gest/Shih Hsiung
Cast: Clarence Derwent, Constance
Carpenter, William Hutchison, Detmar
Poppen and others

11/19-11/21
Ruth Draper in Her Character Sketches
Cast: Ruth Draper

11/23-11/28
Blossom Time
By D. Donnelly/S. Romberg
Producer/Director: Shuberts
Cast: John Charles Gilbert, Diana Gaylen,
George Trabert, Manila Powers and others

12/21-12/23
End of Summer
By S.N. Behrman
Producer/Director:
The Theatre Guild/Philip Moeller
Cast: Ina Claire, Osgood Perkins, Jean
Adair, Van Heflin, Sheppard Strudwick
and others

12/28-01/02/37
Moon Over Mulberry Street
By Nicholas Cosentino
Producer/Director: Standish O'Neill
Cast: William Edmunds, Diane Manor,
Norman Stuart and others

1937

01/04-01/06
Pride and Prejudice
By Helen Jerome, after Jane Austen
Producer/Director:
Max Gordon/Robert Sinclair
Cast: Muriel Kirkland, Eugene Rawls,
Evelyn Bird, Vera Fuller-Melish and others

02/15-02/20
Ghosts
By Henrik Ibsen
Producer/Director: Alla Nazimova
Cast: Alla Nazimova, McKay Morris, Harry
Ellerbe, Viola Frayne and Calvin Thomas

02/22-02/27
The Amazing Dr. Clitterhouse
By Barry Lyndon
Producer/Director: Gilbert Miller
and Warner Brothers/Lewis Allen
Cast: Cedric Hardwicke, Muriel Hutchison,
Clarence Derwent, Helen Trenholme,
Frederick Worlock and others

03/26-03/27
The Good Earth
Motion picture

04/12-04/17
Lost Horizon
Motion picture

05/03-05/05
Ziegfeld Follies
By Ira Gershwin
Producer/Director: Mrs. Florenz Ziegfeld
(Billie Burke) and Shuberts
Cast: Fanny Brice, Bobby Clark and others,
in a cast of 120

05/10-05/15
Close Quarters (Attentat)
By Gilbert Lennox
Producer/Director: Shuberts/Watson Barratt
Cast: Gladys Cooper and Philip Merivale

08/30-09/04
The Life of Emile Zola
Motion picture

09/11-09/13
George and Margaret
By Gerald Savory
Producer/Director: John C. Wilson
Cast: Irene Browne, Morland Graham
and others

09/27-10/08
Tovarich
By Robert Sherwood,
trans. from Jacques Deval
Producer/Director: Gilbert Miller
Cast: Marta Abba, Rudolf Forster, Cecil
Humphreys, Jay Gassett, James E. Truex
and others

10/11-10/16
A Doll's House
By Henrik Ibsen
Producer/Director: Jed Harris
Cast: Ruth Gordon, Dennis King, Sam Jaffe,
Margaret Waller, Paul Lucas and Lorna
Lynn Meyers

10/18-10/23
You Can't Take It with You
By Kaufman & Hart
Producer/Director: Sam H. Harris
Cast: George Henry Trader, Mary Patton,
Dulcie Cooper, Adrienne Earl and others

10/25-10/30
Brother Rat
By John Monks and Fred Finklehoffe
Producer/Director: George Abbott
Cast: Eddie Bracken, Gary Merrill, Jean
McCoy, Reese Alsop, James Gillis and others

11/15-11/20
Victoria Regina
By Lawrence Housman
Producer/Director: Gilbert Miller
Cast: Helen Hayes, Werner Bateman,
Raymond Johnson, Wallace Widdicombe
and others

11/22-11/27
Barchester Towers
By Thomas Job
Producer/Director: Guthrie McClintic
Cast: Ina Claire, McKenzie Ward, J.M.
Kerrigan, Effie Shannon and others

11/29-12/04
Love of Women
By Aimee and Philip Stuart

Producer/Director: Shuberts/Leo G. Carroll
Cast: Leo G. Carroll, Valerie Taylor, Hugh
Sinclair Jr., Heather Angel, Muriel Starr
and others

12/06-12/11
Leaning on Letty
By Wilbur Steele and Norma Mitchell
Producer/Director:
Martin Broones/Russell Filmore
Cast: Charlotte Greenwood, Russell Filmore,
Isabel Withers, Romaine Callender and others

12/13-12/18
Stage Door
By George S. Kaufman and Edna Fisher
Producer/Director: Sam H. Harris/George S.
Kaufman
Cast: Helen Warren, Barna Osterag, Ruth
Strome, Dorothea Andrews and others

12/27-12/30
King Richard II
By Wm. Shakespeare
Producer/Director: Margaret Webster
Cast: Maurice Evans, Lionel Hogarth, Lee
Baker, Frederic Worlock, Winston O'Keefe,
Rhys Williams and Philip Truex

Maurice Evans

12/31 (one performance only)
Henry IV (Part 1)
By Wm. Shakespeare
Producer/Director: Margaret Webster
Cast: Maurice Evans, Frederic Worlock,
Winston O'Keefe, Rhys Williams and
Philip Truex

1938

01/10-01/15
Room Service
By John Murray and Allen Boretz
Producer/Director: George Abbott
Cast: Reed Brown Jr., Whitner Bissell,
James Lane, Keenan Wynn and others

01/17-01/22
The Housemaster (Bachelor Born)
By Ian Hay
Producer/Director:
Shuberts and Ruth Selwyn
Cast: Frederick Leister, Aubrey Mather,
Peggy Simpson, Francis Compton,
Helen Trenholme and others

01/31-02/05
The Abbey Players: Juno and the Paycock
(Sean O'Casey), Riders to the Sea
(J.M. Synge), Silver Jubilee (Cormac
O Daly), The New Gossoon (George Shiels),
In The Train (Frank O'Connor and Hugh
Hunt), Playboy of the Western World (J.M.
Synge), Drama at Inish (Lennox Robinson),
The Far-off Hills (Lennox Robinson)
Producer/Director: Abbey Theatre and
Shuberts
Cast: P.J. Carolan, Maureen Delaney,
Eileen Crowe, F.J. McCormick and others

02/17-02/19
Edna, His Wife
By Cornelia Otis Skinner
Producer/Director: Cornelia Otis Skinner
Cast: Cornelia Otis Skinner (Lulu)

02/28-03/05
Whiteoaks
By Mazo de la Roche, Nancy Price
and Victor Payne-Jennings
Producer/Director: Victor Payne-Jennings
Cast: Ethel Barrymore (Colt), Richard
Carlson, Olive Reeves-Smith, Stephen
Haggard, Lenore Chippendale, Reynolds
Dennison and others

03/07-03/12
Tonight at 8:30
By Noel Coward
Producer/Director: Robert Anderson
and Estelle Winwood
Cast: Estelle Winwood, Jessie Royce Landis,
Philip Dakin, Bramwell Fletcher and others

03/28-04/02
You Can't Take It with You
By Kaufman & Hart
Producer/Director: Sam H. Harris
Cast: Mary Patton, Alan Brixey, George
Henry Trader, Dulcie Cooper and others

04/04-04/09
Yes, My Darling Daughter
By Mark Reed
Producer/Director: Alfred de Liagre Jr.
Cast: Violet Heming, Lucille Watson,
Nicholas Joy, Charles Bryant, Haila
Stoddard and Howard Ferguson

04/18-04/23
Brother Rat
By John Marks and Fred Finklehoffe
Producer/Director: George Abbott
Cast: Tom Ewell, Reese Alsop, Lorna Beaton
and others

05/02-05/07
Julius Caesar
By Wm. Shakespeare
Producer/Director: Alex Yokel/Orson Welles
Cast: Edmond O'Brien, Tom Powers,
Morgan Farley, Larry Fletcher, Helen Craig,
Muriel Brassler and Vincent Donahue

05/06 (one performance)
Bury the Dead
By Irwin Shaw
Producer/Director:
Alex Yokel/Edmond O'Brien
Cast: Edmond O'Brien, Seymour Milbert,
Arthur Hoffe, Vincent Donohue,
Muriel Brassler, Helen Craig and others

09/26-10/01
The Women
By Clare Boothe (Luce)
Producer/Director: Max Gordon
Cast: Lois Wilson, Laura Pierpoint, Edith
Shayne, Dema Byron, Dorothy Draper
and others

10/10-10/15
Shadow and Substance
By Paul Vincent Carroll
Producer/Director: Eddie Dowling/Peter
Godfrey
Cast: Cedric Hardwicke, Sara Algood,
Julie Haydon and others

10/17-10/22
What a Life
By Clifford Goldsmith
Producer/Director: George Abbott
Cast: Eddie Bracken (Henry Aldrich),
Butterfly McQueen, Connie Nickerson
and others

10/31-11/05
I Have Been Here Before
By J.B. Priestley
Producer/Director: Gilbert Miller
Cast: Wilfred Lawson, Ernest Deutsch,
Lydia Sherwood, Eric Portman and others

11/21-11/26
Pins and Needles
By Harold J. Rome
Producer/Director:
Labor Stage Inc./Charles Friedman
Cast: Orin Jannings, Harold Clark,
Ruby Rubenstein and others

11/28-12/03
Spring Meeting
By M.J.Farrell and John Perry
Producer/Director:
C.P. Merivale/John Gielgud
Cast: Gladys Cooper, Jean Cadell, Sheilah
Richards, Robert Flemyng and James
Woodburn

12/05-12/10
Idiot's Delight
By Robert Sherwood
Producer/Director: Phil Baker
Cast: Phil Baker, Olga Baclanova,
Albert Bergh, Homer Miles, Fred Sherman
and others

12/26-12/31
Damaged Goods
Motion picture

1939

01/23, 01/28
Susan and God
By Rachel Crothers
Producer/Director: John Golden
Cast: Gertrude Lawrence, Paul McGath,
Nancy Coleman and others

02/27-03/06
Angela Is Twenty Two
By Sinclair Lewis and Fay Wray
Producer/Director: Henry Wagstaff Gribble
Cast: Philip Merivale, Flora Campbell,
Royal Beal, Barry Sullivan and others
(Sinclair Lewis as "Commentator")

03/13-03/18
The Importance of Being Earnest
By Oscar Wilde
Producer/Director: Richard Aldrich and
Richard Meyers/Estelle Winwood
Cast: Clifton Webb, Estelle Winwood,
Florence McKee, Helen Trenholme, Edward
Roerich, Answorth Arnold and Hope
Williams

03/20-03/25
The Flashing Stream
By Charles Morgan
Producer/Director: Victor Payne-Jennings
Cast: Godfrey Tearle, Margaret Rawlings,
Anthony Ireland and others

03/27-04/01
Skylark
By Samson Raphaelson
Producer/Director:
John Golden/Samson Raphaelson
Cast: Gertrude Lawrence, William David,
Walter Gilbert, Donald Cook and others

04/10-04/15
The Women
By Clare Boothe (Luce)
Producer/Director: Max Gordon
Cast: Helen Carrington, Edyth Shane, Doris
Kelton, Delma Byron and Alice Buchanan

04/29
Life and Loves of Beethoven
Motion picture

10/02-10/07
I Married an Angel
By Lorenz Hart/Richard Rodgers
Producer/Director: Dwight D. Wiman/
Joshua Logan

10/16-10/21
Charles the King
By Maurice Colbourne
Producer/Director: Maurice Colbourne
and Barry Jones/Maurice Colbourne
Cast: Barry Jones, Jessica Tandy, Maurice
Colbourne and others

10/30-11/04
Geneva
By G.B. Shaw
Producer/Director: Maurice Colbourne
and Barry Jones/Maurice Colbourne
Cast: Maurice Colbourne, Barry Jones
and others

11/10-11/11
Charles the King
By Maurice Colbourne
Maurice Colbourne and Barry
Jones/Maurice Colbourne
Cast: Maurice Colbourne, Barry Jones,
Jessica Tandy and others

11/14-11/18
Geneva
By G.B. Shaw
Producer/Director: Maurice Colbourne and
Barry Jones/Maurice Colbourne
Cast: M. Colbourne, Barry Jones and others

11/20-11/25
When We Are Married
By J.B. Priestley
Producer/Director: Royal Alexandra
Theatre/Robert Henderson
Cast: Estelle Winwood, Alison Skipworth
and others

11/27-12/02
Abe Lincoln in Illinois
By Robert Sherwood
Producer/Director: The Playwrights' Co.
(Maxwell Anderson, S.N. Behrman,
Sidney Howard, Elmer Rice, Robert E.
Sherwood)/Elmer Rice
Cast: Raymond Massey, Clarence Chase,
Arthur Griffin, Lewis Martin, Calvin Thomas,
Augusta Dabney, Joseph Wiseman and others

12/04-12/09
Kiss the Boys Good-Bye
By Clare Boothe (Luce)
Producer/Director: Brock
Pemberton/Antoinette Perry
Cast: John Alexander, Ollie Burgoyne,
Helen Claire, Sheldon Leonard and others

12/11-12/16
Chin-Up
By Roly Young
Producer/Director:
Royal Alexandra Theatre and Roly Young
Cast: Ross Hamilton, Pat Rafferty, Red
Newman, Marquette & Lynda and Alex
Morgan

12/25-12/26
Geneva
By G.B. Shaw
Maurice Colbourne and Barry
Jones/Maurice Colbourne
Cast: Maurice Colbourne, Barry Jones
and others

1940

01/11-01/15
Ruth Draper in Her Character Sketches
Cast: Ruth Draper

01/15-01/20
Tobias and the Angels
By James Bridie
Producer/Director:
Maurice Colbourne
and Barry Jones
Cast: Maurice Colbourne and Jessica Tandy

01/22-01/27
Three After Three
By Guy Pollon, Parke Levy, Alan Lipscott
and Johnny Mercer/Hoagy Carmichael
Producer/Director: Shuberts/Ruth Selwyn
Cast: Stepin Fetchit, Mitzi Green, Simone
Simon, Mary Brian, Jack Whiting and others

02/15-02/17
Earl Carroll's Vanities
By Dorcas Cochran/Charles Rosoff
Producer/Director: Earl Carroll
Cast: Ygor and Tanya, Lela Moore,
The Three Nonchalants, Gary Stone,
Susan Miller and others

02/19-02/24
Mamba's Daughters
By Dorothy and Dubose Heyward
Producer/Director: Guthrie McClintic
Cast: Ethel Waters and others

03/04-03/09
Hamlet
By Wm. Shakespeare
Producer/Director: Maurice Evans/Margaret
Webster
Cast: Maurice Evans, Donald Cameron,
Rhys Williams and others

03/11-03/16
Ladies in Retirement
By Edward Percy and Reginald Denham
Producer/Director:
Gilbert Miller/Reginald Denham
Cast: Flora Robson, Estelle Winwood,
Isobel Elsom and others

03/18-03/23
Worth a Million
By Vernon Sylvanine
Producer/Director: Halliday & Kenley
Cast: Charley Chase, Taylor Holmes,
Cobina Wright and Nita Naldi

03/25-04/01
The Streets of Paris
By James McHugh and Al Dubin; additional
numbers by Harold J. Rome, Charles
Sherman, Tom McKnight, S. Jay Kaufman,
Edward Duryea Dowling, James La Ver,
Frank Eyton and Lee Brody
Producer/Director: Shuberts, in association
with Olsen & Johnson
Cast: Carmen Miranda, Luella Grear, Bobby
Clark, Yvonne Bouvier and Della Lind

04/08-04/13
The Little Foxes
By Lillian Hellman
Producer/Director: Herman Shumlin
Cast: Tallulah Bankhead, Patricia Collinge,
Dan Duryea, Carl Benton Reid and Frank
Conroy

04/15-04/20
Margin for Error
By Clare Boothe (Luce)
Producer/Director:
Aldrich & Meyers/Otto Preminger
Cast: Josephine Dunn, Kurt Katch, Sheldon
Leonard, Alexander Clark and others

04/21
Progressive Theatre Party
Director/Producer: Progressive Girls Club

04/22-04/27
No Time for Comedy
By S.N. Behrman
Producer/Director:
Katharine Cornell/Guthrie McClintic
Cast: Katharine Cornell, Francis Lederer,
John Williams and Margalo Gillmore

06/17-06/22
Outward Bound
By Sutton Vane
Producer/Director: Frank McCoy
Cast: Bramwell Fletcher, Daisy Belmore
and Louis Hector

06/24-06/29
Susan and God
By Rachel Crothers
Producer/Director:
Frank McCoy/Robert Burton
Cast: Roy Roberts, Robert Burton,
Violet Heming and Judy Parish

07/01-07/06
Private Lives
By Noel Coward
Producer/Director:
Frank McCoy/Robert Burton
Cast: Violet Heming and Roy Roberts

07/06-07/10
The Curtain Rises
By B.M. Laye
Producer/Director: Frank McCoy
Cast: Roy Roberts, Ethel Britton,
Freddy Sherman and Marshall Bradford

07/08-07/13
Criminal at Large
By Edgar Wallace
Producer/Director: Frank McCoy
Cast: Florence Reed, Romney Brent,
Roy Roberts and Charles Emerson

07/15-07/20
Candida
By G.B. Shaw
Producer/Director: Frank McCoy
Cast: Peggy Wood, Romney Brent,
Roy Roberts and Ethel Britton

07/22-07/27
Pursuit of Happiness
By Alan Child and Isabelle Loudon
Producer/Director: Frank McCoy
Cast: Francis Lederer, Ethel Britton,
Roy Roberts, Adwlyn Bushnell,
Fred G. Brown and others

07/29-08/03
Our Betters
By Somerset Maugham
Producer/Director: Frank McCoy
Cast: Margaret Bannerman, Ethel Britton,
Mary Godwin, Adelyn Bushnell, Marshal
Bradford and others

08/12-08/17
Biography
By S.N. Behrman
Producer/Director: Frank McCoy
Cast: Cornelia Otis Skinner and
Donald Brian

09/02-09/14
A School for Scandal
By R.B. Sheridan
Producer/Director: Frank McCoy
Cast: Ethel Barrymore, Georgie Drew,
Phyllis Joyce, Reynolds Denniston,
Edward Broadley and others

09/16-10/05
Autumn Crocus
By C.L. Anthony (Dodie Smith)
Producer/Director: Frank McCoy
Cast: Francis Lederer, Frances Fuller,
Pamela Simpson and St. Clair Bayfield

10/07-10/12
Tonight at 8:30
By Noel Coward
Producer/Director: Frank McCoy
Cast: Diana Barrymore, Bramwell Fletcher,
Ann Andrews, Rhys Williams and others

10/14-11/03
The Philadelphia Story
By Philip Barry
Producer/Director:
Theatre Guild/Robert Sinclair
Cast: Katherine Hepburn, Van Heflin,
Joseph Cotton, Nicholas Joy and others

11/05-11/09
There Shall Be No Tonight
By Robert E. Sherwood
Producer/Director: Theatre Guild
Cast: Alfred Lunt, Lynn Fontanne,
Maurice Colbourne, Montgomery Clift,
Elisabeth Fraser and others

11/11-11/16
Pins and Needles
By Harold Rome
Producer/Director: Bob Gordon
Cast: Elise Bregman, Freda Fay,
Ida Mandel, Alma Charmat and others

11/18-11/23
Hellzapoppin'
By Olsen and Johnson
Producer/Director: Olsen and Johnson
Cast: Olsen and Johnson, Billie House,
Eddie Garr, Jo and Joanne Readinger

12/09-12/14
Lady in Waiting
By Margery Sharp
Producer/Director: Brock
Pemberton/Antoinette Perry
Cast: Alan Napier, Gloria Jean,
Gladys George, Carol Curtis-Brown,
Lenore Chippendale and Leonard Penn

12/26-12/28
The Male Animal
By James Thurber and Elliott Nugent
Producer/Director: Herman Shumlin
Cast: Eliott Nugent, Elizabeth Love,
Leon Ames, Ivan Simpson, Julie Stevens,
Minna Phillips and others

12/30-01/04/41
A Night of Love
By Rowland Leigh/Robert Stolt
Cast: Helen Gleason, John Lodge,
Marguerite Namara and others

1941

01/16-01/18
The Man Who Came to Dinner
By Kaufman & Hart
Producer/Director: Sam H. Harris
Cast: Clifton Webb, Sally McMorrow,
Doris Diana Dalton, Ruth Sherrill,
Leonore Harris and others

01/20-01/26
The Time of Your Life
By William Saroyan
Producer/Director: Theatre Guild/ Eddie
Dowling and William Saroyan
Cast: Eddie Dowling, Julie Haydon, Ross
Bagdasarian, Edward Andrews, William
Bendix, Charles Cane, Arthur Hunnicut
and others

02/03-02/08
Night Must Fall
By Emlyn Williams
Producer/Director:
Frank McCoy/Guy Douglass
Cast: Florence Reed, Violet Heming,
Douglas Montgomery and others

02/10-02/15
Ballet Russe de Monte Carlo
Producer/Director: Sol Hurok, Col. W.
deBasil's Ballet Russe Company
Cast: Irina Baranova, Tatiana Riabouchinska,

Tamara Toumanova, David Lichine
and others

03/03-03/15
Sim Sala Bim
Producer/Director: Harry Alvin Jansen
and Rombout van Reemsdyke
Cast: Dante (Harry Alvin Jansen)

03/24-03/29
Cabin in the Sky
By Lynn Root, John Latouche, Vernon Duke
Producer/Director: Albert Lewis and Vinton
Freedley/George Balanchine
Cast: Ethel Waters, Dooley Wilson,
Rex Ingram, Archie Savage, Todd Duncan,
Katherine Dunham and others

04/09-04/12
Sim Sala Bim
Producer/Director: Harry Alvin Jansen
and Rombout van Reemsdyke
Cast: Dante (Harry Alvin Jansen)

04/24-04/26
Canadian Ballet
Producer/Director: Boris Volkoff
Cast: Ruth Carse, Lloyd Thornton, Carole
Beames, Patricia Drylie, Janet Baldwin
and John Marsha

04/28-05/10
San Carlo Opera Co.: Carmen, Aida,
La Traviata, Faust, Samson and Delilah,
Rigoletto, Il Trovatore
Producer/Director: Forture Gallo

05/12-05/17
Accent on Youth
By Samson Raphaelson
Producer/Director: Harold J. Kennedy
Cast: Sylvia Sidney and Luther Adler

05/19-05/24
Blossom Time
D. Donnelly/S. Romberg
Producer/Director: Shuberts
Cast: Everett Marshall, Marie Nash
and others

05/26-05/31
Rose Marie
By Otto Harbach, Oscar
Hammerstein/Rudolf Friml
Producer/Director: Shuberts
Cast: Alexander Gray, Nancy McCord,
Hope Emerson and a cast of 60

06/02-06/07
Pygmalion
By G.B. Shaw

Producer/Director:
Frank McCoy/Barry Thomson
Cast: Barry Thomson, Ruth Chatterton,
Helen Gardiner, Earle Grey, Madeline
Grey and others

06/09-06/14
The Night of January 16
By Ayn Rand
Producer/Director: Frank McCoy
Cast: Fay Wray, Robert Wilcox, Hunter
Gardner, Helen Gardiner, Ethel Britton,
Arthur Hughes and others

06/16-06/21
Nancy's Private Affair
By Myron C. Fagan
Producer/Director:
Frank McCoy/Myron Fagan
Cast: Anna Sten, Philip Houston,
John Lorenz and others

06/23-06/28
George Washington Slept Here
By Moss Hart and George S. Kaufman
Producer/Director: Frank McCoy
Cast: Charles Butterworth, Arthur Jarrett,
Ruth Holden, Helen Gardiner and others

06/30-07/05
Rain
By Somerset Maugham
Producer/Director: Frank McCoy
Cast: Lenore Ulric, Robert Wilcox and others

LENORE ULRIC in "RAIN"

ROYAL ALEXANDRA
· THEATRE ·
Week Commencing Monday, June 30th

07/07-07/12
What Every Woman Knows
By James M. Barrie
Producer/Director: Frank McCoy
Cast: Sophie Stewart, Leslie Austen,
Arthur Jarrett, Ethel Britton, Mary Power,
Earle Grey and others

07/14-07/19
Ritzin' the Blitz
Producer/Director: Frank McCoy and Royal
Alexandra Theatre, Robert Cornfield
conducting
Cast: Jack Hennessey and others

07/21-07/26
Old English
By John Galsworthy
Producer/Director: Frank McCoy
Cast: C. Aubrey Smith, John Glen,
Lee Parry and others

07/28-08/02
Mary-Rose
By James M. Barrie
Producer/Director: Frank McCoy
Cast: Sophie Stewart, Bernice Vert, Peter
Boyne, Earle Grey, Peter Boyne and others

08/04-08/09
Meet the Wife
By Lynn Starling
Producer/Director: Frank McCoy
Cast: Mary Boland, Alexandra Brackett,
John Roche, King Kennedy and others

08/11-08/16
George Washington Slept Here
By Moss Hart and George S. Kaufman
Producer/Director: Frank McCoy
Cast: Allen Kearns, Arthur Jerrett,
Ethel Britton, Diana Leslie, John Glen,
Mary Power and others

08/18-08/23
Old Acquaintance
By John van Gardiner
Producer/Director: Frank McCoy
Cast: Violet Heming, Edith King,
Alan Handley, Nancy Wiman and others

08/25-08/31
The Male Animal
By James Thurber and Elliot Nugent
Producer/Director:
Frank McCoy/Richard Beckhard
Cast: Conrad Nagel, Ethel Britton, Eulabelle
Moore, Helen Gardner and others

09/16-09/20
Ballet Russe de Monte Carlo
Producer/Director:
Sol Hurok/Leonide Massine
Cast: Alexandra Danilova, Tamara
Toumanova, Frederic Franklin and others,
in a cast of 125

09/22-09/27
Theatre
By Somerset Maugham and Guy Bolton
Producer/Director: John Golden
Cast: Cornelia Otis Skinner, Arthur
Margetson, Viola Roache and others

09/29-10/18
Fantasia
Motion picture

10/20-10/25
Hold on to Your Hats
By Guy Bolton, Matt Brooks , Eddie Davis
and E.Y. Harburg/Burton Lane
Producer/Director: George Hale, Al Jolson
and Shuberts/Edgar J. MacGregor
Cast: Al Jolson, Buddy Ebsen and others

11/03-11/08
Ah, Wilderness
By Eugene O'Neill
Producer/Director: The Theatre Guild,
Inc./Theresa Helburn, Lawrence Langer
and Eva Le Gallienne
Cast: Harry Carey, Ann Shoemaker, Victor
Chaplin, Zachary Scott, Edmund Dorsay
and others

11/24-12/06
Claudia
By Rose Franken
Producer/Director:
John Golden/Rose Franken
Cast: Mabel Taliaferro, Stephen Chase,
Liesl Neumann, Murray O'Neill, Gage Clarke
and others

12/08-12/13
The Rivals
By R.B. Sheridan
Producer/Director:
Theatre Guild/Eva Le Gallienne
Cast: Helen Ford, Donald Burr, Hailia
Stoddard, Mary Boland, Bobby Clark,
Walter Hampden and others

12/15-12/20
The Student Prince
By Donnelly/Romberg
Producer/Director:
Shuberts/Edward J. Scalon
Cast: Harold Brindel, Herman Madigson,
Walter Peterson, David Newman,
Alex Alexander, Detmar Poppen and others

1942

01/19-01/24
Ritzin' the Blitz
Producer/Director: Melville Keay
Cast: Canadian soldiers' revue

01/26-01/31
Dansation
Producer/Director: George M. Gatts
Cast: Veloz & Yolanda

02/02-02/07
Native Son
By Paul Green, Richard Wright
Producer/Director: Orson Welles, John
Houseman/Orson Welles
Cast: Canada Lee, John Berry, Patricia
Palmer, Stephen Roberts and others

02/09-02/21
Ballet Theatre
Producer/Director: Sol Hurok
Cast: Alicia Markova, Anton Dolin, Michel
Fokine, Irina Baronova and others

03/12-03/14
Rose Burke
By Henri Bernstein
Producer/Director:
Katharine Cornell/Guthrie McClintic
Cast: Katharine Cornell, Philip Merivale,
Jean-Pierre Aumont, Clarence Derwent
and others

03/16-03/21
Hellzapoppin'
By Olsen & Johnson
Producer/Director: Olsen & Johnson
Cast: Olsen & Johnson, Billie House,
Eddie Garr and others

03/30-04/06
My Sister Eileen
By Joseph Fields and Jerome Chodorov
Producer/Director:
Max Gordon/George S. Kaufman
Cast: Leo Chalzell, Betty Furness,
Dorothy Littlejohn and others

04/20-04/25
The Corn Is Green
By Emlyn Williams
Producer/Director: Herman Shumlin
Cast: Ethel Barrymore (Colt),
Richard Waring and others

04/27-05/02
Earl Carroll's Vanities
Producer/Director: Earl Carroll
Cast: Irving Aaronson and his Commanders,
Dabny Scholl and the Girls

05/04-05/09
Blackstone and His Show of 1001 Wonders
Harry Blackstone

05/25-05/27
Blackstone and His Show of 1001 Wonders
Harry Blackstone

06/22-06/27
Meet the People
By Henry Myers, Danny Dare, Jay Gorney,
Ben Barzman and others
Producer/Director: Irving Yates/Danny Dare
Cast: Marion Colby, Ruth Godfrey, Howard
Blaine, Joey Faye, Jack Albertson and others

06/29-07/04
Varieties of 1942
Producer/Director: Berni Vici
Cast: Wally Ward, Young & Kay,
Carl Emney and his Wags and others

07/20-07/25
Stage Door
By George S. Kaufman, Edna Fisher
Producer/Director: Frank McCoy
Cast: Louise Lamont, Ruth Conley,
Enid Croal, Dorothy Eaton and others

07/27-08/01
Romance
By Edward Sheldon
Producer/Director: Frank McCoy
Cast: Elissa Landi, Jack Grogan and others

08/03-08/08
Reflected Glory
By George Kelly
Producer/Director: Frank McCoy
Cast: Gloria Swanson, Douglas Gregory,
Eulabelle Moore, Wendell Corey, Bert
Wilcox, Dorothy Eaton, Harold J. Kennedy
and others

08/10-08/15
No Time for Comedy
By S.N. Behrman
Producer/Director: Frank McCoy
Cast: Francis Lederer, Ethel Britton,
Dean Norton, Ollie Burgoyne and others

08/17-08/22
You Can't Take It with You
By Kaufman & Hart
Producer/Director: Frank McCoy

Cast: Fred Stone, Paula Stone, Daisy
Atherton, Ollie Burgoyne, Peter Mews,
Harold J. Stone, Dorothy Eaton and others

08/24-08/29
Petticoat Fever
By Mark Reed
Producer/Director: Frank McCoy
Cast: Michael Whalen, Cosy Lee, Earle
Grey, Louise Buckley, Dorothy Eaton
and others

08/31-09/05
Mary of Scotland
By Maxwell Anderson
Producer/Director: Frank McCoy
Cast: Elissa Landi and William Harrigan

09/07-09/12
The Moon Is Down
By John Steinbeck
Producer/Director:
Howard Productions/B.D. Kranz
Cast: Conrad Nagel, Robert Ober,
Graham Velsey and others

09/14-09/19
My Sister Eileen
By Joseph Fields and Jerome Chodorov
Producer/Director:
Max Gordon/George S. Kaufman
Cast: Leo Chalzell, Betty Furness,
Dorothy Littlejohn and others

09/21-09/26
Angel Street
By Patrick Hamilton
Producer/Director: Shepard Traube
Cast: Lynn Phillips, Byrn McGrath and others

09/30-10/03
Ballet Russe de Monte Carlo
Producer/Director:
Sol Hurok/Léonide Massine
Cast: Alexandra Danilova, Mia Slavenska,
Nathalie Krossovska, Andre Eglevsky
and others

10/05-10/10
Spring Again
By Isabel Leighton and Bertram Bloch
Producer/Director: Guthrie McClintic
Cast: Grace George, C. Aubrey Smith
and others

10/12-10/29
Tobacco Road
By Jack Kirkland
Producer/Director:
Jack Kirkland/Anthony Brown

Cast: John Barton, Norman Budd, Sara
Perry, Sheila Brent, Lillian Ardell and others

11/02-11/07
Private Lives
By Noel Coward
Producer/Director: Russell Lewis
Cast: Ruth Chatterton, Ralph Forbes
and others

11/09-11/14
Her First Murder
By Robert Presnel
Producer/Director:
Victor Payne-Jennings and Marion Gering
Cast: Zasu Pitts, Richard Taber,
Merle Maddern and others

11/16-11/28
Arsenic and Old Lace
By John Kesselring
Producer/Director:
Walter Hampden/Hugh Rennie
Cast: Walter Hampden, Cecilia Loftus,
Ainsworth Arnold, Arthur Jarrett,
Ethel Britton and others

11/30-12/04
Life without Father
By Lindsay & Crouse
Producer/Director:
Oscar Serlin/Bretaigne Windust
Cast: Percy Warram, Margalo Gillmore
and others

12/28-01/09/43
Angel Street
By Patrick Hamilton
Producer/Director: Shepard Traube
Cast: Lynn Phillips, Byron McGrath,
Georgette McKee, Daisy Belmore
and Ernest Crossart

1943

01/11-01/16
Dansation
Producer/Director: George M. Gatts
Cast: Veloz & Yolanda

01/18-01/23
Arsenic and Old Lace
By John Kesselring
Producer/Director:
Walter Hampden/
Hugh Rennie

Cast: Cecilia Loftus, Walter Hampden and others

01/25-01/30
Claudia
By Rose Franken
Producer/Director:
John Golden/Rose Franken
Cast: Frances Starr, Donald Cook and Dorothy McGuire

02/15-02/20
Watch on the Rhine
By Lillian Hellman
Cast: Margaret Anglin, Walter Gilbert, Katharine Warren and George Spelvin

02/22-03/04
Ballet Russe de Monte Carlo
Producer/Director:
Sol Hurok/Leonide Massine
Cast: Alexandra Danilova, Tamara Toumanova, Frederic Franklin and others, in a cast of 125

03/04-03/06
The Gondoliers
By Gilbert and Sullivan
Producer/Director: Canada Packer's Operatic Society/W.R. Curry
Cast: James Green, Emlyn E. Plummer, Stuart C. Cramp, William Currie, Arthur Sclater and others

03/08-03/11
Porgy and Bess
By Du Bose Heyward, Ira Gershwin/ George Gershwin
Producer/Director: Cheryl Crawford/ Robert Ross
Cast: Todd Duncan, Etta Moten, Avon Long, Warren Coleman and The Eva Jessye Choir

03/15-03/20
Ballet Theatre
Producer/Director: Sol Hurok/Léonide Massine
Cast: Alicia Markova, Léonide Massine, Baronova, Anton Dolin and a cast of 125

03/22-04/03
Tobacco Road
By Jack Kirkland
Producer/Director: Jack Kirkland/Anthony Brown
Cast: John Barton, Sarah Perry, Lillian Ardell and others

04/05-04/10
Ruth Draper and Her Sketches
Producer/Director: Sol Hurok
Cast: Ruth Draper

04/12-04/17
Fantasia
Motion picture

04/22-04/24
Three Sisters
By Chekhov
Producer/Director:
Katharine Cornell/Guthrie McClintic
Cast: Katharine Cornell, Judith Anderson, Ruth Gordon, Gertrude Musgrove, Alexander Knox, Edmund Gwenn and Joseph Wiseman

04/26-04/31
Junior Miss
By Chodorov & Fields
Producer/Director: Max Gordon/Moss Hart
Cast: Robert Allen, Sid Conrad, Katherine Anderson, William Whitehead and others

05/03-05/08
Ecstasy
Motion picture

05/10-05/15
San Carlo Opera Cu.
Producer/Director: Fortune Gallo/ Carlo Peroni

05/17-05/29
Arsenic and Old Lace
By John Kesselring
Producer/Director: Arthur Jarrett
Cast: Cecilia Loftus, John McKee, Arthur Jarrett, Lawrence Hayes, John Powers, Daisy Atherton and others

06/21-07/26
The Vinegar Tree
By Paul Osborn
Producer/Director: Royal Alexandra Theatre/Robert Henderson
Cast: Luella Gear, John Grogan, Richard Temple, Mary Howes, John Richards and others

06/28-07/03
The Late Christopher Bean
By Sidney Howard
Producer/Director: Royal Alexandra Theatre/Robert Henderson
Cast: Pauline Lord, Clarence Derwent, Arthur Jarrett, Cora Smith and others

07/05-07/10
Out of the Frying Pan
By Frances Swann
Producer/Director: Royal Alexandra/Robert Henderson
Cast: Marjorie Peterson, Stanley Bell, John Grogan, Valerie Valaire, Earle Grey and others

07/12-07/17
Little Women
By Marian De Forest and Jessie Bonstelle
Producer/Director:
Royal Alexandra/Robert Henderson
Cast: Erin O'Brien-Moore, Marjorie Peterson, Cora Smith, Dora Sayers, Isabel Price, Valerie Valaire, Earle Grey and others

07/19-07/24
Brief Moment
By S.N. Behrman
Producer/Director:
Royal Alexandra/Robert Henderson
Cast: Glenda Farrell, Dean Norton, Stanley Bell, Marjorie Peterson, Leo Chalzell, Robert Bartron, John Grogan, John Richards and Valerie Valaire

07/26-07/31
Personal Appearance
By Lawrence Riley
Producer/Director:
Royal Alexandra/Robert Henderson
Cast: Dorothy Eaton, Leo Chalzel, John Grogan and Stanley Bell

08/02-08/07
Candida
By G.B. Shaw
Producer/Director:
Royal Alexandra/Robert Henderson
Cast: Elissa Landi, John Grogan, Dorothy Eaton, Robert Barton and Richard Temple

08/09-08/14
Theatre
By Somerset Maugham and Guy Bolton
Producer/Director:
Royal Alexandra/Robert Henderson
Cast: Elissa Landi, Edward Colton, Valerie Valaire, Judson Laire, Roger Sullivan and others

08/16-08/21
Smilin' Through
By Jane Murfin and Jane Cowl
Producer/Director:
Royal Alexandra/Robert Henderson
Cast: Erin O'Brien-Moore, Richard Temple, John Grogan and others

08/23-08/29
Tonight or Never
By Lily Hatvany/Frederick and Fanny Hatton
Producer/Director: Royal Alexandra/Robert Henderson
Cast: Ethel Barrymore Colt, Judson Laire, Stanley Bell, Dorothy Eaton and others

08/31-09/04
Another Heaven
By Margaret Laine, Guy Bolton
and John Golden
Producer/Director:
Royal Alexandra/Robert Henderson
Cast: Clarence Derwent, A.P. Kaye,
with Thelma Schnee, Ethel Morrison,
Elizabeth Inglis and others

09/06-09/18
Abie's Irish Rose
By Anne Nicholls
Producer/Director: Anne Nicholls
Cast: Abe Gore, Bertha Walden, James
O'Neill, Alfred White, Vincent Gardner,
Louise Snyder, Donald Brian and others

09/20-10/02
Fantasia
Motion picture

10/11-10/23
The City That Stopped Hitler
Motion picture

10/25-10/30
The Patriots
By Sidney Kingsley
Producer/Director: The Playwrights'
Company (Maxwell Anderson, S.N.
Behrman, Elmer Rice, Robert E. Sherwood
and Sidney Howard)
Cast: Walter Hampden, Cecil Humphreys,
Julie Haydon, Guy Sorel and others

11/01-11/06
Boston Comic Opera Co.: Trial by Jury,
HMS Pinafore, Pirates of Penzance, Patience
By Gilbert and Sullivan
Producer/Director: R.H. Burnside

11/08-11/13
Blossom Time
By Donnelly/Romberg
Producer/Director: Shuberts
Cast: Barbara Scully, Doug Leavitt,
Roy Cropper, Roy Barnes, Helene Arthur,
William Kent and others

11/15-11/20
Sim Sala Bim
Cast: Dante (Harry Alvin Jansen),
with Moi-Yo Miller and a cast of 35

11/22-11/27
Blithe Spirit
By Noel Coward
Producer/Director: John C. Wilson

Cast: Clifton Webb, Mildred Natwick,
Peggy Wood and Haila Stoddard

11/29-12/04
The Student Prince
By Donnelly/Romberg
Producer/Director: Shuberts
Cast: Everett Marshall, Frank Hornaday,
Laurel Hurley, Detmar Poppen, Nina Varela
and others

12/13-12/18
Three Is a Family
By Phoebe and Henry Ephron
Producer/Director: John Golden, John
Pollock and Max Siegel/Henry Ephron
Cast: Dulcie Cooper and others

12/27-01/01/44
Life with Father
By Howard Lindsay and Russel Crouse
Producer/Director:
Oscar Serlin/Bretaigne Windust
Cast: Harry Bannister, June Walker
and others

1944

01/03-01/08
Tropical Revue
By Katherine Dunham
Producer/Director:
Sol Hurok/Katherine Dunham
Cast: Katherine Dunham and others

01/10-01/15
My Sister Eileen
By Joseph Fields and Jerome Chodorov
Producer/Director: Max Gordon/George
S. Kaufman

01/17-01/22
The House in Paris
Eric Mawby Green
and Edward Allen Feilbert
Producer/Director: H. Clay Blaney,
Wm. Harris Jr./Clarence Derwent
Cast: Ludmilla Pitoeff, Alistair Kyle, Barbara
Kent and Youl Bryner (Yul Brynner)

01/24-01/29
The Doughgirls
Joseph Fields
Producer/Director:

Max Gordon/George S. Kaufman
Cast: Betty Furness, Ralph Meeker, Lenore
Ulric, Royal Beal and Olive Reeves-Smith

01/31-02/05
Fiesta
By Léonide Massine and Eugene van Grona
Producer/Director:
Vincent Youmans/Max Goberman
Cast: Léonide Massine Ballet, Frank Parish
and his puppets and others, in a cast of
162, Deems Taylor (narrator)

02/07-02/12
Tobacco Road
By Jack Kirkland
Producer/Director:
Jack Kirkland/Anthony Brown
Cast: John Barton, Norman Shelly,
Sara Perry, Jane McCloud, Lillian Ardell
and others

02/14-02/19
No Greater Love
Motion picture

02/23-03/04
Ballet Russe de Monte Carlo
Producer/Director: Sergei J. Denham
Cast: Alexandra Danilova, Nathalie
Krossovska, Dorothy Etheridge, Ruthanna
Boris, Maria Tallchief, Leon Danielian and
others, in a cast of 100

03/06-03/11
Ravaged Earth
Motion picture

03/13-04/08
Janie
By Brock Pemberton, Josephine Bentham
and Herschel Williams
Producer/Director:
Frank McCoy/Harry Lowell
Cast: William Sharon, Mary Killen,
Grace Carney and others

04/10-04/23
Fantasia
Motion picture

04/24-04/29
The Old Soak
By Don Marquis
Producer/Director: Frank McCoy
Cast: Guy Kibbee, Joseph E. Bernard,
Valerie Valaire, Muriel Scott, Victor Finney
and others

05/01-05/06
Junior Miss
By Sally Benson, Jerome Chodorov
and Joseph Fields
Producer/Director: Max Gordon/Moss Hart
Cast: Eddie Nugent, Bruce Hall, Lois
Wilson, Elaine Temple, Conrad Janis
and others

05/08-06/03
Kiss and Tell
By F. Hugh Herbert
Producer/Director: George Abbott
Cast: Violet Heming, Walter Gilbert
and Betty Ann Nyman

05/30-06/03
The Family Carnovsky
By Israel Joshua Singer

06/05-06/10
Aren't We All
By Frederick Lonsdale
Producer/Director:
Royal Alexandra/Robert Henderson
Cast: Melville Cooper, Marie Paxton,
Fritzi Scheff, Tom Rutherford and others

06/12-06/17
The Man Who Came to Dinner
By Kaufman & Hart
Producer/Director:
Royal Alexandra/Robert Henderson
Cast: Tom Rutherford, Norman Budd,
Marie Paxton, Peter Boyne and others

06/19-06/24
The Letter
By W. Somerset Maugham
Producer/Director:
Royal Alexandra/Robert Henderson
Cast: Margalo Gillmore, Fredric Tozere,
Robert Ross, Tom Rutherford, Jay Williams,
Wells Richardson, Robert Ross,
William King, Allan Leneck, John Rawley,
Marie Paxton and others

06/26-07/01
Arms and the Man
By G.B. Shaw
Producer/Director: Royal Alexandra/Robert
Henderson
Cast: Madge Evans, Alexander Kirkland
and others

07/03-07/08
Mr. and Mrs. North
By Frances and Richard Lockridge/
Owen Davis
Producer/Director:
Royal Alexandra/Robert Henderson

Cast: Madge Evans, Tom Rutherford,
Ben Lennick, Marie Paxton, Peter Boyne
and others

07/10-07/15
The Doughgirls
By Joseph Fields
Producer/Director:
Royal Alexandra/Robert Henderson
Cast: Gina Malo, Marie Paxton,
Marjorie Peteron, Stanley Bell and others

07/17-07/22
Hamlet
By Wm. Shakespeare
Producer/Director:
Royal Alexandra/Robert Henderson
Cast: Tom Rutherford, Allan Leneck, Rupert
MacLeod, Wells Richardson, Victor Chaplin,
Earle Grey and others

07/24-07/29
Dark Eyes
By Elena Miramova and Eugenie Leontovich
Producer/Director:
Royal Alexandra/Robert Henderson
Cast: Elena Mirmova, Ludmilla Toretzka,
Suzanne Caubet, Victor Chapin,
Richard Temple, Ruth Mitchell, Jane
Moultrie, Marie Paxton and others

07/31-08/05
Hamlet
By Wm. Shakespeare
Producer/Director:
Royal Alexandra/Robert Henderson
Cast: Tom Rutherford, Allan Leneck, Rupert
MacLeod, Allan Wilkie, Rupert MacLeod,
Wells Richardson, Victor Chapin, Earle Grey
and others

08/07-08/12
The Royal Family
By George S. Kaufman and Edna Ferber
Producer/Director:
Royal Alexandra/Robert Henderson
Cast: Tom Rutherford, Marie Paxton,
Kathleen Kidd, Victor Chapin,
Jack Medhurst and others

08/14-08/19
Becky Sharp
By Langdon Mitchell, after W.M. Thackery
Producer/Director:
Royal Alexandra/Robert Henderson
Cast: Haila Stoddard, Tom Rutherford,
Richard Temple and others

08/28-09/02
The Merchant of Venice
By Wm. Shakespeare

Producer/Director:
Royal Alexandra/Robert Henderson
Cast: Ann Andrews, Richard Temple,
Frank Wilson, Marie Paxton and others

09/04-09/08
Hamlet
By Wm. Shakespeare
Producer/Director:
Royal Alexandra/Robert Henderson
Cast: Tom Rutherford, Allan Wilkie, Allan
Leneck, Rupert MacLeod, Victor Chapin,
Earle Grey and others

09/25-09/30
Othello
By Wm. Shakespeare
Producer/Director: Theatre Guild and
Margaret Webster Productions/José Ferrer
Cast: Paul Robeson, José Ferrer
and Uta Hagen

10/02-10/07
Blackstone and His Show of 1001 Wonders
Harry Blackstone

10/09-10/15
Wallflower
By Mary Orr and Reginald Denham
Cast: Betty Blythe

10/16-10/21
Sons O' Fun
By Olsen & Johnson/Jack Yellen and
Sam E. Fain/Robert Alton
Producer/Director:
Shuberts/Edward Duryea Dowling
Cast: The Pitchmen, Marylin Ross,
Jack Shea, June Johnson, Bobby Barry,
Jack Whitney and others

10/23-10/28
Life with Father
By Howard Lindsay and Russel Crouse
Producer/Director:
Oscar Serlin/Bretaigne Windust

Cast: Carl Benton Reid, Betty Linley,
Mary Diveny, Sandy Campbell, Tom Moore
and others

10/30-11/04
The Great Mr. Handel
Motion picture

11/06-11/11
Rebecca
By Daphne DuMaurier
Producer/Director:
Victor Payne-Jennings/Clarence Derwent
Cast: Bramwell Fletcher, Florence Reed,
Diana Barrymore and others

11/13-11/18
Tropical Revue
By Katherine Dunham
Producer/Director: Sol Hurok/Katherine
Dunham
Cast: Katherine Dunham and others

11/20-11/25
Harriet
By Florence Ryerson and Colin Clements
Producer/Director: Gilbert Miller/Elia Kazan
Cast: Helen Hayes, Alberta Perkins,
Richard Wilder and others

11/27-12/02
Errand for Bernice
By Jacques Deval
Producer/Director: Gilbert Miller,
Charles Stewart/Jacques Deval
Cast: Gertrude Lawrence, Stephen Bekassy
and Wendell Corey

12/04-12/09
Gilbert and Sullivan Comic Opera Co.
By Gilbert and Sullivan
Producer/Director: H. Burnside
Cast: Ralph Riggs, Robert Pitkin,
Kathleen Roche, Bertram Peacock,
Catherine Judah and others

12/11-12/16
Blossom Time
By Donnelly/Romberg
Producer/Director: Shuberts

Cast: Ruth Gillette, Earl Covert, William
Marel, Zella Russell, Harry K. Morton,
Peggy O'Neil, Edmund Dorsay,
Victor Morley and others

12/18-12/30
Abie's Irish Rose
By Anne Nicholls
Producer/Director: Anne Nicholls
Cast: Eddie Pascal, Bertha Walden, James
O'Neill, Robert Leonard, Clarence Geiger
and others

1945

01/01-11/06
Fantasia
Motion picture

01/08-01/13
The Great Mr. Handel
Motion picture

01/22-02/03
Blithe Spirit
By Noel Coward
Producer/Director:
Royal Alexandra/Robert Henderson
Cast: Elissa Landi, Alexander Kirkland,
Vicki Cummings, Hildegarde Halliday, Marie
Paxton, Dorman Leonard and Phylis Adams

02/05-02/10
Candida
By G.B. Shaw
Producer/Director: Royal
Alexandra/Alexander Kirkland
Cast: Elissa Landi, Bram Nossen,
Marie Paxton, Dorman Leonard,
A.P. Kaye and Richard Hylton

02/12-12/17
Romance
By Edward Sheldon
Producer/Director:
Royal Alexandra/Elissa Landi
Cast: Elissa Landi, Alexander Kirkland,
Marie Paxton and Bram Nossen

02/19-02/24
Berkeley Square
By John Balderston
Producer/Director:
Royal Alexandra/Robert Henderson
Cast: Elissa Landi, Bramwell Fletcher,
Bram Nossen, Marie Paxton, Ruth Mitchell,

Frances Ross, Dorman Leonard, Derrick
Overholt and others

02/26-03/03
The Student Prince
By Donnelly/Romberg
Producer/Director: Shuberts
Cast: Alexander Grey, Laurel Hurley,
Detmar Poppen and a cast of 50

03/05-03/10
Warsaw Concerto
Motion picture

03/12-03/17
A Doll's House
By H. Ibsen
Producer/Director:
James B. Cassidy/Eugene Bryden
Cast: Jane Darwell, Dale Melbourne,
Frances Lederer, Keven McClure,
H.B. Warner and Lyle Talbot

03/19-03/24
Over Twenty One
By Ruth Gordon
Producer/Director:
Max Gordon/George S. Kaufman
Cast: Ruth Gordon, Jane Sterling, Kip Good,
Clinton Sunberg, Loring Smith, Eddie Hodge
and others

03/27-04/07
Ballet Russe de Monte Carlo
Producer/Director: George Balanchine
Cast: Nathalie Krassovska, Dorothy
Etheridge, Ruthanna Boris, M. Leon
Danielian, Alexandra Danilova, Maria
Tallchief and others, in a cast of 125

04/09-04/14
Four Feathers
By A.E.W. Mason, adapted by R.C. Sherriff

04/16-04/21
Ramshackle Inn
By George Batson
Producer/Director:
Robert Reid/Arthur Sircom
Cast: Zasu Pitts, Helen MacKellar,
Gordon Peters, John Lorenz and others

04/30-05/05
Hamlet
By Wm. Shakespeare
Producer/Director:
Royal Alexandra/Robert Henderson
Cast: Tom Rutherford, George Somes,
Lily Cahill, Richard Temple, Katherine Bard,
Le Roi Operti, James Ganon and others

05/07-05/26
The Merry Widow
By Victor Leon and Leo Stein/Franz Lehar
Producer/Director:
Royal Alexandra/Robert Henderson
Cast: Ruth Altman, Arthur Maxwell,
Alex Alexander, Augusta French, Nils Landin
and others

05/28-06/02
Romeo and Juliet
By Wm. Shakespeare
Producer/Director:
Royal Alexandra/Robert Henderson
Cast: Dean Harens, Katharine Bard, Jessie
Busley and others

Katharine Bard

06/08-06/23
The Vagabond King
By Brian Hooker and W.H. Post/Rudolf Friml
Producer/Director:
Royal Alexandra/Robert Henderson
Cast: Edward Roecker, Ralph Riggs,
Adelaide Abbot, France Bendsten,
Alice Howland and others

06/25-06/30
Anything Goes
Guy Bolton, P.G. Wodehouse, Howard
Lindsay/Cole Porter
Producer/Director:
Royal Alexandra/Robert Henderson
Cast: Vicki Cummings, Arthur Maxwell,
Ralph Riggs, Gedda Petry, Marjorie
Peterson, Alex Alexander, John Rawley
and Earle Grey

07/09-07/14
Design for Living
By Noel Coward
Producer/Director:
Royal Alexandra/Robert Henderson
Cast: Vicki Cummings, Arthur Maxwell,
Michael Ames, Frank Wade, Cosette Lee
and others

07/16-07/21
Too Many Husbands
By W. Somerset Maugham
Producer/Director:
Royal Alexandra/Robert Henderson
Cast: Nancy Carroll, Michael Ames,
Kathleen Kidd, David Powell, Barbara Todd
and others

07/23-07/28
Hay Fever
By Noel Coward
Producer/Director:
Royal Alexandra/Robert Henderson
Cast: Estelle Winwood, Gedda Petry,
Arthur Maxwell, Cosette Lee, Frank Wade
and others

07/30-08/03
Cradle Snatchers
By Russell Medcraft and Norma Mitchell
Producer/Director:
Royal Alexandra/Robert Henderson
Cast: Frances Comstock, Doro Merande,
Arthur Maxwell, Michael Ames and others

08/05-08/10
And So to Bed
By James B. Fagan
Producer/Director:
Royal Alexandra/Robert Henderson
Cast: Eugenie Leontovich, Ruth Altman,
Michael Ames and Alex Alexander

08/13-08/18
The Animal Kingdom
By Philip Barry
Producer/Director:
Royal Alexandra/Robert Henderson
Cast: Haila Stodard, Michael Ames, Arthur
Maxwell, Frank Wade, Jacqueline Susann
and others

08/20-08/25
Little Miss Bluebird
By Avery Hopwood
Producer/Director:
Royal Alexandra/Robert Henderson
Cast: Lillian Harvey, Arthur Maxwell,
Cosette Lee and others

09/03-09/08
Blackstone and His Show of 1001 Wonders
Harry Blackstone

09/17-09/22
Tobacco Road
By Jack Kirkland
Producer/Director:
Jack Kirkland/Anthony Brown
Cast: John Barton and others

09/24
The Six Wives of Henry VIII
Motion picture

09/25
Catherine the Great
Motion picture

09/26
Sanders of the River
Motion picture

09/27
The Ghost Goes West
Motion picture

09/28
The Scarlet Pimpernel
Motion picture

09/29
Elephant Boy
Motion picture

10/01-10/06
Girl No. 217
Motion picture

10/08-10/13
The Student Prince
By Donnelly/Romberg
Producer/Director: Shuberts
Cast: Alexander Grey, Lauren Hurley,
Detmar Poppen, Nina Varela and others

10/15-10/20
The Fall of Berlin
Motion picture

10/22-10/27
Strange Fruit
By Lillian Smith
Producer/Director: José Ferrer
Cast: George Oliver, Earl Jones, Vera Allen,
Melchior Ferrer, Ralph Meeker,
Eugenia Rawls and Jane White

10/29-11/03
Gilbert and Sullivan Opera Co.
By Gilbert and Sullivan
Producer/Director: R.H. Burnside
Cast: Warren Lee Terry, Bertram Peacock,
Ralph Riggs, Beverly Sills, Athena Pappas
and others

11/05-11/10
Ballet Russe Highlights
Producer/Director:
Fortune Gallo/Léonide Massine
Cast: Anna Istomina, Jean Guellis, Rosella
Hightower, Ivan Demidoff, Bettina Rosay,
Yurek Lazovsky, Léonide Massine and others

11/12-11/17
The Hasty Heart
By John Patrick
Producer/Director: Howard Lindsay and
Russel Crouse/Bretaigne Windust
Cast: John Dall, John Burke, Dort Clark,
Lee Kresel, Victor Chapin and others

11/19-12/01
Rose Marie
By Otto Harbach, Oscar
Hammerstein/Rudolf Friml
Producer/Director: Shuberts
Cast: Kendal Kelly, Malcolm Lee Beggs,
Nina Olivette, Victor Carell, Arthur Maxwell
and others

11/24-11/28
Countess Maritza
By Harry B. Smith/Emmerich Kalman
Producer/Director: Shuberts
Cast: Anthony, Allyn and Sonja LevKova,
Carl Randall, Beth Deal, Billy Sully
and others

12/02-12/08
A Joy Forever
By Vincent McConnor
Producer/Director: Blevins Davis,
Archie Thompson
Cast: Guy Kibbee, Dorothy Sands,
Nicholas Joy and Loring Smith

12/10-12/15
Pick Up Girl
By Elsa Shelley
Producer/Director: Harry Baker
Cast: Marguerite Morrissey, Coburn
Goodwin, Evelynne Eaton, Guy Gillette,
Eda Reiss Merin and others

12/17-12/22
School for Brides
By Frank Gill Jr. and George Carleton
Brown
Producer/Director: Frank McCoy
Cast: Jack Sheehan, Helen Twelvetrees,
Kirk Brown, Richard Posten and others

12/24-12/29
Fantasia
Motion picture

12/31-01/04/46
Windy Hill
By Patsy Ruth Miller
Producer/Director: Ruth Chatterton
Cast: Roger Pryor, Kay Francis, Royal Beal,
Jetti Preminger and others

1946

01/07-01/12
A Gift for the Bride
By Andrew Solt and S. Bekeffi,
adapted by Rowland Leigh
Producer/Director: Jules Leventhal and
Shuberts/Rowland Leigh and Andrew Solt
Cast: Luise Rainer, Paul Kaye, Adrienne
Bayan, Jay Rogers, Gloria Humphreys,
Sapleton Kent, Ruth Amos and Wells
Richardson

01/14-01/19
The Great Mr. Handel
Motion picture

01/21-01/26
Life with Father
By Lindsay & Crouse
Producer/Director: Oscar Serlin/Bretaigne
Windust
Cast: Carl Benton Reid, Betty Linley
and others

01/28-02/02
School for Brides
By Frank Gill Jr.
and George Carleton Brown
Producer/Director: Frank McCoy
Cast: Jack Sheehan, Helen Twelvetrees
and others

02/04-02/09
10 Little Indians
By Agatha Christie
Producer/Director:
Arthur W. Kelly/Albert de Courville
Cast: Forrest Orr, Elsbeth Hoffman
and others

02/11-02/16
Windy Hill
By Patsy Ruth Miller
Producer/Director: Ruth Chatterton
Cast: Roger Pryor, Kay Francis and
Royal Beal

02/18-02/23
Deep Are the Roots
By Arnaud d'Usseau and James Gow
Producer/Director: Kermit Bloomgarden
and George Heller/Elia Kazan
Cast: Edith Atwater, Theodore Newton
and Robert Harrison

02/25-03/01
Carmen Jones
By Oscar Hammerstein/Georges Bizet
Producer/Director: Billy Rose/Hassard Short
Cast: Robert Clarke, George Willis, Elton J.
Warren, Coreania Hayman, Jack Carr
and a singing cast of 125

03/05-03/09
Raizin' Kane
Producer/Director: Leaside Lions Club

03/11-03/16
Ballet Theatre
Producer/Director: Sol Hurok
Cast: Andre Eglevsky, Nora Kaye, Alicia
Alonso, John Kriza, Janet Reed, Lucia
Chase, Dimitri Pomanoff, Michael Kidd
and others

03/18-03/23
Dear Ruth
By Norman Krasna
Producer/Director: Joseph M. Hyman
and Bernard Hart/Moss Hart
Cast: William Harringan, Leona Powers,
Herbert Evers, Hope Cameron and others

03/25-03/30
Dansation of 1946
Producer/Director: George M. Gatts
Cast: Veloz & Yolanda, Elizabeth
Talbot-Martin and others

04/01-04/13
St. Francis of Assisi
Motion picture

04/15-04/27
Ballet Russe de Monte Carlo
Producer/Director: Sergei J. Denham
Cast: Alexandra Danilova, Nicholas
Magallanes, Leon Danielian, Peter Deign
and others

04/29-05/02
School for Brides
By Frank Gill and George Carlton Brown
Producer/Director: Frank McCoy
Cast: Jack Sheehan, Ethel Britton ("Jack
Sheehan and 12 Hollywood Pin-Up Models")

05/06-05/11
Dark of the Moon
By Howard Richardson and William Berney
Producer/Director: Shuberts/Robert E. Perry
Cast: Carol Stone, James Lanphier
and others

05/13-05/18
Second Best Bed
By N. Richard Nash
Producer/Director: Ruth Chatterton
and John Huntington/Ruth Chatterton
and N. Richard Nash
Cast: Ruth Chatterton, Ralph Forbes,
Richard Temple, Barry Thomson and
Richard Dyer-Bennet

05/20-05/25
Stop and Go
Producer/Director: Jack Arthur
Presented by Entertainment Committee
of the Citizens' Committee for Troops
in Training
Cast: Company of 125 Canadian Amateurs
from the Wartime Units

05/27-06/02
Goose for the Gander
By Harold J. Kennedy
Producer/Director:
Jules J. Leventhal and Frank McCoy
Cast: Gloria Swanson, Harold J. Kennedy
and others

06/04-06/15
The New Moon
By Frank Mandel, Oscar Hammerstein II,
Laurence Schwab/Sigmund Romberg
Producer/Director: Royal Alexandra
Theatre/Robert Henderson
Cast: Adelaide Bishop, Frank Melton,
Ralph Riggs, Doris Patston, Catherine
Judah, Ray Carroll and others

06/17-06/22
Private Lives
By Noel Coward
Producer/Director: Royal Alexandra
Theatre/Robert Henderson
Cast: Tallulah Bankhead, Donald Cook,
Alexander Clark, Mary Mason and
Alice Pearce

06/24-06/30
The Chocolate Soldier
By Stanislaus Stange/Oscar Strauss
Producer/Director: Royal Alexandra
Theatre/Robert Henderson
Cast: Adelaide Bishop, Nina Varela,
Doris Patston, Frank Melton, Lloyd Harris,
Lucy Greene and others

07/01-07/13
Good Night, Ladies
By Cyrus Wood, Avery Hopwood
and Charlton Andrews

Producer/Director: Royal Alexandra
Theatre/Robert Henderson
Cast: Eddie Nugent, Allen Kearns
and others

07/15-07/20
Private Lives
By Noel Coward
Producer/Director: Royal Alexandra
Theatre/Robert Henderson
Cast: Tallulah Bankhead, Donald Cook,
Alexander Clark, Mary Mason and Susan
Thompson

07/22-08/03
Richard III
By Wm. Shakespeare
Producer/Director:
Royal Alexandra/Robert Henderson
Cast: José Ferrer, Nance O'Neil, Robert
Carroll, Elfrida Derwent, Richard Temple,
Lloyd Harris, John Colt and others

08/05-08/10
Green Goddess
By William Archer
Producer/Director:
Royal Alexandra/Robert Henderson
Cast: José Ferrer and others

08/12-08/30
The Desert Song
By Otto Harbach, Oscar
Hammerstein/Sigmund Romberg
Producer/Director:
Royal Alexandra/Robert Henderson
Cast: Lucille Manners, Gordon Dilworth,
Jack Sheehan and others

09/02-09/07
Merry Wives of Windsor
By Wm. Shakespeare
Producer/Director: The Theatre Guild,
Lawrence Langner and Theresa
Helburn/Romney Brent
Cast: Allan Reed, Jessie Royce,
Romney Brent, Gina Malo, Witford Kane,
David Powell, Charles Francis and others

09/09-09/14
Life with Father
By Lindsay & Crouse
Producer/Director:
Oscar Serlin/Bretaigne Windust
Cast: Edwin Maxwell, Betty Alden
and others

09/16-09/28
Blackstone and His Show of 1001 Wonders
Harry Blackstone

09/30-10/05
Cyrano de Bergerac
By Edmond Rostand
Producer/Director:
José Ferrer/Melchor Ferrer
Cast: José Ferrer, Frances Reid, Francis
Compton, Ralph Clanton, Hiram Sherman
and others

10/07-10/12
Tobacco Road
By Jack Kirkland
Producer/Director:
Jack Kirkland/Anthony Brown
Cast: John Barton, Walter Draper,
Sarah Taft, Virginia Vincent,
Lillian Ardell and others

10/14-10/20
Apple of His Eye
By Kenyon Nicholson and Charles Robinson
Producer/Director: Jed Harris/Walter Huston
Cast: Walter Huston, Doro Merande,
Don Doherty and others

10/21-10/26
Joos Ballet
Producer/Director: Kurt Joos and Arts
Council of Great Britain
Cast: Nigel Burke, Noelle de Mosa, Ulla
Soederbaum, Frederic Bucher, Florence
Read, Suzanne de Courcy, Aart Vergstegen,
Ludmila Mlada and others

10/28-11/03
Hamlet
By Wm. Shakespeare
Producer/Director: Michael Todd
Cast: Maurice Evans, Nelson Leigh, Doris
Loyd, Miles Malleson, Pamela Conroy and
others

11/04-11/09
Mary Had a Little ...
By Muriel Herman, Arthur Herzog
and Al Rosen
Producer/Director: Al Rosen/Leon Errol
Cast: Edmund Lowe, Mary Brian, Claire
Carleton, Fred Sherman, Gerald Oliver
Smith and others

11/11-11/16
A Family Affair
By Henry R. Misrock
Producer/Director: Jesse Long and
Edward S. Hart/Alexander Kirkland
Cast: Ann Mason and John Williams

11/18-11/23
The Student Prince
Donnelly/Romberg
Producer/Director: Shuberts/Walter Johnson
Cast: Frank Hornaday, Detmar Poppen,
Marian Stevens, Nina Varela, John Mooney
and others

11/25-11/30
Pygmalion
By G.B. Shaw
Producer/Director: Theatre Incorporated
and Richard Aldrich/Cedric Hardwicke
Cast: Gertrude Lawrence, Cecil Humphrys,
Ralph Forbes, Katherine Fmmet, Cynthia
Latham and others

12/02-12/07
Theirs Is the Glory
Motion picture

12/09-12/14
Temporary Mrs. Smith
By Jacqueline Susann and Beatrice Cole
Producer/Director:
Vinton Freedley/Jessie Royce Landis
Cast: Luba Malina, Mischa Auer,
Millard Mitchell and others

12/16-12/21
Springtime for Henry
By Benn W. Levy
Producer/Director:
Frank McCoy/Henri Caubisens
Cast: Edward Everett Horton, Matthew
Smith, Muriel Hutchinsona and Elaine Ellis

12/23-12/28
Love Goes to Press
By Martha Gellhorn and Virginia Cowles
Producer/Director: Warren P.
Munsell/Wallace Douglas
Cast: Ralph Michael, Joyce Heron,
William Post Jr., Jane Middleton and
Georgina Cookson

12/30-01/04/47
Fantasia
Motion picture

1947

01/06-01/18
The Voice of the Turtle
By John Van Druten
Producer/Director:
Alfred de Liagre Jr./John van Druten
Cast: Harvey Stephens, Louisa Horton
and Frances Tannehill

01/10-02/01
King Lear, As You Like It, Hamlet,
The Merchant of Venice, Volpone
By Wm. Shakespeare and Ben Johnson
Producer/Director: Advance Players
Association Ltd./Donald Wolfit
and Christopher Ede
Cast: Donald Wolfit, Rosalino Iden
and the London Company

02/03-02/08
The Importance of Being Earnest
By Oscar Wilde
Producer/Director: Theatre Guild and
John C. Wilson and H.M. Tennent Ltd./
John Gielgud
Cast: Robert Flemyng, John Gielgud,
Margaret Rutherford, Pamela Brown
and Jane Baxter

02/17-02/23
The Eagle Has Two Heads
By Jean Cocteau
Producer/Director: John C. Wilson
Cast: Tallulah Bankhead, Helmut Dantine,
Clarence Derwent and Eleanor Wilson

03/03-03/08
Take It Easy
Producer/Director: Leaside Lions Club
Cast: Leaside Lions Club Members

03/10-03/22
Bloomer Girl
E.Y. Harburg/Harold Arlen
Producer/Director: John C. Wilson and

Nat Goldstone/E.Y. Harburg,
choreographed by Agnes de Mille
Cast: Nanette Fabray, Arthur Maxwell,
Olive Reeves-Smith, Mabel Taliaferro
and others

03/24-03/29
Call Me Mister
By Arnold Auerbach/Harold Rome
Producer/Director:
Melvyn Douglas and Herman Levin
Cast: Melvyn Douglas, Betty Kean
and others

04/01-04/12
Ballet Russe de Monte Carlo
Producer/Director: Sergei J. Denhan
Cast: Alexandra Danilova, Frederic Franklin,
Leon Danielian, Ruthanna Boris, Nathalie
Krassovska and others

04/14-04/19
State of the Union
By Lindsay & Crouse
Producer/Director: Leland Hayward
Cast: Neil Hamilton, Erin O'Brien-Moore,
James Rennie, Katherine Meskill, Donald
Kohler and others

04/21-04/26
The Two Mrs. Carrolls
By Martin Vale
Producer/Director: Paul Czinner
Cast: Elisabeth Bergner, Joel Ashley
and others

04/28-05/03
Laura
By Vera Caspary and George Sklar
Producer/Director: H. Clay Blaney and
S.P. and Roy O. Steckler/Clarence Derwent
Cast: John Loder, L.T. Stevens, Hugh
Marlowe, Tom Rutherford, with Tom Walsh
and others

05/05-05/10
Pygmalion
By G.B. Shaw
Producer/Director: Theatre
Incorporated/Richard Aldrich
and Cedric Hardwicke
Cast: Gertrude Lawrence, Cecil Humphreys,
Ralph Forbes, Dennis King and others

05/12-05/24
Oklahoma!
By Rodgers & Hammerstein
Producer/Director: Theatre Guild National
Company and Rouben Mamoulian/Theresa
Helburn and Lawrence Langner

Cast: Edith Gresham, James Alexander,
Peggy Engel, Alfred Webster, Ridge Bond
and others

05/26-05/31
The Two Mrs. Carrolls
By Martin Vale
Producer/Director: Paul Czinner
Cast: Elisabeth Bergner, Joel Ashley
and others

06/02-06/07
Stone Flower
By Pavel Bazhov and Ivan Keller
Producer/Director: Alexander Ptushko

06/04-06/16
The New Moon
By Frank Mandel, Oscar Hammerstein
and Laurence Schwab/Sigmund Romberg
Producer/Director:
Royal Alexandra/Robert Henderson
Cast: Adelaide Bishop, Frank Melton,
Ralph Riggs and others

06/19-06/28
Naughty Marietta
By Rida Young/Victor Herbert
Producer/Director: Alexandra Company
Limited/Ralph and Katherine Riggs
Cast: Lillian Raymondi, Ralph Magelssen,
Ralph Riggs and others, in a cast of 70

06/30-07/12
The Merry Widow
Victor Leon, Leo Stein/Franz Lehar
Producer/Director: Alexandra Company
Limited/Ralph and Katherine Riggs
Cast: Margaret Roy, Ralph Magelssen,
Ralph Riggs, Edith Herlick, Nils Landin
and others

07/14-07/19
Love for Love
By William Congreve
Producer/Director:
H.M. Tennent Ltd./John Gielgud
Cast: Cyril Ritchard, Pamela Brown, Robert
Fleming, Marian Spencer, George Hayes,
Sebastian Cabot, John Gielgud and others

07/21-07/26
Dream Girl
By Elmer Rice
Producer/Director:
Jules J. Leventhal/Jus Addiss
Cast: Lucille Ball, Scott McKay,
Ann Andrews, Hayden Rorke and others

09/01-09/06
Oklahoma!
By Rodgers & Hammerstein
Producer/Director: Theatre Guild National
Company and Theresa Jelburn & Lawrence
Langner/Rouben Mamoulian
Cast: Louise Fornaca, Jean Bledsoe,
Marcella Dodge, Claire Pasch, George
Lawrence and others

09/08-09/13
The Great Mr. Handel
Motion picture

09/15-09/27
Blackstone and His Show of 1001 Wonders
Harry Blackstone

09/29-10/11
New Wine
By Howard Estabrook and Nicholas
Joy/Franz Schubert
Producer/Director: Reinhold Schunzel
Cast: Ilona Massey, Alan Curtis, Binnie
Barnes, Albert Basserman, Billy Gilbert
Sterling Holloway and others

10/13-10/18
Harvey
By Mary Chase
Producer/Director: Brock
Pemberton/Antoinette Perry
Cast: Joe E. Brown, Marion Lorne,
Mary Dallas, Helen Randall, Dorothy Scott
and others

10/20-10/25
Men of Two Worlds
By Joyce Cary, Thorold Dickinson
Producer/Director: Thorold Dickinson
Cast: Phyllis Calvert, Eric Portman,
Cathleen Nesbitt and others

10/27-11/01
The Red Mill
By Henry Blossom
Producer/Director: Paula Stone and
Hunt Stromberg Jr./Billy Gilbert
Cast: Odette Myrtil, Buster West Dorothy
Stone, Charles Collins, Sara Ann McCabe
and others

11/03-11/08
Moonlight Sonata
Motion picture

11/10-11/15
Anna Lucasta
By Philip Yordan
Producer/Director:
John Wildberg/Harry Wagstaff Gribble
Cast: Sidney Poitier, Wesleen Foster,
Rosetta Le Noire, Laura Bowman, Roy Allen
and others

11/17-11/22
Antony and Cleopatra
By Wm. Shakespeare
Producer/Director: Guthrie McClintic
Cast: Katharine Cornell, Godfrey Tearle,
Kent Smith, Lenore Ulric, Ralph Clanton,
Ivan Simpson, with Charlton Heston
and others

11/24-11/29
The Roosevelt Story
Motion picture

12/01-12/06
Colonel Blimp
Motion picture

12/08-12/13
The Barber of Seville
Motion picture

12/15-12/20
Lady Windermere's Fan
By Oscar Wilde
Producer/Director:
Homer Curran/Jack Minster
Cast: Cornelia Otis Skinner, Estelle
Winwood, Bramwell Fletcher, David
Manners, George Thirlwell and others

12/25-01/06/48
Henry V
Motion picture

1948

01/07-01/24
Richard III, Midsummer Night's Dream,
Macbeth, Twelfth Night, King Lear,
Much Ado About Nothing
By Wm. Shakespeare
Producer/Director:
Advance Players Association
Cast: Donald Wolfit, Rosalind Iden,
Eric Porter and others, including 30 artists

01/26-02/08
Dublin Gate Theatre: John Bull's Other
Island (Shaw), Portrait of Miriam
(Michael MacLiammoir), The Old Lady Says
No (Denis Johnston), Where Stars Walk
(Michael MacLiammoir)
Producer/Director: Brian Doherty/Dublin
Gate Theatre Productions/Louis Elliman
Cast: Hilton Edwards, Michael MacLiammoir,
Meriel Moore and a cast of 20

02/09-02/21
Mourning Becomes Electra
By Eugene O'Neill
Motion picture

02/23-02/28
The Student Prince
By Donnelly/Romberg
Producer/Director: Shuberts/Walter Johnson
Cast: Toby Durst, Detmar Poppen, Nina
Varela, Victoria Sherry and others

03/01-03/06
Karnival Kapers
By Stew Michie
Producer/Director:
Leaside Lions Club/Stew Michie
Cast: Members of the Leaside Lions Club

03/08-03/13
Shoe Shine
Motion picture

03/15-03/20
Macbeth
By Wm. Shakespeare
Producer/Director: Brian Doherty and
Theatre Incorporated/Norris Houghton
Cast: Michael Redgrave, Flora Robson,
Whitefield Connor, Beatrice Straight,
Russell Collins and others

03/22-04/03
Ballet Russe de Monte Carlo
Producer/Director: Serge J. Denham
Cast: Alexandra Danilova,
Mathalie Krassovska, Robert Kindgren,
Leon Danielian and others

04/05-04/10
New Tropical Revue
By Katherine Dunham
Producer/Director: Katherine Dunham
Cast: Katherine Dunham, Eartha Kitt,
Lucille Ellis, Lenwood Morris, Vanoye
Aikens and others

04/12-04/17
Blossom Time
Donnelly/Romberg
Producer/Director: Shuberts/Zella Russell
Cast: Everett Marshall, Tony Blair,
Marion Stevens, Elizabeth Houston,
Harold R. Brown and others

04/19-05/01
The Glass Menagerie
By Tennessee Williams
Cast: Helen MacKellar, Meg Wyllie,
Ernest Graves and Ted Erwin

05/03-05/08
Carousel
By Rodgers & Hammerstein
Producer/Director: The Theatre Guild
and Lawrence Langner and Theresa
Helburn/Rouben Mamoulian, choreographed
by Agnes DeMille
Cast: Stephen Douglass, Iva Withers,
Louise Larabee, Eric Mattson, Margot
Moser and others

05/10-05/15
Lucia di Lammermoor
Motion picture

05/17-05/23
Burlesque
By George Manker Watters and Arthur
Hopkins
Producer/Director:
Jean Dalrymple/Arthur Hopkins
Cast: Bert Lahr, Peggy Cass, Fay McKenzie
and others

05/24-05/30
That Winslow Boy
By Terence Rattingan
Producer/Director: Atlantis Productions,
The Theatre Guild, H.M. Tennent Ltd. and
John C. Wilson/Glen Byam Shaw

Cast: Michael Newell, Betty Sinclair,
Mary Lynn, Alan Webb, Valerie White,
Owen Holder and others

05/31-06/12
Rosalinda
By Johann Strauss
Producer/Director: The Royal Conservatory
Opera/Felix Brentano
Cast: Jeanne Merril, Ronald Stewart,
Andrew MacMillan, Beth Corrigan,
Earl Dick and a cast of 100

06/17-06/26
Anna Lucasta
By Philip Yordan
Producer/Director: David Lowe and
Sue Davidson/Harold J. Stone
Cast: Sadie J. Browne, Rosetta Le Noire,
Laura Bowman, Roy Allen, Sidney Poitier
and others

07/05-07/17
Furia
Motion picture

07/19-07/24
Dream Girl
Motion picture

07/26-08/21
Sins of the Fathers
Motion picture

08/23-08/28
Opera and Music Film Festival
Motion picture

08/30-09/11
Blackstone and His Show of 1001 Wonders
Harry Blackstone

09/13-09/18
The King's Jester
Motion picture

09/20-09/25
John Loves Mary
By Norman Krasna
Producer/Director:
Rodgers & Hammerstein/Joshua Logan
Cast: Jan Sterling, Donald MacBride,
Richard Derr, Margaret Bannerman,
J. Richard Jones and others

09/27-10/02
Oklahoma!
By Rodgers & Hammerstein
Producer/Director: The Theatre Guild,

Lawrence Langer and Theresa
Helburn/Rouben Mamoulian
Cast: Wilton Clary, Hy Anzel, Ann Crowley,
Edith Gresham, Murvyn Vye and others

10/04-10/09
The Great Mr. Handel
Motion picture

10/11-10/16
The Silver Whistle
By Robert McEnroe
Producer/Director: Theatre Guild,
Theresa Helburn and Lawrence Langner/
Paul Crabtree
Cast: José Ferrer, Eleanor Wilson,
Robert Carroll and others

10/18-10/23
Escape Me Never
By Margaret Kennedy
Producer/Director:
Monte Prosser/Paul Czinner
Cast: Elisabeth Bergner, Philip Huston,
Katharine Sergava and Griffith Jones

10/25-10/30
Goodbye, My Fancy
By Fay Kanin
Producer/Director: Michael Kanin, Aldrich
& Myers/Sam Wanamaker
Cast: Madeleine Carrol, Conrad Nagel,
Shirley Booth and Sam Wanamaker

11/01-11/06
The Breden-Savoy Gilbert and Sullivan
Comic Opera Company: The Mikado,
Pirates of Penzance, HMS Pinafore
By Gilbert and Sullivan
Producer/Director: Barry Breden
Cast: Charles Goodwin, Ray Thomas,
Leo Leonard, Norman Rederick,
Everett Nygaard and others

11/08-11/13
Japhet
By Ronald Telfer and Pauline Jamerson
Producer/Director: John Yorke/Harry Ellerbe
Cast: Ernest Truex, Vicki Cummings, Sylvia
Field, Judson Laire, Grace McTarnahan
and Morton L. Stevens

11/15-11/20
Man and Superman
By G.B. Shaw
Producer/Director: Maurice Evans
Cast: Maurice Evans, Malcolm Keen,
Dorothy Eaton, Chester Stratton and others

11/22-11/27
The Drunkard or The Fallen Saved
Producer/Director: Brian Doherty
Cast: The New World Theatre Company
with John Pratt, Murray Matheson
and others

11/29-12/03
Escape Me Never
By Margaret Kennedy
Producer/Director: Monte Prosser,
Paul Czinner/Lillian Udvardy
Cast: Elisabeth Bergner, Philip Huston,
Katherine Sergava, Griffith Jones and others

12/06-12/11
The Breden-Savoy Gilbert and Sullivan
Comic Opera Co.: HMS Pinafore, Trial
by Jury, Pirates of Penzance, The Mikado
By Gilbert and Sullivan
Producer/Director: Barry Breden
Cast: Edgar Iversen, Everett Mygaard, Ray
Thomas, Charles Goodwin, Thomas Glynn
and others

12/13-12/18
Annie Get Your Gun
Dorothy Fields, Herbert Fields /Irving Berlin
Producer/Director: Rodgers &
Hammerstein/Joshua Logan
Cast: Billie Worth and others

12/20-12/25
The Drunkard or The Fallen Saved
Producer/Director: Brian Doherty
Cast: The New World Theatre Company,
with John Pratt, Murray Matheson,
The Commodores and others

12/27-01/02
O Mistress Mine
By Terence Rattigan
Producer/Director: Harald Bromley,
Eddie Rich, Dean Goodman/Harald Bromley
Cast: Sylvia Sidney, John Loder, Dick Van
Patten and others

1949

01/03-01/08
Favorite Stranger
By Eleanore Sellars
Producer/Director:
Jules J. Leventhal/Leon Michel
Cast: Kay Francis, Joel Ashley,
Gordon Mills and Paul Langton

01/24-01/29
High Button Shoes
Stephen Longstreet and Sammy Cahn/
Jule Styne
Producer/Director: Monte Prosser
and Joseph Kipness/George Abbott,
choreographed by Jerome Robbins
Cast: Eddie Foy Jr., Jack Whiting, Audrey
Meadows, Marty Barrett and others

02/01-02/05
Yiddish Art Theatre: Shylock and His
Daughter, (Ari Ibn-Zahav/Joseph
Rumshinsky), Hershel, The Jester
(Moshe Livshitz/Joseph Rumshinsky),
The Great Fortune (Sholem Aleichem)
Producer/Director: Yiddish Art
Theatre/Maurice Schwartz
Cast: Maurice Schwartz, Charlotte
Goldstein, Yudel Dubinsky, Jacob Mestel,
Anatole Winogradoff and others

02/07-02/12
To Tell the Truth
By Morley Callaghan
Producer/Director: The New Play Society
(Dora Mavor Moore)/James Mavor Moore
Cast: Don Harron, Herbert Gott, Charles
McBride, Murray Cherkover, Beth
Lockerbie, E.M. Margolese, Marcia
Diamond, Mavor Moore, Henry Karpus,
Lawrence Law, Arthur Garmaise, Charles
Else, Alfie Scoop, John Sullivan,
Lloyd Bochner and others

02/14-02/19
The Desert Song
By Otto Harbach, Oscar Hammerstein,
Frank Mandell/Sigmund Romberg
Producer/Director: Russell Lewis and
Howard Young, Gerald Rado/Glenn Jordan
Cast: Edward Roecker, Gale Sherwood,
Jack Good, Iris Whitney and others

03/01-03/05
Canadian Ballet Festival
Producer/Director: Ballet Club of Toronto,
The Hamilton Ballet, Mildred Wickson Ballet
(Toronto), Neo-Dance Theatre (Toronto),
The Ottawa Ballet, Panto-Pacific Ballet
(Vancouver), Ruth Sorel Ballet (Montreal),
Toronto Ballet, Volkoff Canadian Ballet
(Toronto) and The Winnipeg Ballet

03/02
The Red Ear of Corn
By John Weinzweig
Producer/Director:
Volkoff Canadian Ballet, premiere

03/07-03/12
The Ivy Green
By Mervyn Nelson
Producer/Director:
Hall Shelton/Roy Hargrave
Cast: Hurd Hatfield, Judith Evelyn, Daniel
O'Herlihy, Carmen Mathews and others

03/14-03/19
Helter Skelter
By "Stew" S.G. Michie
Producer/Director:
Leaside Lions Club/Stew Michie
Cast: Stew Michie, Len Brooks, Charles
Knight, Charles Pye, Jack Berry, Bob Leary
and others

03/28-04/02
Brigadoon
By Lerner & Lowe
Producer/Director:
Cheryl Crawford/Robert Lewis
Cast: David Brooks, Patricia Gillette,
Pamela Britton, Robert Smith, Jack Byron
and others

04/04-04/09
Oklahoma!
By Rodgers & Hammerstein
Producer/Director: The Theatre Guild
National Co., Theresa Helburn and
Lawrence Langner/Rouben Mamoulian
Cast: Alice Clift, Jean Ruth, Claire Pasch,
Mary Marlo, Ridge Bond and others

04/11-04/23
Ballet Russe de Monte Carlo
Producer/Director: Serji J. Denham
Cast: Mia Slavenska, Mary Ellen Loylan,
Oleg Tupine, Leon Danielian, Gertrude
Tyven and others

04/25-04/30
Dominion Drama Festival: Hedda Gabler,
Over the Boiler Room, Phèdre, John Loves
Mary, The Glass Menagerie, National 6,
Fortune My Foe, The Emperor Jones,
Les Femmes Savantes, Another Part of
the Forest, The Taming of the Shrew
Producer/Director: Workshop 14 (Calgary),
London Little Theatre, Conservatoire Lasalle
(Montreal), Players Guild (Hamilton),
The Vagabond Players (New Westminster),
La Comedie Nouvelle (Ottawa), Mt. Allison
University, Ottawa Drama League, Negro
Theatre Guild (Montreal), Cours François
Rozet (Montreal), Players Workshop
(Toronto) and Peterborough Little Theatre

05/02-05/07
Born Yesterday
By Garson Kanin

Producer/Director:
Max Gordon/Garson Kanin
Cast: Jean Parker, Scott McKay, Carroll
Ashborn, Welba Lestina, William Foran
and others

05/09-05/14
Present Laughter
By Noel Coward
Producer/Director: John Wilson, Martin
Manulis and C. Edwin Knill/Martin Manulis
Cast: Edward Everett Horton, Marta Linden,
Jane Seymour, Katherine Meskill and others

05/23-05/28
Harvey
By Mary Chase
Producer/Director: Brock
Pemberton/Antoinette Perry
Cast: Joe E. Brown, Marion Lorne,
Helen Gillette and others

05/30-06/04
High Button Shoes
By Stephen Longstreet, Sammy Cahn
and Jule Styne
Producer/Director: Monte Prosser and
Joseph Kipness/George Abbott
Cast: Eddie Foy Jr., Audrey Meadows,
Jack Whiting and others

06/06-06/18
Finian's Rainbow
By E.Y. Harburg, Fred Saidy/Burton Lane
Producer/Director: Lee Sabinson and
William R. Katzell/Bretaigne Windust
Cast: Russ Brown, Mimi Kelly, Jay Martin,
Charles J. Davis, Carmen Guitterez
and others

09/05-09/10
Oklahoma!
By Rodgers & Hammerstein
Producer/Director: The Theatre Guild
Company, Theresa Helburn and
Lawrence Langner/Rouben Mamoulian
Cast: Mary Marlo, Ridge Bond,
Patricia Northrop, Owen Martin and others

09/26-10/02
George Formby and His London Music Hall
Varieties
Producer/Director:
Ernest Rawley/Harry Culley
Cast: George Formby, Cynthia & Gladys,
Guss Brox & Myrna, Medlock & Marlowe,
The Humoresques, The Sensational Harbins
and Alan Clive

10/04-10/08
People Like Us
By Frank Vosper

Producer/Director: William L. Taub, Henry
Sherek and Brian Doherty/Clarence Derwent
Cast: Ann Dvorak, Sydney Blackmer, Ernest
Cossart, Viola Roache, George Spelvin
and others

10/10-10/15
Inside USA
By John Gunther/Howard Dietz and Arthur
Schwartz/Arnold Auerbach, Moss Hart,
Arnold B. Horwitt, Joseph Stein and Will
Glickman
Producer/Director: Arthur Schwartz
and Victor Samrock/Helen Tamiris and
Robert H. Gordon
Cast: Beatrice Lillie, Lew Parker, Eric Victor,
David Atkinson, Olga Lunick, Aileen Stanley
Jr. and 101 others

10/17-10/22
Mister Roberts
By Thomas Heggen, Joshua Logan
Producer/Director: Leland Hayward/Joshua
Logan
Cast: John Forsythe, James Rennie, Robert
Burton, Jackie Cooper, Cliff Robertson and
others

10/24-10/29
That Lady
By Kate O'Brien
Producer/Director:
Katharine Cornell/Guthrie McClintic
Cast: Katharine Cornell, Henry Daniell,
Torin Thatcher, Henry Stephenson,
Joseph Wiseman, Marian Seldes and others

10/31-11/05
Anne of a Thousand Days
By Maxwell Anderson
Producer/Director: The Playwrights'
Company, Leland Hayward/H.C. Potter
Cast: Rex Harrison, Joyce Redman,
John Merivale, Wendell K. Phillips,
Frederic Worlock and others

11/07-11/12
Light Up the Sky
By Moss Hart
Producer/Director: Eddie Rich,
Joseph M. Hyman and Bernard Hart
and Arthur J. Brown/Sam Levene
Cast: Sam Levene, Lynn Bari, Margie Hart,
Glenn Anders and others

11/14-11/19
Brigadoon
By Lerner & Loewe
Producer/Director:
Cheryl Crawford/Robert Lewis
Cast: Susan Johnson, Virginia Oswald,
Hayes Gordon, Virginia Richardson,
Kenneth LeRoy and others

11/24-12/03
Sadlers Wells Ballet
Producer/Director: The Covent Garden
Opera Trust, The Arts Council of Great
Britain and the British Council,
Sol Hurok/Ninette de Valois
Cast: Moira Shearer, Margot Fonteyn,
Robert Helpman, Pamela May, Beryl Grey,
Violetta Elvin, Alexis Rassine and a cast
of 150

12/05-12/10
The Man Who Came to Dinner
By Kaufman & Hart
Producer/Director:
Max Gordon/William McFadden
Cast: Monty Woolley, Mabel Acher,
Mardette Edwards and others

12/12-12/17
The Philadelphia Story
By Philip Barry
Producer/Director: The Theatre Guild—
American Theatre Society/Martin Manulis
Cast: Sarah Churchill, Jeffrey Lynn,
Margaret Bannerman, Hugh Reilly
and others

12/19-12/24
Blossom Time
By Donnelly/Romberg
Producer/Director: Shuberts/Zella Russell
Cast: Webb Tilton, Dorothy Hirth, Betty
Oakes, Anthony Blair, Elizabeth Houston
and others

12/26-01/07/50
Mother Goose
Producer/Director: The New Play
Society/Eric Christmas/Dances Director
Betty Oliphant

Cast: Eric Christmas, Al Pearce, Robert
Christie, Gladys Forrester, E.M. Margolese,
Peter Mews, Jack Medhurst and others
(Proceeds in aid of the Kiwanis Club of
Riverdale)

1950

01/09-01/14
Yosele the Nightingale
By Sholem Aleichem and Maurice Schwartz
Producer/Director: Edwin A. Relkin,
Monte Prosser and Joseph Kipness/
Maurice Schwartz
Cast: Maurice Schwartz, Berta Gersten,
Lucy Gehrmah, Gustave Berger, Anatole
Vinogradoff and others, in a cast of 60

01/16-01/21
The Barretts of Wimpole Street
By Rudolf Besier
Producer/Director: John Kenley/Ted Post
Cast: Susan Peters, Brandon Peters,
Robert Carroll and others

01/23-01/28
A Streetcar Named Desire
By Tennessee Williams
Producer/Director: Irene M. Selznick
and Elia Kazan/Elia Kazan
Cast: Anthony Quinn, Uta Hagen,
Mary Welch, George Mathews and others

02/03-02/11
Royal Conservatory Opera Festival:
Rigoletto, Don Giovanni, La Bohème
Producer/Director: Royal Conservatory
Opera/Arnold M. Walter
Cast: Roger Doucet, Frank Crame, Ernest
Adams, Patricia Snell, Gilles Lamontagne,
Andrew MacMillan, Jan Rubes, June
Kowalchuck and a cast of 100

02/13-02/18
Gilbert and Sullivan Comic Opera Co.:
The Mikado, Pirates of Penzance
By Gilbert and Sullivan
Producer/Director: Canada Packers Operatic
Society/W. Richard Curray
Cast: Emlyn Plummer, Sydney Wrightson,
Arthur Sclater, James Green, Ian Kemp
and others

02/20-02/25
Diamond Lil
By Mae West, Jack Linder

Producer/Director: Albert H. Rosen
and Herbert J. Freezer
Cast: Mae West, Charles G. Martin,
Walter Petrie, James Courtney,
Dan Matthews and others

02/27-03/04
Les Ballets de Paris (Carmen)
Producer/Director: Sol Hurok and Shuberts,
with Arthur Lesser/Roland Petit
Renee (Zizi) Jeanmaire, Roland Petit,
Colette Marchand, Belinda Wright, Gabriel
Houbard, Gregor Mondjian, Stanley Hall,
Mireille Lefebre and others

03/06-03/11
Ballets Russe de Monte Carlo
Producer/Director: Ballet Foundation/
Sergei J. Denham, Maître de Ballet:
Frederic Franklin
Cast: Alexandra Danilova, Frederic Franklin,
Leon Danielian, Ruthanna Boris and others

03/13-03/18
Private Lives
By Noel Coward
Producer/Director:
John C. Wilson/Martin Manulis
Cast: Tallulah Bankhead, Donald Cook,
Barbara Baxley and others

03/20-03/25
Button Busters
By George Mason/Norm Duff
Producer/Director: The Leaside Lions
Club/George A. Mason
Cast: Mayor Tracy Manes, Reeve Bill
Morgan, Lion Knight, Stew Michie
and others

03/27-04/01
Carnegie Hall
Motion picture

04/03-04/15
Brigadoon
By Lerner & Lowe
Producer/Director: Cheryl Crawford/Dances
by Agnes de Mille/Staged by Robert Lewis
Cast: Virginia Oswald, Susan Johnson, Peter
Turgeon, Hayes Gordon, Kenneth LeRoy
and others

04/17-04/29
There Goes Yesterday
By Dorothy Watkins and Jessie Macdonald
Producer/Director: Murray and Donald
Davis/Musical Director: Dorothy
Watkins/Dance Director: Louise MacDonald
Cast: John Pratt, Murray Matheson,
Charmion King, Araby Lockhart and others

05/01-05/06
Springtime for Henry
By Benn Levy/Dorothy Watkins and
Jessie MacDonald
Producer/Director: Donald and
Murray Davis
Cast: Edward Everett Horton,
Murray Matheson, John Pratt, Araby
Lockhart, Charmion King and others

05/08-05/13
On Approval
By Frederick Lonsdale
Producer/Director: Charles Deane
and Richard Doscher
Cast: Edward Everett Horton,
Paula Houston, Margaret Maginnis
and Matthew Smith

05/15-05/20
The Madwoman of Chaillot
By Jean Giraudoux
Producer/Director: Alfred de Liagre Jr.
Cast: Martita Hunt, John Carradine,
Estelle Winwood and others

05/24-06/03
Good Evans
By Norman Evans
Producer/Director: Norman Evans
& His London Variety Company
Cast: Norman Evans, Charles Ancaster
& Wendy, Radcliffe & Ray, Eddie Ready
& Eileen, Teddy Panda and others

06/05-06/10
The Iron Crown
Motion picture

08/14-08/19
The Devil Also Dreams
By Fritz Rotter and Elissa Rohn
Producer/Director: H. Clay Blaney and
C. Peter Jaeger/Reginald Denham
Cast: Bela Lugosi, Clare Luce, Richard
Waring, Francis L. Sullivan and Oswald
Marshall

09/18-09/30
George Formby and His 1950 London Music
Hall Varieties
Producer/Director:
George Formby/Harry Culley
Cast: George Formby, Henri Vadden
& Girls, Harry Bailey, Carsony Brothers,
Herschel "Jizz" Henlere, Mills & Belita,
Marion Sanders and Roger Carne

10/02-10/07
Two Blind Mice
By Sam Spewack

Producer/Director: Harald Bromley
and Morton S. Ries/Melvyn Douglas
Cast: Melvyn Douglas, Mabel Paige,
Laura Pierpont and others

10/09-10/21
Brigadoon
By Lerner & Lowe
Producer/Director: Robert Lewis
Cast: Elizabeth Early, Robert Busch, Susan
Johnson, Orville Sherman, David Tihmar
and others

10/23-10/28
Oklahoma!
By Rodgers & Hammerstein
Producer/Director: The Theatre Guild, Inc.,
Theresa Helburn and Lawrence
Langner/Rouben Mamoulian
Cast: Mary Marlo, Jack Kilty,
Patricia Northrop and others

11/06-11/11
Grand Opera Company of New York
(Alfredo Salmaggi Opera Co.)
Producer/Director: Laurence A.
Lambert/Alfredo Salmaggi
Cast: June Kelly, Claudio Fagerio, James
Eby, Norma Howard, Alessandro Granda
and others

11/13-11/18
I Know My Love
By S.N. Behrman
Producer/Director: Theatre Guild/Alfred Lunt
Cast: Alfred Lunt, Lynn Fontanne, Velma
Royton, Leo Lucker, J.P. Wilson and others

11/20-11/25
One for the Road
By Pat Paterson and Doug Sackfield
Producer/Director: Brian Doherty
and Roy Wolvin/Roy Wolvin
Cast: Barbara Hamilton, John Pratt,
Betty Carr, Gladys Forrester, Don Wolvin
and others

12/04-12/09
Blossom Time
By Donnelly/Romberg
Producer/Director: Shuberts/Zella Russell
Cast: Anthony Blair, Deane Carroll,
Melton Moore, Marjorie Wellock,
Zella Russell and others

12/18-12/23
A Streetcar Named Desire
By Tennessee Williams
Producer/Director: Elia Kazan
Cast: Louise Platt, Phillip Kenneally,
Ellen Davey, Harry Kersey and others

12/25-01/06/51
Babes in the Wood, Bold Robin Hood
By Mavor Moore
Producer/Director: The New Play
Society/Don Hudson/Dances directed by
Boris Volkoff
Cast: Lou Jacobi, Peter Mews, Ted Follows,
Giselle, Andrew MacMillan, Sheila Craig,
David Gardner and others

1951

01/08-01/13
Ti-Coq
By Gratien Gélinas
Producer/Director: Gratien Gélinas
Cast: Gratien Gélinas (Fridolin), Georges
Alexandre, Jacques Auger, Clément Latour,
Fred Barry, Amanda Alarie, Huguette
Oligny, Juliette Béliveau, Denise Pelletier
and others

01/16-01/20
Sadler's Well Ballet
Producer/Director: The Covent Garden
Opera Trust, Arts Council of Great Britain
and British Council, Sol Hurok/
Ninette De Valois
Cast: Margot Fonteyn, Moira Shearer,
Beryl Grey, Violetta Elvin, Alexis Rassine,
Gillian Lynne and others

01/22-01/27
D'Oyly Carte Opera Co.: Iolanthe,
Trial by Jury, HMS Pinafore, Gondoliers,
The Mikado
By Gilbert and Sullivan
Cast: Darrel Fancourt, Martyn Green,
Neville Grffiths and others

01/29-02/03
Mister Roberts
By Thomas Heggen and Joshua Logan
Producer/Director: Leland Hayward/Joshua
Logan
Cast: Tod Andrews, Robert Ross, Rusty
Lane, Lawrence Blyden and others

02/08-02/17
Opera Festival Toronto: Figaro, Faust,
Mme Butterfly
Producer/Director: Opera Festival Toronto,
Royal Conservatory Opera
Company/Herman Geiger-Torel,
Nicholas Goldschmidt

Cast: Andrew MacMillan, Marguerite Gignac, Ernest Adams, Louise Roy, Marjorie Hays, Virginia Lippert, John Asher, Joan Maxwell, Victor White, Douglas Scott, Glenn Gardiner, Beth Corrigan, Jan Rubes, June Kovalchuck, James Shields, Gilles LaMontagne, Earl Dick and others

02/19-02/24
Of Corset's Us
Producer/Director: Leaside Lions Club

02/26-03/01
Oklahoma!
By Rodgers & Hammerstein
Producer/Director: The Theatre Guild Inc., Theresa Helburn and Lawrence Langer/Rouben Mamoulain
Cast: Mary Marlo, Ridge Bond, Patricia Northrop, Owen Martin and others

03/12-03/17
Ti-Coq
By Gratien Gélinas
Producer/Director:
Gratien Gélinas and Fred Barry
Cast: Gratien Gélinas (Fridolin), George Alexander, Jacques Auger, Clement Latour and others

03/19-03/31
Ballet Russe de Monte Carlo
Producer/Director:
Ballet Foundation/Sergei J. Denham
Cast: Alexandra Danilova, Frederic Franklin, Leon Danielian and others

04/09-04/14
Ti-Coq
By Gratien Gélinas
Producer/Director:
Gratien Gélinas and Fred Barry
Cast: Gratien Gélinas (Fridolin) and others

04/16-04/21
Yeoman of the Guard, The Gondoliers
By Gilbert and Sullivan
Producer/Director: Canada Packers Operatic Society/W. Richard Curry
(Benefit for Ontario Society for Crippled Children)

04/23-04/28
Fantasia
Motion picture

04/30-05/05
The Member of the Wedding
By Carson McCullers
Producer/Director: Robert Whitehead,

Oliver Rea and Stanley Martineau/ Harold Clurman
Cast: Ethel Waters, Julie Harris, Brandon de Wilde and others

05/07-05/26
Kiss Me Kate
By Sam and Bella Spewack/Cole Porter
Producer/Director:
Saint Subber and Lemuel Ayers
Cast: Frances McCann, Robert Wright, Benny Baker, Marc Platt, Betty George and others

09/24-09/29
Death of a Salesman
By Arthur Miller
Producer/Director: Kermit Bloomgarden and Walter Fried, Elia Kazan/Del Hughes
Cast: Duncan Baldwin, Sylvia Davis, Ted Jordan, Steven Ritch, John Devoe, Nancy Cushman, Arthur Tell and others

10/08-10/13
Mister Roberts
By Thomas Heggen and Joshua Logan
Producer/Director:
Leland Hayward/Joshua Logan
Cast: Tod Andrews, Robert Herman, Raymond Bailey, Daniel Keyes, Ted Jacques and others

10/15-10/20
Sadlers Wells Ballet
Producer/Director:
Sol Hurok/Ninette De Valois
Cast: Elaine Fifield, David Blair, Svetlana Beriosova, Patricia Miller, Maryon Lane, Sheilah O'Reilly, David Poole, Donald Britton and others

10/29-11/03
Oklahoma!
By Rodgers & Hammerstein
Producer/Director: The Theatre Guild Inc., Theresa Helburn and Lawrence Langner/Rouben Mamoulian
Cast: Mary Marlo, Ridge Bond, Patricia Johnson and others

11/05-11/10
Darkness at Noon
By Sidney Kingsley and Arthur Koestler
Producer/Director: The Playwrights' Company (Maxwell Anderson, S.N. Behrman, Elmer Rice, Robert E. Sherwood and Sidney Howard)/Sidney Kingsley
Cast: Edward G. Robinson, Louis Edmonds, John Morny, Richard Seff and others

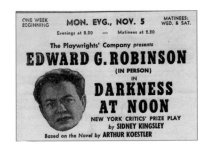

11/12-11/24
Metropolitan Opera: Die Fledermaus
By Johann Strauss
Producer/Director: Metropolitan Opera/Rudolf Bing
Cast: Donald Dame, Jon Crain, Brenda Lewis, Laura Casteeano, Virginia MacWatters, Jack Gilford and others

12/24-01/05/52
Fantasia
Motion picture

01/07-01/12
The Moon Is Blue
By F. Hugh Herbert
Producer/Director: Richard Aldrick and Richard Myers, Julius Fleischmann/ Otto Preminger
Cast: Hiram Sherman, Maria Henderson, James Young and Lester Mack

01/14-01/19
Autumn Garden
By Lillian Hellman
Producer/Director: Kermit Bloomgarden/Harold Clurman
Cast: Fredric March, Florence Eldrige, Emily Lawrence, Laura Pierpont, Calvin Thomas and others

01/21-02/02
Guys and Dolls
By Jo Swerling and Abe Burrows/ Frank Loesser
Producer/Director: Feuer & Martin/ George S. Kaufman
Cast: Allan Jones, Pamela Britton, Julie Oschins, Jeanne Bal,"Slapsy" Maxie Rosenbloom and others

02/04-02/09
Ballet Theatre
Producer/Director: Ballet Theatre
Foundation/Lucia Chase and Oliver Smith
Cast: Alicia Alonso, Igor Youskevitch,
John Kriza, Mary Ellen Moylan and others

02/11-02/16
Tommy Trinder and His Royal Command
Music Hall Varieties
Producer/Director: Variety Club
of Toronto/Tommy Trinder
Cast: Josef Locke, The Elkins Sisters,
Tommy Trinder, Rey Overbury, Suzette,
The Three Hellos, José Moreno & Partner,
Alan and Blanche Lund and Joe Lee

02/21-03/01
Third Annual Opera Festival: The Bartered
Bride, The Magic Flute, Manon
Producer/Director: The Opera Festival
Association of Toronto/
Royal Conservatory Opera Company/
Herman Geiger-Torel/Ernest Rawley,
General Manager
Cast: Marguerite Gignac, John Alexander,
Gilles LaMontagne, Andrew MacMillan, John
Nedra, Ernest Adams, Mary Alice Rogers,
Suzette Nadon, Joanne Ivey, Alexander
Gray, Milton Jiricka, Ralph Roose, Claudette
LeBlanc, Victor Morin, Bernard Turgeon,
Mary Morrison, Robert Price, Jean
Edwards, Lois Marshall, Ruth Gillis,
Joan Maxwell, Jan Rubes, Glen Gardiner
and others

03/03-03/10
Catskill Honeymoon
By Joel Jacobson
Producer/Director: Martin Cohen
Enterprises Inc./Josef Berne
Cast: Michael Michalesko, Irving Grossman,
Julius Adler, Jan Bart, Bas Sheva, Dina
Goldberg and others

03/17-03/22
Trial by Jury, HMS Pinafore,
Yeoman of the Guard
By Gilbert and Sullivan
Canada Packers Operatic Society/
W. Richard Curry

03/24-03/29
The Student Prince
By Donnelly/Romberg
Producer/Director: Shuberts/Frank Cork
Cast: Glenn Burris, Grace Aurelia,
Detmar Poppen, Robert Grandin and others

03/31-04/05
Tommy Trinder and His Royal Command
Music Hall Varieties

Producer/Director: Variety Club of
Toronto/Tommy Trinder
Cast: Josef Locke, Two Valors,
Tommy Trinder, Rey Overbury, Suzette,
The Three Hellos, José Moreno & Partner,
Alan and Blanche Lund and Joe Lee

04/07-04/12
Candida
By G.B. Shaw
Producer/Director:
Thomas Hammond/Norris Houghton
Cast: Olivia de Havilland, Ron Randell,
Terrance Kilburn, Bramwell Fletcher,
Pamela Simpson and Frank Leslie

04/14-04/19
Eroica: The Beethoven Story
Motion picture

04/28-05/03
Affairs of State
By Louis Verneuil
Producer/Director: Richard W. Krakeur
and Fred F. Finklehoffe/Louis Verneuil
Cast: Haila Stoddard, Reginald Owen,
Barbara O'Neil, Shepperd Strudwick, Harry
Bannister and Elmer Brown

05/05-05/10
The Fourth Canadian Ballet Festival
Producer/Director: Classical Ballet Company
(Ottawa), Gotschalks Halifax Ballet,
Elizabeth Leese Ballet (Montreal), The
Winnipeg Ballet, Le Ballet Concert
(Vancouver), the Montreal Ballet, Ballet
Production Club (B.C.), Janet Baldwin Ballet
(Toronto), Mildred Wickson Ballet
(Toronto), Willy Blok Hanson Group
(Toronto), The Toronto Ballet, New Dance
Theatre Group (Toronto)/Conductor Samuel
Hersenhoren

05/12-05/17
The Cocktail Party
By T.S. Eliot
Producer/Director:
Lewis & Young/Norman Lloyd
Cast: Estelle Winwood, Dennis King, Neva
Patterson, Reginald Denny, Harry Ellerbe
and others

05/19-05/24
Long Is the Road (Lang ist der Weg)
Motion picture

06/02-06/21
The Great Morton
Cast: Dr. Robert Morton (one-man show)

08/04-08/16
Goodnite Ladies
By Avery Hopwood, Cyrus Wood
Producer/Director: G. & S.
Productions/Harry Minturn
Cast: Dolores Cross, Joyce Savage,
Patricia Stedman, Bob Ball and others

08/18-09/13
The Great Morton
Cast: Dr. Robert Morton (one-man show)

09/15-09/20
Oklahoma!
By Rodgers & Hammerstein
Producer/Director: The Theatre Guild
National Company/Jerome Whyte
Cast: Ralph Lowe, Florence Henderson,
Victor Griffin, Harold Gary, Jacqueline
Daniels and others

09/22-09/27
Gentlemen Prefer Blondes
By Anita Loos and Joseph Fields/
Jules Styne
Producer/Director: Herman Levin and
Oliver Smith/John C. Wilson
Cast: Pat Wiles, Arte Johnson, Iva Withers,
Harry Stockwell and others

09/29-10/04
Paris '90
By Cornelia Otis Skinner/Kay Swift
Producer/Director: Cornelia Otis Skinner
Cast: Cornelia Otis Skinner
(one-woman show)

10/06-10/11
José Greco and his Company of Spanish
Dancers
Producer/Director: Charles E. Green

10/13-10/18
Bagels and Yox
By Sholom Secunda and Hy Jacobson
Producer/Director: Beckman & Pransky
Cast: Barton Brothers, Ricky Lane and
Velvel, the Yiddish-speaking dummy

10/20-10/25
The Great Morton
Cast: Dr. Robert Morton

10/27-11/01
Paint Your Wagon
Lerner & Loewe
Producer/Director: John Yorke and Wolfe
Kaufman/Daniel Mann
Cast: Burl Ives, Ellen McCown, Edward
Chappel, Andrew Duggan, Gordon Dilworth
and others

11/03-11/08
Ballet Theatre
Producer/Director: Ballet Theatre
Foundation/Lucia Chase and Oliver Smith
Cast: Alicia Alonso, Igor Youskevitch,
John Kriza, Mary Ellen Moylan and others,
in a cast of 100

11/10-11/15
Jane
By S.N. Behrman
Producer/Director: The Theatre Guild,
Theresa Helburn and Lawrence
Langner/Cyril Ritchard
Cast: Edna Best, John Loder, Howard St.
John, Brenda Forbes, Richard Stapley
and others

11/17-11/22
The Constant Wife
By Somerset Maugham
Producer/Director: Katharine Cornell,
Robert Flemyng and John Emery/
Guthrie McClintic
Cast: Katharine Cornell, Robert Flemyng,
John Emery, Margery Maude, Gertrude
Musgrave and others

11/24-11/29
Anonymous Lover
By Vernon Sylvaine
Producer/Director:
Louis Mandel/Larry Parks
Cast: Larry Parks, Betty Garrett
(Mrs. Parks), George Hall and Helen Baron

12/01-12/06
Call Me Madam
By Howard Lindsay, Russell Crouse/
Irving Berlin
Producer/Director: Leland Hayward/George
Abbott, choreographed by Jerome Robbins
Cast: Elaine Stritch, Kent Smith, David
Daniels, Jay Velie, Pat Harrington, Ralph
Chambers, Alexander Clark and Terry
Taylor

12/08-12/13
The Shrike
By Joseph Kramm
Producer/Director: Ermit Bloomgarden
and José Ferrer/José Ferrer
Cast: Van Heflin, Doris Dalton, Kendall
Clark and others

12/15-12/27
Guys and Dolls
By Jo Swerling, Abe Burrows/Frank Loesser
Producer/Director: Feuer & Martin/
George S. Kaufman

Cast: Allan Jones, Pamela Britton, Julie
Oshins, Jeanne Bal, Mike Mazurki, Jack
Prince and others

12/29-01/04/53
Bell, Book and Candle
By John Van Druten
Producer/Director: Shepard Traube
Cast: Joan Bennett, Zachary Scott,
William Windom, Dorothy Sands and others

1953

01/05-01/17
Maid in the Ozarks
By Claire Parrish
Producer/Director: John Kenley/Leslie Cutler
Cast: Bert Wheeler, Betty Bartley, Kay
Hart, Leslie Cutler, Francis Perkins, Dulcie
Cooper and others

01/19-01/24
National Ballet Co. of Canada
Producer/Director: The National Ballet Guild
of Canada/Celia Franca
Cast: Joyce Hill, Lois Smith, David Adams,
Lillian Jarvis, Joan Stuart, Grant Strate,
Robert Ito, Howard Meadows, Celia Franca,
Brian Macdonald and others

02/05-02/07
Charles Dickens and Bleak House
By Emlyn Williams
Producer/Director: Sol Hurok
Cast: Emlyn Williams (solo)

02/11-02/21
Fourth Annual Opera Festival: Mme
Butterfly, Cosi Fan Tutte, The Consul
Producer/Director:
The Opera Festival Association of Toronto
with the Royal Conservatory Opera
Company
Cast: Glenn Gardiner, Theresa Gray,
Nellie Smith, Don Garrard, Joanne Ivey,
Ernest Adams, Jan Rubes, Edward Johnson,
Andrew MacMillan and others

02/23-02/28
The Fourposter
By Jan de Hartog
Producer/Director: The Playwrights'
Company/José Ferrer
Cast: Hume Cronyn and Jessica Tandy

03/02-03/04
White Cargo
By Leon Gordon
Producer/Director: Wallis Clark
Cast: Samia Gamal, Wallis Clark, Anthony
Dearden, David Leland, Royal Dano and
others

03/05-03/07
Royal Winnipeg Ballet Co.
Producer/Director: Gweneth Lloyd
(Director)/Betty Farrally (Ballet Mistress)
Cast: Gweneth Lloyd, Arnold Spohr, Joy
Camden, David Adams, Eva von Gencsy
and others

03/16-03/21
I Found April
By George Batson
Producer/Director: Kenneth Banghart
and Diana Green/Luther Martin Kennett
Cast: John Baragrey, Herbert Evers,
Marjorie Peterson, Louise Larabee,
Evelyn Varden and Constance Bennett

03/23-03/28
The Wizard of Oz
By L. Frank Baum, adapted by Frank
Gabrielson, E.Y. Harburg/Harold Arlen
Producer/Director: The Leaside Lions
Club/Stewart Michie
Cast: Art Passmore, Len Hart, Norm
Meldrum, R. Robinson, Chuck Knight,
Hal Smith, Jack Weiler and a cast of 70

03/30-04/04
Fantasia
Motion picture

04/13-04/18
The Big Leap
By Leo Orenstein
Producer/Director: The Actors'
Company/Leo Orenstein
Cast: Austin Willis, Mona O'Hearn,
Sammy Sales, Allan Bertram,
E.M. Margolese, voices of Lorne Greene
and Michael Cashin and others

04/20-04/25
I Am a Camera
By John Van Druten
Producer/Director: Gertrude Macy
and Walter Starcke/John Van Druten
Cast: Julie Harris, Charles Cooper,
Olga Fabian, Edward Andrews, Harriet
MacGibbon, William Allyn and Janet Dowd

04/27-05/19
Good Night, Ladies
By Cyrus Wood
Producer/Director: Harry Minturn
Cast: Jack Mathieson, Elsie Kerbin
and others

06/01-06/06
Concert Variety
Producer/Director:
Triumph Productions Inc./Anna Sosenko
Cast: Hildegarde, Paul Hartmen and others

06/08-06/13
London's Festival Ballet
Producer/Director:
H.H. Princess Marie Louise/Anton Dolin
Cast: Nathalie Leslie-Krassovka, Anton
Dolin, Sonia Arova, John Gilpin and others

08/24-10/03
South Pacific
By Rodgers & Hammerstein
Producer/Director:
Rodgers & Hammerstein/Joshua Logan
Cast: Jeanne Bal, Webb Tilton,
Benny Baker, Robert Emmett Keane,
Dorothy Franklin and others

10/05-10/17
Maid in the Ozarks
By Claire Parrish
Producer/Director: John Kenley/Leslie Cutler
Cast: Pink Tracy, Connie Stack, Maggie
Trask, Dulcie Cooper and others

10/19-10/24
Ring Around the Moon
By Jean Anouilh
Producer/Director: Jupiter Theatre/
Leonard Crainford
Cast: Bruce Belfrage, Douglas Rain,
Margaret Griffin, Joy Lafleur, David Gardner
and others

10/26-10/31
Love of Four Colonels
By Peter Ustinov
Producer/Director: The Theatre Guild and
Aldrich & Myers/Rex Harrison
Cast: Rex Harrison, Lilli Palmer, Robert
Coote, Stefan Schnabel, Edward Andrews,
Maureen Hurley, Reginald Mason and
Robert Claiborne

11/16-11/21
Ring Around the Moon
By Jean Anouilh
Producer/Director:
Jupiter Theatre/Leonard Crainford

Cast: Bruce Belfrage, Douglas Rain,
Margaret Griffin, Joy Lafleur, David
Gardner, Toby Robins, Jane Mallett
and others

11/30-12/05
José Greco and His Spanish Dance
Company
Producer/Director: Chas. E. Green
Consolidated Concerts Corp.

12/14-12/19
An Evening with Beatrice Lillie
Producer/Director: Edward Duryea Dowling
Cast: Beatrice Lillie, Reginald Gardiner,
Xenia Bank, Shannon Dean and Eadie
& Rack

12/28-01/03
Salzburg Marionettes
Producer/Director: Salzburg Marionette
Theatre/Professor Hermann Aicher

1954

01/11-01/16
Relative Values
By Noel Coward
Producer/Director:
Jupiter Theatre/Leonard White
Cast: Eleanor Stuart, John Colicos,
Guy Verney, Pegi Brown, Douglas Rain
and others

01/25-01/30
National Ballet of Canada
Producer/Director:
National Ballet Guild/Celia Franca
Cast: Lois Smith, Irene Apine, David Adams,
Jury Gottschalks and others

02/01-02/06
Misalliance
By G.B. Shaw
Producer/Director:
Misalliance Company/Cyril Ritchard
Cast: Martyn Green, Katharine Sergava,
Priscilla Morrill, Lee Richardson, Robert
Casper, Hugh Thomas and others

02/20-02/26
Fifth Annual Opera Festival: The Council,
La Bohème, Rigoletto, School For Fathers
Producer/Director: Opera Festival
Association of Toronto/Herman
Geiger-Torel (Musical Director:

Nicholas Goldschmidt)
Cast: Glenn Gardiner, Theresa Gray, Nellie
Smith, Andrew MacMillan, William
Copeland, Charles Couture, Joanne Ivey,
Jan Rubes, Suzette Nadon, Gilles
Lamontagne, James Milligan, Robert Goulet
Jon Vickers and others

03/15-03/20
The Moon Is Blue
By F. Hugh Herbert
Producer/Director: Jody
Associates/Maximillian Slater
Cast: Edward Andrews, Jacqueline Holt,
Michael Lipton and others

03/22-03/27
Stalag 17
Motion picture

03/29-04/04
Guys and Dolls
By Jo Swerling, Abe Burrows/Frank Loesser
Producer/Director: Feuer & Martin/
George S. Kaufman
Cast: Iva Withers, Julie Oshins, Norwood
Smith, Pat Rooney, Jack Prince and others

04/06-04/17
Porgy and Bess
By Du Bose Heyward/Gershwin
Producer/Director: Blevins Davis
and Robert Breen/Robert Breen
Cast: Cab Calloway (Sportin' Life), Helen
Colbert, Jerry Laws, Helen Thigpen and
others

04/19-04/24
National Ballet of Canada
Producer/Director: The National Ballet Guild
of Canada/Artistic Director: Celia
Franca/Musical Director: George Crum
Cast: Celia Franca, Lois Smith, David
Adams, Lillian Jarvis, Oldyna Dynowska,
Robert Ito and others

05/03-05/15
Twin Beds
By Salsbury Field and Margaret Mayo
Producer/Director:
Manny Davis/George Lipton
Cast: Nina Olivette, Betty Bartley,
Jack Harrold, John Shanks, John Armstrong
and others

08/16-08/28
South Pacific
By Rodgers & Hammerstein
Producer/Director: Rodgers
& Hammerstein/Joshua Logan

Cast: Iva Withers, Webb Tilton, Benny Baker, Alan Baxter, Dorothy Franklin, Russ Brown and others

08/31-09/11
Porgy and Bess
By Du Bose Heyward/Gershwin
Producer/Director: Blevins Davis and Robert Breen/Robert Breen
Cast: Helen Colbert, Jerry Laws, Lorenzo Fuller, Joseph Attles, Helen Thigpen and others

09/13-09/25
The Moon Is Blue
By F. Hugh Herbert
Producer/Director:
Jody Associates/John Holden
Cast: Jerome Cowan, Martha Randall, Wayne Carson and Clyde Waddell

09/27-10/02
Dial M for Murder
By Frederick Knott
Producer/Director:
Charles Harrow/Billy Mathews
Cast: Christiane Felsmann, Denis Green, Bethell Long and others

10/04-10/09
My Three Angels
By Sam and Bella Spewack
Producer/Director: Charles Harrow/ Victor Jory
Cast: Royal Beal, Herbert Evers, Jean Jory, Nina Varela, Victor Jory, Kenneth Paine and Howard Hanson

10/11-10/16
José Greco and His Spanish Dance Company
Producer/Director:
John F. Nonnenbacher Jr.

10/18-10/23
Gentlemen Prefer Blondes
By Anita Loos and John Emerson
Producer/Director: George Lipton
Cast: Jet MacDonald, Walter Long, Adrienne Angel, John Shanks, Marion Weeks and others

10/25-10/30
Salzburg Marionettes
Producer/Director: The Salzburg Marionette Theatre/Professor Hermann Aicher

11/01-11/06
Those Fabulous Dorseys
Producer/Director: Gerald Peters

Cast: Tommy Dorsey and his Orchestra featuring Jimmy Dorsey, Lynn Roberts, Bill Raymond and Lee Castle

11/08-11/13
The Caine Mutiny Court Martial
By Herman Wouk
Producer/Director:
Paul Gregory/Charles Laughton
Cast: Paul Douglas, Wendell Corey, Steve Brodie and others

11/15-11/20
Oklahoma!
By Rodgers & Hammerstein
Producer/Director: Broadway Lights, Inc./Rouben Mamoulian
Cast: Vera Walton, Robert Austin, Patricia Marand and others

11/22-11/27
Getting Gertie's Garter
By Wilson Collison and Avery Hopwood
Producer/Director: Max Yorke/Nat Burns
Cast: Nat Burns, Velle Davenport, David Tyrrell, Billie Nelson and others

11/29-12/10
The Dark Is Light Enough
By Christopher Fry
Producer/Director: Katharine Cornell and Roger Stevens/Guthrie McClintic
Cast: Katharine Cornell, Tyrone Power, Christopher Plummer, Arnold Moss, John Williams, Paul Roebling and others

12/27-01/02/55
Ballet Espagnols
Producer/Director: Michaux Moody, Jules Borkon, Les Productions Parisiennes Arts et Spectacles/Teresa & Luisillo
Cast: Teresa & Luisillo

1955

01/03-01/08
Blackstone and His Show of 1001 Wonders
Cast: Harry Blackstone

01/10-01/22
Sunshine Town
By Mavor Moore, based on Leacock
Producer/Director: New Play Society, Mavor Moore/Alan Lund

Cast: Robert Goulet, Joe Runner, Jacqueline Smith, Sandy Webster, Louis Negin, Robert Christie, Beth Amos and others

01/24-01/29
Tea and Sympathy
By Robert Anderson
Producer/Director: The Playwrights' Company (Maxwell Anderson, S.N. Behrman, Elmer Rice, Robert E. Sherwood and Sidney Howard)/Elia Kazan
Cast: Deborah Kerr, Alan Baxter, Don Dubbins and others

01/31-02/12
National Ballet of Canada
Producer/Director: Celia Franca (Artistic Director)/George Crum (Orchestra Director)
Cast: Celia Franca, David Adams, Lois Smith, Irene Alpiné, Jury Gottschalks and others

02/14-02/19
Sunshine Town
By Mavor Moore, based on Leacock
Producer/Director: New Play Society, Mavor Moore/Alan Lund
Cast: Robert Goulet, Joe Runner, Jacqueline Smith, Sandy Webster, Louis Negin, Robert Christie, Beth Amos and others

02/25-03/12
Sixth Annual Opera Festival Company of Toronto: Die Fledermaus, Marriage of Figaro, La Traviata
Producer/Director:
Herman Geiger-Torel (Director)
Cast: Ramsay, Evelyn Gould, Joanne Ivey, Lesia Zubrack, Ernest MacMillan, Jan Rubes, Jon Vickers and a cast of 100

03/21-04/02
The Pajama Game
By George Abbott, Richard Bissell and Richard Adler/Jerry Ross
Producer/Director: Frederick Brisson, Robert E. Griffith and Harold S. Prince/George Hirst
Cast: Eddie Foy, Jr., Fran Warren, Larry Douglas, Buster West, Pat Stanley and others

04/11-04/16
Pajama Tops
By Mawby Green and Ed Feilbert
Producer/Director: H. Clay Blaney and Rex Carlton/Leonard Altobell
Cast: Diana Barrymore, Kurt Richards, Brook Byron, Robert Wilcox and others

04/18-04/30
Guys and Dolls
By Jo Swerling, Abe Burrows/Frank Loesser
Producer/Director: Manny Davis/Al Evans
Cast: Wilton Clary, Marie Foster, Margot
Moser, Bill Jones, Howard Ross and others

05/02-05/14
Edith Piaf
Producer/Director: Cress Courtney
and J.T. Gale
Cast: Edith Piaf, Jacques Peals, Harry
Mimmo, Rivieras, Arnauts and Les Marcellis

06/17-06/29
La Comedie Française: Le Bourgeois
Gentilhomme, Arlequin Pour L'Amour,
Le Barbier de Seville
Producer/Director: Canadian Concerts &
Artists Inc. and the Royal Alexandra Theatre
with the Government of the French
Republic/M. Jean Meyer
Cast: Maurice Escand, Jean Meyer,
Louis Seigner, Jacques Charon, Jean Piat,
Robert Manuel, Georges Chamarat,
Beatrice Bretty and Micheline Boudet

07/04-07/30
The King and I
By Rodgers & Hammerstein
Producer/Director: Rodgers
& Hammerstein/John Van Druten
Cast: Patricia Morison, Leonard Graves,
Fairfax Burgher, Jeff Hall and others

09/05-09/10
The Solid Gold Cadillac
By Howard Teichmann
and George S. Kaufman
Producer/Director:
Max Gordon/George S. Kaufman
Cast: Ruth McDevitt, Al McGranary,
Neil Hamilton, John C. Becher, Neil
Fitzgerald, Reynolds Evans,
Vera Fuller Mellish and others

09/26-10/08
Comedy Show
Producer/Director: Variety Club of Toronto
Cast: Norman Evans, Tessie O'Shea,
Alec Finlay, Betty Jumel, Alistair McHarg,
Granger Brothers and Ernest Wampola
(Benefit for Variety Village for Physically
Handicapped Boys)

10/11-10/15
Ballet Russe de Monte Carlo
Producer/Director:
Columbia Artists Management and
the Ballet Foundation/S.J. Denham

Cast: Frederic Franklin, Nina Novak,
Leon Danielian, Gertrude Tyven, Yvonne
Chouteau, Irina Borowska, Victor Moreno
and others

10/19-10/22
La Comedie Française: Le Bourgeois
Gentilhomme, Arlequin Pour L'Amour,
Le Barbier de Seville
Producer/Director: Canadian Concerts
& Artists Inc. and the Royal Alexandra
Theatre with the Government of the French
Republic/M. Jean Meyer
Cast: Maurice Escand, Jean Meyer,
Louis Seigner, Jacques Charon, Jean Piat,
Robert Manuel, Georges Chamarat,
Beatrice Bretty and Micheline Boudet

FIRST TIME IN CANADA

CANADIAN CONCERTS & ARTISTS INC.
by arrangement with
The Government of the French Republic
has the honour to present

LA
COMÉDIE
FRANÇAISE

ROYAL ALEXANDRA THEATRE
OCTOBER 19 · 20 · 21 · 22

10/24-10/29
Words and Music
Producer/Director: Charles Wick
and Harry D. Squires/Charles Tate
Cast: James Melton, Dorothy Coulter,
Evelyn Taylor, Shirley Givens and others

10/31-11/05
Tea and Sympathy
By Robert Anderson
Producer/Director: George Brand,
Elia Kazan/Sy Milbert
Cast: Maroa Riva, Alan Baxter, Robert
Higgins, Christy Palmer, Laurence Haddon
and others

11/07-11/12
Anastasia
By Marcelle Maurette,
adapted by Guy Bolton
Producer/Director:
Elaine Perry/Alan Schneider
Cast: Dolly Haas, Eugenie Leontovich,
John Emery, Kurt Richards, Carl Don,
Robert Duke and others

11/14-11/19
Ruth Draper and Her Character Sketches
Producer/Director: Charles Bowden
and Richard Barr/Ruth Draper
Cast: Ruth Draper

11/21-11/26
The Seven-Year Itch
By George Axelrod
Producer/Director: Courtley Burr
and Elliott Nugent/John Gerstad
Cast: Anne Kimbell, James Arenton,
Kaye Lyder, Edward Hunt, Eddie Bracken
and others

11/28-12/10
D'Oyly Carte Opera Co.: The Mikado,
Iolanthe, Trial By Jury, HMS Pinafore,
The Pirates of Penzance
By Gilbert and Sullivan
Producer/Director: Bridget D'Oyly Carte
Cast: Donald Adams, Neville Griffiths,
Peter Pratt, Fisher Morgan, Jeffrey Skitch,
John Banks, Cynthia Morey and others

12/12-12/31
Teahouse of the August Moon
By John Patrick
Producer/Director: Howard Lindsay
and Russel Crouse/Maurice Evans
Cast: Larry Parks, Thomas Coley,
Don Lochner, Reiko Sato, John Alexander
and others

1956

01/04-01/14
Tamburlaine the Great
By C. Marlowe
Producer/Director: The Stratford Foundation
of Canada and The Producers'
Theatre/Tyrone Guthrie
Cast: Anthony Quayle, Coral Browne,
David Gardner, Eric House, Tony Van
Bridge, Robert Goodier, Robert Christie,
Ted Follows, Edward K. Holmes, Barbara
Chilcott, Donald Davis, William Hutt,
William Shatner, Peter Wylde, Peter
Perehinczuk, Neil Vipond, Julian Flett,
Deborah Cass, Bruce Swerdfager, Douglas
Rain, Lloyd Bochner, Richard Howard,
Colleen Dewhurst, Louis Negin and others

01/16-01/28
National Ballet of Canada
Producer/Director: Celia Franca

Cast: Celia Franca, David Adams, Lois Smith and a company of 62

02/06-02/18
The Boy Friend
By Sandy Wilson
Producer/Director:
Feuer & Martin/Vida Hope
Cast: Jo Ann Bayless, John Hewer, Eric Berry, Ruth Altman and others

02/24-03/10
Seventh Annual Opera Festival Company of Toronto: Carmen, Don Giovanni, Mme Butterfly
Producer/Director: The Opera Festival Company of Toronto/Dr. Ettor Mazzoleni/Herman Geiger-Torel
Cast: Alexander Grey, Marguerite Lavergne, Jon Vickers, Andrew MacMillan, Regina Renik, Joanne Ivey, Paticia Snell, Patricia Rideout, Robert Savoie, Bernard Turgeon, Ernest Adams, Sylvia Grant, Don Garrard, Sidney Melville and others

03/26-03/30
Maurice Chevalier
Producer/Director:
Canadian Concerts & Artists Inc.
Cast: Maurice Chevalier and Fred Freed

04/02-04/14
Can-Can
By Abe Burrows/Cole Porter
Producer/Director:
Feuer & Martin/Abe Burrows
Cast: Rita Dimitri, John Tyers, George S. Irving, Ronnie Cunningham, Ferdinand Hill, Richard Purdy, Jon Silo and others

04/16-04/21
Bus Stop
By William Inge
Producer/Director: Robert Whitehead and Roger L. Stevens/Harold Clurman
Cast: Peggy Ann Garner, Dick York, Glenn Anders, Russell Hardie and others

08/27-09/08
The Pajama Game
By George Abbott and Richard Bissell/Richard Adler and Jerry Ross/Choreography by Bob Fosse
Producer/Director: Frederick Brisson, Robert D. Griffith and Harold S. Prince/George Abbott and Jerome Robbins
Cast: Larry Douglas, Betty O'Neil, Buster West, Barbara Bostock, Fred Irving Lewis, Barrie Croft, Jack Straw and others

09/17-09/19
Fujiwara Opera Company of Japan: Mme Butterfly
By David Belasco/G. Puccini
Producer/Director: Fine Arts Enterprises,Inc./Yosie Fujiwara
Cast: Sumi Kawauchi, Masako Toda, Eiko Kuwabara, Keiko Oyama, Kiyoko Maruyama, Kimiko Saegusa, Bernard T. Russell and a cast of 60

09/24-10/13
The Old Vic Company: Richard II, Macbeth, Romeo and Juliet
Producer/Director: Sol Hurok and Old Vic Trust Ltd. and Arts Council of Great Britain/Michael Benthall
Cast: Claire Bloom, Coral Browne, Paul Rogers, John Neville, Richard Wordsworth, Tom Kneebone, Denis Holmes, Peter Needham, Charles Gray, John Woodvine, Keith Taylor, Aubrey Morris, Edward Harvey, Graeme Campbell and others

10/22-11/03
Salad Days
By Dorothy Reynolds/Julian Slade
Producer/Director: Toby Robins, Bruce Snell, Bill Freedman/Barry Morse
Cast: Barbara Franklin, Frank Peddie, Mary Savidge, Jack Creley, Betty Leighton, Maggie St. Clair and Eric Christmas

11/05-11/10
The Happiest Millionaire
By Kyle Crichton
Producer/Director:
Howard Erskine and Joseph Hayes
Cast: Walter Pidgeon, Diana van der Vlis, George Grizzard, Katharine Raht, Ruth White, Lou Nova, Martin Ashe, Ruth Matteson and others

11/12-11/17
A Hatful of Rain
By Michael V. Gazzo
Producer/Director: Jay Julien/Frank Corsaro
Cast: Vivian Blaine, Harry Guardino, Mark Richman, Frank Silvera and others

12/10-12/15
The Boy Friend
By Sandy Wilson
Producer/Director:
Feuer & Martin/Vida Hope
Cast: Jo Ann Bayless, John Hewer, Eric Berry, Geoffrey Hibbert, Millicent Martin and others

12/20-12/28
Waltz of the Toreadors
By Jean Anouilh
Producer/Director: The Producers Theatre and Robert Whitehead/Harold Clurman
Cast: Ralph Richardson, Mildred Natwick, John Abbott, Meriel Forbes, John Stewart and others

12/28-01/02/57
The Chalk Garden
By Enid Bagnold
Producer/Director: Albert Marre
Cast: Judith Anderson, Cathleen Nesbitt, Frederic Worlock, Deirdre Owens, Rosemary Murphy, Stanley Bell and others

1957

01/17-01/26
National Ballet of Canada
Producer/Director: Celia Franca
Cast: Celia Franca, David Adams, Lois smith and a company of 70

01/28-02/02
The Chalk Garden
By Enid Bagnold
Producer/Director: Albert Marre
Cast: Judith Anderson, Cathleen Nesbitt, Frederic Worlock, Deirdre Owens, Rosemary Murphy, Stanley Bell and others

02/25-03/09
Eighth Annual Opera Festival Company of Toronto: Abduction from the Seraglio, Tosca, Hansel and Gretel
Producer/Director: Herman Geiger-Torel
Cast: Edita Symonek, Pierette Alarie, Leopold Simoneau, Jan Rubes, Ernest Adams, Joseph Furst, Ilona Konbrink, Richard Cassilly and others

02/04-02/16
Fanny
Based on Maurice Pagnol/S.N. Behrman and Joshua Logan/Harold Rome
Producer/Director: David Merrick and Joshua Logan/Joshua Logan
Cast: Italo Tajo, Billy Gilbert, June Roselle, Jack Washburn, Nejla Ates, Dulcie Cooper and others

04/01-04/13
The Apple Cart
By G.B. Shaw
Producer/Director: Charles Adams
and Joseph Neebe/George Schaefer
Cast: Maurice Evans, Signe Hasso,
Charles Carson, Mercer McLeod, Stanley
Bell and others

05/03-05/04
Farblonjete Honeymoon
Cast: Molly Picon, Michael Michalesko,
Jacob Jacobs and Jacob Kalich

05/06-05/19
Damn Yankees
By George Abbott/Douglass Wallop
Producer/Director: Frederick Brisson, Robert
E. Griffith, Harold S. Prince/George Abbott
Cast: Bobby Clark, Horance McMahon,
Ralph Lowe, Charlotte Fairchild, Sally
Brown, Hildegarde Halliday, Joe Hilland
and others

08/26-09/07
My Fur Lady
By Donald MacSween, Timothy Porteous,
Erik Wang/James Domville,
Galt MacDermott, Harry Garber
Producer/Director: Quince Productions and
James Donville/Brian and Olivia Macdonald
Cast: Brian Macdonald, Robin Berlin,
Frank Blanch, Donald MacSween, David
Langstroth, Elisabeth Heseltine, George
Carron, John MacLeod, Donald MacSween,
Sheila McCormick and others

09/12-09/21
Ziegfeld Follies
Producer/Director: Mark Kroll
and Charles Conaway/Mervyn Nelson
Cast: Kaye Ballard, Paul Gilbert,
Micki Marlo, Bob Copsey, Patrice Helene,
Lew Herbert, Richard Curry and others

09/23-09/28
My Fur Lady
By Donald MacSween, Timothy Porteous,
Erik Wang/James Domville, Galt
MacDermott, Harry Garber
Producer/Director: Quince Productions and
James Donville/Brian and Olivia Macdonald
Cast: Brian Macdonald, Robin Berlin, Frank
Blanch, Donald MacSween, David
Langstroth, Elisabeth Heseltine, George
Carron, John MacLeod, Donald MacSween,
Sheila McCormick and others

10/01-10/13
Sim Sala Bim
Producer/Director:
Harold Steinman and Gae Foster
Cast: Kalanag (Helmut Ewald Schreiber)

10/21-11/09
Ninth Annual Opera Festival Company
of Toronto: Carousel, The Merry Widow,
Die Fledermaus
Producer/Director: The Opera Festival
Association of Toronto/Herman Geiger-Torel
Cast: Don Gerrard, Lesia Zubrack, Marie
Gauley, Lillian Bozinoff, Elizabeth Mawson,
Karl Norman, Don McManus, Victor Braun,
Andrew MacMillan and others

11/11-11/16
The Middle of the Night
By Paddy Chayefsky
Producer/Director: Joshua Logan
Cast: Edward G. Robinson, Mona Freeman,
June Walker, Nancy R. Pollock, Martin
Landau and others

11/18-11/23
No Time for Sergeants
By Ira Levin, adapted from Mac Hyman
Producer/Director: Maurice Evans in
association with Emmett Rogers/
Morton Da Costa
Cast: Charles Hohman, Rex Everhart,
Tucker Ashworth, Howard Freeman,
Royal Beal and others

12/02-12/07
My Fur Lady
By Donald MacSween, Timothy Porteous,
Erik Wang/James Domville, Galt
MacDermott, Harry Garber
Producer/Director: Quince Productions and
James Donville/Brian and Olivia Macdonald
Cast: Brian Macdonald, Robin Berlin,
Frank Blanch, Donald MacSween, David
Langstroth, Elisabeth Heseltine, George
Carron, John MacLeod, Donald MacSween,
Sheila McCormick and others

"MY FUR LADY"
TWO WEEKS: AUGUST 26 — SEPTEMBER 7, 1957

12/09-12/14
Auntie Mame
By Jerome Lawrence and Robert E. Lee
Producer/Director:
Bowden, Barr & Bullock, with Juston Sturm
and Richard Horner/Morton DaCosta
Cast: Constance Bennett, Mark O'Daniels,
Kendall Clark, Arthur Barnett, Dulcie
Cooper, James Coco and others

12/16-12/21
The Canadian Players:
Man and Superman, Othello
Producer/Director:
Terry Fisher/George McCowan
(Director: *Man and Superman*)/
Douglas Campbell (Director: *Othello*)
Cast: Mervyn Blake, John Horton, Ted
Follows, Dawn Greenhalgh, Deborah Cass,
Paddy Croft, Irena Mayeska, Alan Nunn,
James Peddie, Max Helpmann, Tony Van
Bridge and Patricia Walker

12/26-01/04/58
Cat on a Hot Tin Roof
By Tennessee Williams
Producer/Director:
George Brandt/Albert Lipton
Cast: Victor Jory, Jean Inness, Olga Bellin,
William Daniels and others

1958

01/07-02/01
National Ballet of Canada
Producer/Director: Celia Franca
Cast: Celia Franca, David Adams, Lois Smith
and a company of 75

02/03-02/15
My Fur Lady
By Donald MacSween, Timothy Porteous,
Erik Wang/James Domville, Galt
MacDermott, Harry Garber
Producer/Director: Quince Productions and
James Donville/Brian and Olivia Macdonald
Cast: Brian Macdonald, Robin Berlin,
Frank Blanch, Donald MacSween, David
Langstroth, Elisabeth Heseltine, George
Carron, John MacLeod, Donald MacSween,
Sheila McCormick and others

02/17-03/22
Stratford Festival Company: Two Gentlemen
of Verona
Producer/Director: Michael Langham

03/03-03/07
Inbal Dance Theatre of Israel
Producer/Director: Sol Hurok and America-Israel Cultural Foundation/Sara Levi-Tanai

03/17-03/22
The Diary of Anne Frank
By Frances Goodrich
Producer/Director:
Kermit Bloomgarden/Garson Kanin
Cast: Francis Lederer, Maria Palmer,
Gilbert Green, Nan McFarland, Lou Gilbert,
Otto Hulett, Abigail Kellogg and others

03/24-04/01
Stratford Festival Company: The Broken Jug
By Donald Harron
Producer/Director: Michael Langham

03/31-04/05
Ballet Russe de Monte Carlo
Producer/Director:
Ballet Foundation/Sergei J. Denham
Cast: Nina Novak, George Zoritch, Alan
Howard, Irina Borowska, Gertrude Tyven,
Miguel Terekhov, Eugene Slavin and others

04/07-04/12
The Firstborn
By Christopher Fry,
with songs by Leonard Bernstein
Producer/Director: Katharine Cornell
and Roger L. Stevens, under the auspices
of America-Israel Cultural Foundation/
Anthony Quayle
Cast: Jack Betts, Katharine Cornell, Robert
Drivas, Anthony Quayle, Mildred Natwick,
Torin Thatcher, Roddy McDowall and others

04/14-04/19
Marcel Marceau
Producer/Director:
International Artists and Jean de Rigault
Cast: Marcel Marceau, Gilles Segal
and Pierre Verry

04/21-05/03
My Fur Lady
By Donald MacSween, Timothy Porteous,
Erik Wang/James Domville,
Galt MacDermott, Harry Garber
Producer/Director: Quince Productions and
James Donville/Brian and Olivia Macdonald
Cast: Brian Macdonald, Robin Berlin,
Frank Blanch, Donald MacSween, David
Langstroth, Elisabeth Heseltine, George
Carron, John MacLeod, Donald MacSween,
Sheila McCormick and others

05/26-05/31
Auntie Mame
By Jerome Lawrence and Robert E. Lee
Producer/Director: Bowden, Barr
& Bullock/Charles Bowden
Cast: Sylvia Sidney, Mark O'Daniels,
Betty Sinclair, Phil Arthur, Shannon Dean,
Winifred Ainslee, Philip Bosco and others

08/27-09/02
My Fur Lady
By Donald MacSween, Timothy Porteous,
Erik Wang/James Domville,
Galt MacDermott, Harry Garber
Producer/Director: Quince Productions and
James Donville/Brian and Olivia Macdonald
Cast: Brian Macdonald, Robin Berlin, Frank
Blanch, Donald MacSween, David
Langstroth, Elisabeth Heseltine, George
Carron, John MacLeod, Donald MacSween,
Sheila McCormick and others

09/11-09/14
Ziegfeld Follies

09/15-09/20
Romanoff and Juliet
By Peter Ustinov/Ballads by Anthony
Hopkins and Peter Ustinov
Producer/Director:
David Merrick/George S. Kaufman
Cast: Peter Ustinov, Henry Lascoe
and others

09/22-09/27
Shakespeare's Ages of Man
Based on George Rylands' Shakespeare
anthology
Producer/Director:
Peter Lawrence and Jerry Leider
Cast: John Gielgud (one-man show)

09/29-10/03
Look Back in Anger
By John Osborne
Producer/Director: David Merrick and the
English Stage Company/Tony Richardson
Cast: Kenneth Haigh, Diana Hyland, Jack
Livesey, Elizabeth Hubbard and Al Muscari

10/13-10/25
Tenth Anniversary Season Opera Festival:
Un Ballo in Maschera, The Tales of
Hoffman, La Bohème
Producer/Director:
Canadian Opera Co./Herman Geiger-Torel
Cast: Teresa Stratas, John McCallumn,
Guiseppe Campora, Ilona Kombrink,
Marguerite Gignac, Patricia Snell,

Harold Mossfield, Jim Hawthorne, Morley
Meredith, Norman Mittleman, Jan Rubes,
Andrew MacMillan and others

10/29-11/01
Le Theatre du Nouveau Monde:
Le Malade Imaginaire, Trois Farces,
The Time of the Lilacs
Producer/Director:
Le Theatre du Nouveau Monde
Cast: Denyse Saint Pierre, Huguette Oligny,
Denyse Pelletier, J.P. Jeannotte, Guy
Hoffman, Jean Gascon and Jean-Louis Roux

11/03-11/08
Two for the Seesaw
By William Gibson
Producer/Director: Fred Coe/Arthur Penn
Cast: Ruth Roman and Jeffrey Lynn

11/25-11/29
The Old Vic Company: Twelfth Night,
Henry V, Hamlet
Producer/Director: Old Vic Trust Ltd.
and the Arts Council of Great Britain,
Sol Hurok/Michael Benthall
Cast: John Neville, Barbara Jefford,
Laurence Harvey, Richard Wordsworth,
Dudley Jones, Judi Dench and others

12/15-12/20
Sunrise at Campobello
By Dore Schary
Producer/Director: The Theatre Guild
and Dore Schary/Vincent Donehue
Cast: Leif Erickson, Russell Collins,
Ann Shoemaker, Michael Meyers,
Lawrence Fletcher, Fran Carlon and others

12/22-01/03/59
L'il Abner
By Norman Panama, Melvin Frank,
Johnny Mercer/Gene de Paul
Producer/Director: Norman Panama, Melvin
Frank and Michael Kidd/Michael Kidd
Cast: Peter Palmer, Wynne Miller,
Jack Prince, Billie Hayes and others

1959

02/02-02/28
National Ballet of Canada
Producer/Director: National Ballet Guild
of Canada/Celia Franca
Cast: Celia Franca, David Adams,
Lois Smith, Lilian Jarvis, Angela Leigh,
Betty Pope, Sylvia Mason, Earl Kraul,
Harold Da Silva and others

03/02-03/07
The World of Sholom Aleichem
By Arnold Perl/Serge Hovey
and Robert de Cormier
Producer/Director: Benjamin
and Lawrence Rothman/Jacob Ben-Ami
Cast: Jacob Ben-Ami, Celia Adler,
Gerald Hiken, John Randolph, Earl Somner,
Muni Seroff and others

03/09-03/14
The Dark at the Top of the Stairs
By William Inge
Producer/Director:
Saint Subber and Elia Kazan/Elia Kazan
Cast: Barbara Baxley, Audrey Christie,
George L. Smith, Don Briggs, Evans Evans,
Sandy Dennis and others

03/18-03/21
Summer of the Seventeenth Doll
By Ray Lawler
Producer/Director: The Crest Theatre
Foundation, The Australia Elizabethan
Theatre Trust/George McCowan
Cast: Barbara Chilcott, Anne Collings,
Latherine Blake, Hugh Webster, Ruth
Springford, Max Helpmann and Jim Beggs

04/06-04/11
Les Ballets Africains
Producer/Director: Luben Vichey/Achkar
Marof, Kante Facelli and Raphael Wigbert
Cast: Suzy Baye, Mansaba Camara,
Marcelle Diallo, Pierrette Diouf, Diene
Doumbouya, Aissatou Mansare and others

04/27-05/05
The Warm Peninsula
By Joe Masteroff
Producer/Director:
Manning Gurian/Warren Enters
Cast: Julie Harris, Josephine Brown,
Steve Holland, Carroll Brooks and others

05/07-05/09
A Boy Growing Up
By Dylan Thomas
Producer/Director: Program
Associates/Emlyn Williams
Cast: Emlyn Williams (solo)

05/18-05/23
Dominion Drama Festival: The Boy Friend,
Ghosts (Ibsen), Teach Me How to Cry
(Patricia Joudry), Victimes du Devoir, Every
Bed Is Narrow, The Diary of Anne Frank,
The Cave Dwellers, Le Militaire Fanfaron
Producer/Director: Halifax Traveling
Players, Marktonian Players (Halifax),
L'Atelier du Proscenium, Simcoe Little
Theatre, Sudbury Theatre Guild, Medicine
Hat Civic Theatre, Ottawa Little Theatre Arts
Guild and La Compagnie Nina Diaconseco

08/17-09/05
Jubilee
By Billy Solly, Dolores Claman,
Joseph Shaw, Donald MacSween,
Timothy Gray, Mavor Moore with others
Producer/Director: Quince Productions
and James de B. Domville/Brian Macdonald
Cast: Corinne Conley, Dave Broadfoot
and Paul Kligman

09/22-09/27
Shakespeare's Ages of Man
Based on George Rylands' Shakespeare
anthology
Producer/Director: Peter Lawrence
and Jerry Leider
Cast: John Gielgud (one-man show)

10/12-10/24
Canadian Opera Company, Eleventh Annual
Season: La Forza Del Destino, The Love for
Three Oranges, The Barber of Seville
Producer/Director: The Opera Festival
Association of Toronto/Herman Geiger-Torel
Cast: Sylvia Grant, Ilona Kombrink, Arlene
Meadows, Sheila Piercey, Patricia Snell,
Barbara Strathdee, John McCollum, Jan
Rubes, Sereryn Weingort and others

11/05-11/07
Look Homeward, Angel
By Ketti Frings, based on Thomas Wolfe
Producer/Director: Theatrical Interests Plan,
Inc./David Pressman
Cast: Miriam Hopkins, Gilbert Green,
Andrew Prine and others

11/12-11/14
The World of Carl Sandburg
By Carl Sandburg,
adapted by Norman Corwin

Producer/Director:
Armand Deitsch/Norman Corwin
Cast: Bette Davis, Gary Merrill
and Clark Allen

11/23-11/29
J.B.
By Archibald MacLeish
Producer/Director:
Alfred de Liagre/Elia Kazan
Cast: Basil Rathbone, Frederic Worlock,
Michael Higgins, James Ray and others

11/30-12/03
Yves Montand
Producer/Director:
Norman Granz/Yves Montand
Cast: Yves Montand, Bob Castella, Jimmy
Guiffre, Al Hall, Jim Hall, Norman Jeffries,
Benny Marton and Dominic Cortese

12/28-01/03/60
The Pleasure of His Company
By Samuel Taylor, Cornelia Otis Skinner
Producer/Director: Frederick Brisson and
The Playwrights' Company/Cyril Ritchard
Cast: Joan Bennett, Donald Cook,
Leo G. Carroll, Conrad Nagel, John Napier,
Carolyn Groves and Jerry Fujikawa

1960

01/25-01/30
The World of Suzie Wong
By Paul Osborn
Producer/Director: David Merrick,
Seven Arts Productions, Inc. and Mansfield
Productions/Joshua Logan
Cast: Tom Helmore, Jeri Miyazaki,
James Olson and others

02/01-02/27
National Ballet of Canada
Producer/Director: Celia Franca
Cast: Lois Smith, David Adams
and a company of 75

02/29-03/05
The Visit
By Friedrich Durrenmatt
Producer/Director: The American Theatre
Society and The Council of the Living
Theatre/Peter Brook
Cast: Alfred Lunt, Lynn Fontanne,
Thomas Gomez, Glenn Anders, John Wyse,
David Clarke, William Hansen and others

03/09-03/19
Gang Show '60
By Ralph Reader
Producer/Director: The Boy Scouts
Association, Greater Toronto Region/
Sam Graham

03/21-03/26
Mary Stuart
By Friedrich Schiller
Producer/Director: Sol Hurok and the
National Phoenix Theatre/Tyrone Guthrie
Cast: Eva Le Gallienne, Signe Hasso, Statts
Cotsworth, Patrick Waddington, Bruno
Gerussi, Paul Ballantyne and others

03/28-04/02
Servant of Two Masters (Arlecchino,
Servitore di due Padroni)
By Carlo Goldoni
Producer/Director: Jerry Hoffman, Canadian
Concerts & Artists Inc. and the Royal
Alexandra Theatre/Paolo Grassi and Giorgio
Strehler
Cast: Piccolo Teatro di Milano: Marcello
Moretti, Warner Bentivega, Narcisa Bonati,
Anglo Corti, Giancarlo Dettori, Vincenzo de
Toma, Bruno Lazarini and others

04/04-04/09
Mark Twain Tonight
Producer/Director: Program Associates,
the Royal Alexandra Theatre
Cast: Hal Holbrook (solo)

04/11-04/30
The Music Man
By Meredith Willson
Producer/Director: Kermit Bloomgarden
Cast: Forrest Tucker, Joan Weldon, Cliff
Hall, Benny Baker, Lucie Lancaster, The
Frisco 4, Jane Linnig, Harry Hickox and
others

05/02-05/07
José Greco and His Spanish Ballet
Producer/Director: International Artists
in Association and Royal Alexandra
Theatre/Roger Machado

08/22-09/03
The World of Suzie Wong
By Paul Osborn
Producer/Director: Manny Davis,
Joshua Logan Production/Neil Hartley
Cast: Romi Yamada, Robert Carle,
Joel Thomas, Joshi Naka, Gia-Mo Wong
and others

09/05-09/17
Peking Opera
Producer/Director:
Tien Han/Lu Chun-chao and Tsen Yi-chou
Cast: 90 acrobats, actors, muscians, mimes,
singers and dancers

09/19-09/24
Ballets Africains de la République
de Guinée
Producer/Director:
Luben Vichey/Kante Facelli

09/26-09/31
Laughs and Other Events
By Stanley Holloway
Producer/Director:
Martin Tahse/Tony Charmoli
Cast: Stanley Holloway (solo)

10/12-10/29
Canadian Opera Company, Twelfth Annual
Season: Otello, Figaro, Night in Venice
Producer/Director: Canadian Opera
Co./Peter Ebert, Herman Geiger-Torel,
Mavor Moore
Cast: Aldo Bertocci, Norman Harper,
Louis Quilico, Ilona Kombrink, Jan Rubes,
Irene Salemka, Andrew MacMillan,
Darlene Hirst, Heinz Rehfuss, Robert Briggs
and Arlene Meadows

11/02-11/05
Love and Libel (Leaven of Malice)
By Robertson Davies
Producer/Director: Canadian Theatre
Exchange and Don Herbert/Tyrone Guthrie
Cast: Dennis King, Tony Van Bridge,
Madeleine Christie, Robert Christie, Barbara
Hamilton, Laurence Hardy, Charmion King,
Roberta Kinnon, Leo Leyden, John Milligan,
Gene Saks, Bruce Swerdfager and others

11/10-11/12
Royal Winnipeg Ballet
Producer/Director: Brian MacDonald,
Michael Conte/Arnold Spohr
Cast: Marilyn Young, Fredric Strobel,
Lynette Fry, Sheila Mackinnon
and a cast of 20

11/14-12/03
A Raisin in the Sun
By Lorraine Hansberry
Producer/Director: Philip Rose
and David J. Cogan/Lloyd Richards
Cast: Claudia McNeil, Douglas Turner,
Diana Sands and others

12/05-12/24
Five Finger Exercise
By Peter Shaffer
Producer/Director: Frederick Brisson
and The Playwrights' Co./John Gielgud
Cast: Jessica Tandy, Roland Culver,
Robert Dowdell, Pinkie Johnstone
and Brian Bedford

12/26-01/07/61
The Dance Theatre of Rio de Janeiro:
Brasiliana
Producer/Director: Mieco Askanasy
Cast: Nelson Ferraz, Nair Eufenia,
Fausta Conceicao and others

1961

01/30-03/04
National Ballet of Canada
Producer/Director: The National Ballet Guild
of Canada/Celia Franca (Director)/George
Crum (Musical Director and Conductor)
Cast: Lois Smith, David Adams,
Angela Leigh, Earl Kraul, Judie Colpman,
Jocelyn Terell, Jacqueline Ivings,
Grant Strate and others

03/06-03/11
Shelley Berman with The Cumberland Three
Producer/Director: Nirene
Productions/Shelley Berman

04/10-04/29
Majority of One
By Leonard Spiegelgass
Producer/Director: The Theatre Guild
and Dore Schary/Dore Schary
Cast: Gertrude Berg, Cedric Hardwicke,
Berta Gersten, Maurice Ottinger and others

05/01-05/06
José Greco and His Spanish Ballet
Producer/Director: International
Artists/Roger Machado

09/12-09/17
Ballet Espagnol
Producer/Director: Sol Hurok/
Antonil Ros Marba and Trabal Altes
Cast: Roberto Iglesias, Rosario Galvan,
Manolo Galan, Lola Grau and a cast of 20

09/19-10/07
The Three Penny Opera
By Brecht/Weill
Producer/Director:
Carmen Capaldo, Stanley Chase,
Lucille Lortel/Carmen Capalbo
Cast: Gypsy Rose Lee, Scott Merrill,
Jane Connell, Mitchell Jason, Didi Van Eyck
and others

10/09-11/04
A Taste of Honey
By Shelagh Delaney
Producer/Director: David Merrick,
Donald Albery and Oscar Lewenstein Ltd./
Tony Richardson and George Devine
Cast: Hermione Baddeley, Fracus Cuka,
Frederick Combs, Roy Shuman and
Bobby Dean Hooks

11/06-12/02
The Tenth Man
By Paddy Chayefsky
Producer/Director: Saint Subber
and Arthur Cantor/Tyrone Guthrie
Cast: Jacob Ben-Ami, Risa Schwartz,
Michael Lipton, David Vardi, Anatol
Winogradoff and others

12/04-12/09
The Captain and the Kings
By Leo Lieberman
Producer/Director: Theatre Guild
Productions Inc. and Joel Schenker
present The Paul Gregory Production/
Joseph Anthony
Cast: Dana Andrews, Charlie Ruggles,
Peter Graves, Conrad Nagel, Lee Grant,
Joseph Sullivan, Gavin MacLeod,
Joseph Campanella and others

12/11-12/24
Toys in the Attic
By Lillian Hellman
Producer/Director:
Kermit Bloomgarden/Adrian Hall
Constance Bennett, Anne Revere,
Scott McKay, Patricia Jessel, Penny Fuller
and others

12/26-12/31
A Thurber Carnival
By James Thurber
Producer/Director: Lee Guber, Frank Ford
and Shelly Gross/Peter Turgeon
Cast: Imogene Coco, Arthur Treacher,
King Donovan and others

1962

01/01-01/13
Advise and Consent
By Loring Mandel, based on Allen Drury
Producer/Director: Martin Tahse,
Robert Fryer and Lawrence Carr,
John Herman/Franklin Schaffner
Cast: Farley Granger, Chester Morris,
Royal Beal and others

01/15-01/20
Bousille and the Just
By Gratien Gélinas
Producer/Director: La Comédie
Canadienne/Gratien Gélinas
Cast: Gratien Gélinas, Paul Berval, Pierre
Dufresne, Beatrice Picard, Paul Guevremont,
Juliette Huot, Monique Champagne,
Jean Lajeunesse, Gilles Latullippe and
Thérèse Arbic

01/22-01/27
From Paris with Love
By Don Driver
Producer/Director: Herb Rogers/Don Driver
Cast: Geneviève, Luc Poret, Danny Carroll,
Norma Doggett, Gus Viseur and Art Merrill

01/29-02/24
National Ballet of Canada
Producer/Director:
National Ballet of Canada/Celia Franca
Cast: Lois Smith, Lilian Jarvis, Earl Kraul,
Angela Leigh, Judie Colpman, Sylvia
Mason, Galina Samtsova, Hans Meister,
Diane Nyland and others

02/26-03/03
The Miracle Worker
By William Gibson
Producer/Director: Martin Tahse,
Fred Coe/Arthur Penn
Cast: Eileen Brennan, C.M. Gampel,
Laurinda Barrett, Thomas Connolly,
Donna Zimmermann and others

03/19-04/07
Little Mary Sunshine
By Rick Besoyan
Producer/Director: Brian Macdonald
Cast: Alex MacDougall, Dan Baran,
Ed Riley, Pat Galloway, Suzanne Lapointe,
Dominique Michel, Tom Kneebone
and others

05/14-05/19
Prescription: Murder
By William Link and Richard Levinson
Producer/Director:
Paul Gregory, Amy Lynn/Myles Eason
Cast: Joseph Cotton, Thomas Mitchell,
Agnes Moorehead, Patricia Medina with
Lucille Fenton, Barry McCollum,
Howard Wierum and Raleigh Davidson

09/08-09/15
Step on a Crack
By Bernard Evslin
Producer/Director: Roger L. Stevens
and Herbert Swope Jr./Herbert Swope Jr.
Cast: Nancy Kelly, Gary Merrill, Margaret
Hayes, Maggie McNamara, Joey Heatherton
and others

09/17-09/22
Get on Board the Jazz Train
Producer/Director:
Manning Gurian/Mervyn Nelson
Cast: Gilbert Adkins, Brown Barker, Danny
Cook, Stoney Marteeni, Rosalie Esther, Jim
Mosby, Oliver Thelma, Spearman Rawn,
Maxwell Sutherland and others

10/01-10/06
The Hostage
By Brendan Behan
Producer/Director: Perry Bruskin and
Joseph H. Schaeffer/Perry Bruskin
Cast: Paddy Croft, Alan Nunn, Sheila
Cuonan, James Cahill, Robert Packer,
Marge Burnett, Dick Sobel, Michael Lewis,
Gavin Payne, Georgia Heaslip and others

10/22-10/23
The Canadian Players: Arms and the Man
(Shaw), Twelfth Night (Shakespeare)
Producer/Director: Tony Van Bridge
Cast: Howard Mawson, Patricia Farmer,
Norman Ettlinger, Jack Medley, Jon Adams,
Mary Benning, Nicholas Simons,
Christine Bennett, Ted Todgeman, Ken
Pogue and others

10/24-10/27
Playboy of the Western World
By J.M. Synge
Producer/Director:
The Original Irish Players,
National Tours Ltd./Dermot McNamara
Cast: Dermot McNamara, Fiona Martin,
Paddy Edwards, Brendan Dillon,
Liam Lenihan and others

11/01-11/10
Moby Dick
By Orson Welles

Producer/Director: Jerry Adler
and Samuel Liff/Douglas Campbell
Cast: Rod Steiger, Bruno Gerussi,
Frances Hyland, Roy Poole, William
Needles, Hugh Webster and others

11/12-12/08
A Shot in the Dark
By Marcel Achard
Producer/Director:
Leland Hayward/Harold Clurman
Cast: Elizabeth Seal, Zack Matalon,
Rene Paul, Valerie French, James Coco,
Bram Nossen and others

12/31-01/05/63
José Greco and His Spanish Ballet
Producer/Director: Roger Machado

01/07-02/02
Mary Mary
By Jean Kerr
Producer/Director:
Roger L. Stevens/Joseph Anthony
Cast: Martha Wright, Biff McGuire, Michael
Evans, Alan Bunce and Elizabeth St. Clair

02/13-03/09
National Ballet of Canada
Producer/Director:
Celia Franca (Director)/George Crum
(Musical Director and Conductor)
Cast: David Adams, Lois Smith, Earl Kraul,
Lilian Jarvis, Galina Samtsova, Angela
Leigh, Jacqueline Ivings and others

03/11-03/23
Pajama Tops
By Mawby Green and Ed Feilbert
Producer/Director:
Havenhurst Productions, Inc./Richard Vath
Cast: June Wilkinson, Cliff Halle, James
Winslow, Leslie Vallen, Don McArt and
Frances Fong

03/25-03/30
Here Today
By George Oppenheimer
Producer/Director: Thomas Brock
and Robert Carson/Thomas Brock
Cast: Tallulah Bankhead, Estelle Winwood,
Richard Kendrick, Patience Cleveland, John
Granger, Jimmy O'Hayes, Isabell Sanford
and Peter Hobbs

04/02-06/08
Spring Thaw '63
By Stan Daniels
Producer/Director:
Mavor Moore/Leon Major, Alan Lund
Cast: Peter Mews, Betty Robertson, Jean
Templeton, Bill Cole, Pam Hyatt, Drew
Thompson, Jan Goldin, Bernard Behrens
and Grant Cowan

09/09-10/05
Never Too Late
By Sumner Arthur Long,
incidental music by John Kander
Producer/Director: Elliot Martin
and Daniel Hollywood/George Abbott
Cast: William Bendix, Nancy Carroll, Will
Hutchins, Janis Young, Larry Fletcher, Kate
Wilkinson, Royal Beal, Robert Carraway
and Robert Fitzsimmons

NEVER TOO LATE
William Bendix ★ Nancy Carroll ★ Will Hutchins
THE ROYAL ALEXANDRA THEATRE

10/07-10/12
Second City: When the Owl Screams
Producer/Director:
The Second City/Bernard Sahlins
Cast: Severn Darden, Andrew Duncan
and others

10/14-10/16
Les Grandes Ballets Canadiens
Producer/Director: Ludmilla Chiriaeff
(Artistic Director)/Claude Poirier
(Musical Director and Conductor)/
Daniel Seillier (Ballet Master)
Cast: Milenka Miderlova, Veronique
Landory, Andree Millaire, Olga Makcheeva,
Margery Lambert and a cast of 30

10/17-10/19
The Canadian Players
Producer/Director: Canadian Players
Foundation/Desmond Scott
Cast: Joyce Campion, Ron Bishop, Ted
D'Arms, Felix Munso, Paul Hecht, Jerry
Martin, Nancy Shaffner, Patrick Blackwell,
Mary Benning, Eric Donkin, Leo Leyden
and others

10/21-10/26
An Evening at the Royal
Cast: Jackie Mason and Billy Daniels

10/27
Toronto Chamber Orchestra
Producer/Director: Jacob Groob
(Founder/Conductor)

10/28-11/23
A Thousand Clowns
By Herb Gardner
Producer/Director:
Fred Coe and Arthur Cantor/Fred Coe
Cast: Margaret O'Brien, Dane Clark, Barry
Gordon, Marc London, Conard Fowkes
and Paul E. Richards

11/25-11/30
Black Nativity
By Langston Hughes
Producer/Director:
Michael R. Santangelo-Barbara Griner
and Eric Frank/Vinnette Carroll
Cast: Marion Williams and the Stars of
Faith, Alex Bradford and The Bradford
Singers, Princess Stewart, Ed Hall,
Hope Clarke and others

12/09-12/14
The Chinese Prime Minister
By Enid Bagnold
Producer/Director:
Roger L. Stevens/Joseph Anthony
Cast: Margaret Leighton, Alan Webb, John
Williams, Douglas Watson, Peter Donat,
James Olson, Diane Kagan and Tish Sterling

12/16-12/28
Obratsov's Moscow State Central Puppet
Theatre: Aladdin and His Wonderful Lamp
Producer/Director: Canadian Concerts
& Artists Inc./Sergei Obraztsov

12/28-01/04 (matinees only)
Kidzapoppin' with Randy Dandy
By Randy Martin, Joseph Torbay
and Nuala Fitzgerald
Producer/Director:
Stagecraft Ltd. and Grasshopper Group
Productions Ltd./Randy Martin
Cast: Randy Dandy Martin, Silly Willy, the
Magic Lady, Michael the Magic Minstrel
and others

12/31-01/04/64
Scottish Memories: Hogmannay Party
Producer/Director:
Donald Keeling (Music Director)
Cast: Andrew Murdison, Pipes & Drums of
the 48th Highlanders, Pipe Major Archie
Dewar, Violet Murray, Highland Dancers
from Alice Wright School of Dancing

1964

01/10-01/11
Dr. Murray Banks: What to Do Until
the Psychiatrist Comes
Cast: Dr. Murray Banks

01/19
Toronto Chamber Orchestra

01/27-02/01
The Hollow Crown
By John Barton
Producer/Director: Royal Shakespeare
Theatre, Stratford-on-Avon/Bonard
Productions/Peter Hall

02/03-02/08
The Canadian Players: Private Lives
By Noel Coward
Producer/Director: Andrew Allan,
Canadian Players Foundation/Eric Christmas
and David Gardner
Cast: William Hutt, Eric Christmas, Amelia
Hall, Zoe Caldwell and Coralee Elliott

02/10-03/07
Stop the World, I Want to Get Off
By Leslie Bricusse/Anthony Newly
Producer/Director: David Merrick, Bernard
Delfont/Anthony Newley/Carmine Coppola
(Musical Director)
Cast: Anthony Newly, Kenneth Nelson,
Joan Eastman, Sherry Jo Miller and others

03/09-03/14
Josephine Baker and Her Company
Producer/Director:
Sherman S. Krellberg/Felix G. Gerstman
Cast: Josephine Baker, Geoffrey Holder
and Aviv Dancers

03/16-03/28
In One Bed and Out the Other
By Mawby Green and Ed Feilbart
Producer/Director: Zev Bufman
and Stan Seiden/Jack Rogotzy
Cast: Jules Munshin, Greta Thyssen,
Rex Robbins, Merle Louise, Dale Helward
and others

03/30-04/05
Théâtre de France
Producer/Director: Canadian Concerts &
Artists with the Government of the French
Republic/Madeleine Renaud
and Jean-Louis Barrault
Cast: Jean-Pierre Granval, Jean Desailly,

Pierre Bertin, Jean-Louis Barrault, Jean
Paredes, Dominique Santarelli and others

04/07-05/23
The Best of Spring Thaw
Producer/Director:
Mavor Moore/Alan Lund and Mavor Moore
Cast: Dave Broadfoot, Barbara Hamilton,
Bill Cole, Jack Duffy, Peter Mews, Dean
Regan, Liane Marshall, Diane Nyland
and Marylyn Stuart

05/25-05/30
Spring Melody '64
Producer/Director: Precious Blood Young
People's Club/Father Dugo/Jack Burns
Cast: Jane Morgan, Pat Doyle, Benny
Silverton, Maurice Pearson, Alec Read
and others

05/31
Toronto Chamber Orchestra

06/12-06/27
Return to the Mountain
By Brian Swarbick
Producer/Director:
George McCowan/Alan Lund
Cast: Peter Donat, John Vernon, Michael
Learned, Jan Campbell, Robert Goodier,
Phyllis Malcolm Stewart and Joe Austin

08/03-08/08
My Fair Lady
By Lerner & Lowe
Producer/Director: Royal Alexandra,
Aries Productions/William Francisco
Cast: Allyn Ann McLearie, George Gaynes,
R.E. Sinclair, Arthur Anderson, Wilson
Robey, Hazel Jones, Jean Muir and others

08/10-08/15
Thursday Is a Good Night
By Abe Enhorn and Donald Segall
Producer/Director: Royal Alexandra,
Aries Production/Bob Herget
Cast: Lawrence Brooks, Mimi Turque,
Michael Lombard, Juliette Randall
and others

08/17-08/22
The Sound of Music
By Rodgers & Hammerstein
Producer/Director: Royal Alexandra,
Aries Productions/Bob Herget
Cast: Lawrence Brooks, Mimi Turque,
Michael Lombard, Juliette Randall, Linda
Rae Hager, Charlotte Povia, Erik Howell,
Judith Leamon, Lois Van Pelt and others

08/29-09/12
Traveller without Luggage
By Jean Anouilh

Producer/Director:
Carroll and Harris Masterson/Robert Lewis
Cast: Ben Gazzara, Blanche Yurka, Mildred
Dunnock, Norma Crane and others

09/11-10/10
Any Wednesday
By Muriel Resnick
Producer/Director: George W. George
and Frank Granat/Henry Kaplan
Cast: Larry Parks, Patricia Cutts, Richard
Roat and Monica Moran

10/12-10/17
Tartans on Tour
Producer/Director:
Concert Arrangements/Ralph Harding's
Tartans on Tour
Cast: Dennis Clancy, The Joe Gordon Folk
Four, Sandra Bald, Jimmy Fletcher, Nichol
Brown, Kathie McBain, Jean Anderson's
Scottish Country Dancers and the 48th
Highlanders' Pipe Band

10/19 11/14
Barefoot in the Park
By Neil Simon
Producer/Director:
Saint Subber/Mike Nichols
Cast: Myrna Loy, Richard Benjamin,
Joan Van Ark, Sandor Szabo, Lou Tiano
and Paul Haney

11/16-11/21
Les Grands Ballets Canadiens
Producer/Director:
Ludmilla Chiriaeff (Artistic Director)/
Claude Poirier (Conductor)
Cast: Andrée Millaire, Lawrence Haider,
Christa Mertins, Armando Jorge,
Margery Lambert and others

11/23-12/12
Pajama Tops
By Mawby Green and Ed Feilbert
Producer/Director: Abba
Productions/Richard Vath
Cast: June Wilkinson, Richard Vath, William
Browder, Robert Osborne, Don McArt,
Sandra Gayle and Maralyn Turner

12/14-12/19
José Greco and His Gypsies
Producer/Director: Roger Machado
and José Greco

12/21-01/02/65
Second City: No Comment
Producer/Director:
The Second City/Bernard Sahlins/Bill Alton
Cast: Bill Alton, Severn Darden, Mina Kolb,
Richard C. Neuweiler and Paul Sand

1965

01/05-01/16
Royal Flush
By Jay Thompson and Robert Schlitt
Producer/Director: L. Slade Brown/
Jack Cole (Director/Choreographer)
Cast: Kaye Ballard, Mickey Deems, Kenneth
Nelson, Louis Edmonds and others

01/18-01/23
The Polish Mime Theatre
Producer/Director: Sol Hurok/Henryk
Cast: Liliana Bobrowska, Elzbieta
Bojanowicz, Ewa Czekalska and others

01/25-02/20
Dear Me, The Sky Is Falling
By Leonard Spigelgass
Producer/Director:
The Theatre Guild/Herman Shumlin
Cast: Gertrude Berg, Roger DeKoven,
Michael Baseleon, Mary-Robin Redd
and others

02/22-02/27
Luther
By John Osborne
Producer/Director: Joel Spector, Julian
Olney and B.B. Randolph/Mitchell Erickson
Cast: Alan Bergmann, Alfred Sandor,
Herman Rudin, John Eames and others

03/01-03/07
D'Oyly Carte Opera Co.: HMS Pinafore,
Mikado, Pirates of Penzance
By Gilbert and Sullivan
Producer/Director: The D'Oyly Carte Opera
Trust, Ltd./Sol Hurok/Isidore Godfrey

03/09-03/14
Seidman and Son
By Erick Moll
Producer/Director: Royal Alexandra Theatre
and James M. Riley/Menasha Skulnik
Cast: Menasha Skulnik, Anna Roman,
Donna Pearson, Raymond Thorne
and others

03/15-03/20
All About Us
Producer/Director: Canadian Players
(Marigold Charlesworth and Jean Roberts)
Cast: Barbara Franklin, Ken James, Bruno
Gerussi, Hugh Webster, Eric House and
Jacques Zouvi

03/22-04/03
Who's Afraid of Virginia Woolf?
By Edward Albee
Producer/Director: Richard Barr, Clinton
Wilder, Sometimes, Inc./Alan Schneider
Cast: Vicki Cummings, Kendall Clark,
Bryarly Lee, Donald Briscoe, Fayne
Blackburn and William Gibberson

04/05-05/29
Spring Thaw '65
Producer/Director: Mavor Moore/Alan Lund
Cast: Barbara Hamilton, Dave Broadfoot,
Bill Cole, Jack Duffy, Gayle Lepine, Liane
Marshall, Peter Mews, Dean Regan,
Marylyn Stuart and others

05/31-06/05
Spring Melody '65
Producer/Director: Precious Blood Young
People's Club/Rev. Fr. L.J. Dugo/Jack Burns
Cast: Jane Morgan, Wally Griffin, Alec
Read, Benny Silverton, Doug Romaine,
Ron Leonard, Ellis McLintock, Gord Braund,
Morris Isen, Johnny Cowell and others

06/08 06/27
Gypsy
By Jule Styne, Arthur Laurents,
Stephen Sondheim
Producer/Director: Royal Alexandra Theatre,
Michael McAloney, Joyce Sloane/
David Davis
Cast: Julie Wilson, Marilynn Allwyn, Jack
Van Evera, Arlene Meadows, Glenn Gibson,
Diane Nyland and Donna Pearson

06/29-07/11
Finian's Rainbow
By E.Y. Harburg and Fred Saidy/
Burton Lane
Producer/Director: Royal Alexandra Theatre,
Michael McAloney and Joyce Sloan/
Vivien Ainslie
Cast: Carmel Quinn, Bert Wheeler,
Jack Hilliard, Diane Nyland, Jay Barney,
Alice Webb, Gabor Morea and others

07/13-07/25
Guys and Dolls
By Jo Swerling, Abe Burrows/Frank Loesser
Producer/Director: Royal Alexandra Theatre,
Michael McAloney, Joyce Sloane/
David Davis
Cast: Jack Carter, Hal Linden, Sandra
O'Neill, Janet McCall and others

07/27-08/08
Can-Can
By Abe Burrows/Cole Porter

Producer/Director:
Royal Alexandra Theatre, Michael
McAloney, Joyce Sloane/Charles Tate
Cast: Lilo, Webb Tilton, Susanne Cansino,
Glenn Gibson, Ferdinand Hilt, Grant Cowan,
Alan Kass and others

08/10-08/22
Annie Get Your Gun
Dorothy and Herbert Fields/Irving Berlin
Producer/Director:
Royal Alexandra Theatre, Michael McAloney
and Joyce Sloane/Larry Leung
Cast: Elaine Stritch, Roger Franklin,
Jack Van Evera, Joan Panton, Sheila
Conlon, Van Luven, Don Young and others

08/24-09/05
Flower Drum Song
By Rodgers & Hammerstein
Producer/Director:
Royal Alexandra Theatre, Michael McAloney
and Joyce Sloane/Larry Leung
Cast: Larry Leung, Franceska Kae, Lucretia
Gould, Sab Shimona, Conrad Yama, Romy
Lee, Francisco Salvacion, Diane Kim, Matty
Rumbaoe, Allen Stewart and Irene Sun

09/07-09/11
The African Ballet
(National Ensemble of Guinea)
Producer/Director: Canadian Concerts
& Artists Inc./Italo Zambo and Bangoura
Hamidou and Amadou Sissoko

09/13-10/09
Luv
By Murray Schisgal
Producer/Director: Claire Nichtern/
Mike Nichols
Cast: Tom Bosley, Dorothy Loudon
and Herbert Edelman

10/11-10/23
Porgy and Bess
By DuBose Heyward/Gershwin
Producer/Director: Royal Alexandra Theatre,
Zev Bufman/Ella Gerber
Cast: Andrew Frierson, Joyce Bryant,
Avon Long, Miriam Burton and others

10/25-11/06
This Was Burlesque
By Ann Corio
Producer/Director:
Michael P. Iannucci/Ann Corio
Cast: Ann Corio, Steve Mills, Dexter
Maitland, Dick Bernie, Harry Conley,
Marilyn Marshall, Gloria Leroy,
Mac Dennison, Harry Ryan and others

11/08-12/04
The Wayward Stork
By Harry Tugend
Producer/Director: Garrick Productions,
Martin Lee/Dan Levin
Cast: Bob Cummings, Lois Nettleton,
Arlene Golonka, Bernie West, Gary Pillar,
Linn Mason, Arlene Walker, Rosalind Cash,
Molly Ardrey and Art Lund

12/06-12/18
Brigadoon
By Lerner & Lowe
Producer/Director:
Royal Alexandra Theatre, Michael McAloney
and Joyce Sloane/Charles Tate
Cast: Ted Scott, Shiela Piercey, Dean
Regan, Brian Crabb, Jan Goldin and others

12/27-01/08/66
What Makes Sammy Run?
By Budd Schulberg
Producer/Director: Royal Alexandra Theatre,
Joseph Cates/Charles Tate
Cast: Sal Mineo, Willi Burke, Ted Scott,
Sean Mulcahy, Bill Janson, Larry Reynolds
and others

1966

01/10-01/22
The King and I
By Rodgers & Hammerstein
Producer/Director: Michael
Myerberg/Darren McGavin
Cast: Darren McGavin, Barbara Williams
and others

01/24-01/29
Fairytale
By Melanie York
Producer/Director:
Michael Myerberg/Darren McGavin
Cast: Darren McGavin, Barbara Williams,
Virginia Wing, Marion Jim, Edward Evanko
and others

01/31-02/12
Teahouse of the August Moon
By John Patrick
Producer/Director: Michael McAloney
and Joyce Sloan/Charles Tate
Cast: Ted Follows, Doug Crosley, Tom
Harvey, Shirley Mai Temple, Vernon
Chapman, Larry Reynolds, Allen Bateman,
John Vidette and others

02/14-02/19
Farther Along: From the Second City
Producer/Director: Bernard Sahlins
and Sheldon Patinkin/Sheldon Patinkin
Cast: Jack Burns, Bob Dishy, Avery
Schreiber, Dick Schaal and Penny White

02/21-03/05
Oklahoma!
By Rodgers & Hammerstein
Producer/Director: Michael McAloney
and Joyce Sloane/Charles Tate
Cast: Robert Kaye, Jacqueline Gooderham,
Wally Griffin, Colin Hamilton, Sylvia Lennick
and others

03/07-03/19
Pal Joey
By Rodgers & Hart
Producer/Director: Michael McAloney,
Joyce Sloane/Charles Tate
Cast: Jane Russell, Joe Bennett, Karen
Jensen, Alan Zampese, Carolyn Kemp,
Tom Harvey, Larry Reynolds,
Donna Pearson and others

03/21-05/06
Spring Thaw '66
Producer/Director:
Robert Johnston Productions/Alan Lund
Cast: Jack Duffy, Marylyn Stuart,
Peter Mews, Dean Regan, Robert Ainslie,
Robina Beard, Pamela Fernie, Betty Hader
and John Rutter

04/04-04/09
A Breath of Scotland
Cast: Johnny Victory, Dennis Clancy,
Will Starr, Jimmy Fletcher, Ivy Carey,
Irene Campbell, John Crawford, The Jean
Anderson Dancers, The Toronto Scottish
Pipe Band with Scotty Porter,
and John Crawford

05/09-05/14
The Owl and the Pussycat
By Bill Manhoff
Producer/Director:
Philip Rose, Pat Fowler and Seven Arts
Productions/Leonard Auerbach
Cast: Eartha Kitt and Russell Nype

05/17-05/22
Pinocchio
Producer/Director: Pinocchio, Inc./
Bobby Clark
Cast: The Magical Marionettes,
102 life-sized marionettes

05/23-05/28
Laughter and Songs from Israel
Cast: Geula Gill and The 4 Ayalons

05/30-06/04
The Subject Was Roses
By Frank Gilroy
Producer/Director:
Edgar Lansbury/Ulu Grosbard
Cast: Martin Sheen, Jack Albertson
and Martha Scott

06/06-06/18
The Loving Couch
By Ray Allen
Producer/Director: Stan Seiden,
Jack Yonchar/Ray Montgomery
Cast: Virginia Mayo, Sabrina and others

07/14-08/20
Like Father Like Fun
By Eric Nicol
Producer/Director:
Leo B. Meyer/Malcolm Black
Cast: Ed McNamara, Roy Shuman, Patricia
Gage, Doris Buckingham, Reid Anderson
and Sylvia Feigel

08/04-08/20
Second City: Farther Along
Producer/Director: Bernard Sahlins
and Sheldon Patinkin/Sheldon Patinkin
Cast: Jack Burns, Avery Schreiber,
Bob Dishy, Judy Graubart and Dick Schaal

08/22-09/03
Any Wednesday
By Muriel Resnick
Producer/Director:
Zev Bufman/Howard Erskine
Cast: June Wilkinson, John Dutra,
Constance Simons, Frank Farmer

09/12-10/22
The Odd Couple
By Neil Simon
Producer/Director: Saint Subber/
Harvey Medlinsky
George *Cast:* George Gobel, Phil Foster
and others

10/25-10/30
We, Comrades Three (Richard Baldridge
and W. Whitman), Right You Are if You
Think You Are (Pirandello)
Producer/Director:
APA Rep/Ellis Rabb and Hal George
Cast: Will Geer, Helen Hayes,
Patricia Conolly, Sydney Walker
and Marco St. John

11/01-11/06
The Wild Duck
By H. Ibsen/Translated by Eva Le Gallienne
Producer/Director:
APA Repertory Company/Stephen Porter
Cast: Donald Moffat, Gordon Gould,
James Storm, Sydney Walker, Dee Victor,
Joel Stuart, George Pentecost and others

11/08-11/13
A School for Scandal
By R.B. Sheridan
Producer/Director:
APA Repertory Company/Ellis Rabb
Helen Hayes, Rosemary Harris, Ellis Rabb,
Esther Benson, Joel Stuart, Paulette Waters
and others

11/21-11/26
Barefoot in the Park
By Neil Simon
Producer/Director:
Saint Subber/Woody Romoff
Cast: Sylvia Sidney, Woody Romoff,
Pamela Grey, Don Fenwick, Andrew Gerado
and Ray Parker

12/08-12/10
The Boards and a Passion
Arranged by George Taburi
Producer/Director:
Strolling Players/Gene Frankel
Cast: Viveca Lindfors, Harris Yulin,
Elizabeth Farley, Roscoe Orman and
Arnold Stiefel

12/12-01/07/67
Generation
By William Goodhart
Producer/Director:
Frederick Brisson/Gene Saks
Cast: Don Porter, Jerome Cowan,
John Luce, Charlotte Glenn, Paul Collins
and John Stewart

1967

01/09-01/14
Mark Twain Tonight
Producer/Director: Cast: Hal Holbrook
(solo)

01/30-02/04
Second City
Producer/Director:
Bernard Sahlins/Sheldon Patinkin

Cast: Valerie Harper, Linda Lavin, David
Steinberg, Omar Shapli and Richard Schaal

02/06-02/18
The Owl and the Pussycat
By Bill Manhoff
Producer/Director: Stan Seiden
and Norman Dolin/Philip Rose
Cast: Pat Suzuki and Robert Reed

02/20-02/25
The City Center Joffrey Ballet
Producer/Director:
The Foundation for American Dance,
New York City Center/Robert Joffrey
Cast: Charthel Arthur, Diana Cartier, Helyn
Douglas, Suzanne Hammons, Susan Magno,
Marjorie Mussman and others

02/27-03/11
The Mad Show
By Larry Siegel and Stan Hart
Producer/Director: Ivor Balding
(Establishment Theatre Co.: Peter Cook
and Eleanor Bron)/Steven Vinaver
Cast: Jay Devlin, Bill Gerber, Lew Horn,
Barbara Rubenstein and Ellen Travolta

03/13-03/18
Philadelphia, Here I Come
By Brian Friel
Producer/Director: David Merrick Arts
Foundation/Hilton Edwards
Cast: Donal Donnelly, Patrick Bedford,
Eamon Kelly, Marin D. O'Sullivan,
Violet Dunn and others

03/20-03/25
A Breath of Scotland
Producer/Director: Ralph Harding
Cast: Will Starr, Dennis Clancy, Jimmy Neil,
George Cormack and Irene Sharp, Stan
Hamilton and His Flying Scotsmen, Sandra
Bald Jones and the Sandra Jones Dancers

03/27-05/06
Spring Thaw '67
By Don Harron/Marian Grudeff
and Raymond Jessel
Producer/Director:
Robert Johnston Productions/Alan Lund
Cast: Dinah Christie, Douglas Chamberlain,
Don Harron, Catherine McKinnon, Barbara
Hamilton, Peter Mews, Diane Nyland, Dean
Regan and Ron Tanguay

05/08-05/13
Bristol Old Vic: Measure for Measure,
Hamlet, Romeo and Juliet
By Wm. Shakespeare
Producer/Director:
Sol Hurok/Tyrone Guthrie

Cast: Jane Asher, Barbara Leigh-Hunt,
John Franklyn Robbins, Desmond Stokes,
Richard Pasco, Frank Barrie, Norman
Eshley, Richard Glyn Lewis, Madge Ryan,
Frank Middlemass, Dawn Grainger,
Christopher Burgess, Bryan Robson,
Marcia Warren, Arthur Blake, Christopher
Serle, Charles McKeown and others

06/05-06/17
The Owl and the Pussycat
By Bill Manhoff
Producer/Director: Stan Seiden
and Norman Dolin/Philip Rose
Cast: Pat Suzuki and Richard Vath

08/21-08/26
The Royal Winnipeg Ballet
Producer/Director: Arnold Spohr
Cast: Christine Hennessy, Gwynne Ashton,
Ted Patterson, Terry Thomas, Marilyn
Lewis, Dianne Bell, Richard Rutherford,
Sheila Mackinnon, Raymond Goulet and
others

08/28-09/23
Wait a Minim
By Leon Gluckman
Producer/Director:
Frank Productions/Leon Gluckman
Cast: Andrew Tracey, Kendrew Lascelles,
Paul Tracy, Michel Martel, Nigel Pegram,
April Olrich, Helene Ireland and Barbara
Quaney

09/25-09/30
Anne of Green Gables
By Don Harron/Norman Campbell
Producer/Director: Mavor Moore,
The Charlottetown Festival/Alan Lund
Cast: Barbara Hamilton, Peter Mews,
Dean Regan, Jamie Ray, Maud Whitmore,
Robert Ainslie, Susan Anderson, Anne
Collings, Diane Nyland, Anne Linden, Flora
Mackenzie, Liane Marshall, Arlene Meadows
and others

10/02-10/07
The Fantasticks
By Tom Jones, Harvey Schmidt
Producer/Director:
David Cryer, Albert Poland/Tom Jones
Cast: John Cunningham, Constance Moffit,
Ty McConnell, Donald Babcock and others

10/09-10/14
Anne of Green Gables
By Don Harron/Norman Campbell
Producer/Director: Mavor Moore,
The Charlottetown Festival/Alan Lund
Cast: Barbara Hamilton, Peter Mews,
Dean Regan, Jamie Ray, Maud Whitmore,
Robert Ainslie, Susan Anderson, Anne
Collings, Diane Nyland, Anne Linden, Flora
Mackenzie, Liane Marshall, Arlene Meadows
and others

10/17-10/29
You Can't Take It with You
By Kaufman & Hart
Producer/Director: APA-Phoenix
Repertory Co./Ellis Rabb
Cast: Dee Victor, Christine Pickles,
Paulette Waters, Sydney Walker,
Joseph Bird, Gordon Gould, Nat Simmons,
Donald Moffat and others

10/31-11/05
Right You Are If You Think You Are
By Pirandello
Producer/Director: APA-Phoenix
Repertory Co./Stephen Porter
Cast: Helen Hayes, Keene Curtis,
Donald Moffat, Dee Victor, Jennifer
Harman, James Greene and others

11/09-11/12
Pantagleize
By Michel de Ghelderode
Producer/Director: APA-Phoenix Repertory
Co./John Houseman and Ellis Rabb
Cast: Patricia Conolly, Ellis Rabb, Keene
Curtis, Nat Simmons, Sydney Walker,
Nicholas Martin and others

11/14-11/19
The Show Off
By George Kelly
Producer/Director: APA-Phoenix
Repertory Co./Stephen Porter
Cast: Helen Hayes, Gwyda Donhowe,
Pamela Payton-Wright, Alan Fudge, Joseph
Bird, George Pentecost, Clayton Corzatte,
James Greene and Gordon Gould

11/21-11/26
Exit the King
By Eugene Ionesco

Producer/Director:
APA-Phoenix Repertory Co./Ellis Rabb
Cast: Patricia Conolly, Richard Easton,
Eva Le Gallienne, Clayton Corzatte,
Pamela Payton-Wright and Richard Woods

12/11-01/06/68
The Impossible Years
By Arthur Marx and Bob Fisher
Producer/Director:
Nederlander-Steinbrenner Productions
and Bob Disher/Sam Levene
Cast: Sam Levene, Abe Vigoda,
Elizabeth Fleming, David Selby, Trudy Van,
Judith Tilman and others

1968
....

01/08-01/13
Grand Music Hall of Israel
Producer/Director: Canadian Concerts
& Artists Inc./Jonathan Karmon
Cast: Nehama Hendel, The High Willows,
Ilan and Ilanit, The Hacarmelins and others

01/17-02/04
The Little Drummer Boy
By Jean Basile
Producer/Director:
Theatre Toronto/Clifford Williams
Cast: Richard Monette, Allan Royal, Gerard
Parkes, Barbara Hamilton, John Colicos,
Hugh Webster, Eric House, Gordon
Thomson, Dominic Hogan, E.M. Margolese,
Colin Fox, Joseph Shaw, David Hemblen,
Guy Bannerman, Maureen Fitzgerald,
Bernard Behrens, David Hemblen, Jack
O'Reilly, Daphine Gibson and Terry Tweed

02/07-02/28
Little Murders
By Jules Feiffer
Producer/Director:
Theatre Toronto/Clifford Williams
Cast: Amelia Hall, Richard Monette,
Eric House, Maureen Fitzgerald, Colin Fox,
Janet Amos, Daphne Gibson, Barbara
Hamilton, David Hemblen, E.M. Margolese,
Jack O'Reilly, Terry Tweed, Hugh Wesbster,
Joseph Shaw and Gerard Parkes

02/28-03/17
Soldiers
By Rolf Hochhuth
Producer/Director:
Theatre Toronto/Clifford Williams

Colin Fox, Richard Monette, E.M.
Margolese, David Hemblen, Dominic Hogan,
Gordon Thomson, John Colicos, Eric House,
Chris Wiggins, Leslie Yeo, Joseph Shaw,
Terry Tweed and Guy Bannerman

03/21-04/07
A Festival of Carols
By John Hearn
Producer/Director:
Theatre Toronto/Clifford Williams
Cast: Chris Wiggins, Anna Cameron,
Pamela Hyatt, Colin Fox, Barbara Hamilton,
Dominic Hogan, John Colicos, Hugh
Webster, Richard Monette and Eric House

04/08-04/13
The Odd Couple
By Neil Simon
Producer/Director: Stan Seiden
and Harry Zevin/Richard Vath
Cast: Don Ameche, Robert Q. Lewis, Bill
Browder, Tom Winston, Paye Johnson, Don
McArt, Carol Lawson and Kerry Slattery

04/15-06/08
Spring Thaw '68
By Roderick Cook and others
Producer/Director: Robert Johnston
Productions/Alan Lund
Cast: Jack Creley, Ed Evanko, Diane
Nyland, Pat Armstrong, Doug Chamberlain,
Roma Hearn, Rita Howell, Bob Jeffrey,
Diane Nyland and Dean Regan

06/10-06/16
Frula Yugoslav Folk Ensemble
Producer/Director:
Robert T. Gaus/Dragoslav Szadzevic
Company of 35 dancers, singers
and instrumentalists

07/01-07/13
Barefoot in the Park
By Neil Simon
Producer/Director: Stan Seiden
and Harry Zevin/Thomas Montgomery
Cast: Virginia Mayo, Margaret O'Brien,
Jack Mullaney, Lyle Talbot and Don McArt

08/08-08/17
The Misanthrope
By Molière
Producer/Director: APA-Phoenix/Ellis Rabb
Cast: Brian Bedford, Keene Curtis, Richard
Easton, Sydney Walker, Christine Pickles,
Patricia Conolly and others

08/19-08/24
The Cocktail Party
By T.S. Eliot

Producer/Director: APA-Phoenix/
Philip Minor
Cast: Nancy Walker, Brian Bedford, Patricia
Conolly, Ralph Williams, Sydney Walker
and Keene Curtis

09/02-09/07
Theatre Royal Windsor:
The Beaux' Stratagem (Farquhar),
An Ideal Husband (Oscar Wilde)
Producer/Director: Theatre Royal Windsor,
Robert T. Gaus/Anthony Wiles
Cast: Robert Cawdron, Jenny Counsell,
Stephen Moore, Richard Gale, Elizabeth
Counsell and others

09/09-10/05
There's a Girl in My Soup
By Terence Frisby
Producer/Director: Saint Subber and
Michael Codron/Harvey Burlingame
Cast: Don Ameche, Taina Elg,
Betsy Von Furstenberg and others

10/07-11/09
Anne of Green Gables
By Don Harron/Norman Campbell
Producer/Director:
Festival Canada and Mavor Moore present
The Charlottetown Festival/Alan Lund
Cast: Barbara Hamilton, Gracie Finley,
Peter Mews, Jeff Hyslop, Maud Whitmore,
Robert Ainslie, Susan Anderson, William
Copeland, Anne Linden, Flora Mackenzie,
Elizabeth Mawson, Jack Northmore,
Betty Phillips and Diane Nyland

11/11-11/23
Sunshine Town
By Mavor Moore
Producer/Director: Mavor Moore,
The Charlottetown Festival/Alan Lund
Cast: Dean Regan, Bill Cole, Peter Mews,
Dorothy Hosie, George Murray, Anne
Linden, Robert Ainslie, William Copeland,
Donald Cullen, Howard Mawson and others

11/25-12/21
A Day in the Death of Joe Egg
By Peter Nichols
Producer/Director: Stan Seiden,
Robert Q. Lewis, Nederlander-Steinbrenner
Productions/Milton Katselas
Cast: Noel Harrison, Mitzi Hoag,
Elizabeth Kerr, Steven Sutherland,
Carol Lawson and Robbie-Lea Jago

12/26-01/04/69
Come Blow Your Horn
By Neil Simon
Producer/Director: Stan Seiden/Richard Vath

Cast: Sylvia Sidney, June Wilkinson,
Sammy Jackson, Jay Lewis, Danny Llorens
and Kerry Slattery

01/09-01/26
Edward II
By Christopher Marlowe
Producer/Director:
Theatre Toronto/Clifford Williams
Cast: William Hutt, Heath Lamberts, Leo
Leyden, Richard Monette, Leon Pownall,
Susan Bell, Kenneth Stearn, Robert Christie
and others

01/30-02/16
In Good King Charles' Golden Days
By G.B. Shaw
Producer/Director:
Theatre Toronto/Richard Digby Day
Cast: Janet Amos, Dawn Greenhalgh,
Richard Monette, Rita Howell, Joseph Shaw,
Giles Block, Donald Ewer, Moya Fenwick,
Nancy Kerr, Brian Petchey and
Barbara Bryne

02/20-03/09
A Servant of Two Masters
By Goldoni
Producer/Director:
Theatre Toronto/Richard Digby Day
Cast: Heath Lamberts, Dawn Greenhalgh,
Richard Monette, Leon Pownall, Brian
Petchey, Diana Leblanc, Barbara Bryne
and others

03/13-03/30
The Killing of Sister George
By Frank Marcus
Producer/Director:
Theatre Toronto/Timothy Bond
Cast: Dawn Greenhalgh, Barbara Byrne,
Amelia Hall and Rita Howell

04/08-04/19
Under the Yum Yum Tree
By Lawrence Roman
Producer/Director: Stan Seiden/Richard Vath
Cast: David Hedison, Edd Byrnes,
Cynthia Pepper and Peg Shirley

04/21-05/24
Spring Thaw '69
Producer/Director:
Robert Johnston/Paxton Whitehead

Cast: Pat Galloway, Tom Kneebone,
Renee Cherrier, Doug Crosley, Judy Lander,
Sam Moses, Jamie Ray and Robin Ward

06/03-06/15
Johnny Belinda
By Mavor Moore/John Fenwick,
based on play by Elmer Harris
Producer/Director: The Charlottetown
Festival and Robert Dubberley/Alan Lund
Cast: Diane Nyland, Bill Cole, Don
McManus, Dean Regan, Anne Linden,
Betty Phillips, Dennis Thatcher, Douglas
Chamberlain, Jack Duffy, Peter Mews
and others

06/16-06/28
Come Blow Your Horn
By Neil Simon
Producer/Director: Stan Seiden/Richard Vath
Cast: June Wilkinson, Sammy Jackson,
Sylvia Sidney, Keefe Brasselle and others

06/30-07/12
There's a Girl in My Soup
By Terence Frisby
Producer/Director: Stan Seiden/Oliver Cliff
Cast: Lyle Talbot, Betty Connor, Del Lewis,
George McDaniel, Rachel Stephens,
Don McArt and Bobbi Spencer

07/14-08/02
The Odd Couple
By Neil Simon
Producer/Director: Stan Seiden/Richard Vath
Cast: Hal March, Jackie Coogan and others

08/06-08/16
Cactus Flower
By Abe Burrows
Producer/Director: Stan Seiden/Richard Vath
Cast: Yvonne de Carlo, John Vivyan,
Nancy Czar, Ike Williams, David Renard,
Sid Conrad, Bell Ellig and others

08/21-08/30
Façade
Producer/Director:
The Global Village
and Inner Stage Limited/G.G. Mills and
Lee Brown
Cast: Bobbie Jo, Tracy Roberts, G.G. Mills
and others

09/01-10/11
Plaza Suite
By Neil Simon
Producer/Director:
Saint-Subber/Robert V. Staus
Cast: Howard Keel, Betty Garrett, Paulette
Sinclair, Mark Hampton and Emil Belasco

10/13-10/18
Harkness Ballet
Producer/Director:
Rebekah Harkness/Lawrence Rhodes
and Benjamin Harkarvy
Cast: Lone Isaksen, Lawrence Rhodes,
Elisabeth Carroll, Helgi Tomasson
and others

10/20-10/25
Rosencrantz and Guildenstern Are Dead
By Tom Stoppard
Producer/Director: Producing Managers
Company/Jacqueline Britton
Cast: Robert Burr, John Church,
Clebert Ford, Michael Aronson,
Margo Ann Berdeshevsky and others

10/22-10/23
Hamlet
By Wm. Shakespeare
Producing Managers Company/Peter Levin
Cast: Robert Burr, Frederic Warriner,
Edwin Owens, Mary Hara, Margo Ann
Berdeshevsky and others

10/28-11/02
Private Lives
By Noel Coward
Producer/Director: APA Rep,
the University of Michigan/Stephen Porter
Cast: Tammy Grimes, Brian Bedford, David
Glover, Suzanne Grossman and J.J. Lewis

11/10-12/06
The Price
By Arthur Miller
Producer/Director: Robert Whitehead,
Robert W. Dowling/Arthur Miller
Cast: Michael Strong, Betty Field,
Harold Gary and Shepperd Strudwick

12/29/69-01/04/71
Hair
By Galt MacDermott, Jerome Ragni
and James Rado
Producer/Director: Michael Butler,
Glen Warren Productions (John Bassett)/
Jerome Ragni and James Rado
Original Cast: Arta Abele, Doug Barnes,
Terence Black, Rudy Brown, Kid Carson,
Avril Chown, Joe Clark, Harriet Cohen, Gale
Garnett, Brenda Gordon, Rachel Jacobson,
Taborah Johnson, Michael Kennedy, Tobi
Lark, George W. Lee IV, Carmen Litke,
Susan Little, Frank Moore, Freddie
Nicolaidis, Colleen Peterson, Betty
Richardson, Clint Ryan, Paul Ryan, Wayne
St. John, Shelley Sommers, Lynda Squires,
Geoff Stevenson, Graham Teear, Laurel
Ward and Robin White

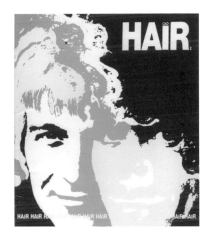

1971
....

01/19-01/30
Borstal Boy
By Brendan Behan
Producer/Director: Michael McAloney
and Burton C. Kaiser, the Abbey Theatre
of Dublin/Tomas MacAnna
Cast: Michael O'hAonghusa,
George Connolly, Bruce Heighly,
Francis Bethencourt and others

02/09-02/14
Israel Folk Co.
Producer/Director:
Canadian Concerts & Artists Inc./Gano Ichiel
Cast: The Beer-Sheva Folk dancers

02/16-03/06
Pinocchio
Producer/Director: Bobby Clark
Cast: 102 marionettes and 8 puppeteers

03/08-03/20
Bob and Ray: The Two and Only
By Bob Elliott and Ray Goulding
Producer/Director: Joseph I. and Johnna
Levine, Hy Saporta/Joseph Hardy
Cast: Bob Elliott and Ray Goulding

03/19-04/24
Butterflies Are Free
By Leonard Gershe
Producer/Director: Arthur Whitelaw, Max J.
Brown and Byron Goldman/Milton Katselas
Cast: Gloria Swanson, David Huffman,
Kristina Callahan and Michael Shannon

04/26-05/22
The Last of the Red Hot Lovers
By Neil Simon
Producer/Director:
Saint Subber/Robert Moore
Cast: Jack Weston, Rosemary Prinz,
Ginger Flick and Marge Redmond

05/31-06/05
The Great World Festival of Magic
and Witchcraft
Producer/Director:
Canadian Concerts & Artists Inc.
presents/André Sanlaville Production
Cast: Ludow, Di-Sato, Yogi Shri Krishna,
Joe Waldys & Partner, Naga the
Mindreader, Omar Pasha and his Company,
Harry Thiery, Rodini, Richiardi Jr.
and his Company

06/07-07/03
1776
Peter Stone/Sherman Edwards
Producer/Director: Stuart Ostrow/Peter Hunt
Cast: Patrick Bedford, Rex Everhart,
George Hearn, Michael Davis, Truman Gaige
and others

08/03-08/07
Vienna State Opera and Ballet
Producer/Director: American Theatre
Productions/Alexander Ursulak
Cast: Judith Gerber, Lisl Maar,
Lilly Scheuermann, Ully Wuhrer,
Michael Birkmeyer and others

08/23-08/28
This Was Burlesque
By Ann Corio
Producer/Director:
Michael P. Iannucci/Ann Corio
Cast: Ann Corio, Jerry Lester, Tami Roche,
Jennifer Fox, Claude Mathis and others

09/13-09/19
A Doll's House
By H. Ibsen
Hillard Elkins
Cast: Claire Bloom, Ed Zimmerman, James
Ray, Patricia Elliott, Robert Gerringer, Kate
Wilkinson and Camilla Ashland

10/06-10/30
Sleuth
By Anthony Shaffer
Producer/Director:
Helen Bonfils, Morton Gottlieb
and Michael White/Clifford Williams
Cast: Michael Allinson, Donal Donnelly,
Philip Farrar, Harold K. Newman and
Roger Purnell

11/02-11/20
Company
By George Furth/Stephen Sondheim
Producer/Director: Harold Prince/
Harold Prince and Michael Bennett
Cast: George Chakiris, Elaine Stritch,
Louisa Flaningam, Robert Goss,
Marian Hailey, Del Hinkley and others

11/29-12/25
Applause
By Betty Comden and Adolph
Green/Charles Strouse and Lee Adams
Producer/Director: Joseph Kipness,
Lawrence Kasha, Nederlander Productions,
George M. Steinbrenner III/Ron Field
Cast: Lauren Bacall, Don Chastain, Beverly
Dixon, Lee Roy Reams, Norwood Smith
and others

Royal Alexandra Theatre

12/27-01/15/72
And Miss Reardon Drinks a Little
By Paul Zindel
Producer/Director: James B. McKenzie,
Spofford J. Beadle, Seath L. Schariro,
Kenneth Waissman and Maxine Fox/
Melvin Bernhardt
Cast: Julie Harris, Kim Hunter,
DeAnn Mears, Bill Macy, Virginia Payne,
David Friedman and Jo Flores Chase

1972

01/17-01/22
La Compagnie Andre Tahon: Marottes
de Paris
Producer/Director:
Arthur Shafman/André Tahon
Cast: André Tahon, Daniel Chassard,
Alain Couet, Bernard Dutant,
Jean-Jacques Le Corre, Jean-Pierre Menager
and Marie-Thérèse Orian

01/24-02/12
Purlie
Ossie Davis, David Rose-Udell/Gary Geld
Producer/Director: Philip Rose
Cast: Robert Guillaume, Patti Jo,
Art Wallace, Sherman Hemsley,
Carol Jean Lewis, Tommy Breslin,
Esther Rolle and others

02/14-02/26
Promises, Promises
By Neil Simon, Hal David/Burt Bacharach
Producer/Director:
David Merrick/Robert Moore
Cast: Ted Pugh, Ilene Graff, Bob Holiday,
Greg Lewis, Jack Drummond, Tom Batten,
Larry Douglas and others

02/28-03/11
The Gingerbread Lady
By Neil Simon
Producer/Director: Arthur Whitelaw,
Seth Harrison/Jeremiah Morris
Cast: Nancy Kelly, Michael Lombard,
Manuel Sebastian, Mimi Bensinger,
Maureen Silliman and Michael Fairman

03/20-04/01
Promenade All
By David V. Robinson
Producer/Director: Fred Coe, Arthur Cantor,
Charles Taubman/Arthur Storch
Cast: Hume Cronyn, Eli Wallach,
Ann Jackson and Richard Backus

04/03-04/15
Captain Brassbound's Conversion
By G.B. Shaw
Producer/Director: Roger Stevens
and Arthur Cantor/Stephen Porter
Cast: Ingrid Bergman, Pernell Roberts,
Eric Berry, Jay Garner, Leo Leyden, Manu
Tupou and others

04/18-04/23
To Live Another Summer
By Hayim Hefer, Dov Seltzer
Producer/Director:
Leonard Soloway/Jonaton Karmon
Cast: Rivka Raz, Aric Lavie, Yona Atari
and Hanan Goldblatt

04/25-04/30
Pinocchio
Producer/Director:
Ruth Productions Inc./Bobby Clark
Cast: 8 puppeteers and 120 marionettes

05/01-06/06
Carousel
By Rodgers & Hammerstein
Producer/Director: John Raitt
Productions/John Raitt
Cast: John Raitt, Linda Michele,
Penny Carroll, Brooks Morton and others

05/08-05/20
The Marquise
By Noel Coward
Producer/Director: Paul Elliott and
Duncan C Weldon/Roger Redfarn
Cast: Glynis Johns, Richard Todd,
Barry Sinclair, Peter Needham and others

05/26-09/03
Godspell
By John Michael Tebelak/Stephen Schwartz
Producer/Director:
Ed Mirvish/Howard L. Sponseller Jr
Original Cast: Victor Garber, Gilda Radner,
Martin Short, Eugene Levy, Jayne
Eastwood, Gerry Salsberg, Avril Marie
Chown, Rudy Webb, Andrea Martin
and Valda Aviks

07/06-08/01
Hair
By Galt MacDermott, Jerome Ragni,
James Rado
Remount/reprise, see 1969/1970

Royal Alexandra Theatre

09/11-09/30
The Rothschilds
By Sherman Yellin/Jerry Bock
and Sheldon Harnick
Producer/Director: Michael Kidd
Cast: Theodore Bikel, C. David Coulson,
Carol Fox Prescott and others

10/04-10/28
How the Other Half Loves
By Alan Ayckbourn
Producer/Director: Peter Bridge and Eddie
Kulukundis/Robin Midgley
Cast: Robert Morley, Jan Holden, Sheila
Steafel, Elizabeth Ashton, Brian Miller and
Ian McCulloch

10/30-11/18
Voyage 'Round My Father
By John Mortimer
Producer/Director: Paul Elliott and Duncan
C. Weldon, Michael Codron/Ronald Eyre
Cast: Michael Redgrave, David Wood,
Amanda Murray, Andrew Sachs and
Connie Merigold

11/27-12/16
Irene
By Hugh Wheeler, James Montgomery
and Joseph McCarthy/Harry Tierney
Producer/Director: Harry Rigby,
Albert W. Selden and Jerome Winskoff/
Sir John Gielgud
Cast: Debbie Reynolds, Ruth Warrick, Patsy
Kelly, Monte Markham, Ted Pugh, Carmen
Alvarez, Jane Sell and Eddie Phillips

12/19-12/31
Goldilocks and the Three Bears
By Paul Elliott
Producer/Director: Paul Elliott and
Duncan C. Weldon/Paul Elliott
Cast: Lionel Blair, John Hewer, Christine
Holmes, Leon Greene, Ben Thomas,
Ronnie Scott-Dodd, the Hassani Troupe,
Jackie Pallo Jr., George Mey, Jackie Barron,
Lionel Blair Dancers and others

1973

01/08-01/27
Emperor Henry IV
By Pirandello
Producer/Director: Sol Hurok and
Elliot Martin/Clifford Williams
Cast: Rex Harrison, Eileen Herlie, David
Hurst, Douglas Seale, Linda De Coff,
Rudolph Willrich and others

01/29-02/17
Twigs
By George Furth/Stephen Sondheim
Producer/Director:
Frederick Brisson/Michael Bennett
Cast: Sada Thompson, Herbert Nelson, Jack
Murdock, Mark Dawson, Dan Travanty, Joe
Mantell, Walter Klavun and Stacy McAdams

02/23-03/17
Cyrano
By Edmond Rostand, Anthony
Burgess/Michael Lewis
Producer/Director:
Richard Gregson/Michael Langham
Cast: Christopher Plummer, Leigh Beery,
Mark Lamos, James Blendick, Patrick Hines,
Arnold Soboloff, Louis Turenne and others

CHRISTOPHER PLUMMER

CYRANO

A NEW MUSICAL

Royal Alexandra Theatre

03/21-03/24
Canadian Opera Co.: Cosi Fan Tutti
Producer/Director: Royal Alexandra/
Herman Geiger-Torel
Cast: Garnet Brooks, John Arab,
Peter Barcza, Donald Oddie, Peter Milne,
Jan Rubes, Barbara Collier, Helly Jedig,
Kathleen Ruddell and others

03/26-03/31
No, No Nanette
By Otto Harbach/Vincent Youmans

Producer/Director: Pyxidium Ltd.,
Cyma Rubin/Burt Shevelove
Cast: Don Ameche, Evelyn Keyes, Ann B.
Davis, Swen Swenson, Lainie Nelson,
Darlene Anders, Tim Heathman and others

04/02-04/21
Grease
By Jim Jacobs and Warren Casey
Producer/Director: Kenneth Waissman,
Maxine Fox, Anthony D'Amato/Tom Moore
Cast: Frank Piegaro, Robin Lamont, Brenda
Gardner, Pamela Adams, Walter Charles,
Mike Clifford, Jerry Zaks and John Travolta

04/23-05/13
The Secretary Bird
By William Douglas-Home
Producer/Director: Paul Elliott,
Duncan Weldon/John Downing
Cast: Patrick MacNee, Lana Morris,
Clive Graham, Joanna Henderson and
Judith Arthy

05/14-05/19
Brief Lives
By Patrick Garland
Producer/Director: Paul Elliott and
Duncan C. Weldon/Patrick Garland
Cast: Roy Dotrice

05/31-06/09
6 Rms Riv Vu
By Bob Randall
Producer/Director: Alexander H. Cohen
and Bernard Delfont/Edwin Sherin
Cast: Jerry Orbach, Jane Alexander, Ron
Harper, Jennifer Warren, Francine Beers,
Emil Belasco, Lynda Myles and F. Murray
Abraham

06/14-07/07
Don't Bother Me, I Can't Cope
By Micki Grant
Producer/Director: Edward Padula
and Arch Lustberg, the Royal Alexandra
Theatre/Vinnette Carroll
Cast: Bryant Baker, Salome Bey,
Leroy Britton, Jo-Ann Brooks, Nell Carter,
Joseph Lee Clark, David J. Hemphill,
Sherman Hemsley and others

09/03-09/22
The Student Prince
By Donnelly/Romberg
Producer/Director: Moe Septee,
Lehman Engel/George Schaeffer
Cast: Harry Danner, Robert Rounseville,
George Rose and others

10/01-10/27
That Championship Season
By Jason Miller
Producer/Director: Joseph Papp/A.J. Antoon
Cast: Forrest Tucker, Phillip R. Allen,
George Dzundza, Joseph Mascolo and
Bernie McInerney

10/29-12/01
Prisoner of Second Avenue
By Neil Simon
Producer/Director: Saint-Subber/Tom Porter
Cast: Shelley Berman, Mimi Hines, Jack
Hanrahan, Ruth Jaroslow, Elsa Raven and
Yvonne Vincic

12/03-12/22
The Day after the Fair
By Frank Harvey, based on Thomas Hardy
Producer/Director:
Arthur Cantor/Frith Banbury
Cast: Deborah Kerr, W.B. Brydon,
Brenda Forbes, Michael Shannon
and Marie Tomillion

12/26-01/05/74
Spellbound
By David Cronenberg and Doug
Henning/Howard Shore and Eric Robertson
Producer/Director: Ivan Reitman
Cast: Doug Henning, Jennifer Dale
and Maya

1974

01/07-01/26
The Sunshine Boys
By Neil Simon
Producer/Director: E. Azenberg/Alan Arkin
Cast: Jack Albertson, Sam Levene, Michael
Durrell, Urylee Leonardos, Jennifer
Richards, Stephan Mark Weyte and Ray Fry

01/28-02/16
Lloyd George Knew My Father
By William Douglas-Home
Producer/Director: Paul Elliott,
Duncan Weldon/James Grout
Cast: Ralph Richardson, Meriel Forbes,
James Grout, David Stoll, Janet Henfrey,
Sheila Felvin, Robert O'Mahoney and
Alexander Archdale

02/18-02/20
The Visit
By F. Durrenmatt

Producer/Director:
New Phoenix Rep/Harold Prince
Cast: Munson Hicks, Peter Friedman, Ralph
Drischell, George Ede, John Glover, Merwin
Goldsmith, John McMartin, Rachel Roberts,
Bonnie Gallup, Charlotte Moore, Robin
Pearson Rose and others

02/21-02/23
Chemin de Fer
By Georges Feydeau
Producer/Director: New Phoenix
Rep/Stephen Porter
Cast: Richard Venture, Rachel Roberts,
George Pentecost, George Ede, David
Dukes, John McMartin, Valentine Mayer,
Charlotte Moore and others

03/04-03/09
The Real Inspector Hound
By Tom Stoppard
Producer/Director:
Kennedy Center/Joseph Hardy
Cast: Robert Vaughan, Noel Craig, Michael
Egan, Connie Forslund, John-David Keller,
Bruce Kornbluth and others

03/22-04/13
Gypsy
By Arthur Laurents, Stephen Sondheim/
Jule Styne
Producer/Director: Barry M. Brown,
Fritz Holt, Edgar Lansbury and Joseph
Beruh/Arthur Laurents
Cast: Angela Lansbury, Rex Robbins,
Zan Charisse, Mary Louise Wilson,
Bonnie Langford and others

04/16-05/11
A Little Night Music
By Hugh Wheeler/Stephen Sondheim
Producer/Director: Harold Prince,
Ruth Mitchell/Harold Prince
Cast: Jean Simmons, Margaret Hamilton,
Ed Evanko, Virginia Pulos, Andra Akers
and others

05/20-05/25
A Community of Two
By Jerome Chodorov
Producer/Director: Ambrose
Productions/Jerome Chodorov
Cast: Claudette Colbert, George Gaynes,
Lou Gilbert, Sylvia Daneel, Peter Adams,
Mary Case and David Winn

05/27-07/13
Grease
By Jim Jacobs, Warren Casey
Producer/Director: Kenneth Waissmann
and Maxine Fox/Tom Moore
Cast: Mike Clifford, Carol Culver, Ray
DeMattis, Candice Earley and others

08/31-09/28
London Assurance
By Dion Boucicault
Producer/Director:
James M. Nederlander, Roger L. Stevens
and Ed Mirvish/Euan Smith
Cast: The Royal Shakespeare Company:
Donald Sinden, Elizabeth Spriggs, Polly
Adams, Roger Rees, John Carter and others

10/02-10/12
Brief Lives
By Patrick Garland
Producer/Director: Paul Elliott, Ellen Brandt
and David Conn/Patrick Garland
Cast: Roy Dotrice

11/11-11/30
Sugar and Spice
By Arthur Marx
Producer/Director:
Michael McAloney/Jed Horner
Cast: Sal Mineo, Jack Kelly, Virginia Grey,
Mary Wilcox, Beri Williams and
Richard M. Davidson

12/02-12/21
The Pleasure of His Company
By Samuel Taylor, Cornelia Otis Skinner
Producer/Director: Paul Elliott and
Duncan Weldon/Peter Dews
Cast: Douglas Fairbanks Jr., Heather
Chasen, Belinda Carroll, Ralph Michael,
George Roubicek, Arsenio Trinidad and
Robert Beatty

12/26-01/04/75
Cinderella
By Paul Elliott
Producer/Director: Paul Elliott, Duncan
Weldon/Lionel Blair
Cast: Lionel Blair, Cheryl Taylor, David
Morton, Barrie Gosney, Dennis Ramsden
and others

01/13-02/01
Private Lives
By Noel Coward
Producer/Director:
Arthur Cantor/John Gielgud
Cast: Maggie Smith, John Standing, Remak Ramsay, Niki Flacks and Marie Tommon

02/03-02/22
The Jockey Club Stakes
By William Douglas Home
Producer/Director: Paul Elliott, Duncan Weldon/Wilfrid Hyde White
Cast: Wilfrid Hyde White, Robert Coote, Dillon Evans, Jill Rose, Ronald Drake and others

02/25-03/22
Odyssey
By Erich Segal/Mitch Leigh
Producer/Director: Kennedy Center Productions, Inc./Albert Marre
Cast: Yul Brynner, Joan Diener, Diana Davila, Catherine Lee Smith, Martin Vidnovic and others

03/24-04/12
Good Evening
By Peter Cook, Dudley Moore
Producer/Director: Alexander H. Cohen and Bernard Delfont/Jerry Adler
Cast: Peter Cook and Dudley Moore

04/15-04/20
Pinocchio
Producer/Director: Bobby Clark
Cast: life-sized marionettes

04/28-05/03
Clarence Darrow for the Defense
By David W. Rintels, based on Irving Stone
Producer/Director: Mike Merrick, Don Gregory/John Houseman
Cast: Henry Fonda (solo)

05/05-05/24
Hedda Gabler
By Ibsen
Producer/Director: Paul Elliott and Duncan C. Weldon, the Royal Shakespeare Company/Trevor Nunn
Cast: Glenda Jackson, Patrick Stewart, Timothy West, Peter Eyre, Constance Chapman, Pam St. Clement and Jennie Linden

06/30-07/12
The Golden Years of Music Hall
By Arthur Lane
Producer/Director:
Paul Elliott/Bill Robertson
Cast: Elsie and Doris Waters, Bob and Alf Pearson, Leslie Sarony, Eddie Molly, Barbara Sumner, The Music Hall Belles and others

07/21-08/02
The Hot L Baltimore
By Lanford Wilson
Producer/Director: Kermit Bloomgarden, Roger Ailes/Jeremiah Morris
Cast: Jan Sterling, Larry Carr, Clement Fowler and others

09/08-09/27
Sabrina Fair
By Samuel Taylor
Producer/Director:
Sidney Gordon/Harold Kennedy
Cast: Arlene Francis, Sam Levene, Russell Nype, Maureen O'Sullivan and others

10/06-10/25
Absurd Person Singular
By Alan Ayckbourn
Producer/Director: The Theatre Guild and The John F. Kennedy Center for the Performing Arts/Eric Thompson
Cast: Patrick Macnee, Sheila Macrae, Judy Carne, Michael Callan, Betsy Von Furstenburg and David Watson

10/27-11/01
The Devil's Disciple
By G.B. Shaw
Producer/Director: The Shaw Festival/Paxton Whitehead and Tony van Bridge

Cast: Paul Hecht, Elizabeth Shepherd, Neil Vipond, Paxton Whitehead, Heath Lamberts, Patrick Boxill and others

11/03-11/08
Relatively Speaking
By Alan Ayckbourn
Producer/Director: Paul Elliott, Cameron Mackintosh, George Borwick/John David
Cast: Dora Bryan, Robert Flemyng, Simon Williams and Phyllida Nash

11/10-11/22
Something's Afoot
By James McDonald, Davis Vos, Robert Gerlach
Producer/Director: Emanuel Azenberg, Dasha Epstein, John Mason Kirby, James B. McKenzie/Tony Tanner
Cast: Tessie O'Shea, Gary Beach, Willard Beckam and others

11/24-11/29
Pinocchio
Producer/Director: Reuben Budrow
Cast: life-sized marionettes

12/02-01/10/76
Same Time Next Year
By Bernard Slade
Producer/Director: Morton Gottlieb, Dasha Epstein, Edward L. Schuman and Palladium Productions/Gene Saks
Cast: Joyce Van Patten and Conrad Janis

01/21-01/31
A Matter of Gravity
By Enid Bagnold
Producer/Director: Robert Whitehead, Roger L. Stevens, Konrad Matthaei/Noel Willman
Cast: Katherine Hepburn, Charlotte Jones, Christopher Reeve and others

02/09-02/28
Thirteen Rue de l'Amour
(Monsieur Goes Hunting)
By Georges Feydeau
Producer/Director: Paul Elliott, Duncan Weldon/Peter Dews
Cast: Glynis Johns and Louis Jourdan

03/02-03/07
Zalmen, or The Madness of God
By Elie Wiesel

Producer/Director:
Moe Septee/Alan Schneider
Cast: Richard Bauer, Joseph Wiseman
and David Margulies

03/15-04/03
Mornings at Seven
By Paul Osborn
Producer/Director: Elliot Martin and
William Putch/William Putch
Cast: Jean Stapleton and others

04/05-04/24
The D'Oyly Carte Opera Co.: The Mikado,
The Pirates of Penzance, HMS Pinafore
By Gilbert and Sullivan
Producer/Director: James M. Nederlander,
the D'Oyly Carte Opera/Michael Heyland
Cast: John Reed, John Ayldon, Meston Reid
and others

04/29-07/10
A Chorus Line
By Michael Bennett, Nicholas Dante,
James Kirkwood, Marvin Hamlisch
Producer/Director:
Joseph Papp/Michael Bennett
Cast: Jeff Hyslop, T. Michael Reed
and others

09/13-10/09
No Man's Land
By Harold Pinter
Producer/Director: Roger L. Stevens and
Robert Whitehead and the National Theatre
of Great Britain/Peter Hall
Cast: John Gielgud, Ralph Richardson,
Michael Kitchen and Terence Rigby

10/12-10/16
Aladdin
By Arnold Miller
Producer/Director: Budrow Family
(Producers)/Ross Petty
Cast: Ross Petty and others

10/19-10/23
Dutch National Ballet
Producer/Director: Cantour/
Rudi van Dantzig

10/25-11/20
By George
By Alan Lund and Gershwins
Producer/Director: The Charlottetown
Festival, Robert D. Dubberley/Alan Lund
Cast: Sherry Flett, Kerrie Keane, Glen Kotyk
and Rudy Webb

11/22-12/18
Very Good, Eddie
By Guy Bolton and Philip
Bartholmae/Jerome Kern
Producer/Director: David Merrick,
Max Brown and Byron Goldman,
The Goodspeed Opera House/Bill Gile
Cast: J.J. Jepson, Virginia Seidel, Travis
Hudson, Spring Fairbank, John Sloman,
Russ Beasley and others

12/27-01/22/77
The Scenario
By Jean Anouilh
Producer/Director: Duncan C. Weldon
and Louis I. Michaels/Stuart Burge
Cast: Trevor Howard, John Bluthal,
Gary Bond, Helen Cherry, Angels Douglas,
Sue Lloyd and others

1977

01/28-02/26
Anna Christie
By Eugene O'Neill
Producer/Director:
Alexander H. Cohen, Hildy Parks
and Roy A. Somlyo/José Quintero
Cast: Liv Ullman, John Lithgow, Mary
McCarty, Robert Donley, Richard Hamilton,
Jack Davidson, Ken Harrison and others

02/28-04/23
Equus
By Peter Shaeffer
Producer/Director: Kermit Bloomgarden,
Doris Cole Abrahams/John Dexter
Cast: Douglas Campbell, Dennis Erdman
and others

04/25-05/21
Rebecca
By Daphne DuMaurier
Producer/Director: Duncan C. Weldon
and Louis I. Michaels/Val May
Cast: Haley Mills, Paul Daneman,
Pauline Jameson and Paul Darrow

05/23-07/02
Side by Side by Sondheim
By Stephen Sondheim, Leonard Bernstein,
Mary Rogers, Richard Rodgers and
Jule Styne
Producer/Director: H.M. Tennent, Cameron
Mackintosh and Paul Elliot/Larry Oaks
Cast: Bernard Braden and Georgia Brown

08/08-08/13
Appearing Nitely
By Lily Tomlin, Jane Wagner
Producer/Director: George Boyd,
Michael Tannen/Jane Wagner
Cast: Lily Tomlin

08/15-09/10
Same Time Next Year
By Bernard Slade
Producer/Director:
Morton Gottlieb/Warren Crane
Cast: Barbara Rush and Tom Troupe

09/19-10/15
Absent Friends
By Alan Ayckbourn
Producer/Director: Claire Nichtern
and Ashton Springer/Eric Thompson
Cast: Eli Wallach, Anne Jackson and
Meg Wynn Owen

10/18-11/12
Chicago
By Fred Ebb, John Kander and Bob Fosse
Producer/Director:
Robert Fryer and James Cresson/Bob Fosse
Cast: Jerry Orbach, Penny Worth, Carolyn
Kirsch, Haskell Gordon, M. O'Haughey,
Edye Byrde and Susan Stroman

11/16-12/17
The Circle
By Somerset Maugham
Producer/Director: Duncan C. Weldon
and Louis I. Michaels, Chichester Festival
Theatre/Peter News
Cast: Googie Withers, John McCallum
and Jenny Quayle

12/26-01/28/78
California Suite
By Neil Simon
Producer/Director: Emanuel Azenberg
and Robert Fryer/Philip Cusack
Cast: Robert Reed, Elizabeth Allen,
Warren Berlinger and Patti Kerr

1978

01/31-03/11
The Wiz
By William F. Brown and Charlie Smalls
Producer/Director: Ken Harper and
Twentieth Century Fox/Geoffrey Holder
Cast: Renée Harris, Ben Harney,
Ken Prymus and Charles Valentino

03/14-03/28
For Colored Girls Who Have Considered
Suicide/When the Rainbow Is Enuf
By Ntozake Shange (Paulette Williams)
Producer/Director: Joseph Papp/Ox Scott
Cast: Latanya Richardson, Brenda J. Davis,
Barbara Alston, Gloria Calomee and
Paula Parke

04/03-04/29
Canadian Opera Co.: The Marriage of
Figaro, La Traviata, The Barber of Seville
Producer/Director: COC/Lotfi Mansouri
Cast: Barbara Shuttleworth, Pamela Myers,
William Danby, Raymond Hickman,
Janet Stubbs, Riki Turofsky, Avo Kittask,
Don McManus and others

05/01-05/27
Tribute
By Bernard Slade
Producer/Director:
Morton Gottlieb/Arthur Storch
Cast: Jack Lemmon, Rosemary Prinz, Tresa
Hughes, Robert Picardo, Catherine Hincks,
Joan Welles and A. Larry Haines

05/29-06/24
Picture of Innocence
By Robert Morley and John Wells
Producer/Director: Duncan C. Weldon, Louis
I. Michaels and Ed Mirvish/Robin Midgley
Cast: Robert Morley, Kenneth Griffith, Lally
Bowers, Derek Fowlds, Heather Chasen,
Bernard Archard and Susie Blake

06/27-07/02
Anne Murray in Concert

07/19-08/12
Oh, Kay
By George and Ira Gershwin, Guy Bolton
and P.G. Wodehouse
Producer/Director: Cyma Rubin and
The Kennedy Center/Donald Saddler
Cast: David-James Carroll, Gene Castle,
Marie Cheatham, Reno Roop,
Alexandra Korey and others

08/15-08/16
Toronto Dance Theatre
Producer/Director:
Peter Randazzo and David Earle

08/17-08/19
Merce Cunningham Dance Company
Producer/Director: Merce Cunningham
Cast: Merce Cunningham, Chris Komar
and others, including 10 dancers

08/21-08/26
Chinese Circus

09/08-10/07
Uncle Vanya
By Chekhov
Producer/Director: Ed Mirvish and
The Royal Alexandra Theatre Company/
Nat Brenner
Cast: Peter O'Toole, Jackie Burroughs,
Charles Shamata, Claude Bede, James
Douglas, Maggie Askey, Maureen McRae,
Peter Dvorsky and Marie Kean

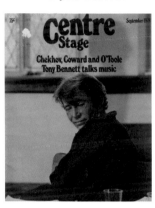

10/09-10/21
Present Laughter
By Noel Coward
Producer/Director: Ed Mirvish and
the Royal Alexandra Theatre
Company/Roderick Cook
Cast: Peter O'Toole, Marie Kean,
Peter Dvorsky, Jackie Burroughs, Barbara
Gordon, Maggie Askey, Maureen McRae
and Charles Shamata

10/23-10/28
Tony Bennett Sings
Tony Bennett

10/30-11/25
The Last of Mrs. Cheyney
By Frederick Lonsdale
Producer/Director: The Kennedy Center,
J. William Fisher, Duncan C. Weldon and
Louis I. Michaels/Frank Dunlop
Cast: Deborah Kerr, Monte Markham,
Donal Donnelly, Marti Stevens, Gavin Reed,
Stephen D. Newman and others

11/27-12/23
Half Life
By Julian Mitchell
Producer/Director: Duncan C. Weldon,
Louis I. Michaels/Waris Hussein
Cast: John Gielgud, Dinah Sheridan,
John Phillips, James Cossins and others

12/26-01/20/79
Dracula
By Hamilton Deane and John L. Balderston
Producer/Director: Jujamcyn Theatres,
John Wulp, Nelle Nugent and
Elizabeth I. McCann/Dennis Rosa
Cast: Jean LeClerc, Leta Anderson, William
B. Cain, Geoff Garland, Richard S. Levine,
George Martin, Malcolm Stewart and
Lauren Thompson

1979

01/22-02/17
Bedroom Farce
By Alan Ayckbourn
Producer/Director: The National Theatre
Company of Great Britian/Peter Hall
and Alan Ayckbourn
Cast: Polly Adams, Michael Gough,
Joan Hickson, Delia Lindsay and others

02/19-03/17
The Gin Game
By D.L. Coburn
Producer/Director: Hume Cronyn,
Mike Nichols and Shuberts/Mike Nichols
Cast: Hume Cronyn and Jessica Tandy

03/19-04/14
Home Again
By Russell Baker and Barbara Fried/
Cy Coleman
Producer/Director: Irwin Meyer,
Stephen R. Friedman/Gene Saks
Cast: Dick Shawn, Ronny Cox, Lisa Kirk,
Mike Kellin and others

04/23-05/19
The Canadian Opera Co.: Carmen,
Cinderella
Producer/Director: COC/Lotfi Mansouri
(Carmen)/Jeanette Aster (Cinderella)
Cast: Lyn Vernon, Frederic de Marseille,
John Ostendorf, Roxolana Roslak, Kathy
Terrel, Susan Gudgeon, Samuel Byrd,
Judith Forst and others

05/21-07/07
Chapter Two
By Neil Simon
Producer/Director:
Emanuel Azenberg/Herbert Ross
Cast: Jerry Orbach, Marilyn Redfield,
Jane A. Johnston and Herbert Edelman

07/11-08/18
A Chorus Line
By Michael Bennett, Nicholas Dante,
James Kirkwood and Marvin Hamlisch
Producer/Director:
Joseph Papp/Michael Bennett
Cast: Buddy Balou, Kenya Benitez,
Gregory Brock, David Cahn, Pam Cecil,
Bebe Neuwirth and others

09/10-10/13
Da
By Hugh Leonard
Producer/Director: Lester Osterman,
Marilyn Strauss, Marc Howard and
Hudson Guild Theatre/Melvin Bernhardt
Cast: Barnard Hughes, Tom Crawley,
Helen Stenborg and others

10/15-12/01
Ain't Misbehavin'
By Richard Maltby/Fats Waller
Producer/Director: Emanuel Azenberg,
Dasha Epstein, Shuberts/Richard Maltby Jr.
Cast: Evan Bell, Debra Byrd, Yvonne Talton
Kersey, Jackie Lowe and Lonnie McNeil

12/03-01/05/80
Deathtrap
By Ira Levin
Producer/Director: Alfred de Liagre Jr.
and Roger L. Stevens/Robert Moore
Cast: Brian Bedford, Betty Miller, Kevin
Conroy, George Ede and Kathleen Freeman

01/07-02/09
I Love My Wife
By Michael Stewart/Cy Coleman
Producer/Director: Terry Allen Kramer
and Harry Rigby/Gene Saks
Cast: Tom and Dick Smothers, with Louisa
Flanigan, Maureen Maloney, Michael Mark
and others

02/12-03/15
Dancin'
Producer/Director:
Jules Fisher and Shuberts/Bob Fosse
Cast: Hinton Battle, Russell Chambers,
André de la Roché, Ronald Dennis,
Cecily Douglas, Anita Ehrler, Lois Englund
and others

03/20
Academy of Canadian Cinema: Genie
Awards

03/21-03/29
The Irish Rovers

03/31- 05/03
The Grass Is Greener
By Hugh and Margaret Williams
Producer/Director: Paul Elliott/Val May
Cast: Patrick MacNee, Jennifer Wilson,
Derek Fowlds and others

05/19-05/24
Spring Thaw, Ha Ha
Producer/Director: Alan F. Gordon
Cast: Rosemary Radcliffe, Mary Ann
McDonald, Paul Brown, Brenda Bradley,
Marvin Karon and Patrick Young

06/03-07/19
Eubie!
By Julianne Boyd/Eubie Blake and
Noble Sissle
Producer/Director:
Ashton Springer/Julianne Boyd
Cast: Billy Newton-Davis, Tenita L. Jordan,
Lynne Clifton-Allen, Luther Fontaine
and others

07/21-08/02
Burlesque USA
By Barry Ashton
Producer/Director:
Michael Brandman/Barry Ashton
Cast: Red Buttons, Robert Alda, Tempest
Storm, Joey Faye and others

08/04-08/16
Bubbling Brown Sugar
By Loften Mitchell
Producer/Director: Gordon Crowe and
Winfield Theatrical Productions/Ron Abbott
Cast: Cab Calloway, Ann Duquesnay,
Bobby Hill, Cecilia Norfleet and others

08/18-08/23
Blue Champagne
By Ken John Grant
Producer/Director: Paquet/Dummett
Associates/Ken John Grant
Cast: Bill Cole, Jayne Lewis, Deirdre van
Winkle and Don Horsburgh

08/26-08/31
Neil Simon Suite
By Neil Simon
Producer/Director: Stockman Briggle
Cast: Paul Lynde and Beverly Sanders

09/02-10/18
The Elephant Man
By Bernard Pomerance
Producer/Director:
Raymond Crinkley, Elizabeth McCann
and Nelle Nugent/Jack Hofsiss
Cast: Ken Ruta, Jeff Hayenga (Merrick),
Concetta Tomei and others

10/20-11/22
Romantic Comedy
By Bernard Slade
Producer/Director:
Morton Gottlieb/Joseph Hardy
Cast: Karen Valentine, Keith Baxter
and others

11/25-12/06
Pinocchio
By Rueben and Charles Budrow, updated
from Bobby Clark/Based on Carlo
Collodi/Marionettes designed and
created by Bobby Clark

12/11-12/14
Makin' Whoopee
By William Anthony McGuire and Gud
Kahn/Walter Donaldson
Producer/Director: National Musical
Theatre Company/G. William Oakley
Cast: Mamie Van Doren, Imogene Coca,
Ted Pritchard, Frank Silvano, King Donovan
and others

12/16-01/24/81
Who's Life Is It Anyway?
By Brian Clark
Producer/Director: Emanuel Azenberg,
James M. Nederlander and Ray
Cooney/Michael Lindsay-Hogg
Cast: Brian Bedford, Pat Galloway, Leon
Charles, Gordon Chater, Stephen G. Arlen,
Delphi Lawrence, Dillon Evans and others

02/03-03/07
I Ought to Be in Pictures
By Neil Simon
Producer/Director:
Emanuel Azenberg/Herbert Ross
Cast: Bill Macy, Alexa Kenin and
Patricia Harty

03/09-03/14
Academy of Canadian Cinema:
Genie Awards

03/17-04/18
Oklahoma!
By Rodgers & Hammerstein
Producer/Director: Zev Buffman/
William Hammerstein
Cast: Christine Andreas, William Mallory,
Bruce Adler, Richard Leighton,
Mary Boucher and others

04/20-05/23
Early Days
By David Storey/Alan Price
Producer/Director:
National Theatre/Duncan Weldon
and Louis Michaels/
Lindsay Anderson
Cast: Ralph Richardson,
Sheila Ballantine, Michael Bangerter,
Marty Cruickshank and others

05/25-05/30
Des O'Connor
Concert

06/01-06/06
With a Touch of Burlesque
By Barry Ashton
Producer/Director: Michael Brandman
and Martin Kummer/Barry Ashton
Cast: Sid Caesar, Imogene Coca, Joey
Forman, Lee Meredith, Mickey Deems,
Josip Elic and others

06/09-06/13
Maggie and Pierre
By Linda Griffiths
Producer/Director: Passe Muraille
and Toronto Theatre Festival
Cast: Linda Griffiths (solo)

06/18-08/29
They're Playing Our Song
By Neil Simon/Marvin Hamlisch
and Carole Bayer Sager
Producer/Director: Emanuel
Azenberg/Robert Moore
Cast: Anita Gillette, Ray Buktenica
and others

09/06-10/17
Say Hello to Harvey
By Mary Chase/Leslie Bricusse
Producer/Director: Mirvish and Michael
McAloney/Mel Shapiro
Cast: Donald O'Connor, Sheila McCarthy,
Patricia Routledge, Joe Silver, Sidney
Miller, Angela Fusco and others

10/20-11/28
Children of a Lesser God
By Mark Medoff
Producer/Director: Emanuel
Azenberg/Shubert/Mark Taper
Forum/Gordon Davidson
Cast: Linda Bove, Peter Evans and others

12/01-01/09/82
A Day in Hollywood, A Night in the Ukraine
By Dick Vosburgh/Frank Lazarus
Producer/Director: Alexander H. Cohen
and Hildy Parks/Tommy Tune
Cast: Frank Lazarus, Jill Cook, Brad
Moranz, Evalyn Baron, Jeff Keller, Mary
D'Arcy, Richard Haskin and Patricia Lockery

01/12-02/20
Billy Bishop Goes to War
By John Gray and Eric Peterson
Producer/Director:
Vancouver East Cultural Centre/John Gray
Cast: Eric Peterson and John Gray

02/22-03/06
Academy of Canadian Cinema: Genie
Awards

03/18-04/17
Not Now, Darling
By Ray Cooney and John Chapman
Producer/Director: Paul Elliott
and Ray Cooney/Ray Cooney
Cast: Leslie Phillips, Andrew Sachs,
Jeremy Hawk, Ann Sidney, Leith Taylor,
Vic Hawkins, Janet Crawford and others

04/26-06/05
My Fair Lady
By Lerner & Lowe
Producer/Director:
Cameron Mackintosh/Alan Jay Lerner
Cast: Tony Britton, Anna Neagle,
Peter Bayliss, Rebecca Caine and others

06/08-07/17
Sweeney Todd
By Stephen Sondheim
Producer/Director: Tom Mallow
and James Janek/Harold Prince
Cast: June Havoc, Ross Petty and others

07/19-07/31
Tintypes
By Mary Kyte
Producer/Director: Gordon Crowe/
Jerry Zaks
Cast: Mel Marvin, Gary Pearle, Beth Fowler,
Timothy Jerome, Catherine Gaines, Zelda
Pulliam and Peter Slutsker

08/09-08/21
Pirates of Penzance
By Gilbert and Sullivan
Producer/Director:
Jan McArt/Bob Bogdanoff
Cast: Barry Bostwick, Andy Gibb, Leo
Leyden, Caroline Peyton, Christina James,
Don McManus and others

09/12-10/23
Mass Appeal
By Bill C. Davis
Producer/Director: Ray Larsen, Manhattan
Theatre Club, Elizabeth McCann and
Nelle Nugent/Geraldine Fitzgerald
Cast: Milo O'Shea and Adam Redfield

10/25-12/04
Blithe Spirit
By Noel Coward
Producer/Director:
The Stratford Festival/Brian Bedford
Cast: Tammy Grimes, Brian Bedford,
Carole Shelley and Helen Carey

12/06-12/24
Aladdin and His Magic Lamp
By Paul Elliott
Producer/Director: Paul Elliott
Cast: Derek Griffiths and others

12/27-02/05/83
Barnum
By Michael Stewart and Mark Bramble/
Cy Coleman
Producer/Director: Judy Gordon,
Cy Coleman, Maurice Rosenfield
and Lois F. Rosenfield/Joe Layton

Cast: Harvey Evans, Jan Pessano, Kathleen Marsh, Robin Kersey, Leonard John Crofoot and Kelly Walters

1983

02/08-03/19
Singin' and Dancin' Tonight
By Alan Lund and Howard Cable
Producer/Director:
The Charlottetown Festival/Alan Lund
Cast: Greg Bond, Jodie Friesen, Barbara Fulton, Susan Gattoni, Amanda Hancox, Brian Harris-Lund and others

03/20-03/26
Academy of Canadian Cinema:
Genie Awards

03/28-05/07
Underground
By Michael Sloane
Producer/Director:
Paul Elliott/Simon Williams
Cast: Raymond Burr, Alfred Marks, Gerald Flood, Patrick O'Connell and others

05/09-06/18
Conduct Unbecoming
By Barry England
Producer/Director: Paul Elliott/Val May
Cast: Anthony Steel, Nyree Dawn Porter, Jeremy Sinden and others

06/27-08/13
Oliver!
By Lionel Bart
Producer/Director:
Cameron Mackintosh/Peter Coe
Cast: Meg Johnson, Jackie Marks, Roy Hudd and others

09/01-09/04
Famous People Players
Diane Dupuy
Producer/Director: Diane Dupuy

09/12-10/22
Master Harold and the Boys
By Athol Fugard
Producer/Director:
Marvin Krauss, Irving Siders and Yale Repertory Theatre/ Lloyd Richards
Cast: James Earl Jones, Ray Aranha, Charles Michael Wright and others

10/25-12/03
Crimes of the Heart
By Beth Henley
Producer/Director: James Pentecost
Cast: Cyd Quilling, Caryn West, Kathy Danzer and others

12/05-12/24
Dick Whittington and His Cat
By Paul Elliott
Producer/Director: Paul Elliott
Cast: Eric Sykes, Ross Petty, Karen Kain and others

12/27-02/04/84
Amadeus
By Peter Shaffer
Producer/Director: Tom Mallow and James Janek/Roger Williams
Cast: Philip Pleasants, Ed Hodson, Mary Jo Salerno and others

1984

02/06-03/17
Piaf
By Pam Gems
Producer/Director:
Paul Elliott/Stephen Barry
Cast: Andrienne Posta, Michael Boland, Tony Boncza, Phil Compton, Roger Fox, Taborah Johnson and others

03/19-03/24
Academy of Canadian Cinema:
Genie Awards

03/27-05/05
Elvis
By Ray Cooney and Jack Good
Producer/Director: Paul Elliott/Carole Todd
Cast: Vince Eager, Bo Wills, J.J. McLean and Gareth Marks

05/14-06/23
The Boy Friend
By Sandy Wilson
Producer/Director:
Cameron Mackintosh/Sandy Wilson
Cast: Glynis Johns, Derek Waring, Peter Bayliss, Paddie O'Neill and others

06/25-08/18
Run for Your Wife
By Ray Cooney
Producer/Director: Paul Elliott and
The Theatre of Comedy/Ray Cooney

Cast: Robin Nedwell, Eric Sykes, Derek Griffiths, Carol Hawkins, Anita Graham and others

08/20-08/25
Acting Shakespeare
Producer/Director:
Arthur Cantor/Ian McKellen
Cast: Ian McKellen

08/27-09/15
Torch Song Trilogy
By Harvey Fierstein
Producer/Director: Kenneth Waissman, Martin Markinson, John Glines and M.T.M. Enterprises/Peter Pope
Cast: Charles Adler, Estelle Getty, Tom Stechschulte, Jonathan Del Arco and others

09/17-10/27
Little Lies
By Joseph Caruso, from Pirandello
Producer/Director: Tony Tanner
Cast: John Mills, Morag Hood, Donald Pickering, Glyn Houston and others

10/29-12/08
Separate Tables
By T. Rattigan
Producer/Director: Ed Mirvish/Stratford Festival
Cast: John Neville, Domini Blythe, Martha Burns, Maggie Askey, Edward Atienza and Andrew Gillies

12/16-12/23
Cinderella
Producer/Director: Paul Elliott
Cast: Geoffrey Hughes, Karen Kain, Ross Petty, Anne Mirvish and others

12/31-02/09/85
Cyrano de Bergerac
By E. Rostand,
adapted by Anthony Burgess
Producer/Director: Mirvish
and Shaw Festival/Derek Goldby
Cast: Heath Lamberts, Marti Maraden, Geraint Wyn Davies, Robert Benson and Susan Cox

1985

02/11-03/23
Gigi
By Lerner & Lowe
Producer/Director: Columbia Artists Theatricals/Dallett Norris

Cast: Louis Jourdan, Betsy Palmer,
Taina Elg, Lisa Howard and others

04/01-05/11
The London Palladium Show
Producer/Director: Paul Elliott/Barrie Stead
Cast: Petula Clark, Allan Stewart, Steve Bor,
Ward Allen and others

05/13-06/22
Brighton Beach Memoirs
By Neil Simon
Producer/Director:
Emanuel Azenberg, Wayne M. Rogers
and Radio City Music Hall/Gene Saks
Cast: Patrick Dempsey, Romy Berk,
Brian Dillinger and others

06/25-08/03
Noises Off
By Michael Frayn
Producer/Director: James Nederlander,
Robert Fryer, Jerome Minskoff,
Kennedy Center and Michael
Codron/Michael Blakemore
Cast: Carole Shelley, Michael Connolly,
Deborah Fallender, Emily Heebner, Edward
Hibbert, Patricia Kilgarriff, Eddie McPhillips,
Allan Murley and Rex Robbins

08/13-08/18
Handy Dandy
By William Gibson
Cast: James Whitmore and Audra Lindley

08/19-08/31
Why Not Stay for Breakfast?
By Ray Cooney and Gene Stone
Producer/Director:
Paul Elliott/Dennis Ramsden
Cast: Ian Lavender, Amanda Bairstow,
Nicholas Bailey and Annette Bowers

09/09-10/19
Seven Brides for Seven Brothers
By Lawrence Kasha, David Lindsay
and Johnny Mercer/Gene de Paul,
after Stephen Vincent Benet
Producer/Director: Theatre Royal York
and Paul Elliott/Michael Winter
Cast: Roni Page, Steve Devereaux,
Paul Reeves, Simon Hayden, Simon Howe
and others

10/28-12/07
Two into One
By Ray Cooney
Producer/Director: Theatre of Comedy Co.
and Paul Elliott/Ray Cooney
Cast: John Thaw, Daniel Massey, Nerys
Hughes, Alfred Marks and Burt Kwouk

12/11-12/22
Mother Goose
Producer/Director: Ross Petty/Tudor Davies
Cast: Andrew Sachs, Tudor Davies, Salome
Bey, Ross Petty and others

12/27-02/08/86
The Real Thing
By Tom Stoppard
Producer/Director: Schwarz/Sewell, Mirvish
and Manitoba Theatre Centre/Guy Sprung
Cast: Richard Donat, R.H. Thomson,
Albert Schultz and others

1986

02/11-03/22
On Your Toes
By Rodgers & Hart and George Abbott
Producer/Director:
Lewis Friedman/George Abbott
Cast: Valentina Kozlova, Leonid Kozlov
and others

03/25-05/03
Ross
By Terence Rattigan
Producer/Director: Brian Hewitt-Jones,
Chris Moreno, Paul Elliott and Theatre
Royal Plymouth/Roger Redfran
Cast: Simon Ward, David Langton, Marc
Sinden, Ronald Curram, Bruce Montague
and others

05/05-06/14
Animal Farm
By Peter Hall, after George Orwell/Richard
Peaslee
Producer/Director:
Mirvish and National Theatre of
Britain/Peter Hall and Alan Cohen
Cast: Charles Baillie, Freddie Boardley,
Pamela Buchner, George Costigan
and others

06/23-08/30
Kismet
Charles Lederer and Luther Davis/
Robert Wright and George Forrest,
based on play by Edward Knoblock
Producer/Director:
Canadian Opera Co./Theodore Pappas
Cast: Samantha Adamson, Dale Azzard,
Wayne Berwick, Janie Brennan, Michael
Burgess, Michael Maguire, Don McManus,
Arlene Meadows, George Merner, Vince

Metcalfe, Rowena Modesto, Ted Pearson,
Avery Saltzman, Irina Welhasch and others

09/08-10/01
The Foreigner
By Larry Shue
Producer/Director: Marlene Smith,
Ernie Rubenstein and Mirvish/Leslie Yeo
Cast: Wanda Cannon, Lynne Gorman,
Peter Huff, Gerald Lenton, Peter Millard,
Clifford Saunders and Ian D. Clark

10/21-10/26
The Berliner Ensemble: The Caucasian
Chalk Circle, The Threepenny Opera
By B. Brecht
Producer/Director: Mirvish and The Berliner
Ensemble

10/31-12/13
The Mikado
By Gilbert and Sullivan
Producer/Director:
Stratford, Mirvish and Brian Macdonald
Productions/Brian Macdonald
Cast: Avo Kittask, John Keane, Eric Donkin,
Richard McMillan, Paul Massel, Arlene
Meadows, Joy Thompson-Allen, Marie
Baron, Stephen Beamish and others

12/17-01/03/87
Goldilocks and the Three Bears
By Paul Elliott
Producer/Director: Paul Elliott and
Ross Petty
Cast: Lionel Blair, Veronica Tennant
and others

1987

01/05-02/14
Pride and Prejudice
By David Pownall, after Jane Austen
Producer/Director: Schwarz/Sewell
and Citadel Theatre/Bill Pryde
Cast: Douglas Campbell, Jennifer Phipps,
Barbara Hamilton, Karl Pruner, Catherine
Disher, Alicia Jeffrey, Mary Ellen Maguire,
John Moffat and others

02/19-04/04
The Women
By Clare Boothe (Luce)
Producer/Director: Mirvish
and Shaw Fest/Duncan McIntosh

Cast: Lally Cadeau, Susan Cox,
Marti Maraden, Irene Hogan, Robin Craig,
Wendy Thatcher, Nancy Kerr, Camille
Mitchell and Frances Hyland

04/06-05/16
I'm Not Rappaport
By Herb Gardner
Producer/Director: Schwarz/Sewell and
Manitoba Theatre Centre/Guy Sprung
Cast: Paul Soles, Leon Bibb, Kathy Michael
McGlynn and others

05/18-06/27
Henry IV, Henry V
By Wm. Shakespeare
Producer/Director: Mirvish and the English
Shakespeare Co./Michael Bogdanov
Cast: Michael Pennington, John Woodvine,
Jenny Quayle and others

07/06-08/29
Sweet Charity
By Neil Simon, Bob Fosse and Dorothy
Fields/Cy Coleman
Producer/Director: Jerome Minskoff,
James M. Nederlander, Arthur Rubin
and Joseph Harris/Bob Fosse
Cast: Donna McKechnie, Ken Land, Lenora
Nemetz, Stephanie Pope, Mark Jacoby and
others

09/07-10/17
Three Men on a Horse
By George Abbott and John Cecil Holm
Producer/Director: Alexandra Productions
and Tarragon Theatre/John Hirsch
Cast: Paul Brown, John C. Capodice,
Michael Caruana, Charlotte Moore Stephen
Ouimette and others

10/26-12/19
HMS Pinafore
By Gilbert and Sullivan
Producer/Director: Mirvish and Brian
Macdonald Productions/Brian Macdonald
Cast: Meg Bussert, Ron Moody, Michael
Brian, Arlene Meadows, Ted Pearson,
Stephen Beamish and others

12/22-12/31
Snow White and the Seven Dwarfs
By Tudor Davies and Paul Elliott
Producer/Director:
Paul Elliott and Ross Petty
Cast: Ross Petty, Karen Kain, Honor
Blackman, David Keeley, Don McManus
and others

1988

01/08-02/20
Biloxi Blues
By Neil Simon
Producer/Director: Mirvish
and Citadel Theatre/Brian Rintoul
Cast: Leon Pownall, Mitchell Whitfield,
Louise Cranfield, Jennifer Dean, Mark
Krause, Eric McCormack, John Oremrod,
Cliff Saunders and Hugh Thompson

02/27-04/09
One Way Pendulum
By N.F. Simpson
Producer/Director: Mirvish/Jonathan Miller
Cast: Peter Bayliss, Graham Crowden, John
Fortune, Betty Turner, Kathryn Pogson,
Brenda Bruce, Ann Way, Stephanie Gorin
and others

04/15-05/26
Sweet Bird of Youth
By Tennessee Williams
Producer/Director: Mirvish and
Williamstown Festival/Nikos Psacharopoulos
Cast: Joanne Woodward, Charles Durning,
Anita Gillette, Terry Kinney and others

05/28-07/09
Broadway Bound
By Neil Simon
Producer/Director: Mirvish
and Citadel Theatre/Kurt Reis
Cast: DeAnn Mears, Frank Savino, Bernie
Passeltiner, David Bachman, Elva Mai
Hoover, Bruce Clayton, Len Doncheff,
Adam Furfaro and Maya Toman

07/16-09/03
Damn Yankees
By George Abbott, Douglass Wallop
and Richard Adler/Jerry Ross
Producer/Director: Mirvish, Marlene Smith
and Ernie Rubenstein/Madeline Paul
Cast: Moira Walley, Avery Saltzman, Davis
Gaines and others

09/12-10/22
Spoils of War
By Michael Weller
Producer/Director: Mirvish and Second
Stage/Austin Pendleton
Cast: Kate Nelligan, Christopher Collet,
Jeffrey de Munn and others

10/31-12/10
The Nerd
By Larry Shue
Producer/Director: Mirvish/Kevin Dowling
Cast: Gary Burghoff, Peter Blais, Catherine
Disher, Ken James and others

1989

01/02-02/11
The Search for Signs of Intelligent Life
in the Universe
By Lily Tomlin and Jane Wagner
Producer/Director: Lily Tomlin
and Jane Wagner/Jane Wagner
Cast: Lily Tomlin

03/15-05/26/90
Les Misérables
By Alain Boublil/Claude-Michel Schonberg
Producer/Director: Mirvish and Cameron
Mackintosh/Trevor Nunn and John Caird
Original Cast: Michael Burgess, Louise
Pitre, Thomas Goerz, Graeme Campbell,
Janelle Hutchison, Vance Avery, Kymberley
Huffman, Loretta Bailey and others

1990

06/08-09/01
Buddy: The Buddy Holly Story
By Alan Janes
Producer/Director:
Paul Elliott, Laurie Mansfield, Greg Smith
and Mirvish/Rob Bettinson
Cast: Paul Hipp, David Mucci, Bobby
Prochaska, Russ Jolly, Philip Anthony, Fred
Sanders, Melanie Doane, Jo Lynn Burks
and others

09/04-10/13
Sarafina
By Mbongeni Ngema and Hugh Masakela
Producer/Director: Lincoln Center Theater
and Committed Artists/Mbongeni Ngema

10/16-10/27
Penn and Teller: The Refrigerator Tour
Cast: Penn Jillette and Teller

10/29-11/03
Famous People Players
Producer/Director: Diane Dupuy

11/09-12/22
The Heidi Chronicles
By Wendy Wasserstein
Producer/Director: Mirvish and
Manitoba Theatre Centre/Bill Glassco
Cast: Nancy Palk, Michael Riley, Joseph
Ziegler, Tanja Jacobs, Mariam Bernstein,
Martine Friesen, Barclay Hope, Maria
Ricossa and Terri Cherniack

1991

01/04-02/16
Kean, or Disorder and Genius
By Jean-Paul Sartre
Producer/Director: Duncan Weldon
and Jerome Minskoff/Sam Mendes
Cast: Derek Jacobi, Kate Duchêne, Ian
McNeice, Nicholas Farrell, Sarah Woodward
and others

02/25-03/06
Time and the Conways
By J.B. Priestley
Producer/Director: Duncan Weldon
and Jerome Minskoff/Richard Olivier
Cast: Joan Plowright, Tamsin Olivier,
Julie-Kate Olivier and others

04/12-05/25
Dry Lips Oughta Move to Kapuskasing
By Tomson Highway
Producer/Director: Mirvish/Larry Lewis
Cast: Graham Green, Ben Cardinal, Gary
Farmer, Billy Merasty, Doris Linklater,
Kennetch Charlette, Tom Jackson, Dwayne
Mantowabi, Carlos Del Junco, Gloria May
Eshkibok, Jack Burning and Herbie Barnes

06/07-07/21/92
Les Misérables
By Alain Boublil/Claude-Michel Schonberg

Producer/Director: Mirvish and Cameron
Mackintosh/Trevor Nunn and John Caird
Return to Toronto following tour
(Winnipeg/Ottawa)

1992

07/26-09/12
Buddy
By Alan Janes
Producer/Director: Tom Mallow, ATP
Dodger, PACE Theatrical, Paul Elliott,
Laurie Mansfield, Greg Smith and David
Mirvish/Rob Bettinson
Cast: Chip Esten and Alex Bourne
(Buddy alternates), Alex Paez, Brian Ruf,
Jo Lynn Burks, Cheryl Allison, Tony Gilbert,
Bobby Prochaska and others

09/14-10/31
The Secret Garden
By Marsha Norman, Lucy Simon
Producer/Director:
ATP/Dodger, PACE, Jujamcyn and
Heidi Landesman/Susan Schulman
Cast: Melody Kay, Kevin McGuire,
Mary Fogarty, Roger Bart, Jay Garner,
Sean Considine and Luke Hogan

11/03-12/19
Lost in Yonkers
By Neil Simon
Producer/Director:
Emanuel Azenberg/Gene Saks
Cast: Mercedes McCambridge, Susan Giosa,
Taro Alexander, Michael Gaston, Phillip
Reese, Eleanor Reissa and Bruce Nozick

12/31-02/07/93
Les Misérables
By Alain Boublil/Claude Michel Schonberg
Producer/Director: Cameron Mackintosh
Cast: Craig Schulman and others (U.S. tour)

1993-94-95

02/12-04/03
Blood Brothers
By Willy Russell
Producer/Director: Bill Kenwright/
Bob Tomson and Bill Kenwright

Cast: Stephanie Lawrence, Warwick Evans,
Con O'Neill, Mark Hutchinson and others

04/12-05/29
The Good Times Are Killing Me
By Lynda Barry
Producer/Director: Mirvish, Ford's Theater
and Second Stage/Mark Brokaw
Cast: Jorge Luis Abreu, Kevin Chamberlin,
Tony Fair, Holly Felton, Harriett D. Foy,
Renée Allison Harper, LaShonda Hunt
and others

06/01-07/17
Guys and Dolls
By Jo Swerling, Abe Burrows/Frank Loesser
Producer/Director: Dodger Theatricals,
Jujamcyn Theatres/Jerry Zaks
Cast: Lorna Luft, Lewis J. Stadlen, Richard
Muenz, Patricia Ben Peterson and others

07/26-09/25
Man of La Mancha
By Dale Wasserman and Joe Darion/
Mitch Leigh
Producer/Director: Mirvish and Citadel
Theatre/Robin Phillips and Susan Cox
Cast: Michael Burgess, Susan Gilmour,
Grant Cowan, Frank MacKay, Brian MacKay,
David Mucci, Blythe Wilson and others

09/29-11/06
Five Guys Named Moe
By Clarke Peters, music of Louis Jordan
Producer/Director:
Cameron Mackintosh/Charles Augins
Cast: Kevyn Brackett, Doug Eskew,
Milton Craig Nealy, Jeffrey Polk,
Kirk Taylor and Keith Tyrone

12/01/93-12/31/95
Crazy for You
By Ken Ludwig, Mike Ockrent and
Gershwins
Producer/Director: Mirvish, Roger Horchow

and Elizabeth Williams/Mike Ockrent
Cast: Jim Walton (later replaced by Dirk Lumbard), Camilla Scott, Barbara Hamilton, Victor A. Young, Terry Doyle (later replaced by Mickey Rooney), David Mucci, Mary Ellen Mahoney, Deann DeGruijter and others

04/30 (one night only)
An Evening with Peter Ustinov
Producer/Director: Duncan C. Weldon, Jerome Minskoff and John McGreevy
Cast: Peter Ustinov (solo)

1996

01/06-02/17
The Master Builder
By Henrik Ibsen
Producer/Director:
Bill Kenwright/Sir Peter Hall
Cast: Alan Bates, Gemma Jones, Victoria Hamilton and others

02/24-04/06
One for the Pot
By Ray Cooney, Tony Hilton
Producer/Director: Mirvish and Shaw Festival/Christopher Newton
Cast: Heath Lamberts, Simon Bradbury, David Schurmann, Robert Benson, Mary Haney, Helen Taylor, Corrine Koslo and others

03/31 (one night only)
Maggie and Pierre
By Linda Griffiths
Producer/Director: Paul Thompson
Cast: Linda Griffiths
(Benefit for Playwrights' Union of Canada)

04/09-05/18
Three Tall Women
By Edward Albee
Producer/Director: Elizabeth McCann, Jeffrey Ash and Daryl Roth/
Lawrence Sacharow
Cast: Marian Seldes, Michael Learned, Christina Rouner and Michael Rhodes

05/27-09/07
Blood Brothers
By Willy Russell
Producer/Director: Bill Kenwright/
Bob Tomson and Bill Kenwright
Cast: David Cassidy, Amy Sky, Michael Burgess and others

09/10-10/05
André Philippe Gagnon
By Stéphan Laporte and Joe Bodolai
Producer/Director:
Mirvish/Stéphane Laporte
Cast: André Philippe Gagnon

10/07-10/12
Darrow
By David Rintels
Producer/Director: Leslie Nielsen
Cast: Leslie Nielsen (solo)

10/24-11/02
Don Giovanni
By W.A. Mozart
Producer/Director: Opera Atelier/
Marshall Pynkoski and Jeannette Zingg

11/14/96-02/01/97
Jane Eyre
By John Caird and Paul Gordon
Producer/Director: Mirvish/John Caird
Cast: Marla Schaffel, Anthony Crivello, Mary Stout, Elizabeth DeGrazia, Sara Farb and others

1997

02/07-03/22
Death of a Salesman
By Arthur Miller
Producer/Director: Mirvish and Manitoba Theatre Centre/Gloria Muzio
Cast: Judd Hirsch, Rochelle Oliver, Richard Clarkin, Jim Bracchitta, Geoffery P. Cantor and others

03/25-05/03
The Glass Menagerie
By Tennessee Williams
Producer/Director: Mirvish and National Arts Centre/Neil Munro
Cast: Shirley Douglas, Kiefer Sutherland, Kathryn Greenwood, David Storch and others

05/07-06/01
Andre Philippe Gagnon
By Stéphane Laporte and Joe Bodolai
Producer/Director:
Mirvish/Stéphane Laporte
Cast: Andre Philippe Gagnon (solo)

05/13 (one night only)
Piano Man's Daughter
By Timothy Findley

Producer/Director:
Mirvish, Harper Collins Canada and Robert Missen Artists/Paul Thompson
Cast: Timothy Findley, Veronica Tennant, Sylvia Tyson, Joe Sealy, Michael Sean Marye and Jack Nicholsen

06/16-10/25
Jolson
By Francis Essex and Rob Bettinson
Producer/Director: Paul Elliott, Laurie Mansfield and Greg Smith/Rob Bettinson
Cast: Brian Conley and Allan Stewart (Jolson alternates), Sally Ann Triplett, John Bennett, John Conroy, Brian Greene, Craig Stevenson, Maggie Ellis, Kit Benjamin and others

10/29-11/02
Orfeo et Eurydice
By J.W. Gluck
Producer/Director: Opera Atelier/
Marshall Pynkoski and Jeanette Zingg
Cast: Buddug Verona James, Barbara Hannigan, Meredith Hall and others, with Tafelmusik Baroque Ensemble

11/25/97-07/26/98
Rent
By Jonathan Larson
Producer/Director: Jeffrey Seller, Kevin McCollum, Allan S. Gordon and Mirvish/Michael Greif
Cast: Luther Creek, Jai Rodriguez, Chad Richardson, Krysten Cummings (Mimi 1), Saskia Garel (Mimi 2), Danny Blanco, Damian Perkins, Jennifer Aubry, Karen Leblanc and others

1998

07/28-09/05
Two Pianos Four Hands
By Ted Dykstra and Richard Greenblatt
Producer/Director: Mirvish/Tarragon Theatre
Cast: Ted Dykstra and Richard Greenblatt

09/09-10/17
Racing Demon
By David Hare
Producer/Director: Chichester Festival Theatre/Christopher Morahan
Cast: Helen Blatch, Peter Bourke, Jocelyn Eisen, Joe Fraser, John Harding, Paul Ireland, Michael Jayston and others

10/22-11/01
The Marriage of Figaro
By W.A. Mozart
Producer/Director: Opera Atelier/
Marshall Pynkoski, Jeannette Zingg,
Andrew Parrot (Conductor)
Cast: Gerald Isaac, Michael Chioldi,
Meredith Hall, Emilio Roman, Laura Pudwell
and others, with Tafelmusik Baroque
Ensemble

11/09-12/19
Fame
By David de Silva, José Fernandez/
Steve Margoshes
Producer/Director: Richard Martini,
Adam Spiegel, Ronald Andrew, Allen Spivak
and Albert Nicciolino/Lars Bethke
Cast: Gavin Creel, Jennifer Gambatese,
José Restrepo, Natasha Rennalls,
Dioni Michelle Collins and others

12/06 (one night only)
Vinyl Cafe Christmas
By Stuart McLean
Producer/Director: Robert Missen
Cast: Stuart McLean (solo)

12/26/98-01/17/99
Slava's Snowshow
By Slava Polunin
Producer/Director: Dodger Endemol
and Dan Colman/Victor Kramer
Cast: Slava Polunin, Angela de Castro,
Sergei Chachelev, Vladimir Olshansky,
Elena Ouchakova and Olga Volkova

1999

01/19-02/06
The Number 14
By Melody Anderson, Peter Anderson,
Gina Bastone, Colin Heath, David Mackay,
Wayne Specht, Roy Surette and Beatrice
Zeilinger
Producer/Director:
Axis Mime Theatre/Roy Surrette
Cast: Peter Anderson, Darlene Brookes,
Colin Heath, David Mackay, Wayne Specht,
Beatrice Zeilinger and Mark Weatherly

02/10-03/20
Proposals
By Neil Simon
Producer/Director: Mirvish and Manitoba
Theatre Centre/Steven Schipper

Cast: Al Waxman, Graham Abbey, Barbara
Barnes-Hopkins, Tim Campbell and others

03/23-05/01
The Master Class
By Terrence McNally
Cast: Elizabeth Ashley, Frances Limoncelli,
Melissa LaFrance and others

05/07-06/19
Our Town
By Thornton Wilder
Producer/Director:
Soulpepper Theatre Co./Joseph Ziegler
Cast: Peter Donaldson, Oliver Dennis,
Nancy Palk, Martha Burns, Diego
Matamoros, Albert Schultz and others

11/04-12/18
Art
By Yasmina Reza
Producer/Director: Mirvish and Manitoba
Theatre Centre/William Joseph Barnes
Cast: Stephen Ouimette, Scott Hylands
and Richard Poe

12/28/99-02/12/00
The Needfire
By Tom Lackey
Producer/Director: Mirvish/Kelly Robinson
Cast: Denny Doherty, John Allan Cameron,
The Campbell Brothers, Joe Dinicol, Jim
Fidler and others

2000-05

02/17-04/01
Enigma Variations
By Eric-Emmanuel Schmitt
Producer/Director: Mirvish and
Emanuel Azenberg/Anthony Page
Cast: Donald Sutherland and John
Rubinstein

05/11/00-05/22/05
Mamma Mia!
By Bjorn Ulveaus, Benny Andersson
and Catherine Johnson
Producer/Director:
Judy Craymer/Phyllida Lloyd
Original Cast: Louise Pitre, Gary P. Lynch,
Tina Maddigan, Adam Brazier, Gabrielle
Jones, Mary Ellen Mahoney, Lee
MacDougall, David Mucci, Miku Graham,
Nicole Fraser, Nicolas Dromard,
Sal Scozzari and others

10/25-11/06
Dame Edna: Back with a Vengeance
By Barry Humphries
Producer/Director: Barry Humphries
Cast: Barry Humphries (solo)

2006

01/10-02/18
The Boy Friend
By Sandy Wilson
Producer/Director:
Goodspeed Musicals/Julie Andrews
Cast: Jessica Grové, Sean Palmer, Paul
Carlin, Andrea Chamberlain and others

03/11-04/23
The Innocent Eye Test
By Michael Healey
Producer/Director: Mirvish and Manitoba
Theatre Centre/Christopher Newton
Cast: Kevin Bundy, Tanja Jacobs, C. David
Johnson, Tom McCamus, Lisa Norton, Paul
O'Sullivan, Gord Rand and Michael Healey

04/26-06/04
Wingfield's Inferno
By Dan Needles
Producer/Director: Mirvish/Douglas Beattie
Cast: Rod Beattie (solo)

09/12-10/22
Legends!
By James Kirkwood
Producer/Director: Ben Sprecher,
William P. Miller, Percy Gibson
and Mirvish/John Bowab

Cast: Joan Collins, Linda Evans, Joe Farrell, Will Holman, Ethan Matthews and Tonye Patano

10/24-12/03
Pippin
By Roger O. Hirson/Stephen Schwartz
Producer/Director: Goodspeed Musicals
Cast: Joshua Park, André Ward, Micky Dolenz, James Royce Edwards, Shannon Lewis, Barb Marineau, Teal Wicks, Jason Blaine and others

2007

01/03-02/11
Orpheus Descending
By Tennessee Williams
Producer/Director: Mirvish and Manitoba Theatre Centre/Miles Potter
Cast: Jonathan Goad, Seana McKenna, Walter Borden, Rod Campbell, Joyce Campion and others

03/20-05/16
e-DENTITY
By Michael Spence
Producer/Director: Theatre Gargantua/Jacquie P.A. Thomas
Cast: Ciara Adams, Joel Benson, Conor Green, Lori Nancy Kalamanski, Alexis Milligan, Diane Niec and Michael Spence

06/01-06/17
Vida!
By Lizt Alfonso and Kelly Robinson
Producer/Director: Lizt Alfonso, Danza Cuba, Peter Sever/Lizt Alfonso and Kelly Robinson

10/31-??
Dirty Dancing
By Eleanor Bergstein
Producer/Director: Jacobsen Entertainment and Mirvish/James Powell
Cast: Jake Simons, Monica West, Britta Lazenga, Al Sapienza and others